The Asians in East Africa

Was sich sagen laesst, laesst sich klar sagen; was man nicht klar sagen kann, kann man ueberhaupt nicht sagen.

Ludwig Wittgenstein

Whatever can be said, can be said clearly; what cannot be said clearly, cannot be said at all.

The Asians in East Africa
Jayhind and Uhuru

Agehananda Bharati

Professional-Technical Series
Nelson-Hall Company

Chicago

For Dr. Francesca Fremantle

ISBN: 0–911012–49–4

Library of Congress Catalog Card Number: 72–85882

Nelson-Hall Company, Publishers
325 W. Jackson Blvd., Chicago, Ill. 60606

Manufactured in the United States of America

Contents

Preface

"jayhind" (Hindi):
*"hail India"—Indian
nationalist greeting*
"uhuru" (Swahili):
*"freedom!" African
nationalist motto*

Minorities are people. This is sufficient reason for sociologists and anthropologists to study them. Minorities are also people with a problem; they are outnumbered by others who do not usually like them—more often than not, they dislike them very much indeed. African leaders and their western mentors speak about plural societies, multiracial societies, or composite societies. Such terms are either taxonomical, in which case they are of no real concern except to those interested in classification for one reason or another; or else these terms are ideologically loaded, in which case they convey a "beware!" to the minority.

Several excellent books have appeared on Indians in Africa so far. Hilda Kuper's *Indians in Natal,* Floyd and Lillian Dotson's elaborate study on the *Indians in Zambia, Rhodesia,*

1

and Malavi, and Stephen Morris' *Indians in Uganda* are important sociological studies. J. Mangat's *History of the Indians in East Africa* is an up-to-date historical analysis of the minority. R. Gregory's monumental *India and East Africa* is the latest study.

The present investigation was less detached in its motivation than these works. The Indians in East Africa are now in a state of profound duress. Their survival as a community is in doubt, impugned as it is by African nationalism now linked to African political and governmental power. Early in 1968, the British Parliament passed strongly restrictive legislation against Asian immigrants from the area; those who sought and obtained British passports are now summarily barred from entering Britain. Enoch Powell epitomizes this trend —there is no doubt that he speaks for his constituents, and for a much larger British public. "They're trying to take over," "Enoch said the blood will flow"—such may be extreme statements made by British informants, but part of the democratic process is that lawmakers tend to heed the will of their constituents rather than humanistic considerations. *The Observer* (July 14, 1968) carries a gruesome but realistic account of the situation; its author, John Heilpern, does not draw any inferences beyond the confines of the city which he observed. Yet common sense suggests such inference: though reason and cosmopolitanism may prevail one day, they may not do so in time for the Asian immigrant problems to be settled in a humanly satisfactory manner.

The Government of Kenya looks askance at Asians who did not opt for Kenyan citizenship. None of the Indians want to 'return' to India or Pakistan, because most of them have never been there and do not regard India or Pakistan as their homes any more than the Algerian French regarded France as theirs—and those older Indians who were born in South Asia or revisited their ancestral places are simply not ready for the belt-tightening which their 'return' to the subcontinent would require.

This, however, is not how the African leadership views

the situation; to put it quite bluntly, the African leaders want the Asians *out*. Yet a community of roughly 360,000, well settled and on top of things until recently, poses more than one problem for the African leaders. Short of pogrom-like action or other drastic measures, some plans for the Asians may or may not be seriously contemplated by the East-African governments; quite probably, individual African leaders may be divided on the issue. I do not think, however, that many of them want the Asians to remain as they are: an expatriate minority population which controls an impressive segment of the East African economy.

Although an anthropologist's work, this study addresses itself to a much wider audience. African studies have attracted a growing number of cross-disciplinary efforts; historians, political scientists, cultural geographers, students of government and public affairs, and planners should consult works done by anthropologists or sociologists. There are also the philosopher and the historian of ideas, for whom hardly anything so far has been written; this study hopes to remedy the neglect. Ideological change in an expatriate community which brings along, consciously or not, a formidable heritage of ideological sophistication and complexity, has not so far been the primary subject of research. The more conservative anthropologists attend to isolated studies in the South Asian context—a village, a caste; and those who regard anthropology as a hard science tend to regard any interest in ideology as alien and improper. Ideology cannot be sampled and quantified like foodstuffs, ritualistic objects, and arrowheads. Sol Tax once commented that anthropology is what anthropologists do. The community investigated in this book is a highly idiosyncratic community if you will. What could be reported about it by mathematically formalized analyses is predictable without these or trivial. There is here no toss-up between an Indological hunch and the display of methodological exercise; rather, this community suggests its own method of research, one that is syncretistic in style and scope. Chiefly, I am concerned with the value orientations of modern Indians. This study is fundamentally just this: an investigation into the stagnation and the changes which the belief system and the value orientations of the Indian expatriates embody.

I am not too enthusiastic about the claim that there must be a single theoretical orientation at the back of an ideological study, or that there ought to be a single set of theoretical presuppositions. I regard these claims as invitations to slant the report, unless 'theoretical' is to be understood as a synonym for 'methodically rigorous'. In this case, the methodology is generated by three disciplines: cultural anthropology, Indology, and analytic philosophy. I have applied 'ordinary language' analysis suggested by such authors as J. L. Austin and R. M. Hare to complex religious and ritualistic phenomena in my *Tantric Tradition* as well as in reporting on certain problems of communication in modern Indian milieux; and a good deal of it will be found to underlie the assessments made in Chapters VI and VII of this book.

The second chapter of this book deals with caste, marriage, and kinship. Indian kinship terminology has not changed in the East African diaspora. The incidental switch of linguistic media, i.e. between Gujarati and Cutchi as shown in Chapter Two, is not terminologically significant, though it is linguistically revealing. Such lack of terminological innovation could be expected where conservatism is strong; and where social change occurs it does not affect kinship terms for a long time. I had to make a choice: had I treated kinship in as detailed a manner as caste, the chapter would have been much larger than it already is. I could have added a separate chapter on kinship, but such addition seemed hardly justifiable, since western Indian kinship terminology and social structure have been studied and well reported by Prof. Karve and others listed in the bibliography. An additional chapter on kinship would have meant straight duplication of material readily available to the specialist and the interested layman. Not so with caste in East Africa; the material analyzed breaks fresh ground: the fascinating fossilization of rules of endogamy, the disappearance of commensality and the virtual relinquishment of trade exclusiveness in the new domicile necessitated a full enquiry. The second chapter does not overlap thematically with my shorter study of the ideology and content of caste among the East African Asians in the Schwartz volume on *Caste among Overseas Indians.* The Cutchi *nyānī* tradition of institutionalized deference to the female child in the agnatic line has never been reported before and is part of the second chapter in this book.

Anthropologists are becoming suspect with their third-world subjects. Anthropologists working in the Indian field have an additional problem: some of their erstwhile informants may read their books and reports about them. The Indians in East Africa are literate people; they are also anxious people keenly aware of what others think about them. This author stood in a peculiarly structured relation to his subjects: as an Indologist and as a Hindu monk, he has access to types of information which are closed to mere anthropologists. On the negative side, I had to be cautious not to reveal the sort of personal information which came to me in the process of pastoral transference, even where it could have added considerably to the depth of my report. Also on the negative side, the Asians in East Africa resent people who concern themselves with things they do not want to be mentioned at all lest they should jeopardize their image with the African rulers and the outside world—such things as the perseverance of the caste system, stagnation in religious and secular ideas, and other topics essential to the anthropologist's work. But these problems cannot be remedied.

The study is *not* an Africanist study; it is that of a transplanted Indian society. There are parallels by way of converging culture themes between Indian and African society, but this was not the occasion for any comparative analysis. The interface relation between African and Asian segments replicates all the problems of pluralistic societies in Furnival's sense of the term, as shown so well in the Dotson volume; but the two societies do not culturally impinge on each other. On whatever analytical level similarities exist, they are always so remote that they are not perceived by the members of either of the juxtaposed societies, even though they excite the anthropologist. Thus, most of the East African inland tribes have a well-defined system of social stratification or hierarchy, and at least one group has a 'caste' structure very like the Indian. The Tutsi of Rundi, a strongly patrilineal society, grade their own members, with the herdsmen of royal descent on top of the ladder, followed by the Hutu as commoners, and the Twa as outcastes. Some of the socially more perspicacious Asians are more than vaguely cognisant of such parallels even if they know little about their operation.

The seven chapters of this book are necessarily uneven in size. The study being primarily one of ideological stagnation and social change, the quantifiable issues have been kept to the barest minimum in the first and shortest chapter. The economic situation is highly complex and merits a separate study by an economist; I therefore selected only the entrepreneurial aspect of it as it meshes with the cognitive theme of this investigation. Interpersonal relations, particularly the exasperatingly complex male-female situation in any Indian society, and interracial relations are, of course, quite crucial; chapters four and five document a highly explosive, often odious interpersonal situation, revealing, it is hoped, some uniquely Indian psycho-cultural syndromes which have puzzled the occidental student. The world view of the Asians absorbs the two final and the largest chapters. The overlap between the religious and the non-religious—I avoid the term 'secular' for several reasons which will emerge in this study —is a fact in the Indian field, and one that is more obtrusive than in any other complex society today. The emphasis on the 'religious' annoys modern Indians, who will deny its importance, much as they will deny the caste structure of their society if they can get away with it.

The field work and the ensuing preparation of this study were supported by the Crosscultural and African Studies sections of the Maxwell School of Public Affairs and Citizenship at Syracuse University; the National Institute of Mental Health financed the field equipment and defrayed my travel expenses. I am indebted to Dr. William P. Mangin, then Chairman of the Department of Anthropology at Syracuse University, for lowering my teaching load and other commitments to the Department during completion of this work. My thanks go to Dr. Stephen K. Bailey and to Dr. Irving Swerdlow, then Deans of the Maxwell School, for all the moral and material support they gave me. Dr. David E. Sopher of the Department of Geography, Mr. Ramsingh Asher, and Dr. Robert Gregory have given me invaluable information during the concluding phase of this work. Most importantly, my gratitude goes to my many friends and helpers in East Africa, who merit more than the cold title 'informant' or 'subject'.

AGEHANANDA BHARATI
Professor of Anthropology,
Syracuse University

CHAPTER ONE

Historical and Demographic Highlights

Anthropology is not anti-historical; but its subject matter is different from that of the historian. Historical or diachronic method is used constantly by the ethnologist, and with the exception perhaps of the more radical adherents to the structuralist-functionalist schools of anthropology inaugurated by Radcliff-Brown and Malinowski in England, ethnographers and cultural anthropologists use both diachronic-historical, and synchronic approaches, the latter coalescing to some degree with a functionalist view of human societies.

Previous to Mangat's and Gregory's exquisite works, some booklets had been published, giving a sketchy outline of the arrival and settlement of the Asians. Substantial, though incidental, material about them is found in Lord Haley's *African Survey,* and in Hill's *Permanent Way;* the two little booklets by Hollingsworth and Delf are bare outlines which do not claim to be more than just that.[1]

A skeletal sketch, however, is in order at this point. When the British began to build the Uganda Railway in order to link the seaport Mombasa with Nairobi and Kampala, they found African labor unavailable or unreliable. However, they had some experience with a system of indenture, whereby labor from one part of the empire was shipped to an area

8

for a definite period. Such large-scale contractual labor or indenture was used by the British in plantation areas as in the Caribbean (Guiana, Trinidad) and in Fiji, as also in other, widely distant parts of the British Empire. The laborers were paid wages that were considerably higher than the livelihood the workers had in their respective homelands. Transportation to the region of indenture and back home after their contracts expired was free, and in many cases, option to remain in the new area as settlers, agriculturists, or in other capacities was granted in lieu of free passage back to the homeland.

It was toward the end of the nineteenth century that the British Government in Africa, negotiating the matter with the British India Government, began to indenture large numbers of Indian laborers to build the Uganda Railway. They built it; and the Railway runs smoothly and efficiently today, an impressive tribute to the Indian laborers. Many of them died of blackwater fever along the tracks; quite a few were picked up by lions. (This situation was vividly illustrated in a telegram sent by an Indian stationmaster to his superior: "Two lions on platform. Train approaching and signal-man up water tank. Lions won't let him down. I very nervously frightened and secure in office. Cannot give 'line clear signal' to coming train. Please arrange matters own personal satisfaction and dispose of lions who greatly bane my existence." J. A. Hunter and D. Mannix, *African Bush Adventures,* London 1954, p. 149.) Not too many of the Indians chose to stay on after their indenture period was over; most of them returned to India. But as the building of the Railroad began, small-scale entrepreneurs from western India, particularly from the Gujarati and Cutchi speaking areas, took sail to East Africa to set up little shops to cater to the needs of the laborers who were paid well enough to buy goods which they could not afford at home—where they were self-sufficient, as farmers or tillers of the soil, albeit on a subsistence economy level.

As early as the late eighteenth century, some Indian

9

traders, particularly Gujarati and Cutchi-speaking Muslims
and members of the trade-oriented Bhatia community from
Bombay northward along the west coast of the subcontinent,
had settled on the island of Zanzibar and along the coastal
strip of the East African mainland, between the large medieval
Arab ports of Mombasa and Dar es Salaam. Those early
settlers did not bring their womenfolk with them at first,
and quite a few lived with African women until the British
indenture began. Some laborers did indeed bring their wives
along, or called for them after a year or two; then only the
older settlers, whose number was much smaller, followed their
example. As the indentured laborers left to return to India,
two groups of Indians stayed on: the first and second generation descendants of the Indian merchant settlers in Zanzibar
and along the coast, and the petty shopkeepers who had come
more recently to supply goods as traders to two communities.
They sold goods "up" to the British and other European
settlers, and "down" to the Africans. They set up their *dūkā*-s
(shops), and this has become a term of economic-ecological
identification for the Indians in East Africa. To the African
and the white, the Asian was the *dūkāwālā,* the shopkeeper.
For the first time in their history, the indigenous East Africans encountered shops where food, spices, and many other
novel goods could be had at one place. Apart from the tribes
in the coastal areas, where Arab trade had been established
for several centuries and where the indigenous population was
familiar with a bazaar-marketing system, few of the tribes in
the interior had known marketing procedure of the sort the
Indians now provided. The British expatriates soon found
that the thrifty Indian shopkeeper could import "luxury"
goods—soap, bicycles and spares, clothing and textiles, beer
and French wine—and would sell them with a very low profit
margin; so that buying from the Indian merchant would not
be much more expensive than having agents abroad ship
goods into Africa from Europe—and it would certainly be
much faster. Unlike the government of South Africa, the
British East African countries' governments did not pass any

segmentizing legislation against Indian immigrants, and there was a free flow from India to East Africa, virtually until *uhuru* less than a decade ago. Just like the American Chinese or the West African Lebanese, the Indians began to call over their kin, consanguineous and affinal, from India, and the population of Asian expatriates grew at a rate of about 30 percent per year for a period of 50 years. This accounts for the regional provenance of the settlers: the majority of the traders who had come were Gujaratis or Cutchis from western India north of Bombay; a smaller number came from the Panjab. The Indian minority up to this day consists almost entirely of Gujaratis and Panjabis, with little or no representation from other parts of India. Again, we have a parallel here with the Chinese in North America: apart from some university professors and Nobel laureates in physics, who may have come from other parts of China, all Chinese settlers—innkeepers, laundrymen, vegetable growers—come from a tiny village cluster in the Taishan area near Canton in Southern China. They too sent for their kin to enhance the size and status of their group, and as marriage partners.

In an area where the most drastic changes in the numerical situation are in progress even as this study is being completed and where statistics, if available at all, have been half-hearted and sporadic, tabular surveys are of doubtful merit. There is even less merit in attempting to grapple with current population figures relating to our community in a year where a large-scale exodus has begun in two of the constituent areas. The figures presented here have been culled from material whose original sources were slanted, either intentionally or through the naivete of census-takers who were either not at all or too much concerned with a specific minority group. Some of the best studies, such as those by Morris and Pocock,[2] concentrated on a single territory. In the statistics available, the term "Asian" sometimes included all people of South Asian descent and no further division could be gleaned from such a cavalier indicator; conversely, we often found such terms as "Goans," "Muslims," "Hindus" used to stand for

"Asians." The breakdown into castes and caste-like communities which alone would be operational for anthropological research in any South Asian culture and society has never been done here. Attempts to obtain such a breakdown meet with opposition and withdrawal—quite understandable in the light of the political situation. In the quest for figures concerning the various castes, we had to rely on statements of those spokesmen and leaders of the various communities who thought they knew the figures. Let me warn readers, therefore, that many of the figures listed below are at best skilled guesses.

Until 1964, Tanganyika and Zanzibar were separate countries, hence older figures were collated separately. After the merger of these two countries into the Tanzanian union, census authorities naturally deemphasized "old" distinctions.

The figures adduced in the tables are necessarily incomplete;[3] some of them report variant figures, and none of them cover all the regions and population groups for all the years. The counting was largely a hit-or-miss procedure, and it appears that the census takers were frequently biased in favor of one or against another subsection, depending on their own ethnocultural background. The nomenclature used diffusely throughout the tables reveals some interesting slants: Thus, the 1949 figures for Zanzibar show "Indians," the figures for 1958 list "Asians other than Arabs," which must either mean people of South Asian or pre-partition Indian stock. Sporadically and unpredictably, the "Asians" are listed as "Indians, Pakistanis, Goans" in one rubric, as "Asians," in another, or again as "Indians and Goans," where it is impossible to say whether or not "Pakistanis" were included. In most cases, the somewhat cryptic term "others" means migrants from the Seychelles, a Creolized Afro-Asian population which has low status and no ethnic recognition in the eyes of anyone in East Africa, either indigenous or expatriate. The terminology "Indian-Pakistani" was quite fatuous in statistical notation used within a decade previous to and after 1947. The ascription "Pakistani" versus "Indian" was adventitious: Muslims were listed as "Pakistanis," Hindus and Sikhs as

"Indians"—regardless of their place of origin or of the location of their collateral kin in present day South Asia, or before partition. Many Muslims in East Africa, of Indian stock, would call themselves "Indian" or "Pakistani" on different occasions, such as responding to different census takers. The bracket term "Asian" for all people of South Asian stock, which now applies to "Indians," "Goans," and "Pakistanis" alike, would have been less misleading than the arbitrary procedure followed in these census resports and population estimates. There is a logical fallacy involved in the use of "Pakistani"—for strictly speaking, any person born previous to 1947 should be called "Indian"; there was India and there was Goa before that time, but no Pakistan. However, the respondents did not seem fastidious about the nomenclature used by the census reports; shortly after 1947, Muslims whose relatives lived in what was now Pakistan began to call themselves Pakistanis, Muslims whose kin lived in the truncated Indian territory began to call themselves "Indian," or, if they felt embarrassed about it, Asian. Although this latter term has come to mean all South Asians settled in East Africa, it became a term of relative comfort at a time when political loyalties were delicate and vague.

To date, the most exhaustive demographic survey of the Indian minorities is that by R. R. Kuczynski in the second volume of the *Demographic Survey of the British Colonial Empire,* published by Oxford University Press in 1949. Although the data is obsolete in 1972, this survey contains a fine array of historical and demographic data, though even here we do not find profiles which would specify age, sex, caste, natality, etc. At the time Kuczynski collected his data, such a breakdown could have been obtained with relative ease, since there was no reason for Asians to blur caste distinctions and other data of personal provenience. As the years go by, such distinctions are being more and more suppressed in any official discourse. This is due not only to the situational anxiety Asians feel if they appear to be subdivided, hence a divided community to the African leadership, but in

13

an equal measure to more general modern Indian attempts to achieve a national and cultural rather than a sectional or 'communal' identification toward the outside world.

As this book goes to press, the situation is undergoing a radical change, quite terrifying to many of those directly involved. Dr. Nyerere has proclaimed his own brand of a socialist state, in which, so he promised in his millennial-style speech in February 1967, there will be no private capital. Starting with the banks, many of the institutions which kept the Asians a wealthy minority and which were their economic *raison d'être* as expatriates, were nationalized in Tanzania. Strictures implicitly against Asians were legalized in all the three countries soon after *uhuru*; the involved questions of East African citizenship, employment in government services, compulsory national service in the colleges of the East African University, and the many overt and covert pressures which will be pinpointed in this book—all these have set the stage for a total reorientation among the Asians. It now appears that Kenya will be the first of the three to see a large number of Asians leave, with a heavy heart and, presumably, a much lighter purse. Government employees from all the three countries have already left in considerable numbers over the past eight years; but the petty merchant who forms the core of the Asian population might have to follow in a not too distant future. It seems likely that this is what the African leadership wants, but we can only speculate about the ultimate survival of the Asians as a large minority in East Africa and any intelligent and informed guess is as good as any other. There are optimists among the Asians, especially among the young, who believe, perhaps naively, that the Africans may yet accept them as Africans because they declare themselves to be Africans; there are pessimists, especially among the older and the not-too-affluent, who believe that although *they* may last, their children will have no place in East Africa. There are many who will stay even if it means great hardship, or martyrdom—the Ismaili community must stay because their late leader commanded that they do so. And there are many,

14

probably the majority of the 360,000, who do not know what will happen, or who do not want to know.

In no large culture-area must the anthropologist divide and subdivide as in South Asia. There is really no such thing as an "Indian society," analyzable in the manner in which "American society" is. Modern Indians and Pakistanis are uncomfortably aware of this and they do not relish the anthropologist's interest in social segmentation. The official version of things as propounded by the more vocal Indians and Pakistanis on the subcontinent and abroad is that there are an Indian nation and a Pakistani nation; that divisions into castes and linguistic groups are unimportant, or, in the diction of radical and of less informed spokesmen, that these things have been "abolished." The anthropologist who insists that division and caste are still there is not the most enthusiastically welcome guest in India and Pakistan, or among East African Asians. Islam does not recognize the caste system; the *Sari'a*, the theocratic law of Islam as handed down by the *ulema*, the official church, assumed that the social structure of the Arabs of the Arabian desert was, or ought to be, universal. In areas where the social structure happened to be similar to that of the Arabs, as in the Turkish areas, the implementation was easy and natural. But in South Asia, the system of social interaction was very different indeed from what Muslim missionaries had encountered en route to India. Islam in South Asia underwent modifications which the more orthodox Arab doctors would not recognize as Islam. On the social side, Islam adapted itself to the Indian caste-system with very little change. The Muslims of South Asia were converts from Hinduism or Jainism; after conversion, they continued to marry within the old endogamous units. And though Muslims, just like many Sikhs, Christians, and Jains today, believe that they have no caste-system, this is simply not the case. All the religions imported into India had to make the supreme social compromise: their followers retained their erstwhile caste-affiliations as their social standard. Muslims just do not marry *any* Muslim in South Asia, although they might present this notion to the outside world; just as a Hindu marries into his own caste, a Muslim marries into his, and caste exogamy in Muslim South Asia, India and Pakistan alike, is about as rare as it is in Hindu India—which means that the incidence of marriage across caste-lines is negligible.

Unlike other regions where large Indian groups settled as expatriates, East Africa has completely preserved the system. There are several reasons for this: in the first place, East Africa is geographically closest to India, and brides and grooms could be shipped freely to supply the growing matrimonial needs of the East African Asians. Whereas the Union of South Africa set up severe restrictions on immigration from India[4] forcing the Indian settlers to marry within the established settlements in South Africa, no such stricture was placed on Indian migrants in East Africa until *uhuru*, when immigration ground to a virtual halt. If the Indian—regardless of his communal background—*can* "marry his son," and his daughter into his own caste, he does so. If he cannot—as is the case in South Africa due to legislative strictures, and in Fiji or in the Caribbean on account of the great distance from the homeland—he silently acculturates by gradually approving liaisons outside his own caste.

At a time when African rulers are formulating part of their antagonism to this minority on the grounds of its ethnic and cultural distance from the rest of society, any admission of fission and of a social fragmentation is resented. In the chapter on caste, which is a focal point in any study of Indian society[5], we will analyze the situation in greater detail. This being a bare survey, we shall now briefly list the various sub-societies which make up the Asian minority of East Africa. There will be no reference to caste in this section, except where there is referential overlap: among the Gujarati Hindus, the Lohanas and Patels form a substantial majority, and the term "Gujarati Hindu" would be too wide even for the purpose of mere enumeration. On the inside view, of course, every Indian society or subgroup, every identifiable

16

section of a linguistic or regional area on the subcontinent is a "caste" (*jāti*); a point which the demographers in Africa overlooked, underrated, or misunderstood, and one which the contemporary Asians in East Africa would like to ignore.

The Gujarati and Cutchi Hindus are the clear majority in the intra-Asian count; they account for roughly 70 percent of the total Asian population of East Africa. Linguistically, the term Gujarati is slightly ambivalent—for many of the people who are classed by other Asians, and often by themselves, as "Gujarati," are actually Cutchi—the region of Cutch borders the Gujarati speaking area in the Northwest, and is bounded by the Sindhi speaking area and the sea—at least this was the pre-partition situation, as most Sindhi speaking Hindus have migrated to India since 1947. Linguistically, Cutchi stands halfway between Gujarati and Sindhi; it is morphologically closer to Gujarati, phonologically closer to Cutchi. Again, the distinction is becoming more and more tenuous in East Africa, as the younger generation has more or less discarded the Cutchi speech form, using Gujarati only, in addition to the *lingua franca* of East African Asians, a kind of pidgeon Hindustani, and English. Cutchi has slightly lower prestige than Gujarati in India, probably due to the fact that Cutchi speakers ranked lower in average caste status, that many of them were Muslims, and that the Gujarati-speaking groups were modally wealthier than the Cutchis.

Among the "Gujarati Hindus," the two most prominent groups are the Patels and the Lohanas; their respective caste status will be discussed at the proper place. Linguistically, the Patels were and are Gujarati speakers; the Lohanas spoke Cutchi in India in earlier days, but the younger Lohana generation in East Africa no longer speaks Cutchi, and looks at old Cutchi speakers with that typical blend of embarrassment, respect, and disdain which we find diffusely present wherever one speech form has gained higher prestige than the other in a linguistically mixed area. Both Gujarati and Cutchi are Indo-Aryan languages, very closely related to Marāthī to the

South, and not quite so closely to the various forms of Hindi-Urdu in the North. The Gujarati script is very similar to Devanāgarī, which is used for Marāthī, Hindi, Nepali, and of course for Sanskrit. Cutchi was not a written language; its folklore was handed down orally, and when it began to be written, the Gujarati script or the Arabic script was used, depending on the regional preference. Sindhi is written in Perso-Arabic characters; hence many Cutchi speakers in that area who were literate preferred the Arabic script.

A small, concentratedly affluent section of the Asian population are Jainas[6]; they are exclusively Gujarati speakers, and are culturally and occupationally quite similar to the Patels.

The Gujarati- and Cutchi-speaking Muslims constitute about one-fifth of the Asian population. There are three groups among them, the Lohana- or Brahmin-descended Bohras, the one-time Cutchi speaking Ithna-Asari, and the Ismaili Khojas, the latter being the followers of the Aga Khan and, as we shall see on many occasions, the most highly modernized and flexible group within the Asian population. Both Khoja groups profess Shi'ism, unlike the majority of South Asian Muslims, who are Sunnis.

The North Indian Panjabis account for slightly over one tenth of the East African Asians. The most numerous and influential among them are the Sikhs, recognizable everywhere by the impressive beards and turbans their men wear, and the silvār-kamīz (pantaloon-cum—long shirt) garment worn by their women—increasingly worn by other Panjabi women, and more recently, by younger middleclass city women in wide parts of Northern India, partially replacing the "slower" sāṛī. The Panjabi Hindus are not really distinguishable, in an anthropologically accountable manner, from the Sikhs, since there is free intermarriage between them and much of Panjabi Hinduism is shared by Sikh ritual and practice, and vice-versa.

The Panjabi Muslims form a small but highly verbal community. Most of them are *Ahmediyas* (also called Mirzais or Qadianis)—a Muslim sect of very recent origin, and one that has drawn much adverse attention in Pakistani politics since the inception of Pakistan.

A small but prominent section of the Asians are Goans or, inelegantly named, Goanese. They are Roman Catholics; their native speech is Konkani, a speech form closest to Marāṭhī, and thus the southernmost Indo-Aryan language of the sub-continent. The younger goans in East Africa do not want to be identified with Indians. They reinforce the differences between themselves and the other Asians by forgetting Konkani and by speaking English only; most of them try very hard not to understand Hindustani when it is spoken around them—which is not easy since Konkani and Hindustani are very closely related, sharing 80 percent common vocabulary. The problem of cultural and political identity is severe for the Goans, more so since Goa's incorporation into India. Goans in East Africa will have to go to India if they cannot continue living in East Africa—for contrary to the official Indian doctrine that all Goans want to be Indians, East African Goans by and large resent the action which amalgamated Goa with the Indian Union. Interviewing ten Goans in four East African cities, I elicited the term "liberation" for India's action only from two; the others used epithets which were not very flattering for the Indian action. The strong dominance of the Catholic Church represented by Goan clergy reinforces these feelings. The Indian notion of secularity, whatever it may mean in India, does not mean anything to the Goans here, and all of them share the notion that India is a Hindu country. As a consequence, they would rather identify with the donors of their religion, the Portuguese, than with the "heathen" rulers of India. It is a long time since I heard this term from an Indian Christian with reference to Hindus. East African Goan clergy use this epithet quite unabashedly for Hindus.

The remaining Asian population consists of small regional groups from many parts of South Asia. Among them, the Maharashtrians are the most highly corporate; they have a

	1948	1952	1956	1957	1958	1959	1960	1961	1962	1963	1964	1966[1]
Tanganyika[2,3]												
(total)	[4]			8,762,470			9,233,000	9,398,800	9,677,500		(150,000)	[2]
				(128,742)								
Indians		56,499		65,830			} 87,300	} 90,500				
Pakistanis & Goans				10,706								
Arabs		13,025		(30,301)					25,200			
Asians									92,000			
Europeans				(4,478)					22,300			
Africans				(93,963)					9,538,000			
Zanzibar[3] (total)	264,262				299,111				300,000			[2]
Indians	15,892											
Africans					279,935					[5]		
Arabs	44,560											
Non-Arab Asians					18,334							
Europeans					507							
Others					335							

Uganda and **Kenya** population table (page rotated 90°)

Uganda						
(total)	4,958,520	5,593,000	5,678,900	6,523,628	6,845,000	7,189,600
Indians	33,767			69,103		⎱ 82,100
Goans	1,448	⎰ 54,300	⎰ 56,600	2,830		⎰
Pakistanis		⎱	⎱			⎰
Arabs	1,457	2,000	2,000			2,200
Africans						7,093,000
Asians					77,400	80,000[6]
Europeans					11,600	9,800
Others					4,600	2,500

Kenya[7]						
(total)	6,000,000[6]	6,531,000	6,450,000	6,550,000	7,290,000	9,097,000
Asians	97,687				8,636,263 (266,794)	183,000 / 36,000 — 182,000[6]
Arabs	24,174	35,000	38,600	39,000	34,048	36,000
Indians, Pakistanis & Goans		165,000	174,300	178,000	176,613 (86,453)	
Europeans					55,759 (21,477)	
Africans						8,836,000
Others					3,901 (3,901)[8]	

[1] The estimated total Asian population in Tanzania, Uganda and Kenya was 362,000.

[2] Tanganika and Zanzibar joined to form Tanzania in 1964. The estimated number of Asians in Tanzania in 1966 was 100,000.

[3] Figures for Dar es Salaam are in parentheses.

[4] Figure not traceable.

[5] Approximately one-fourth of the total.

[6] Estimated total.

[7] Figures for Nairobi are in parentheses.

[8] Non-African.

well-organized association in Dar-es-Salaam and in some other big cities. Most of them are professional men, with some really outstanding doctors and lawyers amongst them. With their kinsmen in the State of Bombay, they share a highly chauvinistic outlook with regard to Indian culture. They are hardly known as a separate community to the African hosts, and I have noticed that quite a few Asians who live and trade in the bush do not know about the existence of any Maharashtrian people as a group in East Africa. Most of the Maharashtrian settlers are high caste, as would be expected from people who emigrate as professionals rather than as traders or farmers; there are *Desastha* and *Citpāvan* Brahmin's among them, and some very few Marathas, i.e., people of the indigenous Maharashtrian warrior castes.

In Dar-es-Salaam, there is a fairly sizable community of Sinhalese, who have their own Buddhist temple in the same area where the Maharashtrians have their association's premises.

Numerically very few, but spread all over the urban areas of East Africa, we find Parsee families, usually highly affluent bankers, lawyers, and even a lady who runs a beauty salon by the up-to-date name "Slimeaze" in midtown Nairobi. The Parsees do not consider themselves as an expatriate group here; most of them commute between India and East Africa, or come on temporary assignments of a commercial nature; the managers of some of the Indian banks, recently nationalized in Tanzania, were frequently Parsees who spent many years in East Africa but who, unlike the other Asians, did not regard it as their permanent home.

Finally, at Mombasa and at some other large cities, there are some Hindu Sindhis—the most homeless of the homeless. As Sindh went to Pakistan, Sindhi Hindus mostly moved to Bombay after Partition in 1947; and a small overflow settled in East Africa, doing managerial business in which they have achieved considerable affluence which, as with their relatives in India, is quite conspicuous.

CHAPTER TWO

Caste and Marriage

A young Kenyan African sociologist, trained at the University of Wisconsin, wrote a short, highly polemical and not too well informed piece on caste in India and Africa, in a recent issue of *Transition*[1]. Though he had obviously read the proper sources—he quotes Iravati Karve, J. H. Hutton, and Taya Zinkin, all anthropological classics on caste—his conclusions are slanted. "In recent years," he writes, "there has been a beginning of a breakdown in the Hindu caste society. This has been due to the declining of belief in religion. The loss in belief works in two ways: first, there is a loss of belief in one's predestined superiority, and second, there is a loss of belief in one's predestined inferiority. . . ." This statement by a young African scholar, who has been exposed to the Asians, is significant and disturbing. He could not have derived his notions from any of the texts he quotes, for none of those authors would accept any of the naive, untutored propositions about caste which modern Indians tend to make, and which they may or may not believe. The African sociologist, in the paragraphs which precede this statement, reiterates the standard definitions of caste as endogamous, partly commensal, partly trade-exclusive corporate units. There is no doubt in my mind that this highly discrepant finale stems from what he had heard, through many years of symbiosis with Asians, in Kenya or at Makerere. For indeed, Asians, as well as modern, English-using people in India and Indians abroad, declare consistently that caste has been weakened or even "abolished," and that this change is due, not so much to legislation, as to the decline of interest in religion. In his conclusion, the African author then suggests that "anyone in East Africa, should be diametrically opposed to any form of precepts that would encourage caste-like behavior in our society. . . . I am in short all the way for the complete destruction of the tribes. . . ." Quite obviously, the author equates Indian "caste" behavior with tribal behavior in Africa. Invectives against the tribal tradition are as much part of the official culture of modern sub-Saharan Africa as is "no-caste" talk in India, and among Indians settled abroad. There is, however, a very radical difference between these attitudes. For the African, the abolition of the tribes, in whatever manner he may envisage it, is a political postulate; no African would *deny* that tribes exist. Not so the modern Indian: he claims and no doubt believes in part, not only that caste should be abolished, but that it *has* been abolished. Caste and tribe are equally complex phenomena for serious anthropolgical study; but modern Indian and African feelings about these two complexes are readily explicable. The verbal opposition to "caste" and "tribe" by Indians and Africans respectively, whatever these two terms do mean to them, overtly stems from a superficially correct apprehension that such limitations and identifications, with their incumbent segmentary allegiances, are detrimental to progress; progress, of course, is conceived in genetically western terms—nationalistic, democratic, socialist, communist, but above all, technological.

I have dealt with the ideology and the continuity of caste in the Asian communities in East Africa in greater detail, in *Caste in Overseas Indian Communities*.[2] In this chapter, I shall examine caste as one of the three interlocking functions of social organization, along with kinship and the family. Let me, however, summarize the main points I have made in that publication:

The ideology which surrounds caste is confined to the critics of tradition; these critics may either be Indian nationalists, or they may regard themselves as part of the Indian Renaissance with its religious and quasi-secular doctrines, as originally propounded by Swami Vivekananda, Tagore, Gandhi, and other leaders. There are many who defend caste— they would point to the cohesion it has given to Indian society, the corporate forces which have yielded those numerous artefacts, socifacts and mentifacts which constitute the culture of India. But they are in a minority; and even they reject the perpetuation of the system as they see it,—or more correctly, as they think others see it: as a conscious contrivance by priests and their descendants, and by other groups with vested interest, to keep the ignorant masses tethered to abject exploitation. In the terminology of modern Indian nationalism, the caste-system, or "casteism," to use a lovely word coined by Mahatma Gandhi, is responsible for the duress of India's "downtrodden masses," a recurrent Vivekanandian phrase. In the political and economic spheres, it is at the core of "fissiparous tendencies" of all kinds; it is also largely responsible for "corruption"—though corruption, as Professor Morris-Jones has shown,[3] is a new *word* rather than a new phenomenon in South Asia. Under Gandhian influence, and in emulation of Protestant notions about executive and managerial honesty, modern Indians feel that creating and devolving the means of livelihood, not by desert, but through kinship allegiances, is "corrupt." Grass-root Indians do not yet comprehend such irritation: must one not support and employ one's brother rather than a stranger? Is it not one's duty to think of one's family and of one's own *jāt*, i.e., one's extended kin, one's caste rather than of other people who just happen to be around? East African Asian business, too, was conducted and transmitted exclusively on kinship and caste-lines until the mid-twenties; not that economic enterprise was strictly a one-caste affair, but certain culturally similar and linguistically identical sections tended to pool their resources rather than invite partners from other groups. There was no established business liaison, say, between a Sikh and a Bohra, and few between Bohras and Ismailis, in spite of the fact that the two latter groups were Muslim. Under duress, this kind of economic exclusiveness has been abandoned, by and large. Facing the problem of sheer survival in East Africa, Asians of all castes are no doubt ready, at least in principle, to discard the traditional type of economic transmission, i.e., along caste and kinship lines. When a Patel businessman told me "we do not have to enter business liaisons with Ismailis," he was probably speaking out of a habit which he had cognitively rejected. Obviously, when Asian leaders urge their fellow Asians to make Africans their business partners, there is an unspoken implication that inter-Asian segmentation should be a matter of the past.

What, then, do modern Asians mean when they say—or even hope, that caste should be "abolished"? In the first place, their use of the term is not the anthropologist's use; for the latter, caste in South Asia is synonymous with the primary social structure in South Asia, covering India, Nepal, Pakistan, Ceylon, and several South Asian communities in the emigration. The large, still growing anthropological and sociological literature on caste[4] shows excruciatingly obvious disagreement, which is natural when a phenomenon so complex as caste is to be reported. But virtually all social scientists concentrating on the area share a minimal denominator: caste, *jāti* or *jāt* in the Indian vernaculars, is the name of an endogamous, commensal, and trade-exclusive unit. The degrees of adherence vary from region to region, as well as diachronically: trade exclusiveness is no longer part of the system at some places, or it never really was in certain areas. Commensality is being constantly eroded, in the cities and in marginally urban areas, but endogamy seems to endure as the steadiest factor contrasting the East African Indian system with virtually all other Indian emigrant groups in the world.

However, the modern Indian is not concerned with "this

sort of caste," as an Indian guest professor of economics at
Nairobi informed me; for the post-Gandhian Indian, "caste"
is that noxious bundle of conservative, uncritical, superstitious,
irrational, and immoral ideas which prevents India from
becoming a modern nation; to the modern Indian, caste
means the disjointed, faction-centered grouping which does
not let Indians see India as a nation. Asians in East Africa
share the same view. In other words, all East African Asians
feel about "caste," and understand "caste" in the same manner
modern Indians think and feel about it: it is bad, it should
be abolished or curtailed. Just how this could be done, however, is by no means clear to anybody.

In the first place, Indians in India and East Africa do not
know the elementary distinction between the theoretical,
literary four-fold *varna* scheme—propounded in the scriptures
and taught by the religious specialists up to this day—and
the operative *jāti* situation. Somehow, all seem to think—as
do the "orientalists" and "Indologists" who study texts and
ignore people—that the four-fold scheme, the literary division
into the *bráhmanas* (priests), *ksattrīyas* (rulers, warriors,
governors), *vaisyas* (merchants) and *śūdras* (laborers), was
the actual, historical standard in ancient times, and that the
jātis, the thousands of endogamous and "fissiparous" castes
somehow descended, multiplied, and degenerated from the
old scheme. Unfortunately, all this is nonsense. It is idle to
speculate about the origin of the *jāti* system, the endogamous
segmentation of Indian society. The quest after origins has
proved futile in many branches of modern anthropology, not
so much because theories of origins cannot be proved, but
because they cannot be disproved—not because they may all
be wrong, but because they may all be correct. Thus, when
modern Indians speculate about the origin of the caste system, they think in literary or quasi-literary terms, trying to
catch the origin of the *varna* classification; it was color (the
literal meaning of *varna*)—the higher the lighter, the lower
the darker—or personal and social qualifications and achievements which decided caste status. Yet, what they *see* when

27

they look around at people has nothing whatever to do with *varna*: here are hundreds of endogamous mutually suspicious sections which constitute the villages of India and Pakistan, or the various Asian groups in East Africa. It would be a bit like looking for Harvard University, and trying to find one building that *is* Harvard University. There is no such building at all—there are many, plus many things which are not buildings, which constitute Harvard University. The somewhat craggy buildings and grounds, some undusted skeletons, a magnificent library complex, the unpredictable janitorial services, etc., might be viewed as a *degeneration* of the noble notion of Harvard University, but it is obvious that the seeker set out with the wrong premises in the first place. There never were *varnas* in actual India except in the books; there always were *jātis*.

The four-fold *varna* division, stated in the canonical *Purusasūkta* of the Veda, might have been conceived of as an ideal model, a normative guideline, rather than as a division of Indian society at any time. Modern Indians, when asked to what caste they belong, may indeed say, "I am a Brahmin," or "I am a Rājput," which is a synonym for a *ksattrīya*; but this is due to the exalted status of the two uppermost *varnas* and the prestige accruing to the priestly and the royal states. The Brahmins and the Rājputs do not account for more than a fraction of the total population; but this is the fraction that gets around, and that has been exposed to modernity because their grandparents and parents were hired as administrators by India's rulers, foreign and indigenous, since 1300 A.D. The vast majority of the Indian population does not speak English, and does not know about the pretenses and expectations of their more sophisticated, cosmopolitan brothers vis-a-vis the agents of modernity. If you ask a villager anywhere in India or Pakistan who he is, his identification will be in terms of his *jāti*—or *qaum*[5]—a Kāyasth, a Nonia, a Nāyar, a Sārasvat, or any of a hundred other *jāti* designations. Most of these *jātis* are below the *brahmin* and the *ksattrīya;* hence to say, "I am a Vaisya," would be a vacuous reply carrying no operational information.

28

At all times in India there has been a ubiquitous process of "upcasting": groups whose status was low, have been trying to climb—as groups, for such ascent is impossible for the individual unless he migrates hundreds of miles and dissimulates his background. "Upcasting" is accomplished by imitating the higher caste groups around them. This imitation follows a definite pattern all over the subcontinent; it implies corporate withdrawal from professional or ritualistic actions which *pollute,* replacing them by avoidance behavior similar to that of the higher castes in the area. Constant physical contact with organic matter—hides, meat, human and animal cadavers—is defiling, and castes that have or had to handle these substances are the lowest on the rung of the ladder; rituals involving animal sacrifices ranked lower, were more polluting and less pure than vegetarian rituals. In matters of matrimonial alliance, the remarriage of widows has been a mark of the tribals and of low castes; hence a group which wants to "upcaste" itself has to decree that its members abandon widow remarriage. Once a caste has convincingly, consistently, and for a sufficiently long period, desisted from eating meat, from remarrying its widows, and from animal sacrifice, it hopes to be and often will be regarded as a "purer" i.e., higher, group. It may eventually achieve higher caste ranking. In order to speed up the procedure, rituals which used to be the prerogative of the high castes are being introduced, brahmin specialists are hired to perform them, and gradually, the ceremonial style, language, and the total ritualistic setting changes, adapting to the more complex, more standardized, and more highly literary forms of the traditional high castes. This is part of the process of "Sanskritization." It does not mean that the people involved in the process try to understand the Sanskrit language; it does mean that they tend to avail themselves increasingly of the ritual whose literary codification is in Sanskrit.

Caste (*jāti*) status derives from a set of norms which can be stated in terms of degrees of ritualistic defilement or purity:[6] those castes which are traditionally connected with the polluting activities just mentioned, particularly through

29

contact with flesh or meat, alive or dead, are in a state of permanent ritualistic pollution; whereas those castes whose traditional activities avoid such contact, are in a state of relative ritualistic purity. Caste ranking in South Asia, an extremely difficult job, has to take account of degrees of pollution. Rules of commensality provide parallel norms: the rule of thumb is that a person cannot accept ritualistically relevant *cooked* food—for instance, boiled rice—from members of castes below his own, though he can cook and give food to members of lower castes. In my own diction, Indian caste ranking entails the prohibition to eat down, but it allows to cook down—in wealthier households all over India, the cooks are often brahmins, where their employers are not. As Professor McKim Marriott has shown,[7] the most reliable way of ranking caste in any particular region is to observe over a sufficient period of time, and then to tabulate who eats ritualistically relevant food from or with whom. Members of a specific caste in an area may claim, for instance, that they are *ksattrīyas* of some kind, but if other *ksattrīyas* do not accept cooked food from them, then their caste ranks below the refusing caste.

How does this operate in East Africa? The situation is similar, though much simpler. It is simpler not because people have abandoned caste rules—as their spokesmen claim—but because the castes which constitute East African Asian society are few in number, and their status had been completely known and defined in India at the time when the settlers arrived. There is no doubt in the minds of any Gujarati in the three countries, be he a Muslim, a Hindu, or a Jain, that the Patels rank above the *sutāria* (carpenters), and other craftsmen's castes. There are about two dozen castes, which seems a lot to both Africans and whites when they come to know about them; but this is a very small number indeed when compared to the number in comparably sized and populated areas in India. The castes in Asian East Africa are well defined, and there is no group which is not clear about its own image vis-a-vis the other *jātis*.

This does not mean, however, that attempts at "up-casting" are not made. A highly educated lady, a member of one of the richest families in East Africa, has made it one of her life's ambitions to dig into the past of her caste and to prove that its original status was royal, warriorlike, and that its ancestors had been *kṣattrīyas,* not merchants as they are now. Objectively, the lady was wrong; but it is impossible to say whether or not she knew this. I had long discussions with her, spiced with exquisite, strictly vegetarian food, at the home of her brother, which was decorated with the finest artifacts brought from India with selective finesse. "Our ancestors," she said, "fought against Genghis Khan when he attacked India; they fought so hard that there was a stream of blood spreading from the camp of the attackers to that of the defenders; blood *(lauha)* it was, hence our people are called the Lohana." Unfortunately, Genghis Khan never got anywhere near India. The Lohanas rank slightly below the Patels, their status in India is well below the actual *vaiśyas* of the *banyā* or merchant caste, and the word "Lohana" is not derived from *lauha* at all, but probably from *lohā,* "iron," with the suggestion that they might have been iron smelters or blacksmiths at one time. But the veracity of this and similar legendry is quite beside the point: the effort at upcasting continues in all conceivable ways.

The criterion of commensality, once a minimal denominator in India, has all but broken down in East Africa. Officially at least, everybody eats with and from everybody. It is arguable that this is due at least partly to the fact that African cooks have been cooking food in the more affluent Asian households. Pocock has shown[8] that the high caste Hindus in East Africa treat their African domestic servants somewhat like "clean *śūdras*" would be treated by equivalent castes in India. This refers to the domestic servants, not to the high-land tribals: it seems certain that some of the African tribal groups, particularly the Masai, Chaga, and other "tall and fair" tribes, might be considered as of higher status, if the question arose. However, few of these have ever served as domestics in Asian homes. Once cooked food is accepted routinely from cooks of much lower caste ranking, commensality rules have ceased to operate; and in the case where non-Indians do the cooking, it is formally extinct. I observed some exceptions during *prītibhoj,* i.e., religious or life-cycle feasts, where a Gujarati Hindu or Jain *yajamān* (patron of the feast) would feed a large number of fellow-Hindus of all castes. The women of the house who belong to the host's caste would do the ritualistically relevant cooking—i.e., they would prepare the rice or some other staple. However, African servants prepared virtually everything else, the vegetables, the various sugar and milk dishes, and the *dāl* (pulses). At no such occasion would meat be prepared and served, even where the family is otherwise non-vegetarian, as in the case of the majority of the Panjabis. Yet, the use of African cooks at a religious festival is not yet entirely common usage: interviewing ten heads of Lohana, Patel, and Jain families in different East African cities, I found that three rejected the idea that their African servants would be asked to cook food for the *prītibhoj* and other ceremonial occasions; they did not believe it when I told them that I had witnessed such cooking at other places; three of the ten informants were indifferent, but said they would prefer their womenfolk to do the cooking rather than the Africans, "because they cook cleaner"—which statement simulated a denial of ritualistic considerations; four said that Africans in their houses had learned to cook good and clean food and that they did much of the cooking at large feasts, "because the members of the household could not manage it alone."

I attended five *prītibhoj* in four different cities during my sojourn in the field. In only one case—that of a wealthy Patel merchant who had spent several years in Europe—were non-Hindus invited to participate in the feast; at that ceremonial banquet, there were two Ismaili men and their wives among roughly 150 guests. The men and the women ate separately and successively in the same hall, the men eating first. All sat in a *pangat,* i.e., several "lines" or rows, on the well-cleaned floor. At another feast, men and women were served simultaneously, but sat in different courtyards belonging to the house where the banquet was given. The food was distributed by members of the household and by caste mates, and no African would walk along the *pangat*. Asking several men who had given *pritibhoj* more than once, I found that most of them were ambivalent about inviting non-Hindu Asians. Two said they always did; one said it was unthinkable. At all such feasts, especially when the occasion is the marriage of a son or daughter, the non-Hindu Asian, and frequently the European business associate and friends of the host, were invited and fed separately in the salon or in some other ritualistically neutral part of the house, but not in the *pangat*. This follows an Indian pattern—the commensality rule can be tested only in ritualistically relevant areas

The sexes are seated separately at a *priti-bhoj* or ritual Love feast.

of the house: Muslims, Europeans, and even Africans would be invited to partake of the food, but not in the ritualistic feeding zone, the *pangat*. American travellers and Peace Corps volunteers in India often report that they were asked for dinner at many places, but the more perceptive among them did notice the difference—they would be served tea and sweets, or even the staple meal, in a part of the house which was removed from the ritualistic zone; orthodox South Indian brahmins, for instance, eat in the kitchen, which is virtually a part of the shrine area in the house; when non-brahmins are invited, they are served coffee and sweets, and occasionally the staple food, in other parts of the dwelling.

Trade-exclusiveness has been a radical criterion in India until recent times, and more so in rural than in urban regions. And of course, many caste names are occupational names; the comparison of this aspect of caste structure with the medieval guilds in Europe is tempting and not quite inapposite. No doubt, if a caste name *means* a particular trade, then that trade must have been the traditional occupation of the group in question, at one time or the other, even though it is no longer followed today. Thus, the Patels of the Gujarat and of East Africa were land-owning peasants of India, "Patel" being a synonym of *Patidār* which means precisely this—a landholder or a tiller of the soil which he owns himself, or with which his ancestors had been enfeoffed by some ruler.

The "small castes" *(choti jāt)* of the Gujarati Hindus are immediately recognized by their caste-names, which are straight occupational designations: the *mūci* are cobblers, the *sutāria* carpenters, and the *soni* goldsmiths, slightly higher than the other *"choti jāt"* sections in the caste ranking. Among the Sikhs, the Rāmgarhiā are the lower ranked section, the Jats being the higher. In India, the latter are the dominant and politically most powerful group in the Panjab. But though the Rāmgarhias were craftsmen by tradition, their caste name is a loconymic, Rāmgarh being the name of a village cluster in the Panjab. It is important to remember that the traditional caste designation does not mean that all or any of its present-day members follow the indicated occupation. Yet, the lowest ranking do, because members of higher *jātis* would not engage in polluting occupations. *Mūcī* "cobblers," for instance, are the only people that make shoes or repair them, because contact with hides and leather is among the most highly defiling kinds of work. Some activities are hierarchically neutral, particularly agriculture; so are the new occupations which center upon engines and all imported machinery. In India, all the castes now represented in East Africa were farmers in addition to whatever other occupation they followed, from the Brahmin to the *choṭī jāts*. In urban India and Pakistan, as well as in East Africa, members of all castes do the types of work germane to their own and higher caste traditions. But all refrain from activities which were identified with castes ranking below them. For example, a modern *mūcī* (cobbler) might also act as a tailor *(darzī)*, or he might be a clerk. In India, he will probably also till a small plot of land. But a Lohana, in India or East Africa, will not do the work of a tailor or of a cobbler, even if that work happens to be more lucrative. In other words, the rule is that one may work "up," i.e., one may do jobs which were the domain of higher castes at one time; one may not work "down," as this would inevitably lower the whole group's status. The process of "upcasting" consists largely in abandoning the polluting activities with which one's own low caste status was previously identified. A cobbler caste in Bihar gave up the making of shoes about thirty years ago, though its members still produce ritualistic drums which are also made of animal hides; yet this is less polluting than making shoes out of leather; one section of those Bihari *mūcīs* (cobblers) did not heed the decree of the caste council and continued their old trade. The result was that the two groups stopped intermarrying with each other—and two new endogamous groups emerged from one original caste, on the grounds of a section of its members' refusal to give up an old trade known to be polluting.

In East Africa, we do not find any such phenomena as the above. Whatever the background of the settlers was—trade, agriculture, or landholding, all of them have become traders. The *choṭī jāt* Gujaratis, the traditional *mūcī* (cobbler), *sutāria* (carpenter), and *darzī* (tailor) continued their respective trades, since they proved economically profitable, with no idea of upcasting through a change of occupation entering the expatriate's mind. A good number of *choṭī jāt* people gave up their former occupations when they succeeded in making better money through straight trading. Among the *dūkā* owners in and around the cities and in the bush, about a fifth were *choṭī jāt* people. There is absolutely no economic discrimination between traders of different castes. They eat together in areas where the number of Asians is limited; they attend each other's parties, participate in the religious and life cycle festivals, and seem to merge in each other's activities in all matters but marriage; for of course, they remain strictly endogamous. Among the Panjabi Sikhs, the Ramgarhias are comparable to the *choṭī jāt* of the Gujaratis, by way of regional caste ranking; the Sikh farmers, or people of farming-cum-martial descent, the *jāt,* would be analogous to the Patels and the Lohanas among the Gujarati and Cutchi groups.

There were some few untouchable families in East Africa, mainly Panjabi. The euphemistic name for untouchables in Northern India previous to Gandhi's pervasive Harijan nomenclature[9] was *Vālmīk*-s: so named after the mythical seer *Vālmīki,* author of the great Hindu Epic *Rāmāyana,* who reportedly belonged to a very humble caste. Vālmīki has become the tutelary deity of several untouchable groups in the North and in the Panjab, with shrines recently dedicated to him: recently, because the promotion of "Great Tradition" mythological identifications was part of the strategy for the emancipation of the untouchables around the turn of the century.

Some of the sweepers employed by Panjabis—Hindus, Sikhs, and some Muslims in East Africa—were Vālmīks; but even before *uhuru* Africans began to take over most of the menial jobs around the house and the *dūkā;* and by 1964, vir-

36

tually all of the Vālmīk families moved back to India. It was therefore not possible for me to check assertions of complete commensality with Panjabi groups who employed Vālmīks; had they been around, would Jāts and Rāmgaṛhias have eaten with them at the *gurdvāra,* just because the Vālmīks were Sikhs, too? I believe they would not. The official reason given might have been that one simply does not eat with one's domestic servants, irrespective of their caste and background. And yet, at all important religious festivals in India and in East Africa, servants do sit in the *paṅgat* if they are Hindus; none of them, however, are untouchables, for though the *choṭī jāt* people have low caste status, they are well within the system of commensal acceptability by caste Hindus in East Africa, and increasingly in the urban areas of Gujarat today.

The minimal criterion of Indian caste is endogamy. This will appear quite often in subsequent chapters because it cuts across a large number of themes. It is part of the official talk, of the modernistic ideology and its jargon, to deny that endogamy persists—just as it is in urban India. Most Indians who live abroad, in Europe and America, and the younger East African Asians, would deny that they marry into their own caste exclusively. They feel that caste endogamy, though a fact known to everyone at home, should not be revealed to outsiders; it is shameful, it is reactionary, it is "not important," it is not the thing that is done in technologically and scientifically advanced countries. Once this denial has been rebutted, as it would be by anyone who knows the situation, the next apologetic step takes the form "a friend (sister, cousin, etc.) of mine married someone from quite a different caste," "most of my friends marry outside their caste. They marry whom they want to marry," etc. All this is simply false. There are complex psychological and cultural reasons today which explain this response pattern which seems mendacious to the non-Indian. In actual fact, there is no statistically significant inter-caste marriage in East Africa. It is almost impossible to give an exact estimate, but risking the opprobrium of all Asian modernites in East Africa I would state that there cannot be more than five hundred (or 1.8 percent) living couples in the three countries, whose marriage was across traditional caste lines. In some communities, the proportion is slightly higher—the Ismailis seem to top the small count—in other communities it just does not happen at all, as among Sikh Rāmgarhias and *choṭī jāt* Gujaratis. Quantitatively, the present situation seems to be equivalent to present day urban areas in the regions and in the caste groups from which the settlers originated. Indian social scientists and western anthropologists who study the South Asian situation have not so far produced substantial information about inter-caste marriage;[10] its occurrence is too infrequent and sporadic to warrant a modal investigation which social scientists would want to undertake.

Roughly a hundred Ismaili men and about fifty Asians of all other communities have married occidental women. To my knowledge, only three Asian women have married foreign males—whites, that is. There is no Asian woman who has married an African, and there are only about five Asian males who have been officially married to African women, whatever the number of previous informal alliances of Asian males with indigenous women might have been.

One could speculate about the reasons why Asians respond so vehemently to the suggestion that endogamy has not broken down, and that there have been few inter-caste marriages in East Africa. All people of Indian origin know that endogamy is the crucial criterion of caste *(jāti)*; they fear that the outsider's familiarity with the caste situation jeopardizes their political future and impugns their cultural advancement. They feel quite strongly that the system is both obsolete and highly dysfunctional. To them, the suggestion "Asians do not really marry across caste lines" implies "Asians are not giving up the caste system with its 'fissiparous tendencies'," they are not really becoming modern, in spite of their claims to the contrary. In their East

African setting, any reference of the fact of endogamy and caste structure, however objective, creates apprehensions that such knowledge will work against the community in its dialog with the African leadership. "If a person has a toothache," an Asian dentist told me, "and you tap him in the area of his pain, he will feel it; but if you tap exactly his infected tooth, he will jump with pain." He meant this to be—as I think it was—a rather apposite simile for the caste and endogamy question: Asians are sensitive about the system; they are even more sensitive about the core of that system, i.e., the rules of endogamy. And although the more vocal in the community would employ the Gandhian dialectic, which avers that it was not caste that should be given up, but the *feeling of discrimination on the basis of caste (jātibhed*—a Sanskritized term used in the nationalistic idiom), they still know that this is *not* what caste is all about; they know that caste *(jāti)*, if anything at all, is the rule of endogamy which persists even in the technologically advanced milieu in Africa.

At least three of the most knowledgeable Asian leaders took offense to my frequent queries about caste in East Africa. Their reactions ranged between refusal to accept the *fact* of caste endogamy ("all people nowadays marry whomever they like; my best friend married a member of some other caste") and, for the more realistic among them, playing down the facts as either unimportant or harmful or both; "no one talks about caste these days"; "we are trying to get away from caste, and you remind us of these bygones"; "if you talk in terms of caste, then people will not advance," etc. This reaction pattern is replicated by modern Indians anywhere in the world. The more perspicacious in a modern Indian audience understand the need to study "caste" once the goals of social analysis have been explained; but they usually suggest that there are more interesting, and more important things to be studied about modern Indian society. "Why do you study these old things—you have not studied India during the past five years—there have been so many changes—no one is interested in caste any longer," "Why don't you describe the steel factory in Jinja, or the cotton ginnery in Kampala?" etc. Or "how would you feel if a foreigner started writing and talking about the American caste system, about negroes and whites. . . ." etc. That there are indeed many foreigners and natives who do just that, seemed to be quite unknown to the Asian critic; but then, why should it be known to him? River valley dams and steel factories are important, but they are not the anthropologist's business. Whatever ennui this book might create among its Asian readers, there is nothing that can be done about it. "Caste," i.e., the Indian social structure, does not disappear by decree, nor by the contention, however justifiably stated and reiterated, that "caste should not be thought of," or spoken about.

I shall begin with the Hindus, who are the majority, then move on to the Jains, then to the Sikhs who are traditionally closest to the Hindus. I shall then proceed to the various Muslim groups. It would be perfectly admissible to class the Goans as a caste, for they fit into the central criterion for a caste—they are endogamous. They themselves, however, reject any identification as Indians. The Goans of East Africa do not regard their ways as Indian ways. The other Asians reciprocate the Goans' feelings. Although two traditionally different and socially distant communities as, say, the *choṭī jāt* Gujarati Hindus and the Panjabi Muslims, view each other with the indifference that stems from cultural disparity, they would still regard one another as part of an Indian cultural body, but neither of them would include the Goans, not because they are Christian, but because they reject their Indian background altogether, going so far as to gradually renounce their Konkanī in favor of English, thus opting out from the radical cultural criterion of identity in East Africa, the speaking of an Indian language at home.

The two most numerous and economically influential groups are the Gujarati Patels and the Cutchi Lohanas. Patels are easier to spot in the East African area: most of them carry their caste names, i.e., Patel, Amin, or one of about half a dozen names which indicate their being Patels. The Nairobi telephone directory has 16 pages of Patels, the Dar es Salaam directory over 3 pages. The Lohanas have about a dozen *gotra*-names[11] and in addition to these, they share some occupational indicator names with other Gujarati and Cutchi groups. Structurally, these two groups are very similar to each other. They also have the closest inter-caste contacts in East Africa. Short of Patel-Lohana intermarriage—less than a dozen cases have been confirmed for all the three territories—they share each other's social and ritualistic life to the largest thinkable extent. In the Cutchi-Gujarati caste ranking in India, Patels stand slightly above the Lohana; in East Africa the few marriages between members of the two groups seem to bear this out: Patel men married Lohana girls, unwittingly following the Indian tradition of permissible hypergamy: men may at times marry slightly beneath their caste status, but women may not. However, ranking between these two large, powerful groups in East Africa is a purely theoretical procedure. Unless a conservative spokesmen of either group were pressed to make a ranking assessment, neither would claim higher status for his group. However, when the question of origins does come up vis-a-vis some history-oriented spokesmen of any caste, they will claim higher original status than *any* caste within their *varna,* or even above it. The most typical example, perhaps, are the powerful, numerous Kāyasths in North India. They rank ceremonially between *śūdras* and *vaiśyas;* but their own legend places them squarely above the *vaiśyas,* as *kṣattrīyas* on a par with Rājputs. Rājputs do not accept them as their equals, but this is beside the point. In East Africa, I encountered only half a dozen Kāyasth families, and none of their elders knew otherwise than that they were a caste of *kṣattriyā* status. In Bengal, the Kāyasths (Bose, Ghose, Mitra) were declared to be *śūdras* by a court order around the turn of the century; North Indian *kāyasths* were neither affected nor impressed by this decree.

Lohanas and Patels in East Africa are merchants with

a sprinkling of civil servants whose number is on the decline, as their jobs are being taken over by indigenous Africans. Also, those numerous Patels and Lohanas in Kenya who chose British rather than East African citizenship are bound to leave the region sooner or later, unless some close relative, who has Kenyan citizenship, can absorb them into his business or otherwise sustain them. Some 4,000 Asians left Kenya between 1965 and 1968, roughly one-fourth of whom were Lohanas and Patels.

And now to the Patels proper. Whatever their rural, land-holding background in Western India, their identification in East Africa is that of merchants. The North Indian word for merchant being *banyā,* this term has become a lexical indicator for all Asians in the area: and although the actual *banyā* caste (such as the Aggarwal group in Northern India, the Marwārīs and most Rajasthani and Gujarati Jains) is not strongly represented in East Africa in comparison to groups whose background was agricultural, the functional use of *banyā* as "a trader" has come to stick. Not only do the Africans refer to all Asian traders by this term—even to the Sikhs, for whom *banyā* would be an inappropriate appellation in the Panjab—but most Asians have somehow come to accept the word as a generic occupational term. A young Patel woman said "we are all *banyās,* even those who do not have *dukās.*" When I asked her if she knew any real *banyās,* she obviously did not understand the question; not, as a modern friend later suggested, because "these distinctions no longer mean anything," but because she did not know the distinction between *banyā* as a caste designator, referring to certain endogamous groups in India, and the term as simply meaning "a trader." I then pressed this matter to a logical conclusion, and asked her if her father would allow her to marry any *banyā?* She said yes, and I continued "even if he is a Lohana or a Jain?" She hesitated a while, and then said "no, only if he is a *real banyā,* a Patel like ourselves." A similar answer would have been elicited, no doubt, from any young man or woman of her background, belonging to any of the constituent Gujarati or Cutchi groups. Mr. S. G. Amin, former President of the Kenya Congress, was an established leader among the Patels and, of course, among the Asians of Kenya in general until *uhuru*. I asked him if he considered himself and the Patels as *banyās;* he rejected this quite strongly, giving the factually correct answer, i.e., that *banyās* are a distinct group, separate from Patels. He was of course aware of the African, and the average Asian use of *banyā* for any Asian trader; but this, he said was "due to a gross misunderstanding of our society." Mr. Amin was right; a modern man does not necessarily have to blur facts as they are known to him, even if he believes that reiteration of these facts is harmful or reactionary. I found that apart from tradition-bound elders in all the Gujarati groups, it was the intellectually and politically alert modernites, men with considerable empathy and reading, who separated facts about caste and social structure from the official fiction introduced by the Indian nationalist movement and by the agents of the Hindu Renaissance. It is conceivable that most modern Asian remonstrances against "caste" really stem from ignorance rather than from reformatory zeal.

The Patels in the Gujarat consist of two endogamous sections, the *Karwā* and the *Lewā*. In intra-caste ranking, the *Lewās* stand slightly above the *Karwā*, which seems to be supported by the fact that of six *Karwā-Lewā* intermarriages in the Ahmedabad area, contracted over the past decade, only one was a *Karwā* man and a *Lewā* woman liaison; the other five were *Lewā* men and *Karwā* women, following the pervasive pattern of patrifocal hypergamy. Among the *Karwā* and the *Lewā*, there are several subsections. The most highly self-conscious are the *chaṭṭagāoñ* "six villages" section from the Charottar area near Ahmedabad. These designations refer to certain village clusters in the area, i.e., *daśagāoñ* "ten villages," *chaṭṭagāoñ* "six" etc. In India, these sub-groups are again endogamous: people belonging to any one of these hexadic or decadic groups do not marry outside that group; but within the group, there is village exogamy as in most parts of India—which means that a *chaṭṭagāoṅ* person does not marry a partner from the village of his patrilineage; he must marry into one of the remaining five villages within the "six villages"-cluster. A *dasagāoṅ* man does not marry into the village of his patrisib, but must marry into one of the remaining nine villages, etc. This is the situation in India. In East Africa, the procedure has been highly simplified. In the first place, there are hardly any *Karwā* Patels in the area; in fact, the only *Karwā* I met were a school teacher who had been hired from India and his wife. Most Patels hail from the Charottar area near Ahmedabad, with Baroda (Varodra in Gujarati) taking the second place. Charottar has been the center of the *Lewā* section of Patels for at least four centuries; Patels settled in Baroda much more recently. In line with the Indian (and Chinese) expatriate aggregation pattern, the first *Lewā* Patel settlers in East Africa brought their own kin from India, all of whom were from the Charottar region. Within the *Lewās* settled in East Africa, the *chaṭṭagāoṅ* "six village"-cluster descendants seem to regard themselves, and are regarded by the other Patels, as slightly superior in status. However, the village-exogamous pattern of the *chaṭṭagāoṅ* area in India has completely broken down. *Chaṭṭagāoṅ Lewās* in East Africa can marry any *Chaṭṭagāoṅ* mate, regardless of whether the partner's ancestry was from the same village or not. However, marriages between *chaṭṭagāoṅ* and other *Lewā* are still rare in East Africa. Young Patels, people whose marriages were arranged within the last ten years, hardly know that *chaṭṭagāoṅ* Patels did not marry other *Lewās* in the past generations, nor in the Gujarat today. The older and the more conservative do know it, and marriage negotiations are conducted along the old endogamous lines. However, if an economically advantageous match can be contracted outside the *chaṭṭagāoṅ* circle, there is sufficient resilience to accommodate such a liaison.

None of the informants I asked knew the etymology of the designations *karwā* and *lewā*. "I don't have a darned idea," a *Lewā* sophisticate told me. I suggested that these terms may have been loconymics at one time. But the informant did not know of any area or village whose name might resemble these two designatory terms. On the other hand, he was aware that the *Lewā* hailed mainly from the Charottar area.

The Patels in East Africa, of course, do not refer to themselves as Lewā except on the rare occasions when questions of origin and descent are discussed. All Asians, Africans and whites, simply refer to them as "the Patels." Non-Patels tend to think that the Patels are the most affluent and powerful. They are possibly the most highly corporate group among the Hindu Asians—with the Ismailis topping all in the degree of cohesion and corporateness. This notion probably prevails because most Patels use "Patel" as their official surname, and the sheer number of people called Patel in every sphere of East African life is quite obtrusive. "Most Asians are Patels" is a statement which I have heard from non-Asians in East Africa, quite a few times, at different places. There is no doubt that they are among the three economically most successful of the Asian communities in the area. Though most Patels are merchants, the better informed among the non-Gujaratis assess the Patels' status with more precision. A Panjabi Ārya Samāji man, when asked whether the Patels were genuine *banyās* like the Aggarwals in the Panjab and Uttar Pradesh, said after some reflection "Are the Patels *banyās*? No, actually they are not; they are like *khattrīs*. The Lohanas are another business class here, they are different (from the Patels). Here there are no real *marwārīs*" (*Paṭel banye hain? Nahīn Paṭel banyā to nahīn, khattrī log jaise hain na; Lohānā bhī business class ilādā hai un se lekin aslī marwāri idhar hain hī nahīn.*) I found such unpremeditated musings by informed outsiders most helpful. Most northern Hindus, with the exception of the actual *kṣattrīya* class (the Rājputs) think that *khattrīs* are *kṣattrīyas*. This is due to the phonetic similarity of the two words, especially in the North Indian idiom, where they sound identical. The formal criterion for a group belonging to the "twice-born"[12] used to be that their men underwent the ritual of initiation and the investiture with the sacred thread *(jenēu)*, the *upanayana* ceremony. Until the turn of the century Patels did not wear the sacred thread in India or in Africa; neither did the Panjabi *khattrī* in the Panjab or in Africa. This has changed, due in part to the influence of the *Ārya Samāj* and in part to the ubiquitous phenomenon of Sanskritization.[13] Many groups whose members did not consider themselves as entitled to the rite of the "twice-born" now do so with a vengeance. If many Patels in East Africa at this moment do not plan to have their sons initiated, it is due to the general psychological stress which the whole community is experiencing, a state not conducive to more than such minimal ritualistic observance as marriages or funerals. But hardly any Patel in East Africa knows that his ancestors did not wear the *yajñopavita* in India, believing it is due to modernization that people no longer wear it today. If we have to interpret a *jāti* in terms of the theoretical, traditional *varṇa*-scheme at all, the Patels would probably fall between *vaiśyas* and *śūdras.* The Patels themselves, as well as all Indians who are interested in tradition and who are rudimentarily familiar with the canonical writings, believe and affirm strongly that the *varṇa* system handed down from Vedic times was the actual system of social stratification, and that this system is dying out or has been "abolished." Due to the influence of the *Ārya Samāj* and other modern reform movements the fourfold *varṇa* scheme is now said not to refer to status by birth, but is status acquired by skill or talent: a learned person is a brahmin; a heroic, courageous person, a *kṣattrīya;* a person who runs good and honest business is a *vaiśya;* and a man skilled in arts and crafts, a *śūdra.* Gandhi taught this with much emphasis and during all periods of his political life. It is the official account of things, and any other suggestion is rejected as wrong or hostile. It seems to follow quite naturally, then, that wealthy groups would "upcaste" themselves in the one scheme which they know and which they take for granted, even when they claim that it no longer exists, or that it is about to fade out. Yet actually, there is only one region on the sub-continent, the area of Rājasthān, where all the four castes are represented in line with the otherwise purely theoretical *varṇa*-scheme. The Patels would not fit either the *kṣattrīya* or the *vaiśya* category, because they are not ritualistically entitled to wear the *yaj-ñopavita*. But then, the Hindu Renaissance has quite consciously blurred these distinctions: not only Patels, but erstwhile untouchables now often undergo Vedic ceremonies, and insist on wearing the sacred thread. So far, however, the anthropological criterion still obtains: actual *kṣattrīyas* in the rural setting and in the grassroot milieux of India will not accept cooked food from Patels, and of course, they would not regard Patels as eligible marriage partners.

The Cutchi Lohanas, too, claim *kṣattrīya* status and they too are not accorded this status by actual *kṣattrīya* castes. Lohana leaders seem more concerned about upcasting than Patels which may or may not have anything to do with their slightly lower ranking compared to the former.

The organizational side of the Patels in East Africa is more complex than meets the eye. Like all the Asian groups, the Patels have their long established socio-religious service societies, which function both as ritualistic control agencies—even though with rapidly decreasing efficacy—and as secular coordinating organs covering virtually all fields of life, but especially education. There are very few schools which bear the name of a Patel organization *per se;* and after *uhuru,* no parochial schools can operate on communal bases. There are quite a few excellent schools, elementary and high, which are run or financed or under advisement of one or the other Patel service society. But this does not show in the recruitment of staff or pupils. If any part of the Asians' activities has been modified to adapt itself to the rules and the needs of post-*uhuru* Africa, it is educational management. Virtually all castes had their own schools, but if ever there was a degree of discrimination against pupils and faculty nothing of it shows today. In two elementary schools and one high school financed and controlled by a Patel association in Nairobi, only 7 and 10 percent, respectively, of the pupils and the faculty were Patels—which is low even for the total school-going population of that city. There were few African children in that school, but that may be due to the emergent feeling of African parents in the cities, who wish to choose schools which are not dominated by Asians, if they can. Asians have profound respect for educational efforts of any sort, and the parochiality which may be evident in other walks of life is at its lowest in matters of education. This, incidentally, is a thing which even the most chauvinistic, anti-Asian Africans admit: Asians have a strong love for learning.

The two most significant caste organizations of the Patels are the Patel Club and the Patel Brotherhood. Both of these organizations have premises in the major cities of East Africa. Both recruit members freely, without any reference to the social, or even the economic background of the members. Membership in neither of them is automatic or compulsory—most young male Patels join at a time when their fathers suggest it to them.

The difference between the Brotherhood and the Club, however, is significant on ideological grounds. To put it quite briefly—the *Brotherhood* is the conservative, vegetarian, teetotalling, religiously involved association. The *Club* does not object to meat-eating, liquor consumption, card-playing, and other activities which are traditionally frowned upon. The buildings of the Club are modern, and their interior decor quite often plush. Two of the Club premises have large bars with a wide range of untraditional potions. Although membership is open to both sexes, one hardly sees women in the precincts of the Club—and even less so, of course, on the Brotherhood premises. At some annual functions, or if some visitors are to be feted, some members bring their wives; but if you walk into the Club premises on weekdays, you will see men between twenty-five and sixty clustered around the tables, relaxing on the sofas, or contemplating a "peg" of whiskey at or near the bar. Then, of course, there is the inevitable bridge, and it is here that the division of the sexes seems to be breaking down. Some Patel ladies are fine bridge players, and their partnership and post mortem advice is sought, or given unsolicitedly, as is the case anywhere in the pursuit of that noble game.

The Patel Club does not restrict membership to Patels—in theory, anyone can join. But in fact, hardly more than a token number of the members are not Patels but Lohanas or other Gujarati Hindus. I do not think there is any Muslim member in any of the Clubs—each of which, incidentally, is fairly autonomous in its management, centralization of the Patel Club being ideological rather than actual. But office bearers in at least two of the Patel Clubs are Lohanas. However this may be, the important thing about the Club is that it provides a precinct and a forum for those Patel men who want to perpetuate social corporateness, who do not want to be alienated from their communal background and who feel that this sort of modern, liberal, comparatively indulgent organization provides a forum. "All modern people enjoy a glass of whiskey," a functionary of one of the largest Patel Clubs told me, "but most of our people think it is wrong. Still, when you do things together, in view of your friends, it is not so bad. We can be like western people, and still remain Indian."

The Patel Brotherhood is a very different kettle of fish. Most of its members are over forty; the Brotherhood does not have the ecological layout of the Club. There are Brotherhood precincts in many cities, but the members usually meet in houses of other members, the actual quarters being intended for business meetings, rather than for socializing. Also, the fact that a man joins the Brotherhood rather than the Club implies that he does not care for socializing in the modern sense. Officially, no Brotherhood member would have a drink; virtually all of them are vegetarians. This of course does not mean that Brotherhood members never drink; but they feel, in line with the more conservative view, that drinking is and remains a vice, and that if it has to be done,

it should be done solitarily. The danger of alcoholism as a
sequel of lone drinking does not seem to be known to the
conservative, or for that matter to any Asian. Drinking, like
virginity, does not stand evaluation in terms of degree: if
a person drinks, it does not make much difference how
often he drinks. Teetotalling and vegetarianism are implicit
rules of behavior in the Brotherhood. Club members drink,
and in most recent years, they have begun to flaunt their
freedom from feelings of guilt connected with drinking; those
Brotherhood members who drink do so with remorse, and
not *coram populo*.

Most Patels have remained vegetarians in East Africa.
I suggest that about one half of the male Patel population
consume alcoholic beverages—whereas I do not think that
more than a handful of Patel women ever have a drink,
that small number belonging entirely to the highest economic strata. I would think that about one third of the
adult male Patels in East Africa eat meat irregularly, though
probably not more than a few hundred Patel women do.

I obtained confirmation on four cases of Patel-Lohana
hypergamous matrimonial alliances. The interviewed were
people who had been married to each other for over five
years. All the four men were Patels, the women Lohanas.
Three out of the four men assured me that "there are hundreds of cases like ours" all over East Africa. When I asked
the men (these interviews were conducted separately, although in the same city) if they knew of cases where the
women were Patels and the men Lohana, they said there were
a few cases but they did not know them. I believe that alliances between Lohanas and Patels are slightly more frequent than between any other Gujarati Hindu group. This
has to do with life-style affinities between Lohanas and Patels;
these two groups feel most comfortable in each other's presence and social contacts between them are frequent, natural,
and strainless. Yet, even some very young and modern people
were quite aware of the atypicality of such intermarriages.
"A few years ago," a Lohana girl told me, "a Patel boy loved

a Lohana girl very much. She got pregnant, and their parents arranged for a magistrate wedding" (i.e., a civil ceremony). "But when they got a boy, then the Hindu wedding was conducted later, and they are quite happy now." This, of course, was mighty irregular. Middle class Asian girls do not get pregnant before marriage; if it does happen, it bodes utter tragedy for all the involved. If this case was true, it was indeed exceptional.

Let us move to the Lohanas. When seen contrasted to their previous Indian setting, the Lohanas have done very well for themselves. In India, Patels at the time of the first migration to Africa were modally better off than Lohanas, largely because they had been closer to urban centers than the predominantly rural Lohanas in the Cutchi speaking areas of Western India. Although Patels were landowners by caste and tradition, their moorings on the land were probably not quite so strong as the Lohanas'. Also, apart from having been more urban than the latter, Patels pride themselves on being more urbane than other Hindu groups in that general area of India. But by far the two richest families in East Africa are Lohanas, and this is known not only to Asians, but to most African and white urbanites.

Mr. Mulji Madhvani came from India as a petty trader around the turn of the century. "He carried samples of clothing on his head, peddling it from door to door," a Panjabi informant told me. Though this was not quite true, it is the stereotype of the Indian entrepreneur who starts from scratch. The Madhvanis now own substantial light industry in Uganda and to a lesser extent in Kenya, and they run their production on modern lines, with little waste. Estimates about their total worth vary greatly, ranging from a cautious three million to a hazardous twenty million dollars, all told; the Mehta family, also headquartered in Uganda, is a not too distant runner-up; they too are Lohanas.

We have seen that caste ranking is difficult in the Gujarati Hindu context; but basic rank identifications are strong and spontaneous. The test is easily made—the anthropologist working in Indian society must select a person who is neither very interested in nor very knowledgeable about such matters; an apparently paradoxical procedure. In Africa, such persons are easily found: all the young with an English education qualify as informants. Thus, when I told a Lohana girl of about nineteen, that the Indian film actress Nanda belonged to the *mūcī* (cobbler) caste, the young lady got quite irritated and retorted "No, no, she is from a good family." Good family, in Gujarati grassroot diction, means Lohana, Patel, or Brahmin; Muslims and non-Gujarati's are culturally so distant that such assignations could hardly be elicited at all from such an informant. Yet the same young Lohana woman mused about a friend (Lohana) who had fallen in love with a *choṭi jāt* girl in India: "When love comes, caste does not count, nor does the family." A little later she said, "when the family is concerned, then love must stand back." Such vacillation concerning considerations of kin versus modern romantic attitudes is quite pervasive in modern urban parlance. Judgments regarding interpersonal relations based on competing loyalties do not evoke premeditated response. This is very different indeed from situations in which the individual is not personally concerned: when "caste" is said to have been "abolished," or when "everyone marries whomsoever he or she likes nowadays," the reference is to an assumed principle or to other people, not to the speaker or his own family.

The Lohanas are not so conspicuously organized as the Ismailis, yet their leaders in East Africa are deeply conscious of the need for organization, even though the older ones among them are painfully aware that the young generation neither cares nor wants to care. Mr. Thakurbai Kalidas, President of the All East African Lohana *maṇḍal* (organization, circle) at the time of my field work, granted me an extensive interview in his simple, austere office at Kampala. The President's tenure is five years, and it is usually a senior, respected, pious, tradition-conscious, and fairly affluent Lohana man who is elected to this post, which is honorary and tedious. The President chairs the supreme council of the Lohanas, which coordinates some 30,000 Lohanas in the three countries. Mr. Kalidas gave me approximate figures; he thought there were some 40,000 Lohanas adults in the whole area, about 14,000 in Uganda, slightly more in Kenya, and roughly 7,000 in Tanzania; there are hardly any in Zanzibar at this time, and even before the Okello upheaval in 1963-64, this was the least represented community on that island. The Lohanas, so the President told me, were all Cutchi speakers, and still are, though the new generation in East Africa hardly speaks it, their ancestral language having been absorbed in the more stylish, more prestigious Gujarati. Quite a few of the Lohanas had their ancestry in Saurashtra, where a patois of Gujarati is spoken, though all Lohanas originally resided in Cutchi-speaking areas. There is an unconscious attempt at deemphasizing the Cutchi background of the group. The fact that the Ismaili Muslims have been speaking Cutchi with no embarrassment or diffidence might have prompted the Lohanas *not* to perpetuate it. Ismailis were converts from Lohanas—a fact known to all Asians in East Africa, Hindu and Muslim.

When I asked Mr. Kalidas about recruitment into the Lohana *maṇḍal,* he said that the *maṇḍal* accepts people of groups other than the Lohanas without any question; there are many Patel members, and even some Muslims (probably Ismaili) in the larger cities. If this is a fact, then it would mean that the Lohana leaders practice wider tolerance than do other Hindu groups. Reflecting on the various Cutchi and Gujarati speaking groups in the old days in India, and on the settlers in East Africa, Mr. Kalidas said "there are many Cutchis among Muslims; there are also Bhatias, both Hindu and Muslim." When I asked him if the Bhatias—Hindu Bhatias that is—were *banyās* or *khattrī,* he said "they are more like *banyās*. But *banyās* (i.e., *banyas̄* by actual caste —Bh.) do not marry them, though they eat and drink with them." Let me add that the President himself is an orthodox and mature person, who supports the principle of strict en-

dogamy. When I asked him whether the Lohanas in East
Africa observed such strict endogamy as the *Ka̤rwā* and *Lewa*
sections among the Patels, he said that there were many sub-
groups among the Lohanas, but that the only restriction was
that a man may not marry into his own *gotra*.[14] This is
no different from any other Hindu society. According to
Mr. Kalidas, there are forty-six *gotras* among the Lohanas.
This is the total number in India, but only a fraction seem
to be represented in East Africa. Such *gotra* names as
Madhvani, Mehta, Dalal, he said, are the most frequent in
East Africa; but in India, there are the Makhejas, Karkarals,
and many others.

Now "Mehta" is not a *gotra* name at all—it is a functional title given to people of various castes under the Muslim
rulers and into British times. So when I asked the President
whether Mehta was really a *gotra* like, say, Makheja, he hesitated and said "Mehta is what other people here in Africa
call a *clerk*." After several conversations with Lohanas who
were sensitive to traditional matters, it became quite clear to
me that there was considerable confusion about categorical
differences in family names. Obviously "Mehta," meaning
master or clerk in Persianized North Indian vernacular, is no
more a *gotra* name than "Dalal," which means a broker or
"Kapadia," a cloth seller; but Mehta and Dalal are more
frequent surnames than Madhvani and other proper *gotra*
names. A *gotra* being a patrisib with a mythological apical
ancestor—a *ṛṣi* or seer of Vedic times—it must have a Sanskrit
or Sanskrit-derived name, which is patently impossible with
such names as "Mehta" or "Dalal"; and yet, most of my informants thought that these were genuine *gotra* names. There
is a simple test for clarification: as a *gotra* derives its name
from the mythical ancestor, one should ask a tradition-oriented
informant who the *ṛṣi* at the apex of the *gotra* was. But here,
my best subjects hedged—for they were as conscious as I of the
obvious fact, that terms meaning broker or clerk do not
connect with any ancient seer. The replies which I got in
three cases were second-thought responses: "We Mehtas," a

Lohana gentleman whose surname was Mehta said, "belong to a group called the *Rārhīya gotras."* This was an important aside. It seems probable that the Lohanas class several genuine *gotras* under one regional bracket, which makes it possible to widen the range of matrimonial alliances. A term like *rārhīya* "of the region," which means exactly the same as the Maharashtrian *"desasth"* designating a large section of brahmins in that area, or *rār* in Bengal, comprising one of the two major Brahmin groupings in Eastern India, mitigates the stringent rules pertaining to *gotra,* which is the minimal exogamous segment in India. Once the *gotra* is deemphasized through this process of merging into a larger, non-exogamous unit, it becomes easier to create alliances which would have been impossible in the traditional setting in earlier days. In other words, when stress is successfully shifted from an exogamous unit *(gotra)* to an endogamous unit like *rārhīya, desasth, rār,* etc., designating a region of provenance rather than a patrisib, then rules of exogamy are liberalized. This becomes even more important in East Africa, where the selection of Lohana *gotras* is limited. However, this specific process must have started in India quite a while ago, probably a century or so before the first migration to East Africa.

An important clue, perhaps providing an alternative to this hypothesis, was furnished by another Lohana leader. When asked why people change their *gotra* name into some sort of vocational designation, he said "when they go to war, they change their names." In other words, people who enlisted in some sort of mercenary service during Moghul rule —as early as in the sixteenth century—may have been called by their rank or their function rather than their names, just as a man is as likely, or more likely, to be called "Sergeant," "Quartermaster," or "Sparks" rather than "Mr. Smith" by his officers or his comrades. Mehta, Dalal, and other Lohana names I encountered might easily be construed in this manner. As an afterthought, the same informant then added "Lohanas were *ksattrīyas* (warriors) from the beginning. And those who carried flags ahead in battle were Lohanas, and the *roars* which they emitted sounded like *rār rār*—hence they were then called *rārhīya.*" This statement was amusing and informative. Amusing, because the quasi-morpheme *rār* could not possibly have been known to Cutchi speakers before any of them became familiar with the English verb "to roar"; there is no morpheme resembling "roar" and connoting the act of roaring in any Indian language. It is an interesting linguistic attempt of upcasting on the side of a caste which is diffident about its rank; this sort of etymologizing feeds into the claim of warrior-status, since warriors roar when they charge. However, it is obvious that *rārhīya*, like *rātha* in Maharashtra or *Rār* in Bengal, derives from the Indic morpheme *rāstra* "land, region, country." And just as in the case of the *Desasth* brahmins of the Maratha country, or the *Rār* brahmins in Bengal, the word signifies a group that was indigenous at a time when other groups settled alongside, referring to the original population as *desasth* or *rār*—meaning "local." Here as elsewhere in Hindu India, there is prestige in proved migration from another area, particularly from the North. In Kashmir and the Panjab regions complexions are thought to be light—the correlative implication being that the local residents were darker, hence of lower caste status. Let me stress that the historicity or legendarity of these assumptions are quite irrelevant—it is the ascription that counts, not the actual history. When I asked a senior Lohana man where his ancestors had come from, he said "from Kashmir, from the Panjab . . ." and after a while "it is from the Panjab that we came." The reason why this informant corrected himself, finally claiming the Panjab rather than Kashmir as his ancestral home, was subtle: he knew that the only non-Muslims in Kashmir were brahmins, or the ruling Dogra who were not Kashmiri. The Panjab was full of *ksattrīyas* or *ksattrīya*-like castes, and anyone migrating from there could safely claim warrior background for his community.

Each major caste-group in East Africa has its own printed periodical. It may either be published in East Africa itself

—mostly in Gujarati (for example, the Ithna Asari periodical *Federation* which is distributed from Arusha, a Gujarati paper in spite of its name), sometimes in English; or else, the caste publication comes from India, heavily subsidized by its community members in East Africa. The Lohana publication is called *Hitaisī*—"well-wisher." It is the "newspaper" for the whole Lohana community, one of its most regular readers told me. It contains matrimonial advertisements just like all Indian papers; it helps to find brides in India if, for one reason or the other, no East African Lohana girl seems eligible. *Hitaisī* has a regular column containing social and cultural news about the community in East Africa; this is a permanent feature, and quite significant: though most of the subscribers live in India, this column provides current information about that section of the Lohanas which has acquired name, fame, and wealth abroad. The paper is now in its sixth decade of publication. For a while, the Lohana Maṇḍal President himself used to write this column, which features "social, educational reports—about here and about there, which are read and discussed by our people here and there,"—"here," meaning in East Africa, "there," in India.

As I traced the Lohana self-image in depth, certain specific acts of identification provided some clues. A Lohana businessman in Mwanza told me "It is our custom to don the *yajñopavīt* (the sacred cord of the "twice-born" castes) for one day just before the lad gets married." Yet he dodged the question as to whether Lohanas were actually entitled to it in western Indian traditions. "In East Africa hardly anyone wears it nowadays," he said, obviously referring to castes which did originally wear it; "among the old people, one or two wear it, but the *new generation* (he used the English phrase) doesn't, and the boys don't even know its meaning. They don't know that it means *purity*." The informant confused the final part of the word *yajñopavīta* with *"yajñapavitra."* But there is no such term—*yajñopavīta* parses into *yajña* "ritual, Vedic sacrifice" + *upavīta* "donned," i.e., "donned for ritualistic purposes." Language and culture theoreticians will be pleased with this sort of statement: we might see in it an unconscious reaction by the speaker against the lexical meaning of the word: "to be donned for the Vedic sacrifice" suggests the prerequisite twice-born status; but a factitious rendition of *yajñopavīta* as "that which purifies for the ritual"—with the final morpheme misread, ignorantly or intentionally, as -*pavitra* "pure," takes the edge off: for after all, anyone who is "pure" *should* be worthy of the ritual. This is highly typical of reformed Hindu parlance. From Swami Dayananda through Vivekananda and Gandhi right up to this day, there has been a conscious attempt to explain the caste hierarchy as one of merit, not of birth. There is not only no support for this view in the canonical scriptures, but the contrary is stated quite clearly. The traditional view, reiterated even in the non-canonical *Bhagavadgītā,* is that one should do "the work for which one is born." Just how conscious these processes are with a modern Lohana informant in East Africa is an arguable matter.

When I told this informant that I had seen brahmins wear the sacred thread *(yajñopavīta)* in East Africa, plus some Ārya Samājists during their morning and evening observances, he said: "No, everyone should wear it; but nowadays the young educated men don't think it is necessary." When I mentioned the fact that most Ārya Samāji males, regardless of their original caste, tend to wear it for the minimal daily ritual, he nodded assent (he was not an Ārya Samāji), then adding "the Ārya Samājis think that all Hindus should wear it; why, even Muslims should wear it, *if they are pure.* If you think a man is pure, he should wear it." Once more, an avowal of the need for purity as the only qualification. Etymological dissimulation is an important instrument in the Indian apologetic strategy.

Although there are proportionally few Lohanas who belong to the Ārya Samāj, quite a few influential Lohanas sympathize with this fundamentalistic, iconoclastic sect. A senior Lohana man had just returned from Porbandar, India—

the city where his father had lived and, incidentally, Mahatma Gandhi's birthplace. "There is a school for Harijans now;[15] all of them do the *sandhyā* (minimal ritual observance) in the morning, all of them wear the sacred cord."

Another Lohana man in Uganda mused "in former days, Lohanas stuck to themselves; but now they have come out of their shell, we are just like *banyās* (merchants)."

The legend of Northern origin persists; the same man said "when our ancestors lived in the Panjab, some were farmers, a few were in business, some in the military and the civil services. But now we are all over the place; there are some 20,000 families in East Africa, in Malagasay, and Mozambique, and Mauritius; some have even ventured into the Congo. They all do business. But in the bush, it is the *banyās* who have shops, not the Lohanas." This was not correct—the Lohanas are among the most adaptable. The toughest shopkeepers in the bush represent virtually all castes. Yet, the operational self-image as *banyās* is quite strong: the Lohanas were not merchants originally; and though they are no doubt among the most successful today, this informant obviously felt that only a man who was a real merchant, by tradition, would practice the frugality and sustain the hardships of the bush.

Yet another male Lohana aged about forty said that Lohanas and Bhatias—the first Indians who had gone to Zanzibar before the Railroad was built and before the British assumed sovereignty—had intermarried during the first decades of their earliest African residence. Why did they stop doing so? "On religious grounds; they were Vaisnavas (worshippers of Visnu); we were Saivas (worshippers of Śiva)." Again, this is a fanciful statement on all counts. Many Lohanas are Vaisnavas, and the official *kuladevatā*, the tutelary deity of more than half of the Lohana houses, is the Mother Goddess (Ambā). It is quite possible that traditionally more knowledgeable Lohanas make a distinction between the *kuladevatā*, the "inherited" deity of a family, and the individual choice of some other deity, by a member of the community. He may well worship Viṣṇu, although his family deity is Śiva or the Mother Goddess. When I asked this particular Lohana what he would think of his son marrying a girl from another caste, he said "If my boy wants to do such a thing, I cannot stop him; even in India, *havā badal gayā* (the air has changed"), i.e., people no longer can enforce strict endogamy on their children.

The Jains of East Africa are culturally so close to the Lohanas and Patels that no one but the Gujarati expatriate Hindu could tell the difference. The situation in East Africa constitutes an interesting shift due to historical accident: Gujarati speakers who came to the area did not structure their prospective neighborhood. Caste distribution is quite unlike that in India, even though caste ranking has remained unchanged. Most of the Jains in India are merchants by caste, and the Jain population in Rajasthan as well as in the parts of the Gujarat bordering Rajasthan intermarry quite freely with Marwari and other merchant-caste Hindus, much as Panjabi Hindus intermarry with Sikhs of compatible caste levels. However, there are two Jain communities in the Gujarati-speaking area which did not originally belong to the merchant stratum. They are the *Navnīt Vanik* and the *Vissa Oshval* Jains. Unlike most Jains, these two groups were agriculturists in India. This might have affected their caste ranking negatively: the founders of Jainism expressly prohibited their followers from doing agricultural work of any sort; for agriculture, though on a much smaller scale than military occupation, involves killing—the destruction of microbes, insects, and other living creatures of the soil. Of all autochthonous Indian religions, Jainism—a very archaic creed, probably slightly older than Buddhism—stresses non-violence above any other virtue. Jaina monks wear the famous cloth-band around their mouths lest they should inhale and thereby destroy living things; in Mombasa—the city with the finest Jain sanctuary and with the most affluent Jain community in East Africa—the priests, as well as those devotees who are more directly involved with the ritual, cover their mouths during the various observances in the shrine. Yet, all East African Jains are either

Vissa Oshvals or *Navnīt Vaniks*. The latter term clearly means "milk merchants," and several leaders told me that their ancestors sold milk, but never engaged in agricultural pursuits proper. Vissa Oshval leaders do not make such a claim. I believe it is perfectly possible that some of them did in India, though the majority were traders at all times, just like the *banyā* Jains who form the great majority of Jains in western India. Interestingly, though, few East African Jains seem to know or remember that the western Indian Jains are mostly true *banyās,* and that there is free intermarriage between *marwārī* and other *banyā* castes and Jains in the Gujarat and in Rajasthan. It appears that the East African Jains identify more nearly with Lohanas and Patels than with *banyās*; this, of course, is due to the scarcity of actual *banyā* caste people in East Africa, and in an equal measure, to the close proximity and the socio-economical symbiosis with these castes in the area.

Of the two main divisions of the Jains in India, i.e., the *Digambara* or "heavenclad," (i.e., naked),[16] and the *Śvetāmbara* "white clad," only the latter are represented in East Africa. Again, this was not planned, but was a migratory accident: the region in the Gujarat from which people went to East Africa, did not have any significant *Digambar* Jain groups; and, as happens with all migrant communities over a long period of time, the first immigrants called their own kin to augment the expatriate community. The first Jains who came were *Śvetāmbara,* as are most Gujarati Jains, and it is their descendants and spouses who now constitute the Jaina population in East Africa. The *Śvetāmbara* again have two subsections, officially distinguished by religio-ideological concepts: the *Deravāsi* section espouses the use of icons in their formal worship, the *Sthānakvāsi* supposedly excludes representational idols. In fact, however, both of them use icons centrally or peripherally in their delightful shrines. There is a difference in the liturgical texts, but this does not affect actual Jain life. However, as would be expected, the *Deravāsi* and the *Sthānakvāsi* are both endogamous groups, based on

61

one-time doctrinal differences which generated separate castes in India. In East Africa, there has been some intermarriage between *Sthānakvāsi* and *Deravāsi,* and here the *Sthānakvāsi* seem to have made the compromise: their number is very small; the proportion of *Deravāsi* to *Sthānakvāsi* Jains in East Africa being roughly 9:1, the *Sthānakvāsi* simply merged, or are in the process of merging, with the *Deravāsi* majority. This merging is not a case of hypergamy as in the Lohana-Patel liaisons mentioned earlier, for the two Jain groups hold equal rank in India.

The Jains are probably the most highly localized group; the center of Jain culture in Africa is no doubt Mombasa, the ancient port city of Kenya, with an estimated 5,000 families loosely clustered around their new, magnificent temple, which is one of the tallest and most attractive buildings in the city, a replica of the famous shrine at Dilwara in the Gujarat. The managers of the temple told me that their ancestors had been either brahmins or *ksattrīyas* who were converted to Jainism, hence the name "Visa Oshvāl," which they thought derived from *Viśa ujjvala* "the resplendent people."[17] This is folk etymology. It is not likely that their ancestors were brahmins, though there is more than a chance that some might have been *ksattrīya*-like groups previous to Muslim conquest. The statement was a defense against suspicions of lower origin. Since most Jains in India are *banyās,* merchants of high caste-status, the agricutlural minority would tend to claim higher origin than the regional majority whose present ranking is higher than theirs.

More will be said about the high formalization of Jain ritual in the area. I was greatly surprised when I saw the tantric syllable nexus *hrim*[18] engraved on a temple stele, and the *mantra "raksam kuru kuru"* painted on the cover of a liturgical volume displayed prominently in the temple office. The non-Jaina groups, even the most highly ritualized Gujarati Hindus in the city, hardly know that their Jaina friends conduct elaborate ceremonies including occasional dance and impersonation of deities at some of the high festivals.

The Jains run a network of well coordinated educational institutions; the former parochial schools that were started and run by them—either jointly by the *Deravāsi* and *Sthānak-vāsi* or by the larger *Deravāsi* service associations, boys' clubs, scout-like organizations, and other youth groups—impress the most casual and the most critical observer. There is a gentle dignity and some eagerness in the religious and the secular procedures about the shrine. Apart from such highly esoteric occasional festivals as the foundation ceremonies of a new shrine, the regular worship, conducted on Sundays—all Asians follow the "English" weekly schedule of work and rest—is well disciplined, the shrines are crowded but in an orderly manner, and the audience participates with real enthusiasm.

A high percentage of the Jains use Shah as a surname. In fact, both Africans and the more interested whites seem to identify the "Shah-s" with Jains, some even with Gujarati merchants in general. Although the Jains constitute but a small fraction of the Gujarati-speaking groups, their wealth is universally known, admired or envied as the case may be, by other Asian and non-Asian groups. In India, the image of the Jains is that of rich people "because they have been traders for thousands of years—because their religion barred

Jain maidens dressed as *Indrani,* goddesses, take part in a high ceremony.

them from agriculture"; but this stereotype hardly obtains in East Africa, where all Asian groups are merchants. No doubt, the Jains are as thrifty and hard-working as other Gujarati groups, but it seems that their zealously guarded corporateness adds to their general well-being; and though the average Jain male and female do not appear to be as prone to personal religious involvement as parallel Hindu groups, their acquaintance with doctrinal matters—and Jaina theology is complex on all counts—is often quite thorough.

We shall frequently mention the "small castes" *(choṭī jāt)* throughout this study. This is a generic term for a group of castes which are well represented in East Africa. For reasons explained earlier in this chapter, they have preserved trade-exclusiveness as a structural criterion, whereas endogamy has remained the only feature of the other Indian communities in East Africa. Let me repeat: caste integrity implies *not* doing work which has been traditionally stigmatized as beneath any specific caste status. Members of any caste may work "up"—they may and attempt to switch to activities which had been linked to castes higher than theirs—the aforesaid device of the all-Indian process of "upcasting." It accounts for much of the chagrin spokesmen of modernity experience when they face the actual situation: once a person has learned, or has followed a nonpolluting job for a while, he will not revert to his former defiling activity even if that activity is more lucrative. Gandhi, Nehru, and all other modern leaders tried desperately to disabuse people from this "superstition"; it did not help a bit. The notion that there is dignity in manual labor, so powerfully advocated by Gandhi and the Congress leadership, is hard to sell, as it is totally alien to India; Gandhi's sermon that the holy scriptures of Hinduism imply the dignity of physical labor was patently wrong; and there is no telling whether he knew it or whether he only wanted his people to believe the opposite. Whatever the case, manual jobs are done by people whose ancestors had done these jobs, so long as either some leaders or the majority of their caste-mates continue to pursue these occupations. A person belonging to a *chotī jāt*—or say, among Panjabi Sikhs, a Rāmgarhia, a member of the artisan caste—may well aspire to and succeed in doing any job above the type that had been customary in his caste; but once this has been accomplished, he will not revert to his erstwhile occupation. Now the *chotī jāt* people in East Africa have been artisans and craftsmen; their caste names reveal their occupation—the *mūcī* are cobblers, and *mūcī* means "cobbler" the *darzī* are tailors, *darzī* meaning just that. These sartorial crafts are viewed as being on one level, and though in India at least the cobbler *(mūcī, mocī)* ranks pretty well at the bottom of the artisan groups due to his handling of animal hide, all these craftsmen constitute the *chotī jāt* "small caste" in East Africa, and no one else, of whatever caste, will think of making shoes, tailoring, etc. A good number of *chotī jāt* people have dissociated themselves from their one-time trade; there are well over two dozen men in the professions, and several hundred families have moved into trade and commerce. Some of them have gained affluence on a par with the wealthiest higher caste people. It would be quite fatuous to speculate if a higher caste person would choose to learn a "trade" if he were to become poor. This sort of change does not take place in East Africa; and where it does in India, no one moves "down" to be a craftsman. None in East Africa except the *mūcī* knows how to make shoes and how to repair them, none but the *darzī* tailors suits and repairs garments for wages. Viewed from inside, it is simply that the traditional crafts have been passed down lineally from father to son, and save for those relatively few who have moved up and out from the crafts, *chotī jāt* people continue their work. It is much more lucrative than in India, and few *chotī jāt* members in East Africa are poor by parallel Indian standards. Many live in poor housing conditions—but then, many wealthy Patels, Lohanas, and others do too. Housing is no reliable index of wealth among traditional, thrifty Hindus anywhere. In interviews with numerous *chotī jāt* men and women in the three East African countries, these feelings seem to be shared: we are poor, our work is humble, but it is good work; we make a living, better than did our grandparents in India, and better than our relatives in the Gujarat today. We do hope that our sons will go to better schools, and will become merchants, or even lawyers or doctors; yet, it is safer, more secure, for us not to aim too high.

Would *choṭī jāt* people mind if higher caste folks were to take to their crafts? Again, this is a vacuous question; it is not conceivable to any *darzī* or *mūcī* or *sutāria* (carpenter), that a Patel or a Lohana would want to. There is also a strong notion that you have to be born into a craft in order to be able to master it. "Everyone can learn to manage a *dūkā*," a middle-aged *sutāria* in Tabora, Tanzania, told me: "I can direct as big a shop as Bh.-bhai (the name of a wealthy Patel merchant in the city); but he cannot learn to do the work I do; it is in my bones."

The generic term for all Indians who actually do artisanry is *fundi*. It is a Swahili word, and it covers all sorts of skilled laborers, especially the *mistrī* or masons; and it refers to Gujarati and Panjabi speakers. The word has become fully Indianized: it is used as a term of reference about *choṭī jāt* people by Indians, as they speak Gujarati or Panjabi.

In secular and religious custom, there is no difference between *choṭī jāt* Hindus and the middle-class *jātis*. At private *bhajan*-s and other domestic rituals and religious assemblies, *fundis* are as welcome as brahmins, and there is no discrimination of any sort. *Prasād*[19] is freely distributed to them as to the higher castes at private religious gatherings and in the temples. The manner in which they conduct their worship is identical with that of Patels and Lohanas of the same economic status. Neither Patels and Lohanas, nor the *choṭī jāt* people, of course, can officiate sacerdotally in the shrine—only the brahmin does that—but in the view of the brahmin the *choṭī jāt* worshipper is entitled to the same religious benefits as the Patel or the Lohana. Patels, Lohanas, and *choṭī jāt* people visit the same temples, chant the same religious songs, and share the same ritualistic food when distributed by the temple officiants. This does not mean complete commensality: though higher caste Hindus under fifty might accept food cooked in *choṭī jāt* houses, the latter would still feel reluctant to invite older, more tradition-bound members of higher castes to a meal cooked in the *choṭī jāt* house; but commensal restrictions are disappearing fast. Compared with all other castes in East Africa, the *choṭī jāt* structure remains closest to the Indian rural setting.

There is one section of *choṭī jāt* people who could hardly be recognized as such by the outsider. The goldsmiths *(sonī)* are wealthy, here as in India, and·this is due to their entrepreneurial operations: some family members actually perform the craft, while others market the product, thus assimilating completely to the dominant trading groups in the area. My *Sonī* informants at Dar es Salaam were among the wealthiest Asians in that city; the elder of the family, a man in his late fifties, was the head of a sizable gold and jewelry concern; he held high office in the local *Ārya Samāj* —though most *choṭī jāt* people identify with the more conservative, *sanātani* type of Hinduism, the ideologically more alert have been espousing the *Ārya Samāj* which rejects discrimination by caste in ritualistic matters. This *sonī* elder had never practiced the craft himself, though he said he had learned it when he was very young. In his two workshops, the foremen who were practicing goldsmiths were his two parallel cousins. The labor force—he employed over twenty men—were all *Sonīs,* most of them belonging to his *kutumb,* —his kindred or extended agnatic kin. His eldest son was to take over the marketing operation of the business after his retirement. Among the *choṭī jāt* represented in East Africa, the *sonī* probably rank highest, as their work implies physical contact with pure materials, i.e., gold and other precious metals.

The wider Indian rule that low caste status often follows from or implies lenience toward meat eating does not obtain among the East African groups. In line with the predominant Gujarati traditions, very few *choṭī jāt* people eat meat, whereas the more modern Patel and Lohana males often do. The diet of Gujarati and Cutchi Hindus is vegetarian, and meat eating, wherever it occurs, must be considered exceptional. This contrasts sharply with the Panjabi situation, where most males, i.e., Sikhs, *khattrīs,* and some others, eat meat, and only religious conversion, particularly the affiliation with the *Ārya Samāj,* prompts individuals to renounce their meat diet.

Those who feel that language and area are the most significant factors in the comparative study of Indian social groupings would probably feel that the Gujarati and Cutchi Muslim groups should be treated now; but I think that the religio-cultural component is more central in anthropological taxonomies involving Indian society. No doubt Gujarati Hindus find it easier to *speak* with Gujarati Muslims than, say, with Sikhs or other Panjabis—yet their social structure, their ritualistic involvements and their total outlook on life are much closer to those of Northern Indian Sikhs and Hindus, than to those of the Gujarati and Cutchi Muslims, in spite of the fact that none of these groups were converted to Islam more than 300 years ago. I shall therefore pass on to the North Indian Hindu sections and then return to the Gujarati and Cutchi Muslims to wind up this chapter.

"North Indian," in East Africa, means Panjabi. There are a few isolated families who came from Uttar Pradesh or other parts of Northern India. There are about a dozen Bengali families spread over the entire territory; they are not really taken as part of the Asian expatriates, since they came after the turn of the century and hold executive or professional jobs of one kind or another.

In terms of ideas and belief systems, it is almost impossible to list any fundamental differences between the Sikhs and Panjabi Hindus. Until the late twenties, before Sikh nationalism embarked on its successful career, Sikhs hardly regarded themselves as separate from the Hindus. Mostly, they wanted to be seen as the militant, pious, devout protectors of Hinduism against the Muslims. There is excellent literature on the Sikh religion and Sikh ideology,[20] but their doctrines are unsophisticated when compared to Hindu theologies—and this simplicity has worked well for the Sikhs. They are certainly the most highly adaptable Indians anywhere. In East Africa, as in the Panjab, there is no hard-and-fast dividing line between Sikhs and Panjabi Hindus. In the first place, Panjabi Hindus, when they are not Ārya Samājis, feel more comfortable in the Sikh ritualistic milieu than with the elaborate forms of Hindu ceremony prevalent among the Gujarati and Cutchi groups in the area. Panjabi Hindu women chant passages from the Sikh scriptures, and the pattern of simile and parable which they use is derived from the Sikh gurus rather than from the medieval Hindu lore of other North Indian areas. The Sikh gurus themselves, especially Guru Nānak (1469-1539), the founder of Sikhism, were very much part of the late medieval Hindu *bhakti* movement centering on intensive devotion to a personal deity. Even more relevant with regard to the Panjabi groups is the fact that many Hindu families "make" their eldest son a Sikh—they let his hair grow, he ties a turban around his head, and he wears the iron ring *(karā)* on his right wrist—this is a purely Sikh emblem. To balance this, many Sikhs below forty, in the East African cities, have become "mechanized," a frequent facetious term used by North Indians for Sikhs who have shaved and are thus no longer outwardly recognizable as Sikhs.

The only salient distinction is of a more narrowly anthropological kind. The two main castes representing the Sikh population in East Africa are not replicated among the actual Panjabi Hindu groups in the area. All Sikhs were farmers, many of them part-time or full-time soldiers in their short, powerful history. The two *jatis* represented in East Africa also form a clear majority in those areas of the Panjab where the migrants came from. They are the *Jat,* farmers proper, and the *Ramgarhia,* a carpenter and tradesmen's caste, bracketed as *fundi* in East Africa. In the Panjab, there are Sikh and Hindu *Jats,* though only Sikh *Rāmgarhiās.* In India as in East Africa, these two groups are endogamous; and interestingly, this is one of the very few cases (the *banyā*-Jain and Hindu of Rajasthan and bordering Gujarat being the other), where marriage cuts across religious denomination, adhering to the primary *jāti* rule of endogamy. In other words, *Jaṭ* Hindus in the Panjab marry *Jaṭ* Sikhs quite freely. *Ramgaṛhiās* and *Jaṭs* do not intermarry, regardless of their religious background. "*Rāmgaṛhiā*," is a loconymic; it derives from the area of Ramgarh where their ancestors were converted to Sikhism, allegedly from a former Brahmin caste. Now the ranking of *Jaṭs* and *Rāmgaṛhiā* in the Panjab is quite unequivocal, and though there is complete interdining between all Sikhs, excluding only the outcaste *Vālmīks* or sweepers, there is no intermarriage and there is very little downward trade extension, as discussed earlier in this chapter. Thus, whereas most *Rāmgaṛhiās* in India are farmers, or landless agricultural laborers, in addition to following their caste-linked occupations (carpenters and other skilled crafts), hardly any *Jaṭs* do professional artisanry. Again, this does not mean that a *Jaṭ* Sikh would not touch tools or gadgets: the very opposite is the case. Sikhs—and that means mostly *Jaṭs*—are known as enthusiastic drivers and excellent mechanics not only in India, but in all parts of the world where they have settled in numbers. But the motor engine is a strange animal; it came to India late, long after ideas of caste-linked trade had been interiorized; hence work on the modern power gadget is ritualistically quite neutral—*Rāmgaṛhiās, Jaṭs,* and Brahmins would handle a car and its accessories without a thought. The *Jaṭ* is a farmer with a semi-legendary background of heroism and soldiering—and he will not professionally do the work done by the *Rāmgaṛhiā*, i.e., carpentry—"*fundi*-type" jobs in the East African parlance; though of course, he will repair his house and his plough with all the artisan's tools, when needed, and he will do it very well indeed. He acts a bit like the executive of a United States industrial chain who putters around the house, driving in nails and painting roofs on Sundays. He does not regard any of this do-it-yourself work as his profession, or as his calling, except in a nostalgic mood.

Sikhs in East Africa do business, regardless of whether they are *Jats* or *Rāmgarhiās;* but their image as businessmen is less noxious to Africans and whites than that of the Gujarati Hindus. Some of the Sikhs do trade in remote locations in the bush, and non-Sikh informants reported that "they live like the Masai, dress like them, buy hides from them, eat their food, and sleep with Masai women." If this is true, it is certainly atypical of the majority of the Sikhs. A number of *Jats* have bought up considerable tracts of rich farm land from departing South African and other white farmers in the former "White Highlands" of Kenya between Eldoret and Nakuru, and those *Jats* are probably the most highly "fulfilled." After all, the self-image of the Sikhs is that of farmer-soldiers; the notion of being merchants is a late accidental superimposition, as it were. Less than one-third of the *Rāmgarhiās* in East Africa are actual *fundis;* they work as foremen on construction sites, they have private carpentry shops, and they serve as mechanics of all sorts in most townships in the area, as well as in the large cities and in the bush. The *"mistrī"* Sikh, always a *Rāmgarhiā,* is the most popular *fundi:* as a master mason, as a craftsman of the highest skill, his fame is undisputed. A small number of *Rāmgarhiās* have moved up and out from the humbler occupations of their kinsmen, and some have reached top executive and administrative positions in East Africa.

Although the number of *Jats* is much smaller than that of *Rāmgarhiā* Sikhs in East Africa, the total wealth of the *Jats* seems to exceed that of the more numerous *Rāmgarhiās.* Strikingly, the *gurdvāras* or temples of the *Jats* are large, spacious buildings in most cities. The large *gurdvāra* in Nairobi is an edifice visible from many miles and certainly one of the architecturally most powerful, yet simple and elegant, structures in that city. In all cities, the *Rāmgarhiās* and the *Jats* have separate *gurdvāras.* The *Rāmgarhiā gurdvāra* is recognizable by a small onion-shaped cupola, usually

71

green in color. On days of worship—Sundays usually, in accommodation to the secular way of spacing the week after the western model—you can see the small *Rāmgarhiā gurdvārās* packed to capacity, whereas the much larger *Jaṭ gurdvārās* are frequently too large to be filled by devotees on any occasion.

Lastly, quite a few civil servants and middle to upper echelon employees at banks, in light industry and business management were Sikhs—mostly *Jaṭ*—up to the time when Asians began to be replaced by indigenous Africans in most of the civil and in some private services. Just as they do in Northern India, the Sikhs in East Africa "spend what they earn," as a Gujarati businessman put it. This and similar statements are not necessarily meant as reproaches. By and large, the modern Sikh is popular with other Asians, and relatively more popular with non-Asians, than other Asian groups, the Ismailis with their very special status excepted. Sikh women are among the best dressed in East Africa; most men eat meat and enjoy a good strong drink (women don't consume alcohol, though some of the more westernized occasionally join their husbands with a drink). So long as they

The *Jat* Sikh *gurdwāra* (temple) in Nairobi.

72

wear turbans, Sikhs do not smoke either in India or abroad.

There is intermarriage between certain smaller sections of Sikhs and Panjabi Hindus: the merchant-like castes (Malhotra, Bauri, and some half a dozen others) marry Sikhs of the same ranking, although there are few Sikhs belonging to this caste type in East Africa. Hardly any Panjabi Hindu group is strictly endogamous; rather, endogamy incorporates larger segments and a greater number of possible target groups for marriage alliances. The *Rāmgarhiās* are endogamous by default as it were, because none of the Panjabi Hindu groups consider them as eligible partners for conjugal liaisons. Still, there is possibly no closer social interaction, short of marriage, between any Asians groups than between Panjabi Hindus and Sikhs.

The stratification of the Panjabi Hindus as viewed from inside is somewhat ambiguous, and possibly quite as complex as that of the Gujarati sections. In the first place, it appears that village exogamy was practiced by East African Panjabis to a much larger extent than among the Gujarati settlers. The North Indian—though by no means all-Indian—rule is that a man must take a wife from a village other than his own. In East Africa, this meant that the brides' and the grooms' fathers *in India* must have lived in different villages. It does not matter at all whether the domicile in Africa is the same or different—this question does not even arise: it is the ancestral villages in India that count, and strictly speaking no match can be arranged between a girl and a boy whose agnatic ancestors came from the same village —though it is quite irrelevant whether the two were born in Nairobi, or Kampala, or in different African cities. Very few Panjabis are conscious of the rule; grandparents are, and they say they would prefer village exogamy to continue. This is quite different from the *Visa Oshwāl* and *Navanīt Vanik* Gujarati Jain tradition: members of either groups may marry into their own village, though of course not into the other community, if both communities were represented in the same village in the Gujarat.

Panjabi Hindu bride in Nairobi.

Cross-cousin marriage is unknown, officially at least, among Panjabi Hindus. It is the preferred marriage form in the Dravidian area; in fact, certain Brahmin groups in the Telugu and Tamil speaking areas contract niece and maternal-uncle marriages, which are said to be so auspicious that no horoscope need be consulted if such a marriage is to come about. To the North Indian and the Gujarati alike, the very idea of cross-cousin marriage is horrifying, since both parallel and cross-cousins are classed as brothers and sisters. This goes for Hindus only; Mulims in both Pakistans may marry cross—and parallel cousins, since the Prophet himself married his parallel cousin. A Panjabi Hindu doctor in Nakuru, Kenya, said "This sort of thing (i.e., cousin marriage) used to happen at the place from which my wife came. This is due to Muslim influence—for Muslims marry their sisters." The statement reflects North Indian kinship sentiment, which is patri-Hawaiian: agnatic collateral cousins are ascriptive siblings with incest rules applying between them.

A fair number of Panjabi *Sūds* and *Bowris* are spread over the territory; their ranking is not easy to establish. They do not regard themselves as *khattrīs,* and they cannot be classified as proper *banyas* (merchants) in *jati*-terminology. A knowledgeable teacher belonging to the *Sūd*-caste claimed that *"Sūd"* was a *gotra* name; but he could not prove this by traditional standards: a *gotra* is a patrisib with a mythical ancestor, usually a *ṛsi* (Vedic seer). I suggested to Mr. Sud that if his name were indeed a *gotra* name, there would have to be a *ṛsi* whose name was etymologically connected with *"sūd."* My suggestion that *"Sūd"* might stem from *śūdra,* a man of the fourth estate in the classical hierarchy, was not accepted, because the term *śūdra* has a pejorative ring in the North where stratification has always been weak. In the South, certain Śūdra groups—particularly the Nayars of Kerala—have high ritualistic and high dominant social status. The same informant told me that *Sūd* was a generic name, and that Sūds, Baurīs, and Khoslas belonged to the same caste.

There is an Urdu periodical service publication called *Sūd Hitaiśi,* published in the Panjab; it has the same function as the various Gujarati caste organs. *Sūd Hitaiśi* addresses itself to Sūds, Baurīs, Khoslas, and about a dozen other sub-*jātis;* this implies that the groups involved must have been classified as belonging to the same *jāti* during some period. As Richard Fox has shown,[21] there is a strong tendency for originally heterogeneous segments to combine into larger groups for political rather than communal purposes, a trend which has gained strong momentum in India since independence. A Khosla businessman, who had just returned from India, told me he had heard that there had been forty *gotras* among the Suds, but only twenty were now extant. Such statements are frequent in India: we were more, but we lost size and power.

This leads me to a hypothesis which should be tested by fellow anthropologists in the Indian field: it appears that loss of status is explicable not only through alleged defilement, but also as loss in numbers. Vocal Hindus, scholars and lay people alike, aver that the total corpus of the original Vedic hymns has long been lost; that the Holy Writ, in its present form, is but an infinitesimal fraction of the original treasure. Analogously, I think, the loss of corporate strength through the disintegration of *gotras* or patrisibs may be held responsible for the loss of power. It is a fact that the various branches and recensions of the Veda had indeed been the property, quite literally, of different priestly families. The notion that each group of ritualistic texts has its own *ṛṣi* "seer," is based, in part at least, on historical facts. Each *gotra* recited, studied, and transmitted the hymns, from father to son; the canonical texts were not committed to writing for fear of pollution and falsification, even long after the introduction of writing in India. All other things were written down but not the Vedic word.[22] Thus, if a *gotra* missed out on male offspring for a generation or two, it simply died out—and with it the collection of those orally transmitted hymns which only members of that *gotra* knew. It seems quite plausible, then, that the Indian notion of certain *jātis* having been larger at one time, in the sense that there were more *gotras* constituting them, has an objective base, even though this is not known to East African Hindus. The idea prevails among Indians that India had more rather than fewer people in her richer past. Modern Asians know that overpopulation is the problem of our day. And yet, when it comes to traditional parlance, all this common-sense knowledge is set aside: our *jāti* had more *gotras*, more people, it was more powerful, higher in status, more wealthy, etc., than it is now; since spokesmen of all *jātis* claim the same, India must have had a larger population than now!

My Sūd informant—a man of about forty, who spoke excellent English and very beautiful Hindi—rare for Panjabis even in India—granted that *khattrīs* were now higher than Suds, but insisted that Suds had originally been *khattrīs* or even Rājputs; that they had lost their status and dignity when they lost out in numbers—some were killed in warfare, others were converted to Islam, others married too low to preserve their rank. The orthodox anthropological view is that loss of caste status always presupposes some ritualistic pollution at one time in the history of the *jāti* which claims nobler antecedents. But perhaps these examples seem to permit an alternative: not so much, or not only through pollution, but also through alleged loss of number and hence prestige, a caste may sink lower in any regional ranking.

There are roughly two hundred Panjabi Brahmin households in East Africa. They belong to the *Jānalā* brahmin section, and though they rank higher than several other Panjabi brahmin groups, they are not ritualists; religious specialists are recruited from other brahmin sections. Though there are a few regions in India where non-ritualists rank higher than the religious practitioner, I doubt if this is the case with Panjabi brahmins. *Jānalā* brahmin informants claimed that raw food is given to the ritualists by *Jānalā* brahmins at ceremonial occasions, and that cooked food used to be given occasionally by ritualists to *Jānalā* brahmins in the Panjab, though not in East Africa. In East Africa, the situation is somewhat blurred: the upper castes, but particularly the brahmins, are supposed to invest their young males with the *jeneu,* the sacred cord of the "twice-born." This initiation ceremony is less and less frequently performed in East Africa, except among followers of the *Ārya Samāj.* Non-reformed groups have all but abandoned Vedic rituals except marriage in their new habitat, and the gift of raw and cooked food that was part of the ceremonial complex has lost its significance. Food—cooked food that is—is given to one and all at festive occasions; the brahmin who performs the wedding in East Africa is given money, cloth and other goods; but the specific gift of cooked and uncooked food to the brahmin is no longer an integral part of the ceremony, having merged into the amorphous feeding process which includes all those who are present.

Though the trend in India has been that theological differences between founders of sects resulted in the formation of separate endogamous groups after some time, this tendency was weak in the Panjab, where a more cavalier attitude in doctrinal matters obtained. We have already seen that Sikhs and Hindus intermarry provided they belong to an older common *jāti*. In modern Panjab and among the East African Panjabis, all who are not Sikhs or Muslims are either "unreformed" *sanātani* or reformed *Ārya Samājis*—the ideological difference between the two is considerable, and will be discussed in some detail in a later chapter. But contrary to the more pervasive India pattern, this has not resulted in *Sanātani* and *Ārya Samāji* endogamy. *Sanātani* and *Ārya Samāji* Panjabis, here as in India, intermarry quite freely, if their original *jātis* are compatible. The parallel of *banyā* Hindu and Jain intermarriage in Mewar, Rajastahan, and parts of the Gujarat has been pointed out; but although the theological differences between Jainism and Hinduism are much greater than those between *Sanātani* and *Ārya Samāji* Panjabis, the Hindu and Jaina doctrines are so overgrown with mutual ritualistic borrowings that they are no longer a factor for ideological stress. This cannot be said about the *Sanātani* and the *Ārya Samāji* teachings: the former claim to be traditional, they use idols, and they follow what "modern" Hindus regard as "superstitious" or obsolete religious ways. The *Ārya Samājis* are iconoclasts. To the critical observer, however, they appear to be equally conservative, if not more so than the *Sanātanis*, just as the early protestants and puritanical protestantism in general tended to out-moralize the older and more lax, though more highly ritualistic, Catholicism in Europe.

Since the turn of the century, Panjabis of low caste origin, when they converted to the *Ārya Samāj* which rejects the traditional stratification, tended to call themselves "*Ārya*," hoping that this might convey high ritualistic status. Some went farther than that—they assumed the surname "Sharma," which is a general brahmin caste indicator. *Ārya Samāj* doctrine holds that all who practice the Vedic ritual are equal to brahmins. Eager converts of low caste origin grasped the chance to upcaste themselves and their offspring. However, this did not quite work: Hindus in the Panjab know that "Sharma," as the caste or surname of a Panjabi, may mean only that he or his father was an *Ārya Samājis*. There are, of course, as many *Ārya Samājis* among genuine Panjab brahmins, proportionately speaking, as among non-brahmins; but brahmins who have accepted the *Samāj's* teachings tended to retain some other brahmin caste indicator, as Bhargav, Dvivedi, Tripathi, etc., for fear of being taken as non-brahmin converts to the *Ārya Samāj*. The *Ārya Samāj* might have become an endogamous caste in the traditional sense, but the *Samāj* is too new, and too well known. There are new sects in Central India, inaugurated at about the same time as the *Ārya Samāj*—in the mid-fifties of the last century—but they did not acquire national status, nor did they carry any *propaganda fidei* outside their local boundaries; hence in the image of their neighbors, they were simply a new *jāti* which followed some religious teacher. The *Ārya Samāj*, with one of the most highly efficient missionary organizations in India and abroad, is too well known as an ideological faction rather than as an ethno-cultural segment: most North Indians know that the *Ārya Samāj* accepts people of all castes, and that it is therefore not a *jāti* in the sense, say, in which rural Bengalis have come to regard the urban *Brahmo Samāj* as a *jāti*.[23]

All South Asians identify light pigmentation with higher caste status. Ideally, all men and women of *khattrī* origin are said to be "fair"; if a person is dark-skinned and calls himself "Sharma," people shrug their shoulders and smile knowingly, saying: "So, he is that sort of a Sharma" (i.e., an *Ārya Samāji* "brahmin"). This does not imply any criticism of the *Ārya Samāj*, but only of dark-skinned people who exploit the institution to upcaste themselves. That there are many very dark-pigmented genuine *khattrīs* and brahmins and very light colored low-castes all over India, especially in the Panjab, disproves the stereotype, but the fact is either unacceptable or ignored. When I referred to an *Ārya Samāji* woman of light pigment, as possibly of brahmin or *khattrī* background, an old Panjabi man said "not at all, it is all lipstick and makeup—her father was a carpenter," the implication being that she was actually a low-caste woman trying to put on airs. The syllogism is typical of the all-Indian pattern of caste ascription by sight: dark colored people are of low caste origin; a particular person is dark colored, hence he or she is of low caste origin. Correspondingly, light colored people are of high caste origin—a particular person is light colored—hence he or she is of high caste origin.

As in the case of modern urbanites in India, East African Panjabi men under forty-five often deny that they know their caste. I do not believe that they really do not know it, and when a Mr. Khosla said "I do not know what caste the Khoslas belong to," I took it as an elliptical statement in line with the apologetic strategy of modern India: caste is bad, caste does not really exist, and if it does, it shouldn't, hence one should not know what one's caste is, as cogitating on one's caste status would make one "old-fashioned," "superstitious," or "reactionary."

The circle is almost complete, and we now turn to Gujarati speakers who are not Hindus. One community stands out from the rest, in virtually all matters that count in this day and age: the Ismailis, or more completely, the *Khoja Shi'a Ismaili,* followers of His Highness the Aga Khan, linear descendant of the Prophet's confidant and kinsman Ali. This section will assess the Ismailis' place in the structural map of the Asian communities in East Africa.

All Ismailis are descendants from converted Lohana Hindus; hence, their original language was Cutchi, just like that of the Lohanas. In East Africa, however, and again in analogy to the Lohanas, Cutchi has been all but given up by the Ismailis of this generation. Almost all Ismailis, however, understand it when they hear it, except perhaps the very young —people below the age of twenty-five might find it hard to understand and impossible to speak Cutchi. Better informed Ismailis are aware of their Lohana antecedents, but without any feelings about it. Ismailis are Muslims; this is obvious. And yet, interviewing over a hundred East African Ismailis, I found that their primary identification was as Ismailis, *not* as Muslims. Only two of the interviewed gave "Muslim" as an immediate response to the question about their religion and their cultural fealty. There is nothing strange about this. All Asians, as well as Africans and whites, have been referring to these people as Ismailis, never as Muslims. In East Africa, the term "Muslim" means many things and many persons— Arabs, Africans, and Asians—but *not* Ismailis. All people, including the Ismailis, *know* of course that they *are* Muslims; in fact, there are few who would not think that theirs is the most authentic kind of Islam. But the identification as Ismailis, as a group very different from all others, is funda- mental, and has been reinforced over the past five decades, since the late Aga Khan applied himself and his considerable resources—material and spiritual—to the rebuilding of a com- munity which until his days had been just one Shi'a sub- community in Asia. In an excellent study, H. S. Morris[24] has analyzed the institution and the person of the Aga Khan; it is a true case of "divine kingship" believed axiomatically by all Ismailis. The late Aga Khan turned away from Indian Islamic traditions and models quite consciously, through the process of *taqīya* "dissimulation": the Imam, Allah's mes- senger in the world, may dissemble earlier behests if that is necessary for the betterment of the faithfuls' lot, and if that is what he intuits from the written and the oral traditions. He knew that his East African votaries would be the eco- nomic stronghold of the Ismaili organization, if only they could be made to disregard and disavow the crucially retarding features of Indian traditionalism—*purdah* with its sartorial and social strictures, and looking upon India and Southwest Asia as the spiritual home of the community. Spiritual de- centralization was his target.

Like all other Asian groups, the Ismailis are endogamous; still, a high proportion of those few Asians who do marry outside their fold are Ismailis. Ismailis who have gone places have brought home European and American wives—though there are very few Ismaili liaisons with non-Ismaili Asians, Muslim or other. Somehow, the most emancipated members of this most emancipated community seem to feel that if the step out of the tradition is to be made, one might as well make a very large step. Yet the explanation is perhaps not quite as simple: a European or any non-Indian is so strange an animal that solidarity feelings seem less directly challenged than by impermissible inter-Asian liaisons. Psychologically, this pattern is perhaps analogous to the case where an Indian urban woman would rather have a male English physician deliver her baby or treat her malaria, if no Indian woman-doctor is around—the foreign man is a no-man, hence he poses no intra-cultural threat.

As if to compensate for their relatively open society, the Ismaili are ritualistically exclusive. The mosques of the most conservative and orthodox Muslims are left wide open to anyone, of whatever religious background. Not so the *jamāt-khāna*, the "assembly-house," as the Ismailis call their place of worship in conscious distinction from the *masjid* (mosque) of the other Muslims. No doubt, of all Asian communities, the Ismaili leadership most effectively disseminates theological information and instruction. Their preachers may not be learned Muslims in the traditional sense, but they are eager and active. Most importantly, they are in no way handicapped by vestigial archaisms—they wear western dress, all of them speak English, some of them fairly well; all of them talk to anyone who asks them. Religious catechism was part of the instructional program in H. H. the Aga Khan's schools, from primary through the final grades of high school, until *uhuru*, when all schools were deparochialized, at least officially. Still, in 1964, at a large and excellently run high school in Dar es Salaam, there was a teacher specially hired for "religious drill," which meant regular classroom lectures to the pupils and individual counselling with a religious orientation.

The Ismailis are a *jāti* by all the standards supplied in

this chapter. They are strictly endogamous. Occasional liaisons with non-Asian wives can be viewed as instances of hypergamy, in accord with the Muslim rule that a male may marry any woman who accepts the faith and with the Indian element of hypergamy to back it. Some, though not all, of the foreign-born wives become Ismailis, though nobody thinks of this as a crucial issue. The Shah of Iran (and Muslim rulers elsewhere at all times), marries the loveliest girl in the realm —or the most fertile, as the case may be, and no questions, or hardly any, are asked about her background. It is for this reason, I believe, that Ismaili-European marriages have been contracted, and are occurring more frequently. To the western eye, the Ismailis—particularly the wealthy ones— seem to be culturally most similar to and compatible with occidentals. Other Asian Muslim groups do not seem attractive or compatible to prospective European mates: they are openly conservative, and do not concede women equal status—they do not even go through the motions of doing so, unlike other Asian "modernites." Yet, there is less ideological objection on the side of any Muslim groups, against marrying non-Asian women—a matter of much graver concern to Hindus and Jains. To the unwary westerner, the Ismailis simply seem to be the most highly westernized, and other Gujaratis, the most conservative Asians. The kind of conservatism and ritualistic exclusiveness which the Ismailis observe is less evident to the outside world than that of most Hindu groups, because the Hindus are *known* to be more exclusive. Yet even the beginner in oriental studies knows that Islam—all forms of Islam, including the Ismaili doctrine—is less catholic *qua* doctrine than the Hindu teachings. Socially, however, the Hindus are the most, the Ismailis the least exclusive Asians in the three countries of East Africa.

If viewed from a purely Islamicist angle, the group most closely akin to the Ismailis is the one that shares most of its doctrine. Like the Ismailis, the *Ithna A'sari*, the "twelfth" (i.e., the followers of Hassan and Hussein, and the "twelfth" Imam), are Shi'a, the full official names of these two groups being *Khoja Shi'a Ismaili* and *Khoja Shi'a Ithna A'sari,* respectively. And yet, scarcely two other sections could be more different from each other in their life-styles. Where the Ismailis pride themselves on total modernization on the basis of the late Aga Khan's courageous *taqiya,* "dissimulation," of traditional orthodox moulds for the benefit of the community *and* of the faith, the Ithna-A'sari insist on sheer tradition. Not only do they not encourage the education of women, but they make it quite clear to the questioner that this would be against the teachings of the Prophet. Their printed organ *Federation,* published in Gujarati from Arusha, Tanzania, is edited like a modern magazine, but it extolls orthodox values, and decries the waywardness of the young: that they no longer attend at prayers, that they are becoming absorbed by non-Islamic ways of thinking, and worst of all, that many of them drink and look at women with eyes of desire. Yet, the main target of Ithna-A'sari censure is the Ismailis—not their doctrine, for that is known to be virtually identical with their own—but their un-Islamic ways: they act and talk like 'Englishmen,' they send their children to schools and colleges abroad which divert them from the ways of truth and worship, etc.

To other Asians as to Africans, the Ithna-A'sari *are* the most conservative of all. "The Ithna-A'sari of Zanzibar," an Afro-Arab student from that island reported, "come out in procession on the *A'sura* festival day of Muharram every year—chaining their bodies with chains which have nails and spikes on them; they hit themselves as they run, scream, and perforate their chests and bodies. When I was a boy at school, my Ithna-A'sari schoolmates proudly displayed their wounds—and they said that it was a 'Sacrifice for God.'" No African or Arab Muslims would ever dream of doing such things, he mused. But, whether or not this report was true, the fact remains that this community seems to represent many things from which African and Asian Muslims want to get away as impediments to modernization.

Several middle-aged Ithna-A'sari leaders whom I interviewed made no secret about the fact that they did not want their daughters to get any but an elementary Muslim or Quranic education. "Education spoils women" they maintained. To "spoil" a woman of any age, in Indian parlance, means primarily to make her interested in men—and secondarily, to make her "proud" and potentially disobedient to the males under whose care and control she spends her life.

On the ritualistic side, there is a positive compensation: the best *azzan*[25] is chanted by Ithna-Aṡari *maulvīs*—in fact, their Arabic is so chaste that some "America-returned" neighbors thought that it had been prerecorded on tape by some Arab, and then played back from the minaret of the Ithna-Asari mosque! I was impressed by an Ithna-Aṡari Muslim sermon, conducted for a wider Asian interdenominational audience in exquisite Urdu.

If marriage across caste lines is rare among other Asians, it is unheard of among the Ithna-Aṡari with not a single case of inter-caste alliance reported.

The Bohra Muslim community holds a middling position, as it were, with regard to conservatism and modernity. By and large, the Bohras are more modernistic, more entrepreneurial, and more highly oriented toward imported values, than the Ithna-Aṡari, but less so than the Ismailis. Some sophisticated non-Ismaili subjects suggested that the "modernness" of the Ismailis as a group is a veneer—that their women's sartorial adaptation to occidental styles and their men's "getting around" was a cover-up for deep-rooted ideological conservatism. One of the wealthiest and most influential families of Tanzania is Bohra. According to most Asian informants, the Bohras are just another Gujarati merchant community, and their forebears are said to have been *banyās* or Cutchis, possibly Lohanas. But according to some of their leaders' statements, the Bohras ancestry was Gujarati Brahmin. It is hard to decide if Brahmin descent is historically feasible. I tend to think that any group which claims Brahmin descent is more likely right than those who claim *kṣattrīya* antecedents when contemporary society no longer accepts them as *kṣattrīyas;* the *kṣattrīya* bracket is wide and vague and so diffuse that almost any powerful group can claim *kṣattrīya* descent. Most of the political blocs which were created in Northern India over the past thirty years were combines of various castes claiming *kṣattrīya* or Rājput descent. But to claim brahmin background is uncomfortably specific; in addition, it no longer seems desirable in a society where the priestly norm is losing much of the prestige it once had. Hence any group which does claim brahmin antecedents probably has some facts to build on. Such may have been the case with the Bohras.

The Bohras hold, as do all Shi'a groups, that God's revelation is a continuing process, and that his messenger lives on Earth at all times. With the Ithna-Aśari, the Bohras believe the real *Imām* is hidden. This contrasts with the Ismaili conception of the *hāzir-imām,* the physically present leader of the faithful, of 'Ali's lineage, sharing his wisdom and his honor. For historical and political reasons, the *Imām,* so the Bohras or "Daudī" believe, must remain in hiding lest he should be assassinated like Hassan and Hussein, the founders of the Shi'ite dispensation. However, there is an appointed caretaker for that hidden *Imam,* for the Bohras. He has the exalted Arabic title *"Da'i-ul-mutlaq of the Daudi Borah:"*[26] The late *Da'i,* His Holiness Dr. Syedna Tair, lived in state in Bombay. His pious followers regarded him as a learned and holy person; his opponents—among the Bohras themselves—thought he was a ludicrous, anachronistic wastrel, who had learnt his Arabic lore by rote, and who squandered his followers' money. Two of my informants, extremely rich Bohras, and parallel cousins, held these opposing views: one of them thought the *Da'i* was worthy of respect and support; the other said "I refused to give him a cent; and if he had approached me for funds, I would have spat out in front of him, and told him to go to hell."

The Bohras, the third Gujarati Muslim community, are equally endogamous; they are less tradition-bound perhaps than the Ithna-Asari, and apparently more conservative than the Ismailis. The Bohra men have abandoned their headgear, the round onion-shaped turban that was worn by them in Bombay, a distinct mark of that group.

The last, and smallest, Muslim group in East Africa is the Panjabi Muslims. Most of them are regular *sunni,* not distinct from the official Islam most commonly accepted and professed on the subcontinent. But there is a small, vocal minority among them—the *Ahmedīyas,* also called the *Qadianis,* after their shrine at Qadian. This sect was founded less than a century ago; its followers have become endogamous, in line with the Indian pattern, in a very short time, perhaps more by default than by intention: other Muslims mistrust them, not for theological reasons, but due to political recrimination and diatribe meted out to them by orthodox groups over the past fifty years. The opprobrium on the *Ahmedīyas* in Pakistan today is not replicated at all in East Africa. In fact, little about it seems to be known. Within the Muslim communities, both Asian and African, the *Ahmedīyas* are well respected as people who not only take Islam or their version of it seriously, but who are prompted by their teachings toward true brotherhood. It is the *Ahmedīyas,* and only they, among Asian Muslims, who go to the Africans as missionaries, who readily accept them into their fold, and who would be the least opposed to eventual intermarriage. The fact that very few *Ahmedīya* Asian-African liaisons have been contracted up to date is due to the ingrained Indian resistance to it. The *Ahmedīyas* decidedly do not think of themselves as a separate social unit, though they regard their teachings as a special branch of Islam, in a doctrinary sense. This is a unique situation; for the other Asian Muslim groups, the Indian model obtains, doctrinary and ritualistic affiliations coalesce with endogamy. The only Asian woman M. P. in Tanzania in 1964 was *Ahmedīya* and no Muslims, Asian or African, held it against her in any manner; most of her votes, incidentally, were African. Hindus, however, distrust the *Ahmedīyas.* Any group which undertakes vigorous proselytization is suspect to modern Hindus anywhere, a historical consequence of five centuries' exposure to Muslim and Christian conversion backed by political power. "The Qadiani *maulvīs*," an otherwise gently speaking Panjabi Hindu of about fifty said, "would do anything to convert people; they would beat them up and kill them, if they could."

Ahmedīya missionaries have learnt Swahili and other Bantu languages rather better than other Asians; many preachers can conduct Muslim service and sermon in Swahili, an accomplishment which is not paralleled in any other Asian community. These preachers think nothing of moving into the bush and sharing the hardships with their prospective or actual converts.

We have now come to the end of our survey of the Indian castes which constitute the Asian minority in East Africa. Let me summarize the remaining small groups present in the area. Zoroastrian Parsis, Maharashtrians, and Ceylonese live in small numbers in some of the large cities. Most of them stay with one foot in India as it were; many commute frequently, most of them get their brides from India or Ceylon, because their number is too small to emulate the marriage patterns of the larger Asian sections. Some younger people have married girls of their choice—Indian and non-Indian, though never African. They are not really regarded as part of the community, any more than the occasional visitors from India, who come for a year or longer on a terminable contract basis. Some of the finest East African Asian intellectuals belong to those tiny splinter groups; these men do not identify with the dominant Asian population. In fact, it is by these young and bright semi-aliens that African contacts are sought, found, and cherished, though there has been no intermarriage so far. The small but vocal Maharashtrian segment is different: it has some highly motivated Hindu activists among its members, whose attitude is nationalistic and parochial.

Kinship Terminology

I stated in the preface that I would not deal in depth with kinship, since excellent material has been published, and listed in the bibliography. There are, however, two peculiar points of interest, which must be discussed briefly as we conclude this chapter—points that have not been studied in Indian kinship literature so far. The first is unique to East Africa. North and West Indian societies usually belong to a kinship type called patri-Hawaiian; i.e., briefly, that both parallel and cross-cousins are referred to and addressed as siblings, both on the father's and the mother's side, though there are more important ties with these classificatory siblings on the father's side, since almost all Indian societies have strongly agnatic features. In address, therefore, both parallel and cross-cousins are called "brother" and "sister." Terms of reference differ only in the degree of further elaboration or specification; thus, in Gujarati, the cousin—any cousin—on the father's side would be referred to as *pitraibhāī* "brother through my father's line" on the mother's side as *māsiaī bhāī* "brother through my mother's line." These terms are virtually identical, semantically and lexically with slight variations, in the languages of Northern India, i.e., the Indian languages of Indo-European stock. However, in East Africa, there has been an interesting merging of kinship terms between two languages i.e., Cutchi and Gujarati, the languages spoken or remembered by the majority of the Asian settlers. Linguistically, Cutchi and Gujarati are close, yet their kinship terms are as different as, say, Spanish terms from Italian. In India, these differences have remained unchanged in the two languages. In spite of the fact that kinship terminology is more resistant to linguistic change than almost any other vocabulary, there is a notable merging of Cutchi and Gujarati terms in East Africa. Thus, the husband's mother is called *sasu* in Gujarati and *sas* in Cutchi, but most Cutchis in East Africa use *sasu*. Conversely, sister's son is called *bhanej* in Gujarati, and *bhanejo* in Cutchi, but Gujarati speakers tend to use the Cutchi *bhanejo*. One possible reason for this may be that Gujaratis (Patels, and perhaps Jains) have had most of their business and social contact with Lohanas, (Cutchi speakers) in those societies where the Lohanas are either more numerous or wealthier, and where wedding guests spoke Cutchi; wedding talk contains a lot of kinship terminology.

Let me list a small sample of kinship terms where this linguistic merger has taken place in East Africa.

	Gujarati	Cutchi	East African Gujarati-Cutchi
Fa Bro Da	*ben*	*bhen*	*ben*
So So	*dikro*	*potro*	*dikro*
So Da	*dikrī* (address)	*dhī* (address)	*dhī*
Wi Br	*sāro*	*sālo*	*sālo*
Hu Fa Mo	*dādījī*	*dādas*	*dadas*
Hu Si	*nanand bī* (address)	*nanan* (address)	*nanan*

The other peculiarity—shared by Lohanas in East Africa and India—is a type of institutionalized deference to the female child, not paralleled in any other community in India. The focal term here is *niānī*, which has been preserved in Africa in spite of the high degree of specificity which the pattern involved in India. Among Cutchi-speaking groups (which includes those whose members no longer speak Cutchi, having switched to Gujarati as their chief medium), all female children in the agnatic segment are referred to as *niānī*. Bhatias refer to the male children of the agnatic segment as *niānā*—*ā* being the masculine, *ī* the feminine gender suffix in most North Indian vernaculars—but the special treatment discussed here does not extend to the *niānā*. In all other Indian societies, boys not only occupy an economically more advantageous position in the family, but they also carry almost all other corporate functions of their agnatic kin group. It is the son-in-law who is given unquestioned respect in his wife's natal house, whenever he appears there. This holds for Cutchi groups as well. Yet among Cutchis, both Hindu and

Ismaili, the *niāṇī*-female children are given ritualized emotional deference by their ascendants. Among the more highly tradition-bound, both the father and the mother of a girl, as well as her paternal uncles and aunts, render to her the ceremonially highest possible homage, by touching her feet while greeting her. In the old days, this probably occurred whenever a *niāṇī*-relative returned to her natal house from her husband. In East Africa, it is still practiced among conservatives, and by almost all Cutchis on ceremonial occasions. This spectacle strikes non-Cutchis as very curious indeed: that a male person, even though he may be quite senior, master of a family and of fortunes, should show her "too much respect," as a Panjabi observer remarked ("too much," is Indian English for "very much" and does not imply surfeit or excess of any sort). Touching the feet of a person is a token of extreme reverence; it was done, and is done in many parts of rural India, to parents, "saints," and other charismatic persons, but only Cutchis touch the feet of the *niāṇī*.

Originally a Hindu custom, it has been vestigially preserved among Ismailis and other Cutchi-speaking Khoja Muslim groups. A very modern young Ismaili woman from Dar es Salaam reported that when an Ismaili woman recovers from a grave illness, she will call seven poor girls into her house and feed them sumptuously, give them presents and make them comfortable and happy in many other ways. These children are called *niāṇī*. *Niāṇī* status is ascribed to them for the purpose. She may or may not invite her actual *niāṇī*-kin, but the explanation for not doing so was that the real *niāṇī* have all the wealth and the food of their family at other times, and feeding them on such an occasion of gratitude would not be meritorious and ritualistically redundant. Among corresponding castes in Cutchi-speaking India, both in rural and urban settings, the situation today is virtually unchanged: on ritualistically relevant occasions, the father bows to his daughter, the brother to his sister, paternal uncles to their brothers' daughters. It would be quite out of order for a Lohana or Bhatia daughter to bow to or touch the feet of her father, sibling brother, or paternal uncles, which was the expected behavior in all other Indian societies. In East Africa, the frequency of such hierarchically enjoined salutations has no doubt decreased. Still, where there is no actual bowing or touching of feet, the emotive tone of these relations persists. The Lohana as well as the Ismaili father entertain a ritualistically informed attitude toward their *niānī* daughters, sisters, or fraternal nieces. The non-*niānī* relations, as between a man and his wife's brothers' or sisters' children, are modally identical with those in other Indian societies: here, ritualistic and secular respect and the involved salutation-performance is regulated by age, and by seniority and juniority within the kin-group.

When Asian subjects were questioned about such specific kinship behavior responses, their first reaction was almost invariably the denial of such behavior. This, of course, depended on the background of the informant: the more conservative his image of the group, the less direct would be his denial; conversely, the more emancipated the image of a group, the stronger his denial. Thus, my Ismaili informant at first denied that there was a special type of salutational behavior prescribed and enacted toward *niānī* kin. On further probing, a modified answer was given: there are *niānā* and *niānī* relatives, the *niānā* being male, sons or siblings or fraternal nephews, the female being daughters, sisters, or fraternal nieces—but no distinctive behavior was indicated; then, the specific ritualistic deference given to the *niānī*, but not to the *niānā*, was granted; next, salutational behavior was remembered for the ascending generation, and finally, occasional instances of such action among contemporary Ismailis were recalled and admitted. From Lohana informants, there was no denial of such memory from the outset, but the account was given as if it referred to the older generation "My grandfather used to touch my mother's feet when I was a boy, because she was his *niānī*." Now almost all East African Ismailis know that their ancestors were Lohanas. The Ismaili style of life is patently closer to the Lohana style in matters of social interaction than to other Indian *sunni* Muslim groups. Yet Ismailis feel that theirs ought to be Islamic kinship behavior, rather than Lohana or other Hindu kinship orientation. Structurally, however, this is just not the case. Ismailis view and act toward kin very much as Lohanas do, *not* as other Muslim groups act. No Indo-Pakistani Muslim society interacts according to the original Arab Muslim rule; all interact in accordance with whatever Hindu or Jain groups their forbears were converted from. To harness Gandhi's political dictum for anthropological purposes, we can say "Indian Muslims are first Indians, then Muslims." Ismaili informants tend to play down their ancestral Hindu background. The religiously more involved, especially professional religious teachers in the community, would claim that such customs were Muslim in origin—and in most cases, that is what they may well believe. I once saw a mansion at Dar es Salaam, whose name, inscribed above the main door, was *Om Habibā-bād*; when I asked an Ismaili preacher about the meaning of this name, he said *Om* was a *mantra* from the *Qur'ān*! It is quite conceivable that he really believed there were *mantras* in the *Qur'ān*. The fact that the *mantra*-complex is purely Hindu-Buddhist-Jain was probably not known to him.

The classificatory *nīanī* of the Ismaili, the seven unrelated poor girls invited and feted at special occasions, seem to serve a function in East Africa which is provided by a different caste in India. When a Bhatia or Lohana person in India recovers from an illness, or when another particularly auspicious, non-predictable occasion arises, several members of the *Caraṇi* caste are invited and fed and ritualistically propitiated. The *Caraṇi* rank slightly above Lohanas and Bhatias, but well below Brahmins, although the attitude toward them at such occasions resembles that entertained toward Brahmins when invited to attend obsequial and obsequial-memorial rites (*śrāddh*) in all parts of Hindu India. It would seem that the absence of *Caraṇi* in Africa has resulted in creating a substitute *nīanī* situation. This, incidentally, is perhaps the only remnant of the *jajmāni* system ubiquitous in India and studied in detail by anthropologists working in Indian society.[27] Other than that, there is no obligatory inter-caste service of a ritualistic kind, mainly because the Asians are city people who pay cash to the ritualist—the *jajmāni* system breaks down as it enters urban areas, even in India.

The most amazing sequel of the *niāṇī* complex among Cutchi speakers is the post-marital situation of the daughter. In the first place, the Indian high-caste tradition of a high dowry or, in anthropological terms, of a bridegroom price, is not accepted by the Cutchis. A nominal dowry is given, but with the understanding that it should serve solely to assist the departing daughter and help her when in need at her husband's house. The painful negotiations and the menaces implicit in the North Indian dowry complex (*dahez*) have been felicitously eschewed by the Bhatia and Lohana castes. Both in India and in East Africa, it is the groom's people who transfer wealth for the bride to her parents; this is a regular bride-price, and there are very few segments of high-caste-Hindu society where this ancient custom is still followed. The *niāṇī* is the dearest and the most respected person in her father's house; if she has to leave, as she must when she gets married, she has to be ransomed in good faith, as it were. Once she has moved to her husband's house, her own parents will not even take food at their daughter's conjugal estate; if they come for a visit or for business, neighbours of the husband's house will provide food, perhaps even shelter, for the visiting parents of the wife. This is a radical extension of the ceremonial respect the *niāṇī's* agnatic kin entertain toward her throughout her whole life.

CHAPTER THREE

Economic Problems: The Asian Entrepreneur

In my quest for a model that would explain to me the phenomenon of the Asian entrepreneur in East Africa, whom I regard as the core of the immigrant economy, I found Professor F. Rigg's study most helpful. His definition of 'entrepreneurs' can hardly be improved upon:

> ". . . those who seek to unite factors of production-capital, labor, management, technology, security, and 'access'—in order to produce and distribute goods and services, regardless of the scale of their activities; they range from small merchants to millionaire industrialists." (p. 143)[1]

Yet the situation of the Asian entrepreneur in East Africa is at variance with the type envisaged by Riggs, so that apart from the definition and some striking parallels which might be encountered in any entrepreneurial situation, a new model for the "degree of access" would have to be found for the East African area. "Exclusion" and "intrusion" as subtypes of "low degree access," and introduction and assimilation as subtypes of high degree access, presuppose the social and economical juxtaposition of an elite and an entrepreneur who may or may not be part of the elite. Up to this day there is none but a potential indigenous economic elite in East Africa. Riggs' scheme does apply, however, to Indian entrepreneurs

95

in other regions of the world, including South Africa, and wherever there *is* a non-Indian elite to which the Indian entrepreneur could *in principle* assimilate, be introduced, intrude upon, or be excluded from.

In an unpublished paper prepared for the International Development Research Center at Indiana University (IDRC), Professor Spulber[2] has made a lucid analysis of the situation of the Chinese entrepreneur in Indonesia. There are distinct parallels between the Hokkien and Hakka trade-oriented settlers in Indonesia and the Gujarati Patels and Lohanas in East Africa on the one side, and the craft-oriented Kwong-Fu Chinese in Indonesia (Spulber, p. 31) with the Panjabi and Gujarati *fundi* (artisans) in East Africa, on the other. Willem F. Wertheim has made a fine sociological analysis of the trading minorities in Southeast Asia, in what he modestly calls his "no-Gook" anthology.[3]

Just as Chinese entrepreneurs are disliked by the Indonesians, restricted by governmental actions, and rejected by the whites (Spulber, p. 32), so are Asian entrepreneurs in East Africa—and the difference is largely one of style, not of degree or intensity. Rejection by the elite where there *is* a substantial elite (South Africa, Burma, Indonesia), restrictions actual or threatened by the host governments, all these are universal features where there is an Asian entrepreneur with a different mother-tongue from that of the hosts and the elite.

The Chinese in Indonesia pioneered in the marketing of rice, (Spulber, p. 37); the East African Asians were the first to import and distribute cereal; they promoted the export of sisal. In both cases their very efficiency has made the host nations suspicious, alleging either conspiratorial designs—which may have been part fact and part fancy with the Chinese in Indonesia, or draining their locally earned wealth to Britain and other places abroad—which is again part fact and part fancy—with the Asians in East Africa.

Some other parallels are important and obvious: the Chinese, partly as "associates" of Europeans, partly on their own, traced possibilities of exploiting resources which had not been recognized by the autochthonous population or its feudal elite, introduced new products and new techniques (Spulber, p. 38), and created new tastes and hence new markets among the indigenes; the same, without any modification or omission, applies to the Asians in East Africa.

The phenomenon of technological dualism is generated by different opportunities facing the export-oriented foreigner and the subsistence-level-retaining native population; this situation is extreme in East Africa, as the tribal African and the coastal people had been less conscious of marginal needs than say, the Indonesian in his small, overpopulated territory. The tribal areas in East Africa are large and underpopulated; pastoral economy and subsistence level agriculture are easily pursued. It seems to me that the hunger for unknown goods is stronger in an overpopulated underdeveloped region living on a subsistence economy than it is in an underpopulated area with the same economy, and that conversely, the efforts of the alien entrepreneur have to be greater to generate tastes and demands in the underpopulated region than they have to be in the overpopulated area which experiences more intensive all-over economic duress. Consequently, the dualism in East Africa created by the Asians is potentially more explosive than that established by the Chinese in Indonesia or Thailand.

Indonesian private enterprise exhibits an ideological opposition to both Chinese and Europeans; in East Africa, there is no indigenous private enterprise, but the ideological syndrome was created, and is now operative with the East African politician-nationalist who has incipient entrepreneurial traits and who sees a ubiquitous threat in the presence of the Indian entrepreneur whose comfortable, gadgetized, and outward-oriented ways he wants to emulate, or more exactly, inherit. Like the Indonesians, the East Africans now display straight xenophobia, and what might have been an objectively negotiable target of economic criticism—the white and the Asian entrepreneur—turns into an ideological enemy. Jomo

Kenyatta and Dr. Nyerere have been referring to the Asians as "bloodsuckers," "leeches," and a number of other unflattering terms. Their initial motivation was political rather than economic—getting the popular vote is aided by invectives against the Asians, and the scapegoat rhetoric has become part of the political parlance of African leadership. It is no longer the egotistic, ruthless monetary self-enrichment and the theft of the land committed by the Asians, but rather their disdain, their feeling of cultural and racial superiority, and their pretentious one-upmanship based on regular features, straight hair, lighter skin colour, and written traditions, which are pointed out to the emergent African nationalists.

During the decade previous to East African independence Asians did indeed support the East African nationalists,[4] but this support is often interpreted by the Africans as a bribe and as a means of ingratiation, whereby the wealthy Asians would find a comfortable niche to stay on and enhance their wealth in East Africa after *uhuru*. It cannot be gainsaid that this allegation is partly justified. Consciously or unconsciously, many Asian entrepreneurs tried to purchase a measure of security or a warranty for survival in the critical pre-*uhuru* days. Perhaps this pattern of buying security is common to all alien entrepreneurs.

The Europeans in East Africa—farmers, merchants, industrialists, and administrators—were entrepreneurs in a unilateral sense rather than in the bipolar fashion stipulated by most studies on alien entrepreneur groups. They were real competitors to the Asian entrepreneurs, as in the case of sisal marketing in cities like Tanga, where Europeans started the industry and where the Asians moved in. The Greek sisal and coffee estate owners in Tanganyika, the British importers or industrialists ran their own show, crossing the Asians' path only by way of one-way catering: Asians contracted and delivered many of the local raw materials, imported some from abroad (often from India, more recently from Japan); they also furnished those marginal services which

98

did not require highly specialized technological skills or mechanical knowledge. Almost all of the sisal estate managers who have to handle machinery are European up to this day, and so are most sisal engineers who are the Asian entrepreneurs' highest salaried employees. Europeans who built a sisal plant bought machinery from Britain or Germany. They hired labor from the indigenous African population. They contracted for buildings, housing, machinery, offices, furniture, and the laborer's clothing, from the Asian. Where Asian entrepreneurs created highly developed industries of their own, they started from scratch, on a very small scale, and quite independently.

The stereotype image of the Asian trader in East Africa as an economic go-between linking an African and a white clientele is misleading. The Asian trader looked for his customers wherever he could find them, and the fact that some of his goods, intended for the whites—"luxury goods" like razor blades and tropical helmets *(ṭopī)* for men—were also bought by Africans, is as incidental to the system as the occasional American tourist buying a *kanga* (the coastal African women's dress) from an Indian merchant.

If the model suggested by Riggs (ibid., p. 143), is to be extended to the East African situation, the term "elite" would simply have to be qualified, and "potential elite" read for "elite." There was no elite in East Africa which operated like the gentile in Rumania, or the indigenous elite. Nor was there anyone analogous to the "upstart" in monolingual and ethnically homogeneous countries in the west.

Even if we try to squeeze the territory for a few instances, they would in no way establish an entrepreneur-elite dichotomy. The Chaga and, to a lesser extent, the Masai in Tanganyika, or the Kikuyu and Jaluau in Kenya, have been among the Indian entrepreneur's clientele, and they also own large cattle herds and (in the case of the Chaga) sizable coffee estates. But the Chaga (and Masai) coffee-and-cattle wealth is not of an entrepreneurial type. The affluent Chaga coffee owners are feudal managers on all counts. Beneath them, there are tribals, who may have been actual serfs to the Chaga elite in pre-contact days, and here we do find some groups of squatters and others who have been engaged in low menial services to the Chaga feudals; between them and their feudal masters there is no doubt a patron-client relation. But there is no elite-entrepreneur relation between the Chaga, or other tribals, and the Asian entrepreneur. Though the Chaga (as other tribals) *have* their socio-political elite, and though their leaders form a definite all-East African elite today—many of them have gone into politics and have achieved high status in political and administrative careers —they are *not* an elite to be contrasted with the Asian settler, entrepreneur, or conservative petty-trader. *All* Africans have been and still are customers of Asian businessmen, and Africans provide labor and indirect service to the Asian entrepreneurial effort. Among the laborers in the cotton gins in Uganda, we find many Baganda tribesmen, and on the Indian sisal and coffee farms in Tanzania there are quite a few Chaga.

Thus, no elite-entrepreneur polarization emerges unless we redefine the African customers' and the African servants' relations to the Asian entrepreneur. The "potential elite" consists of the African nationalist politicians in office and close to it, and the young Africans who return from college in Europe, America, and Russia, to step into government and trade, and who, during the next few decades, hope to replace the Asian and the white businessmen. Once this situation has come about—as it has in certain metropolitan areas—we shall indeed be able to speak of foreign entrepreneurs, Asian and others, if any are left. They are not wanted by the "potential elite," and it remains to be seen whether the Asian and the white entrepreneur can survive; at this moment, it seems more likely to me that some of the "potential elite" will usurp entrepreneurship to themselves, possibly modeling it on the Asians' entrepreneurial precedent of the past.[5]

In coffee marketing there was no clash, nor any entre-

preneur vs. elite (or quasi-elite) conflict between the Asians
and the Chaga, because marketing has long been directed
by government appointed boards, and both the Chaga and
the Asians, as well as Greek and other European coffee
growers, have had to sell their crop through these boards.

Asians were barred from buying land under the British,
and it is only since *uhuru* that some have bought farmland
from departing white farmers (British and South African) in
the former "white" highlands of Kenya. These lands were
sold to any interested buyer. Most of the Asians who bought
land from the whites were Sikhs of the *Jat*-caste, the professional, hereditary peasant class from the Panjab. For them,
buying land was a matter of great prestige; as previous to
uhuru all Jats were traders like other Asian settlers. Among
the Jats, there are some genuine entrepreneurs, as for instance

Indra Singh Gill, a very wealthy Sikh businessman, does a
sirsasan **(headstand) during his 5 AM yoga exercises. He**
began as a railway clerk forty years ago.

the fabulous Indar Singh Gill in Jinja, Uganda, who began as a stationmaster about twenty-years ago, and who is now a highly eclectic industrialist owning and managing sawmills and other enterprises. Quite recently, he set up a number of his male relatives on the highlands, had them buy wheat acreage (the largest farm of over 3000 acres belongs to his nephew), while some others bought themselves into coffee and tea in continental Tanzania. In addition, he sent some relatives to India to buy sugar cane land near Pilibhit, U.P. far away from the Panjab where his family originated. The fact that Indar Singh delegates large-scale farming and the office of entrepreneurially oriented agriculture to relatives in the descending generation is significant; the Jats had been farmers before they came to East Africa two generations ago, and to farming they return—albeit to a highly modernized entrepreneurial form of it, with bulldozers, tractors, new hybrid crops of wheat and other cereal, and extended marketing across the Indian Ocean.

The Jat-Sikhs' return to the land under these new conditions is a rather special case—they form a tiny fraction of

A Sikh rancher in the Kenya highlands and his African worker repair a tractor.

the total Asian minority in East Africa. These farmers have no doubt improved the adjacent Africans' image of the Asians. In all other areas, the Africans view the Asians as parasites, as self-centered, impolite, humorless petty traders who want nothing from them except their pennies. On the whole, the British, even during the Mau Mau period, were less detested than the Asians, because the British on the Highlands were farmers, occupationally closer to the Africans. That the Indians in India are predominantly farmers was not known to them—nor did the Asian settlers attempt to convey this image to the Africans. But the Jats around Kibos and Eldoret in the Kenyan highlands have succeeded in breaking the stereotype—the African tribals in the area (Nandi and Kipsigi) still recognize the profit-orientedness of the Asian farmer, but profit obtained through the sale of crops is not as noxious to the African. While he views alien entrepreneurship with envy and distrust, these are feelings bound to decrease, or even to turn into appreciation, where the Asian entrepreneur confines himself to agricultural enterprise or where he succeeds in camouflaging his cultural interests.

Much, if not most, of the available literature on the Asians in Africa was produced by economists, who investigated the economy in the territories in conjunction with the Asians' role.[6] The extreme thriftiness of the Indian trader, his willingness to live on a narrow profit margin, and most of all, the complete absence of any desire for leisure or hobby, —based to some extent on the anti-hedonistic background of Gujarati lower urban middle-class Hinduism—made him the ideal merchant in his own image; but as an unfortunate though probably inevitable sequel, he became the object of suspicion and hatred to his African clientele, and of disdain to the whites to whose needs he catered in a demure, tenacious, but socially remote and withdrawn style.

After the First World War, the Asians in Tanganyika profited greatly from the auctioning off of ex-German property, and their economic progress in all the four areas was steady. They enjoyed a real surge after World War II, which was the signal for the Asian potential entrepreneur at large. Soon the Asians virtually monopolized the import-export trade where goods from east of Aden were concerned and, figuratively speaking, the Asians have come to be the department store for all who live in Africa—Africans, whites, and their fellow Asians. In spite of a history of intensive and quite overt government restrictions on all sorts of licensing, purchase of real estate, distribution, etc.,[7] the Asians have succeeded, and have created more per capita wealth than Indians have in India or elsewhere in Southern Asia. This has to be attributed to their thrift, no doubt, but also to an astounding economic optimism which was discrepant with their political hopes. Even now, when the Asians are under formidable political pressure, this optimism is retained in a large measure. A wealthy entrepreneur in the import of foreign and gourmet food, a Panjabi Hindu businessman told me, "the Africans are stopping all import licenses; and even if they didn't, who would buy Geisha Oranges and Nova Scotia salmon except the Americans and British who are leaving this country for good? The only imported things Africans and Asians buy are apples, and now they stopped trade with South Africa . . . but we shall make the Africans like, buy, and eat Nova Scotia salmon and Geisha Oranges and smoke cigars, just as we made them use pepper and spices."

A German anthropologist put it this way as long as thirty years ago,

> The mystery of their success must be attributed, (1) to the generally excellent family life; (2) to the simplicity of their life, a kind of economic asceticism; (3) to the saving of money which they send home to India; (4) to the reciprocal economic aid within the sphere of related families; (5) the Indians settled on the main lines of traffic. . . (6) the Indians know English and often European reading, writing, and reckoning, as they have been trained in Indian schools after the European fashion. . .[8]

In this statement, only (5) is wrong today; before World War II there was a residual tendency among the small shopkeepers to "live near the line"—the Arabs stuck to the old caravan routes. (3) has to be modified: very few people send money to India, which is financially quite insecure and economically worse off than East Africa. The East African shilling is tied to the pound, and was the chief currency up to the free port of Aden. The Indian rupee is not negotiable at this time. Most businessmen, and certainly all the more successful entrepreneurs, send their money to Britain or Switzerland, though a few bank it in the dollar area. The Asian businessman in East Africa does not look at the dollar or the sterling bill with the awe his kinsman in India and Pakistan does.

In 1960, the average Asian per capita earnings in Kenya were about 480 pound sterling per annum, as compared to over 1300 pound for the Europeans, and about 75 pound for the African.[9] This meant three times the earnings of socially and economically equivalent groups in India. Kenya is the richest and economically most variegated of the East African countries, closely followed by Uganda, which seems to be catching up with Kenya at present.

The sisal industry and all the sisal land were in the hands of non-Africans—Greeks and Asians. To my knowledge there is not a single indigenous African sisal farm owner controlling over 20 acres of sisal (European and Asian sisal farms average 2000 acres, with 100 the lowest and 5000 the largest estates). In 1960, the Asians produced 22.95% of the total sisal production of Tanganyika.[10]

In Uganda, one of the world's centers of the cotton industry, Asians had a large share of the market and seemed to be on their way to achieving the ginning monopoly. Progress toward this goal was radically halted by the government of independent Uganda, as cotton cooperatives were given the first right to buy from the cotton boards at controlled prices. The Asian cotton industrialist is now restricted to less than 10% of the land's cotton, and the Ugandan government has made it quite clear that the non-indigene will have to move out; cotton ginning and marketing were among the most profitable entrepreneurial features among the Asians. They are now phasing out of the cotton business—or more correctly, they are being phased out. In the capital city of Kampala, the Asians held 97.5% of the cotton trade previous to these government measures, when 80% of all the African traders made an annual profit of 50 pounds or less.[11] One firm of Asian cotton magnates, started from scratch by a poor immigrant in 1923, is now worth $15 million, and the three sons of that incredible "early" entrepreneur from Cutch, now handle over half a dozen interconnected industrial plants, and the marketing process.

The changing interpersonal and interracial relations between the Asian entrepreneur, the Asian non-entrepreneurial conservative businessman, his white counterparts, and the majority population, especially the "potential elite," are subtle and complex. To some of these problems we must now turn.

Since there is no indigenous large-scale entrepreneur as yet in East Africa, the Asians share certain functions with the whites—banking, insurance, import-export, and light industry. Transport, apart from governmental transport agencies like rails and airlines, was almost entirely in Asian hands, but Africans have begun to move in. Though most of the employees at European banking houses are Asian, several sectors of the Asian minority run their own banks, which are pretty much on a par with the European firms. The Ottoman Bank, the Baroda Bank, and the Bank of India are really branches of Indian and Pakistani banks, some of which were nationalized in India a few years earlier. But the banking business in a wider sense—loans, mortgages, etc.—is very largely Asian, their clientele being about three-fourths Asian, one-eighth African, and one-eighth white.

Asian entrepreneurs could not go into agriculture until *uhuru*, as they were legally barred from buying farmland. However, the British decided around 1930 to let Asians buy some sugar cane land at the lower fringe of the Highlands, in the swampy, hot area of Kisumu. Large tracts of sugar cane land are now owned and most effectively managed by

Sikhs; their farms at Kibos near Kisumu cover approximately 40,000 acres, and they are the sole suppliers of cane for the Mewani sugar mills, a Gujarati Asian factory started by a genial entrepreneur, again from scratch, around 1910. These Sikh cane growers satisfy all the definitional postulates for entrepreneurship set by Riggs.[12] The term "access" in the definition must be given a curious twist in the context: the elite is here constituted by the Asian "old rich" quasi-elite (old: 1910-).

Trade as a function of the entrepreneur is, of course, a very wide term, but the trade pattern followed by the Asian entrepreneur can be readily typified: the basic unit is the *dūkā*, and the trading entrepreneur takes his departure from the *dūkā* as an indefinitely expansible unit. Almost all of the successful entrepreneurs started off with a small *dūkā*— or their fathers or paternal uncles (who are ascriptive "fathers" in the Indian social systems) did—and prestige attaches to reiterations of the kind "X started with a small *dūkā*, now he owns millions and runs this and that factory, industry, etc." In other words, there is no special prestige on non-

Dukas or shops can be seen through East Africa.

entrepreneurial, "old" wealth, mainly because there really is no such thing as "old" wealth, the oldest being three generations old. There was not a single wealthy Indian who transferred his business from India to East Africa; all the Indian wealth in the area is locally-created wealth. This, of course, is more grist to Professor Spulber's mill: traders who remain poor or just "so-so" in their native economy often flourish as entrepreneurs abroad, particularly when they join an economically rising minority in the new setting. In fact, statements about white industrialists seem to be mildly derogatory; the phrase *we to pahile se amīr the* (i.e., "those people, the white industrialists, were rich to begin with" implying "so what's so great about them") are frequently heard in East African-Asian parlance. This is quite different from the Indo-Pakistani scene, where old wealth is much more respected than entrepreneurial wealth—old wealth being identified with feudal, *"rājā"* or *"zamīndār"* (landholder) wealth, which has economic charisma, so to speak, whereas new wealth is despised as ill-gotten by necessity.

Under the British, there were many Asians in the upper echelons of governmental, administrative, and judicial services. The lower ranks were practically monopolized by them and until 1962, over nine-tenths of the clerks in the governmental offices, in all sections excluding the military, were Asian. This has radically changed since *uhuru,* and the Asians are on their way out. There are about six Asian members of Parliament in all the three countries (Tanzania, Uganda, Kenya), and their votes were not Asian votes, but African and white.

One genuine political entrepreneur was Chanan Singh, a man with exceptional talents and an exceptional career. As a young man, he sold clothing and other merchandise "from house to house"; he studied law on his own, borrowing books from various sources; he then passed several examinations, and became a governmental secretary when he was about 40. During the first two years after Kenyan *uhuru,* he was Parliamentary Secretary to Premier Kenyatta, but as the Africans did not want an Asian that close to the top, he was promoted to a Judgeship in the Kenyan Supreme Court. He is an unchallengeable authority on the Asian minority in general, and extremely well informed about African and Asian-in-Africa economics. There is still an Asian senior minister in the government of Tanzania, and a junior minister in the same government who has now moved out into UNESCO. But both in politics and in governmental services, the Asians are on their way out. The official formulation of the African governmental employment agencies has been that "Kenyan (or Tanzanian, or Ugandan) citizens" will be entitled to apply for government service. This has given rise to much anguished speculation about the advisability of taking out East African citizenship. Deadlines from two to four years were set by the individual governments, and government service contracts may not be renewed for people who have not become East African citizens by then. "Africanization" is the official policy, but the term is ambiguous, and the great question before the minds of roughly 10,000 Asian government servants in East Africa, on all levels of administration, was whether "Africanization" really meant East African citizens' employment and promotion, or whether it will not eventually be "blackenization." Such latent racial discrimination makes the Asians apprehensive. There have indeed been occasional statements made by spokesmen for government employment offices that people of "indigenous African background" will be given preference in hiring. There is no doubt that the political-administrative power elite is purely African now, and that the potential economic elite will be recruited either from this elite, or from people directly sponsored by the political elite.

There are no organized pressure groups left which would safeguard the Asian entrepreneurs from the potential power elite. The various Asian parochial organizations previous to *uhuru* provided some informal inter-Asian control: the Patel Service Society would see to it that Patels were not pushed out from competition, say, by Ismailis. As to the

Asians' entrepreneurial status vis-a-vis the white entrepreneurs, the all-Asian political organizations, foremost among them the Kenya National Congress and its equivalents in the other countries, were indeed well-appointed pressure groups which wielded their controlling influence through political channels and through the anti-colonialist rhetoric which was so successful in India; in fact, this rhetoric was conducted simultaneously with that in India and the channels of political communication between India and the Indians in East Africa were intact. However, even before *uhuru* the various political bodies among the Asians openly renounced any further political activity, and whatever residue of those one-time political factions survived has been reduced to a somewhat pathetic "cultural" existence, largely exhausting its function in the reception of visitors from India and Pakistan—who invariably exhort the Asians to be of good cheer, to "integrate" with the Africans, whatever that means, to make Africans their business-partners, to teach them how to conduct business, and to do their share in developing their African homeland. The same advice is given freely by the former Asian political leaders to the Asian businessmen, with the difference that the Africa-born Asian leader, just like the Africa-born Asian non-leader, abhors the idea and the suggestion that the Asians should "integrate" with the Africans in the manner implied by visiting leaders from India and Pakistan and by African leaders: i.e., through intermarriage. Such "integration," it can safely be said, is totally impossible on any scale, for the next four or five generations, at least, if the Asians survive that long as a community.

The next problem which the entrepreneur faces is the protection, by the governments in question, of the property rights, contract enforcements, access to licenses and permits, and foreign exchange. *De jure,* there is at this moment no discrimination in the extension and preservation of property rights between any of the ethnic groups living in East Africa, the only exception being Zanzibar, where hundreds of wealthy Asians, mostly Ismailis and Bohras, were summarily expro-

110

priated. Zanzibar has come to be paradigmatically traumatic for all Asians in East Africa, and it is difficult to conduct any sustained conversation with Asian businessmen without this one query coming up: what is the guarantee that things are not going to happen here (i.e. in Kenya, the other parts of Tanzania, Uganda) the way they did in Zanzibar? The question is not paranoid as I first thought when I went into the field. There is indeed no such guarantee, and African leaders hardly hesitate to let their African constituents know —and the Asians as well—that there not only can be no such guarantee, but that the "foreign bloodsuckers" should quit. In theory, the term encompasses whites and Asians, but it aims obliquely at the latter, simply due to the not entirely unfounded notion that the whites can go home and make money elsewhere, while the Asians cannot, and will try to stay on and keep exploiting East Africans. Though this has never been officially stated in so many words—the closest to such a summary notification were some of the speeches and articles by Tom Mboya—this is what the political power elite— and, *a fortiori,* the potential business elite—wants: business and entrepreneurial opportunities must go to native Africans; Asians and other aliens, regardless of their citizenship, will have to leave their big and small businesses or integrate completely—which means sharing all wealth, and possibly inter-marrying with Africans. The more optimistic Asian entre-preneurs hope that the initial chauvinistic fervor of the African leadership will subside and that they will come to terms with the Asians who have the economic know-how which the Africans lack (this is a fact no one could dispute in an un-emotional state of mind). The less optimistic, however, do not believe that they can survive as an affluent, entrepre-neurially oriented community; they fear that the Africans will sooner or later insist on physical integration and that they will pass confiscatory legislation.

The objective evaluation between the two extremes would no doubt lie somewhere in between, but on heuristic grounds I tend to incline toward the Asian pessimist's view. It is

true that inceptive chauvinistic and other radically ethnocentric attitudes tend to quiet after awhile; this has happened in India, so much so that British visitors are extremely
popular now, even such former "enemies" as Lord Mount-
batten or the Queen. However, the danger as I see it lies
in the possibility that the speed of events may overtake the
gradual process of adjustment intrinsic in post-liberty xenophobia, especially where these attitudes are reinforced by
patterns of economic duress: the British and the powerful
white, in general, have left Africa, but the Asian is sitting
right there as a prime target. He is not willing to go, and
this is well known to the Africans. The mere presence of
the Asian—the fact that the big cities look like wealthy
Indian settlements rather than African towns, with the best
cars and the most prominent and most visible business houses
being run and owned by the Asians, makes them such a
target. "They are an eyesore to us." a young Kikuyu who
had just graduated from an American college told me in
Nairobi.

As to the possibility of sudden radical legislation amount-
ing to displacement or expropriation, that too looms large,
and some African politicians are vaguely flirting with the
thought of seizing non-African property by some sort of
confiscatory legislation, if not by condoned pogrom.

Until 1965, permits were available to all residents without
any discrimination—licenses to run shops, gas stations, and
small businesses of all sorts; the same held for import licenses,
crucial to Asian business and to the Asian entrepreneur, whose
mainstay is the import of manufactured goods. Luxury articles are bound to be checked very soon, and quite a few
items have already been barred from import—since "luxury"
is situationally defined, any import item may fall under the
ax. Although there is no ethnic discrimination in the gradual withdrawal of· import licenses, the Asian businessman is
hit the hardest because he has monopolized foreign food
import. This is well known to the finance ministries and
their adjunct offices in the East African countries, and the

112

very fact of entrepreneurial monopoly now stands against the survival of Asian entrepreneurship: the Africans do not have to enact any discriminatory legislation, since all restrictive action in the process of issuance automatically "discriminates" against the Asian who alone needs the licenses.

Dr. Kyano, the Berkeley graduate Finance Minister of Kenya, admonished the Asians to take Africans on as executive business partners with the implication "or else. . ." In June 1964 he contacted the various Chambers of Commerce and let it be known that he did not want to see the word "Indian" or "Asian" in the telephone and trade directory any longer; the Asian Chamber of Commerce was consequently changed into Central Chamber of Commerce. It was suggested in a meeting of Asian businessmen that the Asian Importers Association be changed into "Importers Association," a characteristic statement; there are no non-Asian im-

An African lawyer confers with his Asian assistant.

porters in sufficient numbers to institutionalize importers' associations. The fact that Africans have not as yet made any significant entry into the business world and that there are no African entrepreneurs in any sense comparable to the Asian aggravates the situation, for it makes African leaders contemplate means to change the situation abruptly.

However, "nostrification"—that somewhat inexorable euphemism—has not really set in. Apart from Zanzibar, where there have been extensive "nostrifications"—plus, of course, complete expropriation of the clove estates from the Muscat Arabs who had been the sole proprietors (about 7000 Arabs were killed in the process in 1963)—Asians have not been forced by any legal or para-legal action to leave their residences or to abandon, sell out, or transfer their businesses. In the bush, the small *dūka*-owners have indeed begun to move out, as there have been well-organized boycots of Asian shops in several tribal areas, and also on account of the rapidly growing indigenous cooperatives. But this process set in much earlier than *uhuru*, though the present developments, no doubt, accelerate it. We must distinguish between the conservative Asian shopkeeper and the entrepreneur, and while the former is hard-hit by the events, and is bound to lose his established livelihood sooner or later, the entrepreneur with his great maneuverability and his typically multi-local enterprise has not been so directly affected.

The economic situation is undoubtedly the catalyst for confrontation and conflict. But there is another less obvious base to such conflict. In most areas of immigration and settlement the Indians encountered hosts who had a codified tradition of learning and communication, who had built edifices of stone, of thought, and of worship. There was no such encounter in East Africa. Though the Asians did not tell the Africans, "we had books and temples and philosophy and you had nothing of the sort," intra-Asian parlance upholds that the Asians came into a cultural vacuum, and that the Africans are not grateful for the gifts the Asians brought: refined tastes—sartorial, gastronomical, and ecological—and a more expansive look at the world. The Africans are viscerally aware of these attitudes, and the neglect and impoliteness, as well as the mercatorial exploitation the Asians wrought upon them, are felt to be clustered up with this latent disrespect toward the autochthonous population. Candid Asians tend to admit that there has been exploitation or, as they would put it, that the Asians came to make money, with little altruistic motivation. But the less perspicacious Asian rationalizes and would like to believe that the benefits accruing to the African population were so great that they far outweighed the obnoxity of the original motivation of the Asians.

The Asian regards himself as superior due to the ancestral culture on which he draws for his life cycle ritual, his spiritual solace, and his literary edification. The African leadership is aware of it, and it impugns the Asians' claim that Africa is their real home.

Short of discriminatory legislation or expropriation, there seems to be one way for the Africans to eliminate the Asian entrepreneur, and that is through guided creation of indigenous African entrepreneurship. The personnel pool is certainly at hand: over 5000 young East Africans are studying abroad—in Europe, Russia, America, and in India. It does not seem too important that only a fraction of these are studying economics and business administration; they are all exposed to the competitive ways of highly entrepreneurial societies. In addition to these, there may, of course, come to the fore some Africans who have never had any formal schooling; most of the original Asian entrepreneurs were not educated men, some were virtually illiterate. And even though the scope for sheer entrepreneurship has diminished in East Africa as elsewhere, the aggressive small trader will feel encouraged by the turn of events in his native land, and genuine African entrepreneurs will emerge from the *dukas* in the bush and in the city, where Africans have been watching their Asian employers, and learning from them. It is the students abroad and the occasional uneducated but perceptive employee of the Asian and white merchant who constitute what I called the "potential entrepreneurial elite," backed by the political and administrative services which are almost completely Africanized by now.

I also maintain that there is more than potential rapprochement between the Asian entrepreneurs and the African potential elite—through their children who have begun to meet and talk at school. But the danger of an avalanche of political, expropriatory, and eventually pogrom-like action launched by the chauvinistic, powerful, charismatic lowbrow looms large at any time. It will be important for the West to court the few intellectual groups, even though their inspiration stems from the left; supporting the ethnic chauvinist, who may or may not consent to show a Tshombean front to the West, will probably be counterproductive in the long run.

CHAPTER FOUR

Interpersonal Relations: Men and Women

Anthropologists working in South Asia have shown that, as a rule of thumb, male-female and other interpersonal relations tend to be more formal, more strained, and less personal at the top of the social hierarchy, and less formal, more relaxed, more personal at the lower end. The South Asian tribals who have not been absorbed by surrounding "Great Tradition" are undoubtedly the least formal with regard to male-female interaction.

In East Africa, the situation is simpler. There are few informal relationships among any of the constituent groups, between male and female relatives, consanguineous and affinal. The proverbial license between the *jijā* and the *sālī* in India and Pakistan is known to the East African Asians, but this knowledge is purely academic. The Hindi proverb *sālī ādhī gharwālī* "wife's sister is half a wife" is known and quoted by Panjabis whose idiom is very close to Hindu-Urdu, but it is not acted upon. The mild horseplay that is prevalent among these affines in certain North Indian groups is simply not replicated in East Africa, and if any male, or worse, any female, would act it out, quoting cultural precedence in the old country, he or she would be severely censured and penalized.

As in high-caste South Asia, men do not smile at women, regardless whether they are their wives, their affinal relatives, or unrelated women. It would be regarded as highly improper if a man showed any sort of affection or tenderness to his wife in public or in front of his own consanguineous kin. He would be characterized as a weakling, or as a potential lecher, and as one who wants to hurt his parents. One of the most pervasive complaints about the Africans, especially the domestic servants who are always in full view, is precisely that they act "shamelessly"; boys and girls smile and walk hand in hand, husband and wife cast tender glances at each other and do not try very hard to disguise the fact that they enjoy each other's company. All this is pointed out with serious bitterness by Asian women, and with disdain by many Asian males. There is an exact parallel here to the Indian situation in areas where there are low-caste groups and tribals, as for example in the Santhal Parganas near Hazaribagh in Bihar. The caste-Hindus, both Bihari and Bengali, point out with disgust that the Santhal, the Mundas, and the Oraon—the three tribal groups in that area—"live with their women in a shameless manner—they talk and laugh all the time and they enjoy in the field" (verbatim from a high-caste Indian informant in the area—"to enjoy" without an object clause being the modern Indian English code for "to make love"). This is another instantiation of Pocock's and Morris' findings[1]—Asians in East Africa view the African native very much as high-caste Hindus view low-caste, tribal, or "scheduled" groups in India.

Married couples avoid any show of affection or interest in each other when in the company of other people, but particularly when the husband's elders are around. Very modern and westernized Asian couples now often make a show of what they think would contrast them from others, by their terms of address: men and women who have been abroad, when speaking English, have begun to call each other "darling" or "my dear." Yet, the terms of reference and address in the Indian languages are still as indirect as they are on the subcontinent: though teknonymy is quite rare[2] today except among the *"choṭī jāt,"* low-caste artisan Gujarati groups, there is hardly any direct address by the wife to the husband, and the traditional Indian paraphrases are very much in use. Thus, Gujarati women would address their husbands by a polite indirect personal pronoun, or simply by some sort of non-semantic expletive, a sound to attract attention; no wife except some English-speaking socialites would address her husband by his first or any other personal name. The only exceptions I have actually witnessed were among Ismailis, where some women did indeed address their husbands by their first names; these were young women under thirty, highly westernized, whose Gujarati was interspersed with so much English when conversing on day-to-day chores that the European manner of addressing the husband by his first name emerged as an alternative form of address; thus, during one evening one of the ladies addressed her husband three times by "Ali-jī" ("Mr. Ali," polite—the *"jī—* in North Indian vernaculars functions like the *-leben* in orthodox Yiddish speech), but at least a dozen times by more conservative circumlocutions such as "I say," "have you heard," etc. Husbands quite often address their wives by their first names, but this has been the usage in the equivalent social groups in India and Pakistan for a long time. However, even in the husband-to-wife address indirect locutions are more frequent, though again, teknonymy has virtually vanished from the East African Asian speech pattern.

Though far less rigidly than among the Rajasthan Thākurs described by Carstairs,[3] the large, wealthy, and conservative Gujarati and Panjabi joint-families do not concede their men any sexual identification so long as the father or a much older brother live in the house. In other words, until the young man has gained status and age in the agnatic hierarchy, he has to pretend, more or less, that he does not have, or better, that he does not enjoy any sexual contact with his wife. It is expected that the first child is born, at the latest, two years after marriage, but hope prevails

119

that the young husband performs the necessary actions with a sense of duty combined with mild disgust. For the women, it is not only impossible, without incurring severe censure and even punishment, to disclose in any manner that they enjoy their husband's conjugal approaches, almost all senior women regard it as their duty to instruct the younger women about the utter depravity of sex. A lady doctor, a Gujarati woman trained in England, told a Peace Corps volunteer, a very attractive nurse who worked at a hospital in Mwanza, Tanzania, "you are lucky that you are not married and that you are a virgin. Women do not enjoy it. It is only for men. You are a young unmarried girl and you do not know these things. I suffered much. But I honored my husband and got used to it and did not tell him that I disliked it. I don't mind it so much now, I just do it like a duty, but it is horrible for women." When senior women instruct their own daughters in this manner, their warnings are much more severe. It is amazing that the lady doctor, who had been exposed to the occident, would talk in this strain to a modern American girl, without suspecting the potential psychological and social assessment about the speaker which an occidental college woman is likely to make on hearing such a harangue.

There is a lot of indirect tutoring, both in the girls' natal house and in her husband's home, to make her realize that a good woman should *not* enjoy sexual relations; that she should submit to her husband only out of a sense of duty. Older women of the conjugal house seek and find opportunity to impress this point upon the young women. A Patel woman of about forty told me that when she had just been married, her husband's older sister once took her aside and warned her not to expect pleasures in marriage. When she told her sister-in-law that her husband's approaches were not unpleasant to her, and that she did enjoy his company as soon as he had allayed her initial fears, the other woman became furious; she censured the young wife for trying to ingratiate herself with her husband, and to deprive his kinswomen of his affection.

The tradition followed by the wealthier Panjabis and by several Gujarati groups requires married women to wear ornate, richly colored and highly decorative *sārīs* until one year after the wedding. This causes considerable anguish among mothers-in-law, and their ambivalent feelings tend to make for a harsher treatment of their daughters-in-law. A woman who had three married sons, the youngest having been married a week before this interview, complained "the women must wear fine dresses for a year; but it is bad, all these old-fashioned customs should be abolished. With these gaudy raiments on, these women constantly attract their husbands and the glances of other men in the house, and the young men aren't worth anything, they forget their duties and begin to drink and gamble. . . ." As in India, mothers often resent attractive daughters-in-law. Most young women—particularly those of a more conservative natal background—play the game and act demurely, by not drawing their husband's attention toward them in the presence of other people, and by "wearing the fine *sārīs* with a sigh," as a young woman told me, apparently without any facetious intent. But women who have been exposed to occidental education and to a lot of "sundowner" and "club-type" environments quite often enjoy annoying their in-laws, particularly when they are sure of their husband's support. Many young men have made the psychological shift to their wives, unheard of a generation ago and extremely rare in South Asia even today— from undivided attachment to the consanguineous group, and total submission to their parents. The traditional attitude requires that the young man side with his mother against his wife, when the occasion arises. But with a good amount of intuition, many young Asians have felt that this shift is the first genuine step toward emancipation on the interpersonal level.

A most enjoyable example of this shift toward individual autonomy and interpersonal liberation occurred in Kisumu, Kenya, in the house of a wealthy and highly conservative Panjabi Hindu merchant. To begin with, his son had married beneath his own caste. This in itself is permissible, though not too popular; in the traditional setup men can and always did marry hypergamically, i.e., slightly beneath their own subcaste. The marriage had been an arranged one, as the lower-caste girl's family was extremely wealthy; also, the two had played tennis and drunk tea together before negotiations began. The young couple told me that theirs was actually a love-marriage, but that their parents, on both sides, made it appear as though it had been arranged "like a good marriage." Then, two days after the wedding, which was conducted in style, with all the Vedic ritual, and with about 1,500 well-fed guests, the young couple decided to do something quite unprecedented: they went on a regular honeymoon—for three days—to a lovely resort near the foot of Mt. Kenya. This caused a stir all over the city; the boy's mother shut herself up and sulked for many weeks; the father was in despair, fearing the censure of his own peers. During a *satsaṅg*,[4] the speaker said "nowadays people have fallen from the ideal of pious sonhood; instead of taking the Name of the Lord *(Hari-Om)*, they go on a *honeymoon*" — ("Hari-Om" and "honeymoon" sound almost alike in the Panjabi phonetic setting).

Although the notion that women neither should nor do enjoy the sexual act is part of the official culture, more modern women of less than thirty-five are interested in the subject in a manner that would hardly be approved by their less sophisticated peers and elders. It could never be predicted which modern informant would identify with the official culture, and which would approach the problems involved in an objective, sympathetically interested manner. The Gujarati lady doctor told the Peace Corps nurse that sex "is a horrible, disgusting thing for the women," but quite a few much less educated women gave different responses. "Husbands know nothing about how to please a woman. They think it is not important. They do not read enough books" a Panjabi woman of twenty-eight, mother of four, confided to me. "It is said in the old Sanskrit books that love is an art, but men do not know that. They think only of themselves and they think this is right. They think a woman who is *śauqīn* [interested, eager] is immodest and bad," a Sikh woman of about forty explained. There is no or very little foreplay involved in the sexual act, and of over a dozen husbands interviewed at different places, eight thought that anything but the direct, swiftly executed pro-creative act was "useless," "unnecessary," or "immoral" and that these things were "bad habits." And like Carstair's Rajasthani village *banyā* woman said to her husband[5] "I do it only to please you," most of the East African Asian women share this sentiment. The modal idea of married women could be summarized in such a statement as "a woman does not enjoy it; she does not enjoy it at first; but then she gets used to it. She does not mind. It is her duty to keep her husband happy." An Ismaili woman at Dar-es-Salaam, aged about thirty-two, with three children, said: "he (my husband) loved me very much and often at first. But nowadays he is so tired when he gets home. When they made him the President of the . . . he began to work too much. Now he is so tired. He says to me that you and I should love like brother and sister now. We have enough children." Did she feel uncomfortable or put out at this lack of attention? "Well, sometimes it does harm me. . . . I get annoyed, sometimes . . . so I make up my mind, and it is not too bad. He thinks too much love is bad for me. We should be like brother and sister." Did she try to change his mind? "I went to the Hindu *paṇḍit* who gave me *golī* (any sphere-shaped Indian medicine, here probably some traditional mild aphrodisiac) to put into his tea. He loved me very much again for a week. But then he found *golī* in his tea and threw it away and was very angry." She then continued saying once more "we have enough children now. We should live like brother and sister." When I suggested they really didn't have to, with all the modern contraceptives including oral pills freely available at all the better pharma-cists in Dar-es-Salaam, she said, "my husband will not do that. He says it is a dirty thing, and it is a sin. God will

123

punish if we use." Both she and her husband had been in Europe twice, once for two years at a stretch.

There is no premarital sexual consummation of any statistical significance among the Asians in East Africa. Sons of the very wealthy who have their own cars do drive to rendezvous sites in the suburbs of the city. The Baha'i shrine charmingly perched on a peak overlooking parts of Kampala is a famous place for the trysts of young Asians, both Hindu and Ismaili, but there is hardly any degree of intimacy except for the mildest sort of necking. A young woman referred to as a "club-type" by some of the older people, said "many boys of the . . . community test girls. They try to kiss them and touch them, but if the girls let them do it, they turn away from them and spread a bad name for the girl. Nobody wants to marry her then and her parents are unhappy." A "club-type" is the East African Asian designation for any girl who speaks with men, has been seen participating in social dance, or is reported to drink in the company of men. "No one wants to marry them. They are bad in the house, they do not look after the house, they hate their parents-in-law," an elderly Sikh businessman said, referring to a group of young Sikh girls whom he knew. When a boy asks a girl for a kiss or any intimacy, she must say "I am not this type of girl. Look for someone else, not me."

Among young, unmarried men and women from medium to high income families, and across caste lines, there is considerable theoretical interest in sexual matters, none of which ever occurs to the older generation. The more ortho-dox among the older people suspect this in a vague manner, and it is conceivable that their complaints about young people no longer sharing the values of the tradition build on some knowledge of the young people's interest. A highly sophisticated Hindu doctor in Mwanza told me that he had given a lot of thought to these matters, and that he had spoken with dozens of young people, men and women, and had spoken professionally with married women of all age groups. He believed that of the married women in East

Africa, not more than 5 percent ever experienced an orgasm in their married life. As to the young unmarried "who have begun to experiment," there is at least the knowledge that a woman can experience something as intensive as the man —and among young people, especially those who use English as their medium of discourse rather than Gujarati and Panjabi, there is fairly free talk about sex across the dating lines. This situation appears to be reinforced by two factors: first, there is a lot of easily available sex literature in English, at stores owned by Asians in all the cities; English-speaking parents buy the books and their growing children obviously read them, and discuss what they have read—with their peers, as they could obviously not talk about them with their elders. Secondly, the numerous movies made in India[6]—India has the second-largest movie industry in the world—provide the young and the middle-aged with fuel for their romantic ideations. When talking about romantic love the Arabic-Persian words *muḥabbat* and *iśq* are used invariably, as there is really no Sanskritic equivalent. Adults, well advanced in their vocations, parents of school-going children, as well as the very young, paint pictures of rosy, *schmaltzy* things depicted on a lovelorn, grotesquely unrealistic, yet highly puritanical screen. Most of the movies shown in East Africa are imported from India; Africans seem to enjoy them, at least for their music and dance, more than they do the Euramerican film imports. The actual or alleged romances of the Indian screen-stars seem grist to the Asians' romantic mills.

There is no genuine living tradition of male-female involvement. The erotic lore of ancient India is not known, and reports and pictures from Khajuraho and Konarak evoke profound shock in any Asian audience in East Africa, though people of comparable social and educational status on the subcontinent have come to take these with a shrug or with an emergent aesthetical curiosity, however germinal. I overheard the conversation of two women on the terrace of the New Stanley, the hotel-restaurant "where everyone meets" in Nairobi. From the manner of their mutual address, they

125

were either sisters or perhaps mother and daughter; the older one was around forty, the younger about twenty. I first thought that they were discussing some real-life episode involving lovers of both sexes; but this was not the case—they were speaking about Raj Kapoor and Vijayanthimala, two film-greats; their actual or imagined exploits vis-a-vis each other in the process of making the four-hour movie *Sangam* (the first Indian movie with mild kissing on the screen) were discussed with much the same gusto as graduate students or ex-college women would discuss D. H. Lawrence or Simone de Beauvior in the western world. People who sip tea or coffee at the Stanley are not just rich Asians; they are indisputably modern. The very rich—Lohanas, Patels, and others—do not go to the Stanley much as the Vanderbilts, presumably, do not patronize Schraffts, nor the Rothschilds the Playboy Club.

Just as in urban sophisticated South Asia today, anyone in East Africa who talks about sex has a large and eager audience; and just as in South Asia, he will be despised and called immoral after the session is over. Young and old are bored, on their own admission, with conservative talk and its underlying values, but the conservative and his talk are "honored."

The enjoyment of sex by others is bitterly resented and there is no doubt that much of the negative assessment of non-Asians—African and white—derives from the notion held by the Asians, that Africans and whites enjoy sex and, what is worse, that they are not ashamed of enjoying it and that they do not conceal its pursuit. Referring to their Somali servants, a Lohana woman said with disgust: "these people wallow like animals. Each time they have great fun ... [from the Hindi phrase used, the implication was that they had orgasms each time they made love] and they have only two children, although they have been together in this house for six and a half years." When asked why she thought that they did not produce more children, the woman continued "in former days, they killed them. . . . Now, they

126

do some magic or other dirty things so they don't get children. They don't care for anything." The speaker had five children at the time of the interview. "Dirty things" probably meant *coitus interruptus* or other non-impregnatory loveplay. Asians report vaguely that "Africans do all these things"; the woman could not possibly mean—as a colleague of mine suggested when I referred the matter to him—that the African servants used contraceptives, since they are simply not yet used by African domestic servants.

It has been known for some years now that Freudian categories do not usually fit outside Europe and America. No doubt some sort of an Oedipal transition in the father-son relationship is evidenced in the patrifocal Indian societies—including all East African Indian groups; but none of it explains the strangely ambivalent relations between father and son, and between father-in-law and daughter-in-law. In one way, the male family head in Indian society *does* castrate his son—and I would add, the richer the merrier: an extremely wealthy Soni (member of the Gujarati goldsmith caste) not only watched his 19 year old son's every step in Dar-es-Salaam, but he even had him chaperoned when the young man went to Bombay to spend a year with his paternal uncle, i.e., his father's brother who is a classificatory father. "My father forces me to take over his job soon; but I am not interested in gold selling. I want to study and help society. My father in Bombay (i.e., his actual father's brother) stopped me from going to college. He also did not let me meet any girls, although they wanted to meet me," the young man narrated. This was particularly revealing; for though we could of course explain father's vigilance over son's sexual activities in an Oedipal situation, it seems that the classificatory father replicated the treatment once he took over paternal responsibilities, temporarily or permanently. A vicarious Oedipal transition could possibly be construed in strongly agnatic societies with joint or extended family organization.

Continuing, the young man complained "You cannot talk to girls here" (i.e., in Dar-es-Salaam)—"in Bombay, the

127

girls are quite free, and they invited me to their houses. . . .
banyā (merchant-caste) and even other girls and Muslims,
too." This report was patent imagination. If anything, the
boy-meets-girl situation among *banyās* and similar groups
in Bombay is more rigid than in East Africa. Obviously, the
young man introjected his notions about what was *supposed*
to happen in Bombay, and what does no doubt happen there,
with Parsis and in highly westernized groups very different
from his own, and then came to believe them, or narrate
them as his own experience. "My mother is very broad-
minded," he continued, "she said to me 'Son, if you want
to talk to a girl and you are kind to her, that is all right.'
But my father here in Dar and (the one) in Bombay are old-
fashioned and pious." "Pious" in this context was simply
deferential for "old-fashioned"—for the young man himself
was as "pious" as any of his elders, performing all the mani-
fold religious observances at home. I took him to an air-
conditioned Espresso-shop in the downtown area of Dar-es-
Salaam. He was visibly excited, but tried to look nonchalant.
I ordered an omelette, and his eyes grew large—he did not
expect a Hindu monk to eat eggs, which are non-vegetarian,
and which none of his own kin had ever touched. He then
said he wanted only a milkshake—there were four flavors
listed on the menu, and it took him seven minutes to select
one—it turned out to be milkshake with milk flavor. . . .

The habitually strained relations between mother-in-law
and daughter-in-law have been noted by even casual observers.[6] But the ambivalence of the father-in-law's feelings toward his son's wife has yet to be analyzed. A wealthy Panjabi Muslim merchant in a city in Upper Kenya made at
least two conflicting sets of statements, on the same day,
about his good looking daughter-in-law. She was fair-com-
plexioned, efficient, a good cook—better than his wife, in
spite of the fact that young women who read English novels
these days don't cook a good meal anymore—she was present-
minded *(hāzir javāb)* without being impolite to her affines.
And yet, she was too attractive, she took away his son's mind,

and as Asian women consult with African servants on matters of baby care and cure, I see no reason why some kind of advisory give-and-take should not also occur in matters of magical practice and counsel. The circumspect wife of a medium wealthy Ismaili businessman had this story to tell; "both of them (i.e., her husband's parents) are always trying to harm me. They hide away stones, precious and other stones of all sorts, to do some harm. . . . When I once mentioned these stones casually, but with the intent of letting them know that I knew about their intentions, they removed them to some different place. . . . but once they had gone to cinema and I broke into her jewelry box and saw many of these stones assorted by color, and it frightened me to see all these stones. There was a *mantra* (magical spell) written on a piece of paper in the same box. . . ." We should no longer be surprised at the fact that Muslims use *mantra, yantra,* and other tantric[7] devices continuing their Hindu ancestors' Great and Little Tradition practices. The technical difference is that *mantra* forms part of the Great Tradition ritual in Hinduism and Jainism, while remaining on the folk level among Muslims.

We must not underestimate clinical dangers inherent in such procedures and attitudes; for quite apart from psychosomatic disturbances recognized by anthropologically oriented psychiatry, the demarcation between magic—or sorcery-inflicted harm and actual physical aggression is tenuous. Drugs and potions of all sorts are easily bought and dispensed; a specialist in magic may well give some drug to his client, asking her to put it into her opponent's milk or tea. As in India, powerful barbiturates and virtually all drugs are available on the free market with hardly any effective checks. Female subjects who feared that magic was being used against them did not make any sharp distinction between such uncanny but biologically harmless items of exuvial magic as cotton with menstrual blood, or nail-parings hidden under the husband's bed, and potassium ground into the adversary's tea cup. "I overheard her (mother-in-law) asking him (her son, subject's husband) not to eat anything for a few days which came directly from the kitchen, but only dishes which she herself would feed him." All these techniques are well known to the student of magic and religion in primitive and peasant societies[8]; yet what remains puzzling in this particular milieu is the fact that little has changed in this situation in spite of the impressive technological advance and the ecological, sartorial, and hygienic innovations Asians in East Africa have achieved.

A Panjabi woman asked me to give her some *mantra* "to protect me, my husband, and my children from harm. . . ." When I asked her if she thought her in-laws would really contemplate harming their own son and their grandchildren, she paused for a while and said "all women are dangerous, and when they get angry, they do not know what they do in their rage." Correcting herself after a while, she said "I am an Ārya Samājī, we don't believe in these things. But all others do, and my in-laws are *sanātani* . . . who knows what harm they could do with the help of the priest who is often drunk; but he is bad and powerful and he knows all kinds of *mantras* . . . he has already harmed many people."

Relations between siblings are generally warm and responsive. The only exception is that between the eldest son and his younger male siblings. In line with the conservative Indian tradition, the oldest son, who will be the head of the family once the father retires or dies, assumes a paternalistic attitude in his dealings with younger siblings, especially with his brothers. All siblings indulge the very young. However, there is no restriction on parents' display of affection toward their pre-teenage progeny, as there is in parallel groups in India and Pakistan. Lohana and Patel women in India refer to their children by *peli* or *pelun*, "this here," "that there," lest they should give offense to the child's paternal grandparents who alone are supposed to show open affection to their grandchildren. I have not witnessed such constraint in East Africa, except in the one case of a poor *chotijāt* family deep in the Tanganyikan bush. In India, the restraints

132

against the mother's overt tenderness toward her young, enjoined in order not to "show disrespect" to the in-laws, are by no means confined to rural areas. I have observed and recorded severest censure for child-indulging mothers in the industrial city of Ahmedabad, in a Patel family where one son had just returned from Britain, and the other was studying in the United States. It appears that the increasing pressure which the Asians experience as a community helps to level some of the more frustrating conservative interpersonal patterns—it seems plausible that Asians feel a trans-generational solidarity is needed more than ever, and as the critical generation is the one that has very young children at this time, considerable lenience is shown toward them by their elders in matters of intra-familial etiquette.

Where parallel and cross cousins are addressed as brothers and sisters, the warm interpersonal response of younger siblings is extended to include them. Among both Gujaratis and Panjabis, parallel cousins are treated exactly like siblings, even in houses where there is no longer any trace of the erstwhile joint family structure.

The father-son relation is distant and delicate, and more reserved where there is wealth. Once the boy is past thirteen, the father no longer displays any overt affection toward him; he admonishes him constantly, alone or in front of relatives and friends—not to develop "bad habits," not to be slothful, to be alert, silent, and pious. If the son has gone abroad, or moved permanently to another African city, things change and his father then praises him with limitless panegyric—in his absence. As a rule, one might say that the eldest son who acts as deputy father to his younger siblings by way of gravity and standard-setting scores well with his father and will be less often rebuked than the son who displays playful tenderness to his younger siblings. "He should read his books and study to become a good man"—or words to that effect—were heard many times; on the other hand, if the son *really* takes to books, his father tends to get very upset indeed; the boy will then not be interested in looking after the business, he will conceive dangerous ideas, and he will not respect his father. However, "the Europe-returned" son is never reprimanded; he is always extolled as the person in whom all the hopes of the family are vested. Before a son or a daughter is sent abroad, there is one thing which parents impress upon their child: not to fall in love and not to marry a foreign woman or a foreign man. This is more difficult and more painful to convey to daughters than to sons. In the first place, the father never discusses sexual and related matters with his son, let alone with his daughter. It is the mother, or a married elder sister, who briefs the young girl before she leaves her parental home to go abroad to study: non-Asian men are dangerous; they flatter girls and want to make love to them; they do not want to marry them; and if they do want to marry them, the girl will not be acceptable to her white groom's family; neither will a white spouse be acceptable in the Asian home in case he or she is brought over to settle in East Africa.

The relation between mother and daughter is much more relaxed; it is more easy-going, by and large, than in cognate social groups in India and Pakistan. Mothers who are under forty-five, and who belong to medium or upper income groups, give all the tenderness to their daughters, knowing that they will depart from their natal house to join a husband. But then, things are not as hard as in South Asia where this departure meant more complete separation. Married women do visit their natal homes at regular intervals on the subcontinent, but these visits become more formal and less frequent as the years pass by. With the much greater affluence and the easier transportation within East Africa—quite a high proportion of married Asian women drive cars and hardly any woman thinks much of riding a train or flying on a commercial airline all by herself—mutual visiting is much more frequent than in India and Pakistan.

However, there is no intimate instruction from mother to daughter even in East Africa. Just as in India and Pakistan, there is absolutely no intimation of the daughter's or

134

younger sister's oncoming menarche and just as in the old country, the first menstruation is usually a severely traumatic experience for the young girl. She finds little solace from her mother, for the latter is upset and mortified and in line with the hypertrophic puritanism of modern India, she tends to feel deep shame, aggravated by the fact that she cannot communicate its cause to her daughter. In India and Pakistan, there is the same situational response to the onset of the daughter's menarche in middle-class society. We must never forget that East African-India is *not* village India; it is a segment of the urban or marginally urban population of two regions transplanted into another land—not into another milieu, for the Asians accepted little of the interpersonal freedom of the British whom they morally despised, and nothing from the Africans whose cultural existence they ignored. Neither the African nor the white expatriates' mother gets in any way ruffled on the occasion of a girl's menarche, but in the Asian homes the event is dreaded. I asked several men about it—their rationale was that once the daughter has

Together they giggle. Wealthy Gujarati girls relax in their Tanga home.

135

had her first menstruation "there is no end to our worry—
we must marry her soon; so long as she is a little girl, we
still think of the day as a future day. But when this thing
happens, this reminds us that the time has come to fulfill
our duty" (i.e., to inaugurate the tedious, expensive process
of finding a suitable groom).

A wealthy Lohana girl of about nineteen had been told
by a girlfriend of her elder sister's that "this would happen
soon" when she was about twelve; and when it did happen,
she knew about it and did not cry. When her elder sister
found out that her friend had briefed the little girl; she
became very angry and never talked to that friend again. When
I suggested that rather than breaking with her friend she
ought to have been grateful to her at relieving the possible
trauma for her sister, she said "no, it is a matter of great
shame and one must not talk about it." Another young
woman reminisced that when she "bled for the first time"
she ran to her mother, and the mother was speechless with
shame; all the same, she told her reluctantly, and bit by bit,
that this was what she would have to expect every month
now; when she asked for the reason, her mother told her
"God sends this disease to remind young girls not to entertain
evil thoughts."

Another woman, who had one child at the time of the
interview, had been sent to England as a girl of fifteen, to
attend a boarding school. She had been having her period
for about two years before she went, but it was only in
England when the other girls told her the relevant facts that
she understood it all.

By and large, East African Asian women use modern
hygienic tissue during menstruation. An unmarried Gujarati
girl said that she would like to use Tampax, which was available in the stores at Nairobi; but that she kept using Modess
instead; since the storekeeper knew her father, if she asked
for Tampax, the word would get around that "she knew too
much about these things." Only married women use Tampax—previous to marriage, women have to use Modess or

some other medically less intrusive and less blatantly functional product.

During menstruation, and until the fourth day after, women do not "pray"—i.e., they do not enter the part of the house which is used as a shrine; no one, including their mothers touch them. All the women about the house seem to know each time, and great care is taken to shield the menfolks from the menstruating girl or woman, who stays out of the kitchen. None of the men about the house know of it; and when the men ask the women "why do you not pray today?" they receive some evasive answer. Having been told that men most often do not know the reason for the avoidance of the daily ritualistic acts, I checked it with half a dozen men, both Hindu and Muslim, and found that five of them indeed never got the idea. One of them got irritated at this anthropologist and exclaimed "you so-called scientists make us think of things we never thought of before—always these dirty things. Cannot you study better things about us? What if I asked you to study your mother's or sister's menstruation?"

Among the older and more conservative men, Muslim, Hindu, and Sikh alike, there is more of an overt, traditional concern with the dangers of ritualistic pollution through contact, however indirect, with women in their period. If they knew the situation they would avoid sitting on the same sofa and talking to them. Responses of an nonspecific kind, such as "it may be harmful" or "it is dangerous" were recorded from the more conservative; but further elicitation yielded the vaguest results—no informant was quite clear as to whether it would harm him or the woman, or both; or whether the possible danger was of a clinical or of a ritualistically polluting kind.

The parents-in-law to daughter-in-law relation, then, is delicate and potentially hostile as on the subcontinent. I had expected that this relationship would have undergone considerable change due to the progressive nuclearization of the Asian family. Yet, the mother-in-law in Asian East Africa still regards her son's wife as a perennial intruder who has to be called "daughter" and who merits, by traditional behest, the love a daughter should be given. Of about one hundred families across the three countries, a cross-section sample on a proportionate scale by constituent castes, there were roughly twenty where relations were both overtly and actually cordial. In each of these cases, however, the positive interaction between sons' wives and their mothers-in-law occurred between the younger sons' wives and their mothers-in-law; it appears that there is the greatest potential friction between the mother and the wife of her oldest son. This follows an explicable pattern set in India; there is such an extraordinary degree of emotional investment in the eldest son, who is the first real status-giver to the mother, that his loss to a rival outsider is hard to sustain. By the time a woman has given birth to more children and several sons, this society-linked investment is no longer so overwhelmingly strong. The Indian woman's status in her husband's household rises abruptly when her first son is born, but the birth of further sons seems to yield diminishing returns in status increase.

In half a dozen cases out of the same sample, there was mutual suspicion of alienation of the son's or the husband's affection through sorcery and magic.

Grandmothers and grandfathers indulge their small grandchildren; although mothers in East Africa are not forbidden to fondle their children in the presence of their in-laws, as is the case with parallel groups on the subcontinent, many grandparents consciously disaffect their small grandchildren from their mother. Quite frequently, and *coram populo,* grandparents point with pride to the fact that their grandchildren are more attracted to them, and that they would rather be taken for a ride or be fetched from school by them than by their parents.

There was hardly any evidence of physical punishment or mistreatment. Several informants averred that wife or daughter-in-law beating occurred among the lower castes, i.e., the Gujarati and Sikh *fundi* or artisan groups. Informants of those castes, however, claimed that it was only among the higher castes, especially the poorer families among them, that young women were maltreated, both physically and mentally. Sometimes, the son would enforec unmerited hardship and punishment on his wife, egged on by his mother's constant nagging suggestions.

There is a bare vestige of the former *purdah* system among some Gujarati groups. In India, *purdah* means that the wife has "to show respect," i.e., to cover her head, turn away, sit down, and keep her voice low, in the presence of her husband's father, elder brothers, and theoretically all the male affines older than her husband. I have witnessed actual *purdah* behavior only in four cases, three Gujarati Hindus and one Ithna Ashari family in the bush in western Tanganyika. Otherwise, "respect" is simply shown by not contradicting anything older affinal relatives say even if they are known to be wrong, and by implementing all the requests made by them.

Asian males seek permanent friendly liaisons with other men. There is hardly any limitation for the prospective choice of a close friend, except perhaps on linguistic grounds. Religious denomination and caste do not enter significantly on this level of interaction, for the man who is an active member of his caste organization does not necessarily choose his close friends from among his caste-mates. The linguistic background is a determinant: Gujarati speakers—Hindus, Muslims, and Ismailis—feel comfortable in each other's company, and Panjabi speakers—Sikhs, Hindus, and Muslims—feel the same way about each other. It is not that Panjabi and Gujarati speakers could not converse; far from it, for every male in East Africa knows the *lingua franca,* a Hindustani which grammarians do not recommend; and well over a third of all Asian males know enough English to handle conversation on the levels of discourse required by them. Yet, the linguistic link is a strong one. Moreover, the two chief linguistic groups have totally different, gustatorily incompatible tastes; the Panjabis—again, regardless of whether Sikh,

Hindu, or Muslim—regard the oily, spicy, staple-oriented Gujarati food as unhealthy and unpalatable, and try to avoid it if possible. Gujaratis think Panjabi food is bland and monotonous. The Ismailis form a culinary norm by themselves—their style of cooking is closer to Gujarati cuisine, but their ingredients are closer to Panjabi and North Indian styles, with a heavy stress on meat—i.e., chicken and mutton, and in the coastal areas of Tanzania and Kenya, some fish.

The material substratum for male friendships is liquor. There is not a single group which officially condones drinking, for both the Hindu and the Muslim doctrine regard drinking as evil. The Catholic Goans do not have such a proscription in theory, but they share the South Asian urban puritanism in all matters, including sex and drink; they hardly drink less than other Asian males, but they certainly do not drink more, in spite of the fact that there is no religious injunction against it. The focal drink is Scotch, referred to as "whiskey" by the Asians, following British nomenclature. Bourbon is not known, some ultramodernites have taken to occasional gin and even vodka, but "a drink" is virtually synonymous with Scotch, either with soda, or more frequently without. Beer is drunk, wine is hardly known. It is quite apparent that apart from those infrequent male friendships which center on religious interests, social drinking is the hallmark, outwardly at least, of positive male interaction. It seems to me that much of it is highly ritualized—there are alcoholics among the Asians, no doubt, but their number is negligible. I say this quite categorically—the average Asian cannot hold his liquor. Somehow, the conviction that drinking is basically wicked makes the Asian puritan enjoy the *sin* about it more than the taste, and I have witnessed dozens of strong, hefty men who were high after two or three *"chotā peg"* (roughly the alcoholic content of one double martini), and completely out of commission after two more *"chotā pegs."* Much joint drinking is probably due to conversational insecurity—Asian males do not yet have intellectual interests that could help them communicate joyfully without liquor, and business talk fills only a portion of friend-to-friend conversation. There is some mildly ribald talk, but far less than among Africans, though probably more than among white expatriates. Once these limited topics have been exhausted, liquor generates its own parlance, and the drowsy, repetitive, cognitively vacuous conversation about sorrow and disappointments occupies the remaining part of the friends' meetings. I said that much Asian drinking was ritualistic—several businessmen, wealthy and poor, report that they cannot relax from the day's worries, and cannot enjoy the evening unless they have had their drink. A Panjabi Hindu merchant in Nairobi put it this way: "I know it is wrong; but when I come home after worrying the whole day, I must have glass of whiskey neat. If I do not have it, I cannot think and talk. The evening is useless." His wife told me, on a separate occasion, that she had never touched a drop before she got married, but after their first son was born, her husband urged her to join him once in a while. Then she began to like it; and now she often drinks a glass or two all alone; her husband does not know it, but he would not mind it. Unfortunately, most people in her circle seemed to know it and pointed it out on many occasions; "Mrs. K. is a whiskey expert," a friend of the house said. "Does she make whiskey?" "No, she drinks it quite solidly." If that was true, she certainly concealed it better than the men about the house. It seemed to me that where women did drink, they had taken to it after their marriage, and usually with slightly more than their husbands' consent—it takes quite a bit of initiative for any Asian woman to start. While society censures the male drinker in a somewhat perfunctory fashion, it reprimands and censures most vehemently any woman who is known to drink, regardless of the quantity. There does not seem to be a feeling of distinction between, say, the woman who takes a "peg" with her husband once or twice a week, and a mild alcoholic. There was also a sort of clandestine admiration for the male drinker; although drinking is never sanctioned by any of the Asian religions, it is connived at for men, because it enhances friendship and association, and because "it makes even a hard man soft," a businessman temporarily human. In addition, there is a vague notion that drinking elevates the spirit—such are indeed the teachings of some of the heterodox fringe groups in both Hinduism and Sufi Islam; there is no cognitive knowledge of these teachings among the Asians, but Urdu and Persian poetry channels these anomic, marginally religious attitudes into the tolerance threshold. This is most frequently the case with Panjabis—Hindus, Sikhs, and Muslims—much less so with Gujaratis. Panjabis over fifty have had direct or indirect acquaintance with Persianized Urdu poetry; the *Diwan-e-Ghalib*[9] is read by many Panjabis of this age group, though not by Gujaratis, who do not appreciate this literature due to linguistic strictures. The speech-form most cherished by urban Panjabis is and has always been Urdu, and poetic Urdu means highly Persianized Urdu; Persianized Urdu literature contains *sokhī*, literally "brashness," but the term, well understood by Panjabi men of that age-group and older, has about the same semantic flavor as the Yiddish "hutzbe" for the sophisticated Ashkanazee Jew in Europe or America.

In line with drinking behavior in many societies,[10] by no means all Asian, male interactional drinking also fills a need which is strongly present in such puritanical societies, including the Irish; anything goes *except* overt interest in sex. For the Irish, as for the Hindu and Muslim, it is not so bad to get drunk once in a while: it is warm, friendly, and masculine. But direct interest in women and sex is felt to be sissy and, in the case of South Asia with its supremely puritanical culture, the lowest interest a man can have. The German proverb: *wer niemals einen Rausch gehabt, das ist kein braver Mann*,[11] and the Chinese proverb which says "how stupid is a man who does not drink"[12] would strike a kindred cord in the Asian male middle-class mind. When Asian males drink together, they are protected, by a temporary screen as it were, from elements in their surroundings which frighten them and which menace their security and their identity: their women—wives, mothers and other women, their business opponents, and more recently, the African rulers. A Bohra businessman agreed, albeit reluctantly, when I suggested that men who drink take revenge on their society which constantly imposes strains and strictures and which bars an outgoing joyful relation between people, especially between men and women.

Men hardly seem to conceive of the possibility that they might just sit together and talk; and I have this *obiter dictum* from a wealthy merchant: "what is there to be talked about? We talk business the whole day, then our women bother us and we must talk to them. Now we enjoy" (i.e., drinking together). The cold fact is, of course, that the man was right. There is little to be talked about in a society which has been cut off from the mainstream of its cultural origin, and which has not had the time to develop discursive interests. I spent many evenings with men and women who did converse on important matters—but they are a tiny elite of roughly fifty people in all the three East African countries, people who read and wrote for *Transition,* who subscribed to *Commentary* or *Encounter.* They too had drinks as they talked, but talking was the focal event to them; neither did they feel guilty about drinking.

The alternative to conversational entertainment in the evenings is the traditional, religious way—there are *bhajans* and *kīrtans* among the Gujarati Hindus, and all Ismailis attend prayers at the *Jamātkhāna* on Friday. The religiously inclined have formed their religious groups, and they spend most of their free time in religious pursuit and in religious conversation. I would estimate that about one in fifty of the Hindu population use a religious forum as a vehicle for interaction between non-kin, while over a third of the total male population interact with drink as the focal medium for interpersonal contact.

The alcohol consumption of women is a much simpler problem. Hardly more than 1 percent, if indeed that many, of all the Asian women drink alcoholic beverages. Virtually all Gujarati Hindu women are teetotallers; among Muslims, some modern Ismaili women do drink occasionally; so do some very few Panjabi Hindus and Sikhs; Goan women do not drink; but they sip at whatever their men drink. Young women who have been abroad do not regard drinking as wrong, even if they themselves seldom do it. I interviewed about a dozen Gujarati Hindu girls who had had their schooling abroad; only two of them thought there was something morally wrong with moderate drinking at a sundowner or at some modern-type social function. Less than about one-fourth of foreign-trained or foreign-travelled women drink with the same regularity as their husbands, but almost all "have a drink once in a while." As I indicated earlier, there is no doubt that the women who do drink display relatively higher psychological tolerance than the men.

Mild social drinking and individual, large-quantity consumption which could lead to alcoholism are not distinguished by drinking or abstaining Asians. A medium wealthy Panjabi businessman in Arusha said about a much wealthier Gujarati businessman at the same place "he starts (drinking) at 10 a.m. and goes easy the rest of the day." Trying to decode the ambivalence of this statement, I realized that it had been intended in a vaguely laudatory manner which would not have emerged had I only recorded the original statement. It appears that in this case, as in others, where responses to other people's drinking are elicited, individual drinking is given *less* censure than social drinking; for in the former case, the "shame does not come on the family, no one knows, people only guess." When men drink socially, or worse, when women join them, everything is out in the open, hence reproachable to the highest degree.

Drinking, public or private, is a lesser offense than nonmarital sex. A young Bohra, who had been studying in Britain and in the States, mused "we can forgive a thief, but we cannot forgive a man who enjoys" ("enjoy" without the syntactically required object, is Indian English for "having sexual relations"). "When a man steals, he is hungry, he must feed himself and his family. But when he enjoys, this is selfish; he does it for his own pleasure. It is bad." The notion that

144

there may be nothing wrong with enjoyment *per se,* sexual or other, is not known to Asians, again with the exception of alienated intellectuals who do not identify with the community.

At Tanga, I tried to explain to a group of Hindus what sort of information the cultural anthropologist wants to collect; and specifically, what sort of information I would like to gather during my field work. I tried, in that particular instance, to obtain some ideas as to what behavior the interviewees considered as deviant in their society. I took great pains to explain that I had not come to suggest any remedy or reform, but that I was eager to understand their ideas about deviancy. Judging from his response, the spokesman of that group—a highly respected elderly bank-clerk, seemed to have grasped the notion of descriptivity without evaluation or moralization. But in his translation into Gujarati, addressing a crowd of about fifty people including some women, he said "he wants to know about people who drink and commit *vyabhicār* (adultery, but also just sheer fornication—author's note); he wants to help them." Deviancy could only mean deviation from the acepted sexual standards; I tried—here and at several other occasions in different places—to convey the sociological, or at least a kind of popularistic psychological notion of "deviancy" to Asian audiences; this did not work at all. The term was always interpreted in a moralistic fashion—thus corroborating one of the basic assumptions of psychological anthropology, that deviance simply means any deviation, instantiated by individuals in a culture, from the accepted norm. That norm, in most societies, is couched in traditional or modified traditional-moralistic terms. It was somewhat discomforting to notice that all but those in the medical profession regarded drinking a moral and not a medical problem.

Let us amend and summarize our observations on interpersonal relations among the Asians in East Africa. As might be expected, there is little change in intra-kin attitudes as compared with comparable groups in India and Pakistan.

There is, modally speaking, more interaction between consanguineously than between affinally related persons. In terms of social interaction, there seems to be more between friends, both in terms of voluntary associations—which have been discussed in the chapter on caste and caste-centered organizations—than between affines. In other words, were we to arrange contact intensity on a linear continuum, the consaguineous would score the highest in density and intensity; friendships and voluntary associations of a non-kin type would follow next, and affinal interaction would score lowest. This is radically different from the situation in most Indian villages,[13] but it does not seem too different from the South Asian urban and marginally urban situation; let me repeat that the Asians of East Africa are city people, hence atypical for the bulk of South Asian societies.

In the more tradition-oriented groups, Gujarati Hindus and Jains, and Gujarati Ithna-Ashari Muslims, the father-eldest son relation is strained—it is one of complete obedience matched with considerable covert resentment from son to father, and one of unquestioned dominance coupled with covert resentment from father to eldest son. Sibling relations are warm and supportive, except between younger male siblings and the oldest brother who acts as father surrogate well before he takes over the family's responsibilities from his father. Mother-to-daughter relations are mutually warm and supportive, though there is considerable anxiety on the mother's side before and after her daughter's menarche, virtually up to the day of her marriage out of the natal house. Joking relationships are negligible and much weaker than in equivalent Indian groups. Husband-wife relationships are distant and seemingly detached. Male-peer voluntary, i.e., non-kin, liaisons are strong and highly supportive, with social drinking as the pervasive catalyst. Non-kin interaction between women diverges to some extent from the Indo-Pakistani *saheli* model; close, intimate friendships between women are rare in the lower and middle income groups; voluntary associations most frequently center on religious activities, such

146

as the various kinds of the all-ladies *satsang* or religious meeting conducted at home or in some temples.

Arthur Koestler once said about Gandhi[14] that the one thing the Mahatma resented about God was that He created man as man and woman. In the puritanical milieu of modern India and of the East African Asians, human relations, both kin and non-kin, are ideologically geared to puritanical standards; the value orientation inasmuch as it applies to interpersonal relations operates on a much simpler, hence much more easily predictable scale than among more highly diversified, and less puritanical societies, as say, those of modern Japan, Western Europe, and Israel, where hedonistic motivations are taken for granted in men and women. Since interpersonal relations, in a puritanical society like that of the Asians, are formulated either as relations of duty or of diversion, inevitable contact between kinsmen, consanguineous and affinal relatives and business associates, stand for duty, and voluntary associations stand for pleasure and diversion. The latter are judged in terms of the moral standards involved, and only in these terms—such value orientations as the aesthetical, the ideological, or the nonconformist hardly exist and where they do, as in the case of a handful of Asian intellectuals, they are known to be exceptions which call for censure. In the value scheme of modern Indian society—Indian, Pakistani, Goan, East African Asian—people who want to meet for any reason apart from "duty," viz. apart from kin and business affairs or religious pursuits (*satsang*) are thought to meet for reasons which are basically objectionable and hence covertly or overtly resented. Sex, gambling, and drinking—in this descending order of demerit, are felt to be the only operative motivation for non-duty associations. Drinking is bad, but it cannot be avoided as almost all men *de facto* drink, which they vindicate as part of their business transactions or medical requirements; as gambling includes horse-betting and playing the stock market, it can and is being construed as a justifiable attempt to augment the fortune of the family, to send the children to good schools, etc. Only sex cannot be excused—

147

it is bad enough, as witness the laments of fathers and mothers-in-law, that the young get attracted and enslaved by their matrimonial partners; extramarital sex has no *raison d'être,* where the hedonistic, aesthetical, and similar lines of thought and value orientation are unknown—and as all non-duty interaction is thought to secure censured gratifications, it` has no positively accepted place in this society. The syndrome of awkwardness, fear, shame and guilt which this lack of salutary assignation has caused, is heuristically important for the study of this society—and it explains, to a considerable degree, why the Asians do not feel comfortable between two societies which value hedonism, albeit from very different cultural settings. I believe I have the key to the question which has been asked for many decades by Africans, white expatriates, and by some Asians: why is it that we live together in these lovely lands close to the equator, and yet we cannot *live* together. I think the Africans and the whites have a culturally and psychologically important element in common; they assign positive value to a joyful interaction between men and women, not only on the sexual, but on all levels. The white missionary was not strong enough to spoil the fun, though he kept trying valiantly. The Asian cannot see that the male-female relationship is either morally neutral or morally meritorious: he has no knowledge and no memory of the ancient Indian *ars amatoria* and when news about the erotic temple sculpture seep through to him even as he sips a drink at the New Stanley in Nairobi, he feels as indignant about it as did Mahatma Gandhi who, when asked by M. N. Roy what he thought about these artefacts, retorted "If I had the power, I would tear them down."[15]

CHAPTER FIVE

The Asians and the Others: Race Relations

We have seen that the main cause of friction between the Asians and the non-Asians is economic. Some earlier writers[1] thought that the Asian patterns of employment, business transactions, and other occupational affiliations followed kinship lines as they do in India. This is no longer quite true; I think Professor Pocock put his finger on the facts when he wrote[2]

> In Gujarat certainly wealth and power are important but it is wealth and power for the purpose of standing in a particular system (i.e., the kinship system, caste-grouping, etc.,—my note) where, in a sense, it is status that makes life worth living. In East Africa one has the impression that the *economic motive* (italics mine) is distinct and is the more important. This is not surprising in a community which is characterized by its commercial interests and which, moreover, is cut off from the areas in which prestige and kinship mean so much. In East Africa there is no local kingroup of any significance and the tensions which pervade India are consequently irrelevant. Even the joint-family, where it remains legally joint, is scattered, for economic reasons, over a wide area. In such circumstances, when we speak of factions we speak of individuals in commercial enterprises together with their commercial clients in opposition to other individuals similarly situated.

Until the late thirties perhaps, the economic orientation

was still kinship-directed, but the swift transition to a more pragmatic outlook accounted, I believe, in no small measure for the boom the Asians experienced after World War II.

What had been potentially the most affluent group in East Africa, now definitely turned into the richest. In urban East Africa, more than 75 percent of all buildings and real estate, and about an equal proportion of investments, belong to Asians. Sections in cities like Kampala, Dar es Salaam, and parts of Nairobi have the appearance of an Indian bazaar. On Kenyatta Avenue in Nairobi, the first African-owned shop was opened only in 1966; all other shops and trade centers were Asian. Counting cars passing by at the busiest intersections, I found that 80 out of 100 were driven by Asians in Dar es Salaam, 85 in Nairobi and 82 in Kampala. Asian women are the best dressed—not only those who wear the universally alluring sārī, but also the Ismailis who by a firmān (decree) of the late Aga Khan have taken to western dress for business and pleasure. The men are inelegantly dressed, overdressed, or poorly dressed, but only in a sartorial sense, for the materials are excellent and imported by their own friends and relatives. At least one-half of the movie audiences are Asian when English language movies are shown. The majority of cinemas in the big cities, and over three-fourths of the movies shown in the smaller settlements, are Hindi films with all-Asian audiences, sprinkled with some few African faces—Indian movies are about the only items of modern Indian culture which Africans appreciate; many African townspeople sing and whistle Hindi film-tunes with gusto.

The indigenous Africans have fine folk art, second to nothing in this genre. But the Asian settler is not a villager, and his background was not rural in the sense that he would appreciate rural or tribal art, Indian or African. Asians know about Masai and other East African woodcarvings—the largest dealer in these exquisite pieces of folk art is an Ismaili. His "curio-shop" caters to all tourists, and to their friends and dependents in America and Europe; mail-orders are accepted and promptly carried out for carvings of Masai men and women of all sizes, impalas, rhinos, and the whole tropical menagerie. But there are few if any Asians who see beauty in this craft. "These carvings," a well-travelled Gujarati businessman told me, "were not originally made by Africans; the missionaries introduced the craft to make the Africans do something that would bring them some money."

African drums and folk music are ignored; whatever the Asian might have heard on his business trips into the bush, or whatever records and praise he has heard from aliens, Peace Corps and other, do not impel him to attend to them. But then again, he would not attend to Indian folk music—he wants to hear *filmī* music. Some few Asians have recently developed an interest in classical Indian music, largely through the feedback from Indian radio broadcasts, imported records, and quite recently, the praise given to Ravi Shankar and Ali Akbar Khan by Americans.

Few Asians see autonomous merit in African culture; many think they know *Swahili*, because they can handle communication with servants and with *duka*-customers. But my most knowledgeable Asian adviser asserts that there is hardly any Asian who really knows *Swahili* well. In line with non-linguists all over the world, Asians seem to think that *Swahili* is not a "complete" language. Several Asian informants asserted independently, that *Swahili* does not have words for different kinds of fruit, and that they use the generic "fruit" to cover all species.

African servants—which means the entire domestic servant population spread over Asian houses in East Africa—are "totally unreliable," several informants told me. "Even if a servant stays with you for twenty years," a Panjabi businessman reported, "there is no trusting him. He will tell you he has to go home as his mother died. But after another month he will say the same thing again. They have no memory. And one day, he will not come back at all." What the businessman did not know was that his servant probably belongs to a group where every individual has many classificatory mothers, and that it is quite conceivable that they die, once in a while. The fact that there are classificatory mothers in Hindu society as well does not seem to mitigate such assessments.

All this is known and resented by the Africans, and the resentment is universal. The Asians in turn are aware of the resentment, and their reaction follows several intricate patterns which we shall adumbrate here. The mere statement that pressure of any sort causes counterpressure is truistic and trivial. There was mutual resentment long before *uhuru*, when no political pressure obtained between the indigenous Africans and the Asian settlers. The strain previous to *uhuru* was purely economic with hardly any political overtones. The political ideology was directed toward the British rulers, by both the Africans and the Asians, partly in a cooperative strain, but much more frequently, of course, in a mutually antagonistic fashion. Asian leaders in East Africa claim—and there may be a good amount of truth in their claim—that *their* political ideology and their zest, inspired by the nationalist movement in India, informed the African leaders in their turn. Perhaps the most fascinating but pathetic example is that of Ambu Patel,[3] an Asian businessman who threw in his lot completely with Mr. Kenyatta, becoming the latter's disciple in a truly Indian *guru*-disciple relationship modelled, consciously or otherwise, on the Gandhi-Nehru relation in earlier days. Ambu was not the only person—a number of intelligent, if not intellectual, highly qualified Asian settlers joined the national movement that led to *uhuru*, completely identifying with the African cause. This identification took various shapes, from participation inspired by a liberal and moderate political outlook, to radically fascist or communist forms. Mr. Makhan Singh, an avowed communist whom the British kept confined for many years both in Africa and in India, is one of the most eloquent spokesmen for "complete intergration"; a labor union leader, he still uses non-revisionist jargon and corrects people who call him "sir" or "sardar" and wants to be called "comrade" by both communists and noncommunists. But both he and Ambu Patel were symptomatic of the post-*uhuru* syndrome of attention and neglect: at the first *uhuru* celebrations, Patel was physically thrown out of a bus that carried African freedom fighters to the celebrations; Makhan Singh was consistently ignored, and the only Asian leaders who remained in the government were those who had administrative know-how which could at first not be dispensed with. Ideologically strong supporters and participants in the pre-*uhuru* dialogue whose interest and direction had been purely political lost out. During the past few years, some of the top-echelon Asian politicians in East Africa have been promoted to nominally high positions without power, and removed from the political center: the Parliamentary Secretary to Mr. Kenyatta was given a judgeship. The M.P.'s that did remain in office put integration on their banners. The Asian community at large, with hardly any difference between the various culturally heterogeneous sections of the Asian minority, felt left out, lost and abandoned. Rather than describe the attitude of Asians toward new rulers in a propositional form, I shall try to list the sort of statements that were made by representative Asians, i.e., men in the professions, government servants, and one-time political leaders.

"It was we who taught the Africans nationalism. Before that and along with it, we gave them new tastes and aspirations, and we supplied the goods to fulfill them. In the struggle with the British we formulated the demands and the thesis which finally led to *uhuru*. We supported, financially and ideologically, all the nationalist endeavors of the African leadership. We helped the Africans toward economic emancipation, we built multistoried mansions, etc. And now they want to push us out. They do not appreciate what we did for them, they are ungrateful, and there is no security for us, even from the side of those we supported."

The African story is a different one, as would be expected. In the first place, African leaders deny that the Asians had given them new tastes and aspirations. Dr. Mondlane, assassinated President of the Mozambique Revolutionary Council, Dar es Salaam, and one-time Assistant Professor of Anthropology at Syracuse, once suggested to me that no Asian precedence had been available in Western Africa, which was economically and ideologically more emancipated than East Africa. Had the Asians not been there, and had Africans had the same chances to study and travel, things would have been about the same as in West Africa. No doubt, African leaders admit, Asians gave a lot of money to African leaders; Ambu Patel supported Margaret Kenyatta when her father was in jail, and large sums of money were given to Africans who had some sort of political status. But these were bribes, the Africans aver, and meant to create a safe and secure niche for the Asians after *uhuru*. What the Africans cannot forget is the disdain in which the average Asian had been holding Africans since Asians came and settled, and the rude manner in which the *dūkā*-owner treated his African clientele, trying to squeeze every penny out of them as well. Also, they know that the Asians detest their darker color and physiognomy. The Asian talks of integration, but will he integrate? Of course not. Asian males had African concubines, but can an African approach an Asian woman? If the Asians were serious about integration, they would not object to intermarriage. They did not come and stay with any humanitarian motives, and whatever the salutary by-effects of Asian domicile in East Africa might have been, their intentions were purely commercial and egotistic. In India, so the "India-returned" African students say, the Patels and Lohanas are poor wretches, as hungry as the people around them, in East Africa they have made millions at the expense of the naive, trusting African villager and tribesman and the poor African domestic servant. The fact that Asians gave only menial jobs to Africans, and that most of the domestic servants in Asian houses have been Africans, irks the African urban dweller. Suggestions by African leaders that Asians should take Africans into partnership go unheeded.

In this manner, of course, a large number of noxious

generalizations on both sides could be accumulated, but these samples should suffice.

Antagonism between the indigenous Africans, now identified as the rulers, and the Asians, now a second-class citizenry in the image of the Africans and the remaining whites as well as in their own self-image, would be predictable even for an intelligent outsider. We do not know of any minority anywhere which does not cause and experience friction and stress at some time. Yet the present situation in East Africa must be one of the most severe. We shall now have to analyze the pressures that are objectively present vis-a-vis the Asians, and then list their reactions to actual or imagined duress due to these pressures.

There is no doubt in my mind that, at this time at least, most African leaders want the Asians as a whole out of East Africa. Most African leaders are also aware that any sudden action against the Asians, though probably popular with the African electorate, would be quite disastrous, at least for some more years. There are exceptions among the African leaders—most Asians feel, for instance, that Julius Nyerere and some other leaders meant it when they talked of a complex or multiracial society. (Since 1966, the Tanzanian President has overtly changed his mind; the Asians are the epitome of the exploiting bourgeoisie which his socialist state has to be rid of.) But many Asian leaders feel that there is an element of ineradicable and almost systematic antagonism in all African minds, even where there are asseverations of good will and good hope held out to the Asians. Indigenous African leaders, Asian leaders in responsible jobs, and also Indian and Pakistani visiting firemen exhort the Asians to take out local citizenship. Some have done so, some are waiting for the absolute deadline which is set differently in the three countries, and others just will not take out East African citizenship at all. Their fear is that becoming Kenyan or Ugandan or Tanzanian citizens will not help in the long run; there is a process of "blackenization," an ugly term used by Asians and whites. There is some objective basis to this notion.

155

Indigenous Africans are given some preference in governmental jobs when competing with better-qualified Asians.

Few Asians trust the East African economic future. Most people who save money deposit it in British banks and invest abroad in the sterling area. This is pointed out by African leaders as one of the reasons why Asians cannot be trusted, and that their professed African nationalism is spurious.

The interracial friction has, however, deeper roots than political and even economical mistrust. If we regard culture in purely anthropological terms—and there are over 160 ways of doing this[4]—no harm could be done. But to the Asian "culture" is a value-term; it is the Asians' notion of having settled in a cultural vacuum which frustrates incipient efforts at a genuine improvement of interracial relations.

Some well-meaning Hindus believe that African culture came from India "many thousand years ago"; this notion of India being the primeval center of cultural diffusion is quite pervasive among Indians. In East Africa, this is expressed in the claim that the tall, strong, handsome tribesmen like the Masai and the Chaga "came from the North"—which may be true, if their origin was Nilotic—and that before that, their ancestors had come from India. A highly respected old Hindu scholar impressed upon me that I should put my scholarly skills to work and prove the Indian origin of African culture.

The white settlers were not representative of the best of European culture. The only useful thing they brought was an advanced technology. The literary and ideological background of the white was too poor and too disparate from the Indian tradition to generate any sort of cultural comparison or competition. The only level of socializing, first between Asians and whites, then between Africans, Asians and whites was the "sundowner," and even that was limited due to the racial strictures set up by the whites, in hotels, restaurants, conveyances, etc. What bothers and aggravates Asians considerably is the African and white indifference to the cultural heritage which the Asians believe to have brought with them. Though there were no Sanskrit or other traditional scholars

156

and artists among the Asian settlers, almost all of them had a cherished set of possible references to a rich cultural milieu: the ideology and philosophy of Hinduism and Islam, the rich heritage of literature, music, dance, etc., and organized ritual based on "Great-Tradition" texts of hoary age. More than the British settlers, the Hindu as well as the Indian Muslim participates in a highly sophisticated, socio-centric ritual; kinship is defined and variable according to bulky, erudite, written and oral traditions—and although few of the Asian settlers, or none except their *pandits*, were familiar with these, there was a profound consciousness of their presence. Ritualistic purity extends over food and drinking habits, and although many Asians took to drinking on European lines, most of their food taboos remained intact until quite recently. The Africans and the whites they encountered had no food taboos, hence no ritualistic purity. Starting from this negative image of both the Africans and the Europeans, the Asian in East Africa began to live in a world of his own, a chip-on-the-shoulder world of concealed conceit nurtured by the facts of his thrift and his consequent economic independence.

It might be objected that this identification with a culture dissimilar to that of the environment—a culture to which Indians all over the world refer as "spiritual" which they contrast with western "materialist" culture, was primarily a Hindu concern and that it did not touch the Muslims, who form an important segment of the Asian minority. This, however, is incorrect. All people of Asian origin in East Africa, including even the Catholic Goans, share the matrix of "spiritual" condescension. True, such Asian Muslim groups as the numerically insignificant Panjabi Ahmediyas or Mirzais find it much easier to mingle with the Africans, to live among them as their own kind, but with the prospect of proselytization. Yet, in matters of religious lore and of ideology, all Asians have been taking a one-upmanship attitude both toward the whites and the Africans. Emotional investment in religious matters is ubiquitous and profound, notwithstanding modern Indian disclaimers. Outsiders are often

157

persuaded by the modern and progressive among the Asians that religion and tradition no longer play an important role. But this is either make-believe or sheer naivete on the side of the Asian informant. All Asians in East Africa are tradition-oriented in Riesman's sense, with the exception perhaps of about half a dozen Asian college teachers in the three institutions constituting the University of East Africa. Kindred groups in India and Pakistan today present a proportionately larger number of people who have broken away from tradition-orientedness. The fact is that there are more colleges in India and Pakistan, and that the coffeehouse echelons of highly influential literati in those countries have been exposed to Sartre, Marxism, extensive reading, and stagecraft. These cultured influences are non-existent among the East Africa Asians. At four performances in the Donovan Theatre in Nairobi in the summer of 1964, the audience was nine-tenths percent white; I counted about two dozen African and one Asian—the lady whom I escorted to the play. Yet it is the Asians who, next to the whites, handle English as their operational language; most business, all romantic and other progressive talk among Asians is conducted in English even when the negotiants speak the same Indian vernacular. This has created another conflict: the Asians see themselves as guardians of an ancient tradition which has a metaphysic and a universally valid world view and which both the whites and the Africans *should* understand in order to appreciate the Asians; in addition, the Asian sophisticates—lawyers, senior government servants, doctors, etc., feel the British let them down in spite of the fact that they, the Asians, absorbed and amalgamated the best of the British-originated contributions to the land, i.e., professional skills and managerial know-how. They further resent the fact that they are being discriminated against on the basis of race—that indigenous Africans with lesser qualifications are being given top executive positions in hospitals, governmental agencies and other organizations of professional relevance—positions which had been their unspoken monopoly for such a long time, and particularly during the rise of African nationalism which again they believe they supported or even helped create. The discrimination which the whites set up and institutionalized, barring both Asians and Africans from the main street hotels, club and service societies, is now felt to be directed against themselves, and pointed out with much resentment. "The Jews in Germany," an Asian high court judge in Nairobi reflected, "were relatively better off than we are going to be, for they looked like other people; we don't, and everyone can point a finger at us."

Some of the more liberal among the Asian educated readily admit the exploitation of native customers in the *dūkā* in the bush and the cities, the discourteous treatment given to them, the open flaunting of disrespect toward the African culture and the African physiognomy. But the majority of the Asians do not see it this way: "we Asians," so several small *dūkā*-owners told me, "do not care much for public relations with our customers; we do not treat them politely, we do not court them, that is not our way, whether they are Asian, African, or white." And this is quite true. An influential Panjabi businessman in Kampala told me "we have not been acting properly toward the Africans, we have been acting selfishly; it couldn't be helped—it is no use calling the African *kālā kālā* (i.e., black, black), for God has given the color and they are just like ourselves; we have built houses and all that, but that does not change the bad relations, and Indians will have to mend their ways, and their attitude toward the Africans." Another middle-aged businessman, owner of a medium-size sisal estate near Arusha, said "we should have taught the Africans efficient agriculture, for business is too difficult and they have not learned the main secret of it, namely plowing the money back into their own business They spend it It is easier with agriculture."

African and Indo-Pakistani leaders have suggested to the settlers during the past fifteen years that they should strive for "full integration" if they want to be accepted. Some said it quite openly, as Mr. Apa Pant, former High Commissioner of

India in Kenya—Asians must make Africans their business partners, and they ought to intermarry with the Africans. African leaders have spoken on the same lines. To the first part of this suggestion for a remedy, the reaction has been negative: Africans, in Asian eyes, are incurable spendthrifts, they do not know how to handle money and goods, and if they lose they don't care and they return to eating *posho* and bananas; make an African a business partner, and your own business is bound to go to pot. To the second part, that of conjugal integration, the reaction has been one of anger, disgust, and dismay: Asians do not even intermarry with each other today, and although the progressives believe and preach inter-caste marriage, that is utopia at best. The few inter-caste marriages and the few marriages between Asian men and white women have been censured by all but the very young, and have caused hurt to most of those concerned. Asians talk about a conversation between the late Mr. Nehru and the late Mr. Mboya, when Mr. Mboya asked Mr. Nehru how he thought the Asians could be accepted as Africans if they did not intermarry with Africans? To this Nehru is supposed to have said this very same thing: "we do not even marry each other, why should we marry non-Indians?" (Mr. Mboya visited this author's university in 1967. The tale is not a legend: the conversation did take place, Mr. Mboya informed me.)

There are about 5,000 people of mixed African-Asian origin in East Africa, most of them along the coast and in Zanzibar. The early Bhatia and other western Indian pioneers came to Africa without their wives and lived with local women; their offspring in the first, second, and third generations are ascriptively African, simply by default: Asians do not accept children of mixed parentage as their own; hence, these people identified with their mothers' kin in all matters. Resentment against the Asians on their side is frequent. Asians deny that there are more than a few hundred Afro-Asians. Professor Aidan Southall, one of the world's authorities on East Africa, thinks my estimate of 5,000 is high, and

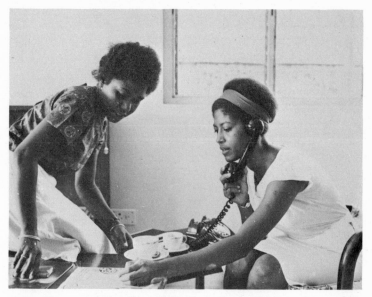

Jotawa or Afro-Asian girls in Dar es Salaam. The African half of their parentage is dominant in their appearance.

told me that he does not believe their number exceeds 2,000. Very few of them are below thirty. The present-day *"joṭāwā"* —a slightly derogatory Gujarati term for Afro-Asians (the word compares, in lexical force, somewhat with the medieval British use of "bastard," or the more recent use of "mongrel") —are for the most part the fourth and fifth generation descendants of those early liaisons.

Once the Asian expatriates began to import their brides from India, new Afro-Asian liaisons ceased to be contracted. Some Gujarati Muslims did actually marry African women— *Swahil* and even upland tribals. There are now only about two hundred Afro-Asians under thirty; their problem seems to be the inverse of that of the older Afro-Asians: they are not readily accepted by the Africans, due perhaps to the fact of their having been brought up in a marginally Asian milieu with Gujarati as their second language, whereas the older mixed groups lived with their African mothers' people, not learning any Indian language, and not in any way identified with their Asian fathers' society. These older *joṭāwā* found it quite easy to be accepted by the Africans. Today, after *uhuru*, the younger ones have, by and large, been identifying with the Africans, and there is no doubt that they will eventually be absorbed completely by the indigenous population. Most, if not all, of the *joṭāwā* between eighteen and thirty-five have married Africans, so that their offspring would have but 25 percent "Asian blood." Genetically, it is interesting to note that the *joṭāwā* usually inherit the African physiognomy, and almost always the kinky hair; in Indian-Euramerican mixtures, the Indian element usually appears to be dominant.

Even today, there are small traders in the bush who live in temporary liaisons with African women. A well known Patel leader in Nairobi told me that when he once toured the bush, his host, a man belonging to the same caste as he, "cleared out the living room" for him, asking two African women "to make other arrangements for this one night." A Bohra trader at Tanga narrated his experience in the countryside, where a distant relative of his evacuated three "lovely African maidens" to make room for his relative from the city for a whole week.

Asians who have had relations with African women display considerable embarrassment when they do report about those affairs, interspersed with such clauses as "it happened long ago, when we were young and immoral"; "but if one has once made love to an African woman," one *dūkā*-keeper, a man of about forty-five mused, "one can never be quite as happy again with another (i.e., Asian) woman. Their (i.e., the African women's) skin is hard and shiny like iron, and she gives too much pleasure" ("too much" being Indian English for "very much").

A non-Sikh Panjabi trader reported that many Sikhs live in the bush like Africans, to exchange cow and other hides for barter; they are as hardy as the Masai, and they live with

Masai women producing children with them—"they live just like the Masai, and Masai women like them. Their children are Masai." Afro-Asian males mix easily with African women; the latter probably do not regard them as Asian at all. But it is quite impossible for the Afro-Asian male to court an Asian woman; the one liaison—a regular marriage according to one source—between a *joṭāwā* male and an Asian girl was much talked about and criticized by Asians at that place. The general Asian feeling seems to be that whatever happened in past decades between Asian males and African women is a thing that should not be discussed; but new liaisons, giving rise to new mixed offspring, should not be encouraged.

A British expatriate businessman, talking about a woman who was partly Asian, and who had been married to an African chief, said "she was extremely beautiful many years ago, and everyone, Asian, African, and white, wanted to make love to her. Many women of mixed blood are exquisitely beautiful." Asian informants often aver that many coastline prostitutes are Afro-Asian mixtures; interestingly, no Asian community envisages the possibility that some of these girls might have been the daughters of men of their community. I was accosted by three girls in Dar-es-Salaam; they looked partly Asian to me, so I addressed them in Gujarati (they had spoken to me in English)—whereupon they looked quite frightened and ran away. When I told a Bohra friend about this occurrence the next day, he said "they must have been part-Ismaili." Just to check the reactions of other communities to this suggestion, I related the episode to an Ismaili man, who got upset and exclaimed that this was quite impossible. If the women were part—or full Asian at all, they must either be Goan, or *joṭāwā*—with some Bhatia ancestry from Zanzibar.

The obverse kind of notion seems in vogue with some men around fifty, who have either had African concubines in earlier days or who have been exposed to Asians, particularly in the bush, who had established quasi-permanent liaisons with African women. Four informants in different parts of

Tanzania told me that tribal African women are tender and delicate, and that they do not like some of the Asians, especially Sikh traders, since the latter are known to be rough and aggressive. All these informants narrated a story which must have somehow diffused from an actual or legendary center: a Sikh trader's penis was so large that he had to place iron rings at the base, lest he would be tempted to enter completely during the sexual act, for the African girl would be grievously hurt; he did approach one, and she had to be taken to a missionary hospital where 18 stitches had to be done to cure her. Then again, a very similar story, possibly a variant of the same narrative, was told by a Sikh trader who claimed that *only* African women could sustain a male with abnormal genital size: when sleeping with his own (Sikh) wife, a friend of his had to use those protective devices lest his wife should come to harm. It is unimportant whether there is any factual truth to this type of tale: what it does prove to the fieldworker is the ambivalence of attitudes toward African women; a love-hate relationship engendered by the peculiar patterns of cultural identity and rejection among the Asian expatriates, discussed throughout this book. The matter is doubly delicate now after *uhuru,* as a sort of *negritude* with feelings of racial pride is evolving and being formulated. Whereas the Asian does not make any bones about not liking the face and color of the Africans, the latter do not usually reciprocate this negative aesthetical attitude. I asked over a hundred Asian men from various places in East Africa, and from all social groups if they thought African women attractive; about one-fourth of them did. Asian women, whom it is almost impossible to ask any such question without a good deal of anthropological subterfuge by indirect interviewing techniques, find the idea of being attracted to an African male reprehensible and repulsive. A highly sophisticated Kikuyu girl studying in the United States put the matter to me quite bluntly: Asians, she said, slept with our women for decades, and thought it perfectly in order to make passes at them. Then why should our men not make passes at Asian women?

When I suggested that Indians were extremely sensitive in these matters through their own tradition, and that this reinforced their negative aesthetic sentiments toward Africans, she said wih a shrug "well, if they don't want to put up with what we had to put up at their hands, they better clear out."

This is at the core of the most traumatic fear syndrome among Asians, young and old: the fear that their women will in the long run be exposed to various degrees of African courtship or sexual attention. It is here that feelings of racial superiority are most bluntly expressed. The Indians in India—and I am using this generalization quite consciously and advisedly—identify physiognomical beauty and attractiveness with the lack of pigment. As in medieval English, "fair" and "handsome" or "good looking" are semantic synonyms in Indian speech. Indians in India and elsewhere, even after having been exposed to different patterns of aesthetic judgment, not only do not recognize the possibility of dark-complexioned attractiveness but they feel embarrassed at occasions when someone suggests or implies it—as when the conversation is steered toward people of mixed African-Indian origin. Praising dark beauty is felt to be almost obscene, and this in diachronic perspective stems from the classical and popular notion in India that dark women are of low caste origin and hence tend to have loose morals and to excel in sexual dalliance. The grudging admission that many Asians in former days did live with African women and begot offspring with them concatenates with that notion: men who did it were lustful creatures whose judgment was of no relevance and should not be emulated by good, that is, nonlustful people. This is the ultimate charge of the Asians against the African autochthonous value orientation: that their morals are loose, that they live with many women and don't feel guilty or ashamed about it.

Africans know about these Indian attitudes; cognitively, they not only do not care, but such attitudes make the Asians all the more unwelcome. On the level where these matters can be discussed, i.e., among scholars and literati, the problems disappear. But this sort of high-level discourse hardly exists as yet in East Africa. The African and the residual Asian leadership are too absorbed in political and economic problems to attend to psychocultural matters.

The actual interaction between Asians and Africans offers. a slightly modified picture to the observer. Apart from the upper middle class "modernized" sundowner situation where Africans, Asians, and whites mix and smile, the two operative types of contact are that between the African customer and the Asian shopkeeper, the Asian householder and his African domestic servants. African servants in the bush are treated very much like the clean śūdra-castes by upper-caste Hindus in the village, and there is no ideological recrimination of any kind.[5] There is an ever-increasing degree of ideological infusion in the city areas, where aloofness on both sides seems to be more studied. Lord Hailey pointed out long ago[6] that the Ismailis had always been more aloof both from Africans and other Asians; this has changed after uhuru and we can assume that the Ismailis and the Ahmeddiyas find it relatively easy today to accept the ideological implications of African nationalism in their houses, as manifested by their African servants. "I cannot call my old servant bwana, as the African leaders suggest we should do;" exclaimed a Panjabi Hindu merchant. "Why not," retorted an Ismaili gentleman of about the same economic and social status, "if they can say bwana to us, we might darn well say it to them too!"

We have a piece of literary corroboration for the highly dysfunctional ambivalence of Asians toward their African hosts. The aforesaid Ambu Patel, one-time associate and admirer of Jomo Kenyatta, edited an anthology of statements in criticism of the latter's detention by the British in the wake of the Mau Mau revolution.[7] Patel no doubt chose correspondents whom he regarded, and who thought of themselves as genuine sympathizers of Kenyatta's cause, well before its consummation in uhuru. Most of the Asian contributors were professional men, and some were political and parochial leaders. In speaking for the release of "Burning Spear" one contributor wrote ". . . for whatever crimes he may have instigated" . . . and "law has a long arm" (p. 8); a barrister-at-law, the late Mr. K. D. Trivedi wrote "from prisons to prime ministership is the order of the day . . . no reason why history should not repeat itself" (p. 159); "misgivings . . . about the part played by Jomo" (i.e., during the Mao Mao situation, p. 178), added another prominent leader. These statements display considerable naivete—the book was compiled when *uhuru* had become a certainty, and when the immediate fate of the Asians after *uhuru* was a big question-mark. In this process, the most vocal Asians did a lot to alienate African leaders, not so much by accentuating and reinforcing the Africans' image of the Asians as ruthless economic exploiters, but by expressing quasi-legalistic sentiments in a patronizing style of speech. Neither was the Asians' notion that their leaders in India had been political or ideological models to the African leadership acceptable to the latter.

Ethnocentrism is hardly the occidental anthropologist's verdict about the ways of untutored westerners alone. The emergent nations not only share it, but it appears that *not* being ethnocentric is felt to be wrong and unpatriotic. Indians today may see beauty and value where they can use indigenous standards; in spite of the elite's admiration of western, particularly British, ways of life, aesthetic judgment about other people derives from Indian models. Some Africans are handsome, Asian settlers would say—because they are tall, light-skinned, "Nilotic," as the Hindu leader said; but "Nilotic," to him meant that their ancestors had originally come from India. An angry aged Gujarati businessman, when asked how his father had come from India to settle in Tanganyika, claimed "we had the shops and sold goods to the Africans when they had nothing; they ran about naked and dyed their faces—whatever valuable things they learnt, they learnt from us." He did not answer my question at all, but burst into invectives against the Africans, because their way of life was not the Indian way of life, *hence* wrong. Indian saints and

167

sectarians also put on a lot of dye, but that was evidently another matter. No doubt the Africans had no shops of the *dūkā* kind, but they certainly had their own well-functioning marketing systems. Such considerations, however, tend to throw some Asians into a rage. "Only people who have a lot of time can write books like this," a Panjabi woman in Nairobi said reproachfully, when I outlined the field-anthropologist's interests to her.

The feelings of the Asians toward the whites are a blend of admiration, resentment, and disdain. In the first place, most Asians think that the whites, in pre- and in post-*uhuru* days, conspired with the Africans to upset and undo the Asians. They are *calāk* (sly, cunningly clever) and must not be trusted; some respondents said the Africans used to be gentle, they used to listen to argument, and they could be trusted before the whites incited them against the Asians.

In all sections of the Asian population, there are people who see things objectively and without panic, though this does not make them any less pessimistic about their future. An extremely knowledgeable and cosmopolitan Sikh lawyer in Mombasa mused "perhaps my little granddaughter, when she grows up, will marry an African; this idea would have been horrible to my parents, and quite unthinkable to me ten years ago. But things change. It is really not the color and the different looks we object to, but the difference in culture; for what do we have in common with the Africans, culturally?" Another professional man said that the daughter of an African statesman had once told him, in a light sociable mood "you Asians do not really fear loss of business or loss of money; what you really fear is being killed, and your women being touched by Africans. That's what you really fear." He then continued saying that it was not so much the actual incidence of pogrom-like action such as had been directed against the Zanzibar Arabs, as the latent menace that kept the Asians on edge and would drive them out of the land, unless these fears were allayed by some sort of official assurance.

168

The few Asian politicians in power identify with the Africans in general and political parlance. Mrs. Mustafa, the Ahmaddiya Asian Member of the Tanzanian Parliament, consistently said "we" in several sustained conversations, where it was quite clear that she included Africans and Asians on the same level of reference. She genuinely resented that there was so little real integration in spite of much Asian talk about it; that Asians were becoming more parochial as the years went by, that they knew little or nothing about the Africans, nor wanted to know anything about them.

Asians recognize a difference between coastal and upland African groups; as I reported earlier, they tend to praise the taller cattle-herding tribes of the interior. Africans hardly know—or want to know—the social and cultural differences between the constituent Asian groups. Neither, of course, do the average whites. This is resented by Asians. "Africans call all Asian women *banyānī* (which correctly refers only to Gujarati women of the merchant class—Bh.)—even to Sikh and other Panjabi women," a Sikh woman complained. "They refer to our *sardārs* (i.e., Sikh men) as *kālāsingha* (i.e., black lion)." The legend goes that during the days of indenture the Africans saw "two kinds of lions" near the tracks: the yellow lions (i.e., the feline beast) and the "black lions," i.e., the bearded, turbaned Sikhs. The true etymology of the term, though, derives from Kāla Singh, the name of an early Sikh contractor who hired fellow Sikhs, then referred to as "Kālasinghas." But the fact is that around the turn of the century, both Sikhs and non-Sikh Asians began to refer to Sikhs by this not unflattering, legend-based title, and in unrefined conversation, this has come to stay. While *singha* "lion" is laudatory for a Sikh, *kālā* "black" is not. Apart from the recent large-scale land purchase by *Jat* Sikhs in the former White Highlands, the Sikh is not perceived as different at all—he is a petty merchant just like the unbearded Gujarati *dūkā*-owner; his martial and agricultural Panjabi background is not known to the Africans.

Except for Peace Corps volunteers and some idealistically

inclined white visitors, there is little positive appreciation of the Asians on the part of older white expatriates, of whatever calling. A highly influential white settler said about the father of an extremely attractive Afro-Asian *"jotāwa"* girl, "he used to beg and come to us for bits of money; he is more Asian than African, he acts just like an Asian—Africans never do these things." He thus assigned undesirable traits in mixed groups to the Asian element. The Asian's image in the minds of the white expatriates is complementary to that entertained by the Africans, though the whites' diction is more elaborate: the Asians are sneaky, mistrustful, they stick to each other and do not mix with others, they are arrogant, they cheat in business, they are cowards, their houses are dirty, they are' obnoxiously thrifty, they lower the living standards of their neighbors because they do not spend any money even though they could afford luxuries and encourage other people's wealth; they are clannish, they monopolize trade within their fold, they are not trustworthy in business nor in social matters. "They live below their standard, they do not let others live up to their own standards, and they think that people who spend what they earn are immoral," a highly perceptive young British sisal-processing engineer remarked.

All human groups entertain stereotypes of their neighbors, but it is from these stereotypes that we can infer much of a group's interaction with other groups. When one Asian businessman said "Africans have to be treated as equals, because they *are* equals," his statement was atypical, yet salutary under the present political exigencies. Most Asians say the opposite: Africans cannot be treated as equals because they are *not* equals—i.e., culturally, by way of economic know-how, etc. A very young Asian woman, who had gone to school in Britain, said without any specific emotion "we hate them, we can't stand them" (i.e., the Africans). But at the same moment she smiled at Pua, her African servant and his pretty young wife "because they are so nice and gentle and very humorous—much more than my brother." Such statements of interactional ambivalence are important; in juxtaposition with

170

an exceptional utterance like the preceding one we learn to distinguish typical from atypical utterances.

Going a step further, we have to attend to unpremeditated utterances of identification and demarcation: when an Asian says "our women" he refers to *all* Asian women if he is talking to a white or an African; he refers to women of his caste and of his linguistic group when he speaks to other Asians; but when he says "your women" to a non-Asian, he implies "your (white) women" or "your (African) women." Asian women are then viewed as of a single kind; so are British, American, Greek, Israeli women and men. I found it quite impossible to elicit common linguistic reference to white and black Americans: even after intensive, teleologically structured conversation, the Asian does not see *how* the Negro could be bracketed with other Americans rather than with Africans.

At a late night party at the delightful Oyster Bay beach at Dar es Salaam, an Ismaili family, whose son had just returned from the United States with an engineering degree, "threw a barbecue," as the young man informed me. By midnight, there was a crowd of at least one hundred people—Africans, Asians, and whites. They danced together with a blissful abundance which only the tropical night will permit; they drank beer and some hard liquor, they laughed and flirted quite eagerly across the race lines. A very lovely Ismaili girl danced with an enormous African student—"isn't he handsome?" she asked her friends with glee. I do believe that such deeds and attitudes might point to future solidarity if occasions of this sort were to occur much more frequently and diffusely; but it is doubtful that they can countervail accumulatively the latent panic that is so much more typical of the Asian's present state of mind.

The Asian self-image

The Asians want to regard East Africa as their permanent home. At the same time they want to be identified with the people whose culture has now become known to the world

171

as rich in such values as non-violence, profound religious speculation, intensive spiritual aspiration, etc.; to the degree that Indian ways of thinking become better known and more fascinating to the West, Indians outside India want their non-Indian neighbours to become aware of this changed state of cultural acknowledgment. This is evident in such statements as that of a Gujarati advocate at Nairobi, who wrote to me,

> . . . wherever in world politics there is talk about peace and spiritual rather than material values, people now think of India as the leader in these things. At the United Nations in Washington [*sic*], whenever someone speaks about uncommitted nations, everyone's eyes turn to the Indian delegation. . . .

In central matters, such as in points of diet, religion, and a quietistic *Weltanschauung,* the East African Indian is hardly distinct from the Indians in the original homeland. His attitude about orthodoxy, doctrine, the importance of traditions, etc., are similar if not identical with the attiude of those in sister-communities in India.

The self-image of Asians in Africa, however, is profoundly affected by their knowledge of the non-Asians views about them. Until about the end of World War II, the East African Indians were both cognizant of and eager to improve their image with the Europeans. This was hard to accomplish. In the first place, with the exception of a few civil servants in the highest echelon who might have served in India and might have become interested in Indian culture, the British did not know, nor care to know about that culture. The British or white Commonwealth settlers in the Kenya highlands did not bother to contemplate either the ancestral or the contemporary glories of India. Asian leaders are painfully aware of the image Europeans entertained with regard to them, and the fact that European opinion about them never changed significantly makes the Asians doubt whether their earlier efforts to accommodate to British tastes were not misplaced altogether. For it is one thing to praise India's democratic institutions, or to laud Gandhi and Nehru, and another thing to revoke what has been said or written in earlier days. In India, the English-reading public has never quite forgotten its grudge against Katherine Mayo's "Mother India," and often when America is to be criticized on an Indian rostrum, that *bête noire* is raised from the dead. Speaking about some early Indian claims for greater influence in the highlands, Professor Hancock wrote in 1937[8]:

> As for the Indian claims, these seemed still to European settlers to be an irritating, but not very alarming, impertinence. The colonists confidently took the offensive against the Indians. Quoting the report of a distinguished sanitation expert, Professor Simpson, they demanded complete residential and commercial segregation of the Indian populations in the towns. They demanded also a barrier against Indian immigration. They asserted in disparaging terms the contract between themselves, the missionaries of civilization, and the Indians, whose influence upon African natives they denounced as degrading and corrupting.

Now the worst affront to the Hindu—of any social status or caste—is the suggestion of physical uncleanliness. In fact, the main rationalization by caste-Hindus of their persisting refusal of commensality with whites in India is the counter-allegation of a similar sort: the whites do not bathe, their clothes don't permit airing, they have "dirty" habits—they eat food touched by others, they don't rinse their mouths after eating, etc. The Hindus' stereotype of the Indian Muslim is quite similar, and a purely traditional nomenclature may be in part responsible for this common front: to the unsophisticated, ethnocentric Hindu both Muslims and whites are *gande,* i.e., "dirty," since, actually or allegedly, they do not take a daily bath and they do not change their clothes daily. Nor do they observe the rules of *"jūthā,"* ritualistic purity of food—i.e., they, the Muslims and the Europeans, pass food from plate to plate and do not reject food that has already been touched, orally, directly or indirectly, by others. Although the Hindus' personal hygiene, prompted by ritualistic traditions, is excellent, and objectively greater than most non-Hindu groups around them, it does not extend to the house outside the kitchen, and less so to roads and the farther sur-

173

roundings. The *dūkā* is as clean or dirty as the *dukān* in India: the poor Kenyan Hindu spits *pān* (betel juice) just as his brother does in the Gujarat, and food for sale is not covered to protect it from flies and other insects. Ritualistic purity begins in the kitchen and ends with the bath, twice daily, and mouth rinsing after each meal. A ritualistically valid bath in Hindu India is not a "bath" in the occidental sense, nor even a hygienically effective bath. Soap and a shower, even where they are available as to most East African Hindus, are not only not ritualistically purifying, but are potentially polluting, as soap is known to have some animal fat in it—Indian brands like *Hamām* make it clear on their package that "pure vegetable oil" has been used in the manufacturing process. The bath to be taken before worship, and, among orthodox brahmins at least, before each meal, and before any ritualistic act, consists of pouring cold water from a *lothā* (a brass vessel) over one's body from the top, and the loincloth or its equivalent must not be removed; nor does the ritualistically valid bath permit contact with the genital and excretory organs—such contact again would cause fresh pollution. This results in a uniquely East African Hindu duplication: being modern, Hindus take modern, hygienic baths, the wealthier women with all the unguents provided by the modern store; but being Hindu, they take ritualistic baths in addition when need arises. Evidently, conceptions of "clean" and "dirty" have the domestic culinary-physical-ritualistic pattern as their only criterial angle for the Hindu. The idea that "dirty"—such as implied in the *Report,* and remembered well by the Hindu leaders in East Africa—may refer to the road around, or the shop and the goods, and may not refer to physical-culinary-ritualistic cleanliness at all, has not occurred to the expatriate Hindu. On the other hand, sanitary behavior other than domestic-culinary-physical-ritualistic does not get credit and is not understood, hence the statement in the *Report,* non-cognizant of the anthropological facts pertinent to Hindu behavior patterns, evoked bitterness in the Hindu audience, and made him reciprocate the charge—equally uninformed—of "dirtiness," directing it at the non-Hindu and the European censor. I maintained that racial feelings among Hindus are tradition-geared and ethnocentric; feelings toward non-Hindus or non-Indians are almost entirely based on the Hindu evaluation of the religious universe of discourse, and on the derivative notion of Indian superiority in religious lore, reinforced during the last two or three decades by the effusive praise given to Indian religious attitudes by the West, including its more bizarre forms as Yoga, theosophy, *Hare Krishna* etc. Projecting a summary of the average literate Asian's attitudes about the non-Asians, some such formulation would emerge: Asians are *obviously* culturally superior to the Africans—since we have an ancient literary-religious-philosophical tradition; we are not *obviously,* but intrinsically superior to the Europeans, because although they have a literary and a technological tradition, they lack *spiritual values,* their culture being *"materialistic-acquisitive-destructive."* The ambivalence in the Asian's ego and alter-evaluation derives from these attitudes. For though India has not invented the things that give "material" pleasures, and does not produce them as efficiently as the West, India has the key to human survival. There is a bucolically ideal, nostalgic value placed on simple, unmechanized living: yet Indians are fascinated by the gadget. The *dūkās,* at least the larger ones, handle auto spares, electric and technologically fairly sophisticated equipment; Indians are excellent mechanics in India and in regions settled by an Indian minority. The Post Office Directory[9] of Kenya shows that over 70 percent of all dealers in mechanical gadgets are Asians.

Replying to my query about cultural and political leadership, and about integration in the emergent African body politic, Mr. R. P. Malaviya, then Attaché at the High-Commission of India in Nairobi, wrote on February 23, 1962:

> The Indian community here has got the same cultural and social organizations as in India, e.g., the Arya Samaj, the Sanatan Dharma Sabha, the Sikh Union, Patel Brotherhood, Lohana Mandal, Surat District Association, etc. They carry on their activities within

these organizations. I have not come across any notable publications with regard to the cultural activities of Indians here, perhaps the need for such a publication has never been felt so far. *Now with the coming of independence to these territories perhaps the greatest problem that will arise will be of the cultural and social integration of the Indians or to put it more precisely the Asian community with the indigenous people* (my italics). As I mentioned before, since the communities are organized into various traditional social and cultural associations they have their own managing bodies besides which there is no special cultural leadership. Normally, the political leaders are also invited to important functions of these cultural organizations to preside over and address. . . .

This last clause is important, and it shows a complete parallel to other non-Indian areas with an Indian minority. There is no longer such a thing as a separate political platform, and it is through the various sectional, parochial institutions that political ideas seep into the community; these do not form an item of particular importance for the general audience, but belong to the routine program of lectures and functions centering on traditional and religious events.

It is hard to say whether the ideas of Indian economical

A famous speaker appears, with garlands and charisma.

and ideological leadership have undergone any radical change in matters of economic relations with the Africans. It seems to me that Lord Hailey's statements written in 1957[10] still apply today, in spite of the fact that he did not then anticipate any such radical and speedy changes in the political structure of the areas involved. I am quoting passages which seem to be valid at this moment much as they were fifteen years ago:

> . . . whatever may have been the relations of the Europeans and Asians of Kenya in the past, it is inevitable that the future outlook of both communities should be affected by a realization of the changes which are now taking place in the position of Africans. . . .
>
> . . . As regards economic matters, however, if there is conflict between Europeans and Asians the issues are of a general nature . . . and do not necessarily raise points of friction between the communities as such. . . .
>
> . . . But though prominent politicians in India have advocated a 'programme of alliance between Indians and Africans,' there is no proof that the Asian community in Kenya has interested itself in any major movement affecting law and order in the territory. It would appear that the Ismaili followers of the Aga Khan have in particular been anxious to stand aloof from any inter-communal movement; they have been warned by their leader that the future of Asians in East African territories lies in Africa, not in India. . . .
>
> It is clear, moreover, that some sections of the Asian community have found reason to realize the effect of African competition in forms of employment which had at one time been held exclusively by their community, and the evidence of the Mau Mau troubles must suggest that some manifestations of African feeling may have consequences which will be fully as damaging to Asians as to Europeans. The leader of the Asian members of the Legislature has expressed himself strongly in favour of the principle of interracial partnership. If this cooperation is achieved in practice, it is to be hoped that its first fruits will be shown in a further relaxation of the measure of social discrimination to which Asians are still subjected in Kenya. . . .

We are faced with a response problem of considerable ideological moment though hardly of much pragmatic im-

177

portance. At Bandung, Indian, other Asian, and African leaders pledged themselves vociferously to the Afro-Asian principle, which turned out to be a situational, geographical bracket rather than any factual link. The ominous fact was that none of its propounders took it seriously except when stating ideology. In a weak moment, a prominent Indian politician confessed to me that, "We and the Africans couldn't care less for each other—our international links are not in Africa, and the Africans' are not in Asia—and China is not Asia." It is only in Africa as an emergent body politic that actual Afro-Asian feelings could be put to test. It is remarkable, however, that none of the Asian leaders in East Africa have capitalized on the Afro-Asian declarations promulgated less than two decades ago. They refuse to be impressed by purely ritualistic declarations. The problems for the community in East Africa are more pressing, and duress is felt by the minority leaders more acutely than by Indian leaders in India.

The only "background" Africans and Asians have in common assumes ideological importance today: they are not Euramericans, and they have not been conquerors and imperialists. This is, of course, not to say that they do not share political motivations—but such common interests as independence, democracy, deparochialization, etc., are not specific to Africa and India.

CHAPTER SIX

Ideas and Perceptions: The Asians' Belief Systems

The analysis of a world view is crucial when a literate society is studied. Not too long ago American and European anthropologists did not pay much attention to such societies, relegating them to such older disciplines as philosophy, history of ideas, and perhaps psychology. Once anthropologists did embark on the study of literate societies their own discipline had not developed its own tools. Professor L. Dumont[1] in Paris, and some anthropologists of the present Chicago school[2] have insisted that there can be no understanding of India, China, Japan, etc., without linguistic and literary knowledge of their languages.

One way of getting at the standard world view of a society was suggested by G.M.C. Carstairs[3] who used autobiographical statements of informants representing the various subsections of the Indian society he studied. My own presentation of the Asian world view is based on numerous interviews with persons of various social and economic levels. Asian reactions toward kinship, religion, political structure, race-relations, radio and television sets were more interesting to me than subjects which the informants themselves would regard as more pertinent—sending their sons abroad, buying a new car, betting on horses in a sweepstake, travel and investment plans for the future. Not that these were of no concern to me—but in order to show where the society has retained its traditionalism, or where conservatism has given way to modern patterns, I suggested topics which would reveal such fundamental attitudes.

Let us begin with the Asian's view of himself. The problem of cultural identification is a vexed one.[4] In village India, matters are relatively simple. Questions of the type "who are you" elicit patterned responses of a highly predictable order; the villager would tell his name, his father's name, he would name the *jāti* (caste) he belonged to, what village he lived in, and on properly conducted, inoffensive enquiry he would easily proceed to expatiate upon the ranking of his own sub-caste, village factions, on the villages from which he gets brides for his sons or which he supplies with brides from among his daughters; he would say which deity his family worshipped, and he would vaguely know that he lived in a large land called India, over which the Moghuls, the British, and now the Indians ruled. Until a decade ago, he would not have said "I am an Indian," but now his children go to school and he listens to the transistor radio placed in the house of the village elder; and he knows that he is also an Indian, or a Pakistani, as the case may be. However, this is as yet a purely academic type of knowledge—the primary identification is with one's kin and caste-group, and with one's ecological unit, the village.

The situation is much more complicated with the Asian settler in East Africa. He wants to be an African—politically, that is, and when the question is one of national affiliation; but that did not always mean that he wanted to be an African citizen, and many of those who took out East African citizenship during the past ten years did so under considerable pressure. Nor does he want to be thought of as an "African" in the cultural sense. He does not regard indigenous African culture as on a par with his own, even where he agrees that there is such a thing as African culture, which the majority of Asians who used the term "culture" in an evaluative sense

180

did not. He does not want to be identified with his caste when his interlocutor is not Asian; yet he would regard his caste status with considerable pride if it were being compared with humbler castes in East Africa and India; the Gujarati Brahmin is extremely proud of being a Brahmin, and he will remonstrate more likely than not if someone suggests he is, say, a Lohana. In other words, the Asian settler does not have a total ego-identification as his kinsman in India and Pakistan; it depends on the circumstances under which his identification has to be verbalized for one reason or another.

When analyzing a specific society's view of itself and the world, we may proceed from particular to more general statements, or we may work in the opposite direction. The first procedure is more fertile in the case of Indian society, due to its strong tendency toward stipulated metaphysical types of identification. Basically, the holy man is the best man, while the good citizen, the good soldier, the successful businessmen rank lower and achieve their status in the evaluative scheme of things only insofar as their ways are closer or more distant to that of the saint, the saint being defined in Indian society as the man who has renounced worldly pleasures and interests. I found that in any survey of Indian ideas, there is a core which seems to inform all other statements—views closer to the core, or more directly related to it in a teleological sense, are more frequent and more prestigious—the mundane specifics of craft, trade, politics, etc., are of less interest and do not always form part of a total evaluative system.

A Marathi businessman in Mwanza, Tanzania—a man who had had considerable influence on the formation of pre-*uhuru* political opinion of his and other Asian communities, said in the course of a conversation on cultural matters "George B. Shaw said that Sanskrit was the most perfect of all languages because every letter is pronounced in exactly one way only." When I tried to point out to him that since Shaw had not been a linguist he should not be taken too seriously in such matters, he said, "I do not criticize, I only say what he said. It is up to you to say evil things about other people." On the surface, this might seem like brisquely non-relevant reaction; but in modern Indian dialog, it carries considerable significance. In the field of communication, the sacred language of India *must* have the first place—it has canonical status, and all other languages are good and rich to the degree that they approximate Sanskrit. G. B. Shaw was a great wise man in the West, and his statement, conceding a first to Sanskrit, was a corroboration for the numinous awe Sanskrit evokes in traditionalist India. My attempt to inject doubt was more to the informant than just a *faux pas*; it was a deep insult, on quite a different level than if Shaw's paradigm had been, say, old Persian, which had the same structural properties as Sanskrit. Hardly any Asians here knew Sanskrit, and what bit the more conservative and religiously inclined did know was the bare minimum of religious reading, and the chanting of some Vedic hymns or of some of the verses of the *Bhagavadgītā*. But "Sanskrit" means a good deal more to the Asian that just the sacred and classical language of India, or even its literature. For the conservative Hindu in East Africa, it is the quintessence of all that is worthwhile, the verbal embodiment, as it were, of charisma, and the ultimate focus of traditional reference. During the life cycle rites, marriage, initiation of high caste boys, and the occasional crisis ritual or a *yajña*,[5] the local Brahmins do indeed chant Vedic hymns. The Panjabi *purohita* (priest, ritualistic specialist) in the East African cities mispronounces all texts most gruesomely; when this is pointed out to him, he more or less agrees but implies that there is no court of appeal or reference anywhere in Africa, that people do not appreciate refinement in ritualistic matters, that he himself learned it in India when he was very young or else from other priests in East Africa who did not know it any better. It is virtually impossible in the territory for Hindu children or adults to study Sanskrit—special arrangements with one or two of the more knowledgeable *paṇḍits* could of course be made, but aren't. Yet, Sanskrit is a theme, a matrix of cultural identification, and Hindus as well as Jains know this—though they would hardly ever formulate it unless they were pressed to do so; but then such pressure would never arise from anyone, person or group, within the local community. M. N. Srinivas, Milton Singer, and other anthropologists have made important formulations of "Sanskritization" in India, and the term is discretely applicable here.[6] Yet, this also seems to be an Indian cultural area where a direct leap from cognitively uninvolved, non-Sanskritic forms of social action to westernization might have been possible. The numerous people and groups which are religiously involved, either because they belong to the more conservative segments of the population, or because they submitted to some form of conversion as will be reported in the chapter on Religion, tend to espouse non-Sanskritized modes of Hindu religiosity rather than the more established scripture-bound forms. The fact that Hīrjī Bābā, a Lohana trader and a genuinely saintly person, today attracts not only Lohanas and Gujaratis, but quite a few Africans, shows that grass root types of Hindu "Little Tradition" behavior can be contagious. The fact is that most of the individuals who are now attracted to or actively engaged in such intensive, committed devotional activities are very much part of the modern, technologically oriented world of their urban African milieu—much more, of course, than in India, where the immediate environment of most religious charismatic leaders and their followers today lacks such direct and diffuse access to wealth and to the consequent technological advancement. It does not seem likely that the younger men and women who are participants in these genuinely Indian grass root type "Little Tradition" pursuits today will approach ideological modernization or westernization via the intermediary stages of Sanskritization, as has been the case in India.

A doctor and his wife, both born in East Africa, both from "very good families" as would be expected, had visited India recently; the doctor, a Panjabi Hindu, had received his M.B.B.S. degree from the University of Bombay. His wife had never been to India; but even before they went, she had been exposed to a considerable amount of religious activity.

183

Her father had been a member of the local Ārya Samāj, her mother was a *sanatani* (conservative) Hindu; in this manner she had been brought up in the Ārya Samāji atmosphere of iconoclasm and Vedic fundamentalism, and her husband in the more conservative, yet more tolerant milieu of old-time Hinduism. When they visited India, they went to Delhi and the Panjab only. This follows an established pattern—Asians, when they visit India, visit only their own ancestral region, i.e., either the Panjab or Gujarat-Cutch, plus the cities of Bombay and Delhi. But the doctor and his wife had heard about a fabulous *pandit* in Hoshiarpur, Panjab, who could not only foretell the future, but could also trace his customer's previous incarnation and the events preceding his visit to him. Of course, the doctor and his wife mused, there are all sorts of astrologers, good and bad, in India, and why, even the local Panjabi priest in the city of Nakuru in Kenya did a fair job with the horoscope, and most of the things he predicted came true. But the Hoshiarpur outfit was of quite a different order. Let me give the doctor's wife's report *verbatim*, in translation:[7] "The *Bhrgu-samhitā* is an ancient text which had long been lost. But this family of *pandits* in Hoshiarpur has a copy of it. They told me that everything about any person's previous existences, his present life, and his future lives are contained in the *Bhrgu-samhitā*, provided his *kundalī*[8] could be found in the book. So we went there, and the *pandit's* son gave us a big packet of *kundalīs*; my husband's was not there, but mine was. Then he pulled out another packet from a seemingly unorganized shelf in some other part of the room, the walls of which were studded with these *kundalīs*. He made his mathematical calculations, and then he told me everything in detail: all he said about my past in this life was true. He did not know who we were, nobody could have told him, we had gone there on the spur of the moment. He couldn't even know that we were foreigners—but he soon found out from his calculations that we did not live in India. Then he told me my past lives, and also that because I was interested in religion now, I would be reborn only twice more

184

and then attain *mokṣa* (liberation)." He gave the doctor's wife two kinds of advice, each of them of a palliative or prophylactic sort: he told her how to prevent threatening sickness by taking some medicines, how to avoid accidents to which she was prone by avoiding situations where such accidents were likely to occur. He charged Rs. 25/— (about four U.S. dollars) and did not accept more from rich people who offered voluntary gifts. He lived there with his three sons, who were all adept in the reading of the *Bhṛgu-saṃhitā*. There were dozens of visitors every day. The demeanor of the Brahmin and his sons was quite matter-of-fact and unassuming.

As this conversation was in progress, another Panjabi woman, a schoolteacher with an excellent knowledge of English, Hindi, and some Sanskrit, stepped in and admitted her own puzzlement at the precision with which the *Bhṛgu-saṃhitā* and that Hoshiarpur *paṇḍit's* *āśram* were operating. That woman was a strict and highly *engagé* follower of the Arya Samaj; this reformed sect has the denial of all miraculous or divinatory phenomena in its statutes. No doubt many close relatives of the schoolteacher were *sanātani* Hindus of the conservative kind, but this did not explain her genuine acceptance of the reports on the *Bhṛgu-saṃhitā* and its workings in the Hoshiarpur *āśram*. Among modern Indians anywhere, there is a gradation of belief in the traditional pattern of supernatural phenomena; some are staunch believers in astrology, spiritual healing, and all sorts of yogic feats which were reported to them by reliable people. But even among those who would like to be viewed as skeptics, there is hardly ever a complete denial of miraculous and supernatural events and the possibility of their ingress into human affairs. It is impossible to predict, in each case, whether a person will hold such beliefs literally or in a toned down form—doctors, engineers, and other professionals as well as the more humble share these beliefs; on the other hand, we have found artisans, farmers, and in East Africa, *fundis,* both Gujarati and Panjabi, who laughed away all such stories as the prattle of women, children, or naive contemporaries. There is no correlation at all between the cognitive state of modernization and the acceptance of large chunks of the supernaturalistic belief-system for any Asian individual. The first president of India, the late Dr. Rajendra Prasad, a saintly person, a polyglott, and a fine legal scholar, was a staunch believer in astrology and reportedly had quite a few professional *jyotiṣī* (Brahmin astrologers) in his retinue; this is known to those Asians in East Africa who feel they have to defend their own trust in these traditional, allegedly non-rational things. It is, however, precisely that alleged non-rationality which the modern Hindu tends to reject. The more verbal the subject, the more structured his efforts to show that astrology, supernatural healing, and all the related syndromes have a scientific basis. He will adduce instances from the Hindu Epics, he will quote what he thinks has been said by Einstein or Darwin. Persons who have a stake in denying any conservatism in their intellectual makeup men, who have studied in Britain or America, and those among the younger generation who have cast their lot with anti-traditional, politicized modernism, were often found to make statements of this form: "I do not believe in astrology and all that; it is superstition. But when my grandfather lived, he met an astrologer who foretold World War II, and *uhuru* in East Africa. . . ."

This response pattern cannot be understood through a merely synchronic approach. The reason for the modern Asian's claim that astrology, divination, and many aspects of the supernatural, which western man has discarded by and large or which he tends to relegate to the primitive or to superstitions and old times, are indeed "scientific," and that by extension, Hinduism (or Islam, or Sikhism, or Jainism) is scientific, is to be sought in a series of historical accidents. It was Swami Vivekananda, B. G. Tilak and the numerous emulators or followers of such leaders who spoke and wrote in this vein, with the force of their charismatic appeal supporting their utterances. That Hinduism is scientific was an *obiter dictum* in Vivekananda's works, and even his American audiences took these statements more or less literally. Tilak, a much more erudite and less naive man than Vivekananda, injected a whole corpus of Sanskrit scriptural lore, partly genuine, partly spurious, to support his claim that the West has had nothing which had not also been created in India thousands of years ago. Socio-cultural studies have shown that the anonymity of a particular teaching frequently strengthens its efficacy. Very few Asians *know* that Tilak and Vivekananda had taken great pains to show that Hinduism was scientific, that the ancient Aryans had not only been "spiritual giants," but also inventors and discoverers. Both Tilak and Vivekananda were eager to prove that India was the original home of the Indo-Aryans, a notion which was rejected by critical scholarship even in their days. But Asians think not only that the home of the Indo-Aryans was in India, but that most of the world's culture somehow began in India in early times. The ahistorical tendency of the Indian tradition has not been modified in Africa—ancient Indian things are said to be 10,000 years old, the Vedas are thought to be as old as 20,000 years. Occasional confrontation with modern indological scholarship which places nothing in Hindu culture beyond 1200 B.C. does not faze them. Somehow, the feeling is that what is good, in all but technological matters, must be very old; and by secondary implication, even technological things must have had their primary models in that very ancient India. Few Asians read Vivekananda in East Africa—there being no Bengali and South Indian sector, the Ramkrishna-Vivekananda Mission did not get a foothold in the area—and hardly any but the few Maharashtrian settlers have read anything by Tilak. But it is the very anonymity of these factually unfounded notions which accounts for their persistence.

Since World War II, *pandits* and other culturally committed people in India have claimed that the atom bomb was invented in India; and that various *astras* (weapons) like the *Brahmāstra* (Brahmā's weapon), *Indrāstra*, *Varuṇāstra*, etc., described in the *Mahābhārata* and the *Rāmāyaṇa* were nothing else but the atom bomb; denial of such ideas immediately labels the doubter as a non-patriot, or as a westernized outsider who does not know true spirituality. This entire pattern has diffused unchanged to East Africa; the very same arguments are proffered when conversation gets there, and on any religious or other forensic occasion these arguments are placed before serenely nodding audiences. The genesis of these notions is interesting, but not really astonishing: since about 1940, the various communities have been inviting Indian speakers for religious lectures; the priests who were hired as ritualistic specialists on temporary contracts and a certain amount of vernacular pietistic literature which is sent to East Africa, account for them. Since there is no intellectual force to countervail jingoistic legend, complete acceptance of the ancient "scientific" pattern seems quite natural.

During a lecture at Tanga, Tanzania, I answered a discussant who had brought up the atom bomb's discovery and use in ancient India, saying that Hindus and modern men should be proud that India did *not* have any of these terrifying gadgets; that India's cultural pride should rest in the traditional emphases on non-violence, etc. My discussant did not reply to this, and I had the feeling that he and most of the audience did not quite catch the first part of the argument. But a middle-aged man got up quite excitedly, and said "that is something quite different; that is a new consideration, and an important one . . . yes indeed, why should we have had any of the wicked things the West is now producing to everybody's destruction?" But there was hardly any reaction, one way or the other, to this afterthought which was atypical. There is a subtler parallel in the field of a possible world view modification. The Ārya Samāj, and other modern Indian reform movements, have denied the phallic complex in Hindu mythology and doctrine. Śiva, the Great God of the ascetics, is ritualistically represented and worshipped only in the form of the *liṅga,* resting in the *pīṭha,* the female counterpart as indicating the cosmic union of male and female in mythological apotheosis. But this the Ārya Samāj and other modern puritanical groups suppress or deny; they claim that the *liṅga* is not a phallus at all, but a *yūpa,* a sacrificial post such as is mentioned in the Veda. The learned Indian argument in the orthodox tradition was that the phallic form of Siva was not priapic, but that it symbolized complete sexual control, and the renunciation of all desires—the state of erection being the closest to total desirelessness immediately preceding or following ejaculatory consummation, the ithyphallic *liṅga* truly represents the Lord of monks and ascetics. I brought this up several times in various Hindu assemblies throughout East Africa. The response was either negative or neutral, assuming that the traditional argument was being understood. The brahmins who function as ritualists in East Africa presumably know the traditional argument, but they do not divulge it to their clientele. On three occasions some elderly man gave assent to the statement, and a Gujarati businessman at Tanga said "all these are true things, but they are only meant for high *adhikāris*" (i.e., people who have achieved maturity in matters of active religious involvement, not necessarily monks, but laymen who have turned to meditation and other "Great Tradition" practices). "One has to renounce first in order to achieve," he continued. The abject fear of anything sexual intruding on the religious was due, to a very large degree, to the puritanizing effect of mid-nineteenth century missionary education in the Indian cities. Vivekananda was no doubt one of the primary culprits, but so was Raja Rammohun Roy a century before him: the missionaries gasped in horror at the lascivity and irreligiosity of erotic sculpture and of some of the religious literature of Hinduism. Conceivably, their Hindu students could have laughed them off; they could have told them something to this effect: just because you are squarely unimaginative, naive, repressed little puritans who cannot appreciate real beauty, manifestations of divinity as we see them, why should *we* reject this part of our tradition?" But nothing of the sort happened; as I have shown elsewhere,[9] the early Hindu Renaissance teachers took the bait; instead of emphasizing what was different between the glorious sensuousness of Hinduism and the impoverished, sanctimonious protestantism of the missionaries at the Scottish Mission School in Calcutta, they felt shame and guilt; and in less than five decades, modern urban Hinduism had erased all that had shocked the missionaries upon their encounter with the heathen. Ever since, Hindu teachers have been at pains to show that Hinduism isn't really different in essence from Christianity—that it is monotheistic, puritanical, good for society, etc. It was this Hinduism that was transplanted into East Africa; apart from some genuinely involved groups among the Gujaratis and the less alienated religious activities of the "Great Tradition" inspired sects, the average Asian who wants to be modern *and* a Hindu espouses the washed-out, unsexed, eclectic forms of Hinduism which congealed in India during the latter half of the nineteenth century, and which are now the official religion of Hindu India—the kind of creed Indian politicians, journalists, teachers, and all those to whom E. Shils refers as the Indian intellectuals[10] profess. The modal views about morality, society, human interaction, and the relation between religion and morality among East African Asians are replicas of the teachings of the Indian Renaissance, which blunted the keen edge of the scholarly, sophisticated, highly individualistic forms of Indian thought which preceded the Renaissance and which are still prevalent among the non-alienated Hindu teachers who do not use English as a medium, but continue their dialog in Sanskrit. Of such teachers, there are none in East Africa. Moreover, any verbalized adherence to the disciplined, ideologically complex forms of the Indian tradition would be branded as reactionary, outmoded, and an impediment to the progress of the Asians and to their "Africanization," an obstacle in the way of modernization and technification.

The naive eclecticism which characterized the Renaissance in India has some interesting ideological corollaries in East Africa. We have already discussed the conviction that Indian culture is primordial, that all the world's great cultures, and the world's great languages, are derived from ancient Indian models. This attitude is tied up with hero worship both in India and East Africa: I used two test-figures in order to elicit the predicted responses—the Bengali-born, all-India hero

Subhas Chandra Bose, called *Netājī*, literally "Herr Führer," by one and all in India *and* Pakistan. He created the Indian National Army under both Nazi and Japanese command.[11] He died of burns suffered in an aircrash over Taiwan toward the end of World War II. This, however, is not believed by Indians, nor by Pakistanis, nor by our subjects. There is the deep-rooted belief that Netājī is hiding out and alive, as a holy man biding his time in the Himalayas, or in China, or Russia. Bose was in no way a statesman of Nehru's calibre, nor a political ideologue of Gandhi's acumen; his political views were an opportunistic blend of leftist and rightist radicalism; he had visited Russia in the thirties, and he had lived in Europe for a couple of years. When he returned to India, he said to a select group[12] "I have seen communism in Russia,

Jingoism begins in childhood. This calendar shows another calendar containing a picture of Netājī Bose, the militaristic hero of modern India.

191

I have seen National Socialism in Germany. We shall have National Communism. . . ." *Sufficit exemplum.* But Netājī was a charismatic leader if ever there was one, and there was hardly anyone, friend or foe, who was not captivated by his charm, inveterate skeptics like the present author not excluded. Netājī knew how to use charisma—even during his lifetime, his image shone from mililons of polychromes, in a fancy-blue quasi-Japanese uniform, emerging from the clouds, I have seen his image topped by God Ganesa's elephant head in several shrines in Maharashtra. It is easy, in fact quite un-avoidable, to get a rise out of Indians anywhere the moment Bose is mentioned. When Patel businessmen in Nairobi had a convention, homage was paid to several Indian leaders, and at a party after the meeting some of the men were musing about Gandhi, Nehru—this happened just a few weeks before Nehru's death—about Johnson, Khrushchev, and other poli-ticians. Then I injected Netājī Bose's name—there was a short silence, and then all of the many guests heaved a great sigh of nostalgic adulation: "Yes, Netājī was the greatest of all. A true hero, an *avatāra,* the greatest statesman. Had he lived, India would not have been divided. India would be a rich country now, and neither the Chinese nor anyone would dare threaten it. And were he alive, we Indians in East Africa would have nothing to fear." What exactly Netājī could or would have done for the expatriate population outside India, was not clear to me or to the speaker; but this is part of the "numinous," to use Otto's term, which attaches to the charis-matic hero once his power is established and consolidated. In India and among Asians in East Africa, it is as yet quite im-possible to say anything radically critical about Subhas Bose—in fact, there are more critics of Gandhi, and certainly very many more of Nehru and other leaders, including Ayub Khan, president of Pakistan in 1964; but to say anything nega-tive or disparaging about Netājī Bose is tantamount to criti-cizing Krsna or Rama or any of the divine heroes of the Indian tradition. On three occasions, Asians asked me whether it was true that Netājī had a daughter in Vienna. When I confirmed this,[13] there was a display of sharply conflicting emotions and of general uneasiness: Netājī's power rested in part in his having been a *brahmacāri*, a chaste man, a saint. The fact that he had begotten a child, and known woman in the biblical sense, was just too much for his devotees, which meant the whole subcontinent. I happen to know Anita, the beautiful, knowledgeable, and charming daughter of Netājī Bose; in India, people gradually got used to her existence, and when she finally visited her father's land as a ravishing teenager of about seventeen, India welcomed her like a latter day divinity. However, she decided on a more earthbound career, and married a brilliant Viennese economist who now teaches at Michigan State University. In East Africa, Asians do not seem to have overcome the trauma of the Netājī complex: not only does he appear to the Asians' mind as the *summum bonum* in Indian statesmanship and as the greatest leader of the age, well beyond Gandhi and Nehru in merit—in addition, the news of his having fathered a daughter before he disappeared was received with disbelief and anguish, and the Asians never quite reconciled themselves to the idea. Most of the people I talked to rejected the news, and when I related my own acquaintance with Bose and later, with his lovely daughter, there was embarrassed silence and a change of topic. A majority of Asians at this very moment still believe that Netājī is alive and hiding out; that the official reports about his death were insidious confabulations; and that he will emerge victoriously one day, when the time is ripe—just what sort of situation would make it ripe is not a thing that is pondered. The idea that Netājī is still alive is shared by the majority of people in India up to this very day.

A somewhat alarming, but by no means astounding parallel to the adulation of Netājī, no doubt an important figure in the Indian struggle for independence whatever the objective qualifications of the man might have been, is to be found—both in India and among the Asian minority in Africa —in a more or less open admiration for Adolf Hitler. Not infrequently, these two persons are thought of and mentioned together when there is a meeting of the radical rightist groups and organizations, like the B.S.S. in East Africa. Hitler's phony use of the swastika and the Aryan myth did a lot to attract Hindus as well as non-Hindus. Not so much the fact that he fought the British with initial success—though that too was no doubt a factor—as his strong mythological appeal, the *avatāra*-like interpretability of his career as filtered down to the Indians, during World War II, plus the ubiquitous notion that he was a *brahmacāri,* a chaste person, that he did not eat meat, and other *bona fide* and *mala fide* tidbits of information that seeped through the grapevine—created a strong feeling of attraction for Hitler, not among ogres or Rockwellian psychopaths, but among perfectly gentle people, many of whom are vegetarians, believers in non-violence and a genuinely religious way of life. Statements and reports about Auschwitz and Belsen are rejected as British-American propaganda fabrications; and hints at Hitler's and his associates' sadomasochistic tendencies are heard with anguish and disbelief. In a large Ārya Samāji meeting at Nairobi, I explained the genesis of the Nazi use of the swastika and of the Nazi rulers genocidally discriminatory use of "Aryan"; the reaction was one of angry dismay. I have discussed the Indian attitude toward Hitler and Nazi Germany in another publication;[14] but the amazing thing is the completeness with which this specific configuration has passed on to the Asians abroad. It is conceivable, even probable, that some additional mythology about Hitler and the Third Reich spilled over from India through the sermons of Hindu holy men visiting East Africa over the past decades. But I do not think that the pattern is predominantly due to such processes of diffusion. I am inclined to believe that the minority's world view is so completely analogous to that of their South Asian kin, that any ideological *gestalt* introjected by its members would be cathected in an identical fashion in East Africa. It is not because Indian visitors talked particularly about Hitler to their East African Asian hosts; but because the Asians read about Hitler through mass media—not from India, but through general reportage, they would select him as an *avatāra*-like culture-hero in exactly the same manner in which he had achieved that image in India. When I read out some anti-Indian, pro-colonialist pro-British passages from *Mein Kampf* to that same audience, their leader finally admitted with a sigh that "the swastika had been misused for politics which is always dirty."

Modernity is not anything homogeneous; it would be a grave error to apply diffuse criteria under the assumption that they apply everywhere, wherever people call themselves "modern," or are called "modern" by others. With Indians, "modernity" means a congeries of several things: interest and participation in technological advance, the utilization of gadgetry, the verbal disavowal of religious interests insofar as they are ritualistic or conservative, contrived nonchalance about sexual matters, the denial of the importance of caste, and cultural nationalism. However, we find that there are numerous exceptions to these modal criteria. I recorded well over two dozen statements which displayed strong disparity between the concept of modernity held by a person, and his or her own ambivalent attitude toward highly traditional things. A young Lohana woman, one of three sisters, remarked about her eldest sister who was a mother of four children: "She looks modern, she thinks she is modern, and she tries to act modern. . . . But in reality she is very *orthodox*." Here we could see that the pair of cognitive opposites was not "modern"-"conservative," but "modern"-"orthodox." Orthodoxy did not necessarily imply any involvement in ritualistic acts; in fact, a large proportion of the wealthier Lohana women do not participate in any ritual except the occasional hearing of religious lectures, and sharing the life-cycle rituals and calendrical festivals, more with a view to putting in an appearance than with ritualistic intent. Orthodoxy does mean, however, that the person discourages emancipated personal behavior within his or her dependent kin-group. In other words, if mothers or fathers do not permit their daughters to participate in ballroom dancing, or to talk to young men or, as the case may be, if they overtly or covertly resist the children's going to college abroad, then Asians will tend to call them "orthodox" rather than "conservative" or "traditional," not because they do not know these terms, but because there is a subconscious reduction of *all* emancipated behavior to fundamentally anti-ritualistic behavior. Conversely, ingroup oriented behavior, effective adherence to conservative rules of social intercourse, is seen as a perpetuation of religious behavior, hence the term "orthodox" or its vernacular equivalents are used rather than "conservative, traditional" and their vernacular equivalents. The daughter of a modern Panjabi family, who held an executive position in an academic institution, offered to drive me home; but her mother insisted that she would come along. This was not entirely due to her chaperoning instinct—she could have sent a servant along; but—and this is what the daughter told me on another occasion, "she did not want to embarrass you; you might have felt uncomfortable driving alone with a young woman, as you are a *sādhu*." Again, this was read as "orthodox" rather than as traditional prophylaxis—the Hindu tradition holds that a *sādhu* must keep away from all female company. Regardless of the fact that the mother, herself a modern woman, knew that I had been teaching at universities all over the world for years, and that I did meet men and women, alone and in groups, on many occasions, the ritualistic rule was extended because a religious identification was uppermost in her mind. In this sense, of course, the Asians' use of "orthodox" rather than "traditional" or "conservative" is objectively justified.

When there is a party for male guests from outside, who do not belong to the host's kin, women usually do not stay in the living room; they serve, or supervise the serving of food and drink, but they do not otherwise participate. This is quite different from the western party pattern in which the ladies collect in one corner to discuss babies, and the men in another to tell each other male things. When Asian male hosts were asked why the ladies did not participate and enliven the party, the answer often was "the ladies are embarrassed because they are not educated. They would not know what to say." This is an institutionalized untruth, for in fact, among the wealthier in East Africa, the women are equally well or better "educated" than the men, in literary matters and in common sense about the world. The real reason is that unrelated men and women should not meet at all, just as men and women, regardless of their degree of emancipation, sit apart in temples, *gurdvāras,* and even at a domestic *sat-sang.*[15] Women just don't sit around at any time; women guests are not expected to stay in the living room for more than a minimum amount of time; they then join the ladies of the house and don't show up until it is time to leave. In addition, Asian males tend to experience strong anxiety in the unstructured presence of women. This the latter may or may not know. "Men are more educated, they know to talk about the things of the world, politics and business. We are not interested in these matters. We are not interested in business," was a middle-aged Muslim lady's reply to my query as to whether she really thought that men were more educated or that the ladies were not educated enough to participate in the party. However, "educated" in the middle class Asian idiom is a catchall for the capacity to talk about anything, over drinks—business, impressionistic politics, factional intrigue—this is "educated" talk, in which women would not like to participate. But the reader who is not an Indianist should not be overly impressed by this somewhat facile use of "educated." Books and world views are not discussed, but the plots of Indian movies are; politics and politicians are commented upon—their corruption, their antagonisms, their affairs; religion is discussed in a broad, generalizing, moralistic fashion; Hindu and Muslim philosophy are not at issue, nor known save to specialists who don't usually go to the typical Asian house party—but Hindu and Muslim leaders are discussed, together with their financial and other affairs, so are the reactions of the local Asians toward these.

At Nairobi, I was pleasantly surprised to chance upon an old colleague of mine; a Brahmin lady who had a degree from the London School of Economics, who had taught with me at Benares Hindu University, and who was now married to a physician, an Asian born in Kenya. She told me a lot about the many changes that had occurred in her life after migrating from India to join her husband. She was not happy about the situation in her in-laws' house. Quite obviously her mother-in-law was jealous of her son's wife's scholastic achievements, her past career in India, and about her "taking too much of her husband's time." The marriage had been arranged through her sister who was married to a wealthy banking executive in another part of East Africa; the doctor, her present husband, had come to "look at her" when she was teaching in India, and the negotiations did not take too long; possibly, the economist felt that she might have to spend all her days as a spinster, and this is something extremely rare and unpleasant even among career women in India. One morning when I visited the Hindu temple, Mrs. M. just emerged from it, and offered me some sweets as *prasād*[16] from the God Hanumān, king of devotees, and simian companion of Rāma, the hero of the Great Epic. Hanumān had appeared to her in a dream the night before; he had not given her any special instructions, but she thought she had better do something about it of her own accord; so she went to propitiate the kindly God, offering some fruit and sweets at his shrine. She then reported that a day earlier she had taken some children related to her husband to the local zoo, "where they enjoyed the monkeys so much"; when I suggested that she might have seen an ape in her dream due to the previous day's impressions, she rejected this with some ennui—how could I doubt the genuineness of this important message? The local *pandit* had also told her, when looking over her horoscope soon after she had come and got settled and married, never to pass by an indication from God. Mrs. M. had done her share of modern critical reading, she was reasonably conversant with Freudian dream theory, and when in Britain for three years, she must have met people who talked about psychology. But this awareness did not seem to countervail

her pre-sophisticated attitude. I think it would be unfair to
class this sort of anachronistic behavior as a sort of double-
think; the Indianist studying modern societies in South Asia
must inject a different tolerance margin into the analysis of
cultural behavior: what seems logically or psychologically incompatible in Western societies may be the rule in India, and
by direct extension, among the Indian expatriates in areas
other than the New World. Mrs. M. did not see any contradiction between a highly sophisticated academic training with
its impact on modernistic discourse, and taking seriously
phenomena of an order which does not mesh with the former.
The old, hackneyed and uninformed travellers' tale about
India being a land of contradictions is no consolation to the
serious researcher, but then if he insists on applying logical
categories to compatible behavior types he will be tempted
to accept some such statement in a refined form. However, the
claim put forward by believers in traditional and ritualistic
patterns that "there is no contradiction" between these different attitudes has to be taken on its face value. There is no
contradiction if you do not wish to see one; and life, after
all, is not basically a matter of logic. The interesting thing
about the case of Mrs. M.—which is not unique—was the criticism her behavior elicited from many Asians who knew her,
including some of her affinal relatives: they happened to
belong to the Ārya Samāj, and as we already know, this iconoclastic sect rejects the worship of the classical Hindu gods.
The unprepared occidentals, as well as the modern Indian
intellectuals who do not heed the religious symbols of their
forbears and of their differently oriented contemporaries,
tend to feel dismay at this dialog: for obviously, they aver,
it does not make much difference whether a person who has
had modern training worships any specific Hindu god and
takes the astrologer's advice, or whether he performs *sandhyā*,
and the fire-cum-*ghee* ritual of Vedic provenance, prescribed
by the Ārya Samāj reformers as incumbent on its active followers, twice a day.

In East Africa, the world view suggested by the Ārya Samāj, not so much by its founder Swami Dayānanda Sarasvatī, but by the consensus of written and unwritten opinion among his later followers, is being more or less identified, among Hindus, with a modern if not secular, view of things. The fact that it is really anything but secular, and that it implies a theocratic way of life, a highly normative piety, and a degree of puritanism in no way different from that of other, more conservative Hindu groups, is not understood. The complete absence of an indigenous secular tradition in South Asia makes it impossible for all but the most highly perceptive to see that the world view of any of the Indian sects, Hindu and Muslim alike, is non-secular, and that the distinction between traditional groups and the more recent reform movements like the Ārya Samāj among Panjabis, or the Swami Nārāyan sect among Gujaratis, is at the most one of degree, not of kind. A genuinely secular view, particularly one with a hedonistic tinge, is seen as foreign and outlandish, and gleaned only by those who have cut themselves loose from the world view of their kin. Talking to the wife of a Panjabi businessman at Tabora, Tanzania, I said something to this effect, assuming she was *sanātani* like her husband; but she proved to have been born in an Arya Samaji family. When I said that the Ārya Samaji notions about interpersonal relationships, particularly that between spouses, in-laws, etc., were quite rigid and that they did not really give any more freedom to either husband or wife than those of the *sanātani* and other orthodox groups, she became quite irritated and said "the Ārya Samāj has many new ideas. But of course it does not allow husbands and wives to speak to each other as if they were lovers (*sic*) . . . this is bad, and the Ārya Samāj does not teach modern things if they are bad. . . ."

There is no such notion as that of a secular morality; Asians of diverse religious background implicitly hold that morality and religion are no separate matters. This, of course, bespeaks the immense alienation from the grass root Hinduism both of the learned and the simple: for the assignation of morality to religious pursuits is a new development in South

200

Asia, due largely to missionary influence since the eighteenth century. In the western world, most people identify religion and morality; but the difference is that intellectuals in occidental countries have known the very crucial difference between the two for several centuries. Asian intellectuals in East Africa—with the exception of the few professional academicians mentioned *passim* in this book—do not envisage the possibility that the two could be distinct *on principle*. The modern Asian argues that if anything in his ancestral religion is worthwhile and negotiable in modern days, then it must belong to the moral realm, for ritual is old-fashioned and redundant. The followers of the Ārya Samāj more than the *sanātani* would identify the moral with the religious, assigning their basic minimal ritual some sort of moralistic status. The half dozen religious specialists in East Africa, the professional *purohit* or sacerdotally employed brahmins, do know and preach that the ultimate aim of Hindu religious life is *mokṣa,* liberation from the cycle of birth and death, *not* the moral life. However, they also know that this knowledge cannot be communicated to their clients in an institutionalized manner, since their social and economic constitution must have moral, pragmatic standards to go by. The classical notion of release from rebirth as the quintessence of Hindu or Jaina religious life may be known to them, but it is in no way operational: therefore, the priestly professional cannot really talk about it except in a marginal fashion, lest he undermine his own function in the expatriate society. In India today, more and more specialists—*sādhus* and monks of all sorts rather than the brahmin ritual experts—speak about, and teach *moksa* to a much more alert, and ideologically more sophisticated audience— witness the hundreds of *āśram*-like institutions all over the subcontinent, with heavy financial support from Indian audiences and from abroad. Thus, when our Panjabi informant got upset about the suggestion that the Ārya Samāj was basically quite as conservative as the admittedly more tradition-bound groups, one of the implications in her mind was that the Ārya Samāj was superior *because* it stresses moral above

201

ritualistic values—her correct correlative assumption being that ritual figured supremely within the *sanatani* groups at the cost of moral emphasis. What she did not, and could not know, was that both the Arya Samaj *and* the *sanatani* groups, at least in East Africa misjudge the complexity and sophistication of Hindu religious traditions, both the learned and the rustic, which distinguish neatly, though not always overtly, between the ritualistic and esoteric redemptor on the one hand, and the moralistic leader on the other. This philosophical naivete was shared by some of the most famous and the presumably most highly westernized; when the late Pandit Nehru delivered the valedictory speech at the opening of the 2,500th anniversary of Buddhism, he said in effect that "Buddhism is good because it is good for Peace." This theme is at the base of the contemporary Asian world view inasmuch as it juxtaposes religious and secular themes. The notion, compellingly obvious to any thinking man in the modern world, that morality must be something totally distinct from religion, and that the value of religion must therefore be of a different order, is simply non-existent among modern Asians, however westernized and emancipated.

There are examples galore. At a religious meeting commemorating the foundation of a temple in Nairobi, there was a "discussion of world religions" slated at the end of the week-long functions. A learned Muslim *mullah* (divine), a young man, Panjabi by origin, who had studied theology in the best traditional school in the Near East, and who mastered Urdu, Persian, Arabic and English with equal eloquence, gave a fiery speech to an assembly that was almost entirely Hindu. He exhorted them to believe in God and worship him with all their might, and he was careful to choose his words with enough generality so as not to offend a Hindu audience in a Hindu shrine; his excellent rhetoric in chaste Urdu drew spontaneous applause, particularly from the Panjabi men in the assembly who love Urdu and highly Persianized diction. In his summary, he said "let us not be deluded, friends, by the wicked life of our days, let us not join those who sin constantly, who steal their neighbors' wealth or cheat them out of it, who take bribes, who gamble, who drink, who commit adultery, who dance in public without shame. . . ." He was referring to social dancing among westernized Asians, pursued and enjoyed by Ismaili and Hindu boys and girls with great abandon, and most delightfully executed. The fact that this preacher listed "dancing" on one moral or immoral level with taking bribes and stealing was quite typical: and no one in the audience as much as winced—not even the young—all of them nodded approval. It was my turn after that preacher's, and I pointed out that dancing and stealing could not be listed as on one level; when I began to elaborate this point, the young Muslim preacher left in a huff, followed by his associates; and there was visible exasperation in the audience— though Hindu, they did feel at one with the Muslim in assigning morally positive and negative values to acts which even a most rudimentarily secular world view must regard as morally neutral; and although I addressed this assembly as a Hindu preacher, in the full regalia of the *sannyāsi* monk, my deliberations were patently unacceptable. After the meeting, I discussed the matter with a bunch of young people, most of whom had studied abroad. They admitted they had felt quite guilty and uncomfortable during the Muslim preacher's lambasts; and they also admitted that they thought he was right—that they really should not indulge in social dance, because this led to "bad things"—"bad things" being such activities as necking or petting, or quite generally, romantic involvement. None of them seemed to understand how these things could possibly be viewed as ethically neutral; and because they were alienated modern youths, they did not know that love and a goodly amount of lust had been perfectly compatible with keen religious participation in the old days in India.

And yet, there is a strange, almost systematic ambivalence in the modal Asian attitudes toward the religious, and toward religious charismatic heroes in particular. It is not, as a superficial observer might assume, a matter of *quod licet Iovi non licet bovi*; nor that the charismatic leader may do things and enjoy life in a manner that would be regarded wicked or at least improper for ordinary men. The actions of the religious leader are not worldly even if they appear to be just that; and those who cannot see the truth are outsiders. When the late Aga Khan visited an East African city, after his weight had been matched in gold, and then again in diamonds (which, meant very much gold and very many diamonds, His Highness having been a 250-pounder in the best years), the Ismaili community invited two white girls to sit by the side of His Highness for dinner—wenches, not ladies of any name—and he was offered the best French champagne to drink. It was a private party, or rather, a party for the top echelon of the Ismaili hierarchy. Somehow the word got into the press the next morning—a non-Asian reporter, who saw nothing objectionable in it, or else an overzealous Asian reporter apparently covered the proceedings. There was a hue and cry—how could anyone dare to write that His Highness had been consuming alcoholic beverage, and worse, that his community should have offered it to him? A refutation was published a day later, which explained that the community had indeed offered His Highness a bottle of champagne to show that only the best of things would do, and as a token of their esteem—but that the champagne turned into water the moment it touched His Highness's lips; an unsolicited inversion of the happenings at the wedding at Kanaa, to a student of comparative mythology, but a necessary improvisation for the benefit of the more fundamentalistic Ismailis. An angry Hindu intellectual, a surgeon of considerable fame, exclaimed with irritation in his voice "when the old man came to M., they put two white tarts, not even good looking ones, one on each side of him; when I asked their local leader what had made him think that His Highness would appreciate the gesture, when he could surround himself with the most beautiful women on earth, white and brown and black and yellow, wherever he went, that fellow said, 'Oh, that is different; he was so spiritual. He would not notice these things. Everything is pure to the pure." Almost all Asians feel that *joie de vivre* and religion are incompatible; they would therefore not face the possibility of such reports being true in the first place. But on a deeper level of psychocultural analysis, there is really no contradiction in the reactions of the modern who assess actions and attitudes as either religious or profane in complete emulation of their erstwhile Christian mentors, and the reactions of their relatives who claimed that the two white girls were intended to be unnoticed decorations and items of hospitality-display, and that Heidsieg-Monopol turned into water as it touched the Aga Khan's lips. This theme is old, and it has been ground into Indian religious parlance through the ages: Lord Kṛṣṇa, full incarnation of the Divine, master of supreme wisdom, teacher of kings, boy-thief of his mother's curds, simultaneous lover of 16,000 married cowherdesses, *jāra cora cūḍāmaṇi* "adulterer, thief, crestjewel," as the medieval Hindu saint-poet invoked him—he and his were the cynosure of the Indian value system. "The mind of these great men," explained the Gujarati *pandit* of a community near Bukoba, Tanzania "is always steeped in the Supreme; whether they meditate in caves in the Himalayas, or whether they drive a Peugeot with two beautiful ladies—nothing touches them, they are always the same, they are one with God." There is no hypocrisy in such statements, nor are they meant to be cynical or facetious. Quite on the contrary, they are very much the formulations of "Great-Tradition" Hinduism, and where the outsider would be tempted to smile at contextual anachronisms, the Asian has pronounced "Great Tradition" doctrine using contemporary variables to fill an ancient function, whose constant is the saint or the sage, the person who has transcended the world and hence the strictures and the criticisms of human society.

So long as a person does not have charismatic status, however, he is judged by the standards of the official Indian culture, which is puritanical and restrictive. A visiting Hindu monk suggested that he would build a modern *math* (monastery) back home in India, with a modern library, a swimming pool, and air-conditioned cells for the monks; what did his host think of it? "I wouldn't let you back into India"—his host retorted; the latter was a young, highly intelligent, cosmopolitan Asian who had been in Europe and America more than once. Being alienated from the cultural grass roots of India, he would not see its institutionally sanctioned ambivalence, the eudemonistic syndrome which is evident to the less alienated when facing the religious hero. To the modernite, there is no religious charismatic leader in the traditional sense—to him, the person who enjoys life cannot be a man of religion; paradoxically, the Asian intellectual, de-Hinduized and de-Indianized, as it were, would regard the naive ascetic as genuinely religious; Lord Kr̥ṣṇa and those who would emulate his exploits today, are frauds to him. It is difficult to find an analogy that would illustrate this situation to the non-indologist. We might think of a contemporary western scene and its dialogue—between professional theologians and laymen in the Christian world. Suppose we select laymen who think they are good Christians, good citizens, good people, church-going believers in the Word, etc.; most of them will tend to be quite rigid in their judgment of other people's morals, especially in the morals of a clergy about which they have doubts—in a sense, this is how the Protestant movements in the West started, and flourished. In contrast to this, there is a highly erudite, intellectual set of theologians. We will find that the latter take life with that ease which seems to go well with much reading, much thinking, and much structured discourse. We know that many priests and ministers in the top echelon of their profession are tenderly fond of such things as wine, women, and music. Now *they* know that all this is compatible with religious doctrine—they are doctrinary experts, they create the rules and standards, and they are not particularly impressed by the austere piety of zealous non-theologians; but the latter take a dim view of the theologians if they suspect laxity—the layman does *not* know the doctrine and its multiple possibilities, hence he takes his early straight-laced catechism seriously, literally. The theologian has many texts to fall back on—for there is not only the Sermon on the

Mount in the Judaeo-Christian tradition; there is also the Song of Solomon. Similarly on the Indian scene, there is of course the simple, non-speculative *Bhagavadgītā* which the modern Hindu reads without criticism, or which he has heard of—the book on which Gandhi said he had moulded his political and personal code of action. The Hindus, and those Muslim sects which follow an eclectic, inclusive pattern like the Ismailis —who quote non-Islamic texts along with the Qur'an and Ismaili doctrine—all these take the simplistic *Bhagavadgītā* as the foundation of Hindu life. But for the scholar, or even for the layman who gets to know the subtler and more versatile Hindu doctrines, there are many other texts and many other traditions which are Hindu—there are the stories of Kṛṣṇa the Lover, there are Śiva and the Goddess represented through phallic-cum-vaginal symbolisms, and there is a gamut of complex, highly eroticized religious teaching; vaguely, the untutored Hindu charismatic leader is aware of these potentialities, though he does not know much about them. But he "lives" them—which is to say, he will act as Kṛṣṇa acted, and he will feel about the joyous things of life the way the texts report that the great legendary and human founders of the Indian tradition felt. From here on, there is no parallel, no possible analogy with the western world: for the Indian religious leader has his guaranteed audience—all Hindus and many non-Hindu Indians revere him as a superhuman entity; "only Śiva can say whether a man who puts on the monk's garb is a genuine monk or a fraud," a learned South Indian gentleman once rebuked a modernite who talked slightingly about some *sādhus*. This guaranteed audience forms the clear majority of the population of the subcontinent. In East Africa, I would guess that about one-half of the total Asian population belong to that audience, the rest vacillate; they may refuse to pass any judgment because they would say that being modern, they neither can nor should concern themselves with these things which they think are on their way out. But the intellectually alienated, a small vocal minority of professional men, journalists, lawyers, etc., hold a highly uncomfortable middling position: they cannot pay homage to the charismatic hero in the manner their less emancipated friends and relatives do; and they do not have the scholastic equipment to crack the code of the Indian leader who refers to holy, traditional precedents. Vaguely, some modernites in Nairobi, Dar-es-Salaam, and Kampala know the myth about the god who made love to 16,000 married cowherdesses; but they do not know enough about the theological implications of a seemingly simple, bucolic legend—nor are they interested in it, because they would think, rightly, that such interests require lots of time and energy, the mastery of Sanskrit being an awesome sort of endeavor even in the eyes of the most skeptical and the most westernized; and that they must use this energy for modern, secular pursuits. In East Africa, the Ārya Samāj seems to fill a gap for some—for though they are aware that its teachings are anything but sophisticated and modern, they are impressed by the official sermon of the Arya Samaj that there should be no idol worship, no superstition, and that men and women should be equal. These ideas, regardless of how they actually operate among Ārya Samājis, are enough to screen out any possible reversion to the more traditional, ritualistically complex and—unknown to one and all in East African Asian society—far less puritanical ways of traditional Hinduism and Indian Islam.

Mr. S. S., a young, bright Hindu journalist in Dar-es-Salaam, third generation in East Africa, talks, reads, and thinks in English; he knows T. S. Eliot and Kafka, but he has not read Kālīdāsa or the Upaniṣads; he has heard about their ancient profundity, but because he identifies them with the old, stagnant ways of people he basically detests—the narrow-minded, unemancipated, ritual-oriented elders—he does not try to draw Kālīdāsa and the Upaniṣads into his own ken. There is a small, although growing group of extremely alert, bright young Asians who live in the three large cities and who are gradually becoming aware of the serious interest occidental intellectuals, artists, and other cosmopolitans have been displaying in things Indian over the past decade. It is known to these young people—and only to them—that Yehudi Menuhin sponsored Ravi Shankar, and that the latter, as well as Ustad Ali Akbar Khan and other top musicians, are being invited to an eager Europe and America; that their stereo records are listened to by thousands of serious musicians and hippies in the West; that famous classical dancers like Balasarasvati, Krishna Rao and Chandrabhaga are asked to and seen with admiration and respect at the finest centers of study and performance in America, Europe and Japan; that Indian literature, Indian erotic and other sculpture, and esoteric Hinduism, together with Zen, are creating numerous converts or at least full-time admirers in the West. There is no reason why this kind of highbrow "pizza-effect"[17] should not devolve upon these young Asians, all of whom are also quite genuinely interested in full integration with the Africans, not in the nominal sense in which the spokesmen of the Asian community proclaim integration, but quite radically: these young people would probably intermarry with Africans if the occasion arose, just as some of them have married European or American girls.

I had been corresponding with a young Panjabi Sikh woman in Dar-es-Salaam before I met her—a brilliant young lady, elegant, cosmopolitan, extremely attractive and quite conscious of being all that. At the end of my letters, I had written the Sikh greeting formula *sat-siri-akāl*, a conservative, thoroughly religious greeting which Sikhs in India and East Africa use when there are no outsiders around, when the situation is a traditional one; and of course, it is the constant greeting formula among all non-literate and/or non-westernized Sikhs. When I finally met the young woman, it was in a "sundowner" crowd, about one-third Asian, one-third African, and one-third white, the latter mostly American students and Peace Corps volunteers. When she was introduced to me, she laughingly folded her hands and said "sat-siri-akāl," a greeting which she never addressed to her peers and relatives, except perhaps the very old. I am quite certain that this would not have happened even a decade ago, when the young and bright felt embarrassed if they were confronted with orthodox patterns of interaction. The awareness of occidental, learned, or aesthetic interest in genuinely Indian matters came to the intellectuals in India roughly twenty years ago. Some three dozen or so young Asians are the only people in East Africa who appreciate this development. Their parents still regard Indian culture or whatever they know of it through the women's *satsaṅg* (religious meetings) and through reluctantly attended minimal ritualistic observances, as a thing that men should not talk about, that should be left to the women, and that stood in the way of modernization as a massive impediment. The same parents have absorbed from the West its most superficial artefacts imitating its sartorial, kinetic, and technological models. The young elite takes western technology and gadgetry for granted and does not feel more attracted to cars and bars than the American college graduate. And again, due to a salutary modification of the "pizza-effect," these young intellectuals no longer regard Hindu, Islamic or Sikh things as causes for social or dialectic embarrassment. It is quite a different sort of Hinduism which they are now concerned with—they will not attend the *satsaṅg* attended by their elders, and they will probably study no more Sanskrit than did their parents. But they *will* regard Indian culture with the same deepening affection which has dignified such Indian artists and intellectuals as Satyajit Ray, Ravi Shankar, and the growing crowd in Calcutta, Delhi, and Madras which reads Kafka, listens to Alan Ginzberg and Ali Akbar Khan, and learns to love or to perform *bharata natyam*. The few Young Turks appear like an unintentional vanguard not only for a resumption of refined Indian presentations, but also as harbingers of a more open society among the Asians in East Africa, for *they* are the ones African leaders respect.

We must, however, return to the statistically relevant bearers of an overtly or covertly conservative ideology, with a thin varnish of modernity. An old Navnit Vanīk Jain gentleman at Mombasa asked me to his house, and I had no idea what sort of a production was in store for me, but I

210

was most elated at the wealth of material the session gave
me. He was the head of a large joint family household, with
four sons, their wives and some twelve grandsons, and about
five unmarried daughters living in the house. He assembled
them all in the largest room, the women sitting on the floor,
and the men lounging on various sofas and chairs. "I am not
a learned man," he apologized; he then proceeded to quote
dozens of Jaina canonical verses in Ardhamāgadhi[18] and in
Sanskrit. He then asked a few standard religious questions,
but without waiting for an answer, he resumed his chanting
which he continued for ninety minutes. All his family sat
around silently, with no one uttering a word. But the corpulent Panjabi Hindu friend, who had taken me to the Jain's
house, pulled away nervously and when he took me home
many hours later he said "He wants to impress his family
that he is up to the *swamiji* in knowledge; he does this same
thing whenever he grabs a visitor from India. Once a distant
relative of his, a banker from Bombay, passed through here
and when the old man started this again, the other one cut
him short and told him to stop that nonsense, to let the
children go to bed and the women do their work, and not to
show off. Then the old man wept bitterly for two days."
Yet, this was an oversimplification. In the first place, many
if not all of the junior members of the house were genuinely
convinced that their father was a serious Jain scholar and a
man on the verge of holiness. Some of the younger men, who
had been chatting in good English quite freely and amicably
before the session began, sat there without a motion, their
eyes closed, and there was no doubt that this was a religious
experience for them. In the daytime, and during their secular
pursuits, all these men, and the old man himself were shrewd,
efficacious businessmen; they would talk "modern" when
speaking to outsiders who were not familiar with the intensive
ritualism at their homes; they would even deny that they were
interested in these old things. At the magnificent Jain temple
in Mombasa, Jain girls dressed as *Indrānīs,* spouses of the
powerful God Indra, adorned with ritualistic headgear, danced

211

in the temple in worship of the *tīrthaṅkara,* the founders of the Jain religion; the mythological implication, not known to any but the most conservative among the Jain audience, was that the *tīrthaṅkaras* had conquered and overcome the Brahmin gods, whose divine spouses were now serving 'the Jina—for "Jīna" and its derivative Jaina means precisely that— "victorious." The Deravāsi Jain priests[19] approach the images of the *tīrthaṅkaras* with pieces of protective cloth strapped over their mouths; so do the women devotees when they get close to the sanctum; and as the ceremony continues for hours, laymen of all ages, following the priests, approach the shrine with identical mouth covers. Now the wearing of this cloth is the ancient rule for the Jaina monk—it prevents him from

Devotees dance in a trance at a Jaina temple inaugural. Ordinarily, they are businessmen.

killing insects by inhaling them—and it is part of the perennial observance of certain Jaina monks in India. The paradox however, was not evident to the East African Jains. Jainism forbids agriculture as this profession involves killing of creatures of the soil. But the two Jaina communities in East Africa, the Navnīt Vanik and the Visa Oshwāl, had been agriculturists in India previous to their emigration—in fact, the *only* agricultural groups among the Jains, who have traditionally been traders. On interviewing one of the priests who lead the formal worship at the Mombasa Jain temple, he explained the matter by stressing the fact of *abhiprāy* "intention": although the Jains here did inhale microbic creatures all the time, the wearing of the mouth-cloth when approaching the sanctum was both a token of their intention, regardless of the fact that it cannot be fully implemented, and of their respect for the founders who were completely non-violent and who never destroyed even a microbe.

At the inauguration of the Jain Temple, young Jain men from Mombasa performed another slow ritualistic dance during the highly complex ceremonies. These boys were called "brahmins" for the occasion—a term which would seem quite inappropriate in the Jain context. There are some brahmin castes performing ritual, but the notion of *brahmin* as a functionary of a higher order by birth is anathema in the Jain doctrine, which is atheistic and which denies the authority of the very texts which are the foci of the brahmins in the Hindu tradition.

The student of Indian society has to find some pattern in these apparently contradictory types of behavior. The young women who acted as *Indrānīs*, the young men who staged a religious dance with a trance-like quality, and who dressed in ceremonial raiment, the worshippers who tied microbic-life-preserving gauze to their mouths, all are modern people in the sense that they participate in the technological modernization which the Asians have helped to create and to use in East Africa. I believe there is some order in these patterns, but it does not emerge through a definitional fiat.

A young unmarried Lohana woman who drove her father's car and who dressed in the most striking *sārīs,* complained about the clandestinely old-fashioned attitudes of young eligible men of wealth. She had felt attracted to a particular young man and he "tested her"—which is shorthand for mild necking which has been in vogue in East Africa since the use of cars filtered down to the young, unmarried generation. But, she continued, this same young man then completely withdrew from her and married someone else—a marriage that had been arranged. This pained her very much, as she had thought he would act differently from his older brothers and from the conservative people around them who insisted on arranged marriages. "I had observed *murakat,*[20] first for my brothers, then for my own desire to make that young man marry me; I also followed the *Sūryanārāyan* vow for many months;[21] a woman who wants the man whom she has chosen herself, for her husband, must perform many hard vows." The same young woman not only had an extraordinary repertoire of modern social dances, including three different versions of the Twist, but she was fairly proficient in semi-classical Indian dance. Yet, she kept performing regular and occasional formal worship *(pūjā)* in her parents house—her mother was ailing, and her father, being a very busy man, could not attend to the domestic worship, so the entire ritualistic commitment of her natal home had devolved on her. Her performance, however, was not only not perfunctory, as one might anticipate in a situation where a time-consuming, tedious routine was entrusted to a young person with presumably very different interests; on the contrary, she made it a point to add ritualistic items of her own; she worshipped different deities on different days of the week, Jagadamba, the Universal Mother, on Tuesdays and Thursdays, the god Brahma also on Thursdays, Visnu and Mahés (Śiva) on the remaining days. She also used different *āratī*-s (concluding hymns) for the different deities; all these were supererogatory acts which require a lot of information-gathering from *pandits* and from older people who have been more exposed to ritualistic pro-

214

cedure than the young, English-educated generation. What has been said about young, modern men—that they tend to deny religious interest even if they perform ritualistic acts at home—does not hold for the women of equal age in the same social groups. In fact, young women of wealthy families and of relatively high caste-status—Patels, Lohanas, Jains—tend to be ritualistically more involved than poor, low-caste women in the same areas who have to labor through the day. Another reason for this apparent paradox is that the latter still live within the more naively conservative framework which assigns ritualistic duty to men, leaving some very minor, subaltern ceremonies to the women. The Hindu Renaissance in India has stressed equal duties for women, implying more direct participation in "Great Tradition" ritual for them. The case of this particular subject exemplifies the Renaissance model diffused into urban East Africa. In Delhi and Calcutta, women of middle and higher income groups now gather for religious purposes under the influence of the reform sects, the Ramakrishna-Vivekananda movement, the Ārya Samāj, and the various imitational organizations that followed in the wake of the large, influential institutions which originated around the turn of the century all over urban India. Thus, our young woman who danced the Twist, drove a car, and indulged in sporadic mild necking, who spoke and read English much better than her own Indian vernacular, performed a highly elaborate, time-consuming ritual, when a woman of the same age, in a poorer income group, in the city or in the bush, hardly performs any ritual at all. Of course, full-scale, time-consuming regular ritual in India has never been part of the "Little Traditions" in villages or in marginally urban India; it requires deployment from domestic chores and considerable leisure, plus the acquisition of pertinent information; and such information itself has never been given free of charge— the brahmin, the *sādhu* and other professionals have to be housed and fed, and a ceremonial fee *(daksinā)* has to be given to them.

Some Gujarati groups, irrespective of their economic

status, tend to accept and to engage in a more intensive and constant type of ritualistic behavior, and the events which generate it seem anachronistic and irksome to Panjabi Hindus, and even to the Gujarati Hindus who do not approve of intensive religious involvement. At Nairobi, a not too wealthy shopkeeper convened a *satsang* in his house every night; there were only four rooms, one of which had been converted into a permanent shrine, with many polychromes, framed and unframed, depicting the various deities, erected over a table, which was covered with incense, flowers, sweet food, cinnabar paste, and other ingredients of formal worship. A pious person, either the host himself or a knowledgeable participant recited a line or two, and the whole audience distributed in the three other rooms joined in the *bhajan*.[22] Once in a while, when a *sādhu* or another religious specialist visited from India or from some other East African town, he was made to preside. His feet were washed with rosewater and milk by the host, the guests bowed, prostrated, and touched his feet, and the atmosphere grew tense and ecstatic as the evening went on. One of the visitors from India, a fairly well-known *sannyāsi*, had a tape recorder and a movie camera with him; as the devotees washed and touched his feet, offering sundry oblations and libations, he handled the tape recorder and trained his Japanese zoom lens on the crowd which worshipped him as tradition enjoins; hardly anyone in the audience seemed to feel that some sort of a *faux pas* was being perpetrated; the worship went on, and the sacred guest's wielding of highly secular equipment did not faze any of the devotees. "It is all *māyā*," an elderly gentleman remarked; I was not quite sure whether he was referring to the anachronistic scene or to the fact that half a *thālī* of the *prasād*[23] had just been dropped to the floor by a helpful, but clumsy young devotee.

During the month of March, Gujarati and Cutchi Hindus celebrate the *Puruṣottam* festival, a complex set of observances and festivities dedicated to Viṣṇu as *Puruṣottama*, a tutelary deity of the Gujarati Hindus. Both men and women take an early bath, before sunrise, in a river or in the sea—prefera-

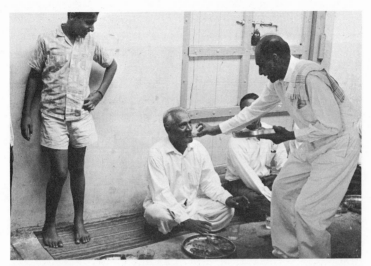

A jovial Brahmin is handfed by his devotees as he chants Sanskrit hymns.

bly the latter; at Tanga, Mombasa, and Dar-es-Salaam, hundreds of devout, silent Hindus took a dip in the Indian Ocean, well before dawn, long before there was any sign of Africans or whites on the otherwise busy streets. Again, a strange bit of anachronism—at Tanga, Gujaratis took their bath within twenty yards from the Yacht Club, a very plush, exclusive club mostly for white expatriates. The more erudite bathers chanted Sanskrit hymns before and after their immersion, and this was followed by a large-scale feeding of guests, a "feast of love" *prītibhoj*, at several homes. Both men and women kept a strict fast before the concluding, joyful event, and this particular fast was taken very seriously by one and all. When I spoke to the manager of the Club, an old-time Englishman who had been living at the premises for an active fifteen years, he looked both baffled and uninterested—a strange physiognomic expression which I noticed on old colonial people's faces when intercultural topics came up. "These Asians will do all sorts of tedious bits," he remarked, but it

217

was quite evident that he was not even aware of the fact that thousands of pious Hindus must have performed their ablutions on the same spot within his earshot at this time of the year, since long before the manager moved in. Living in one and the same place does not mean symbiosis: these were two worlds so incompatible with one another, that any mutual recognition would be traumatic—hence complete ignoring on both sides seemed only a salutary psychological device.

At Tanga, I stayed with a wealthy sisal merchant, a Gujarati Hindu. Rumor had it that he bade the members of his household—a large, joint house with about twenty-five people in residence—not to flush the toilet in the morning until the last person had used it. Water was scarce in Tanga, but not *that* scarce. A not too sympathetic Bohra merchant mused philosophically "That's the way to make a million." The house was a typical Gujarati joint-family dwelling, with several subdivided floors and units with separate entrances; the office, almost totally dark, was on the ground floor; there was a large central courtyard, which accommodated over four hundred people at a time for the *prītibhoj,* which the merchant offered at least twice a year. When it was suggested to him during an evening interview, that a man of his wealth could well afford to have more comfortable lodgings for himself and his family, he chanted, with an abstract mien, and several times to bring home his point, a famous verse from the *Bhagavadgītā: sukhaduhkhasamākṛtvā* . . . "viewing happiness and pain with equanimity . . ." Every evening, from about 9 to 11 p.m., the merchant, his oldest son, all his children and grandchildren assembled in a corridor connecting one of the living rooms with the staircase, to chant prayers in Sanskrit, Gujarati, Hindi, and English. A little granddaughter, a most delightful and lovely child, did some excellent chanting in Sanskrit and English; the oldest son, who would succeed to his father's business, attended and participated every evening, without a smile, but with no sign of impatience or rebellion. It was a genuinely pious family; and one that succeeded in conveying the message of its piety to kinsmen and friends alike. When I asked the merchant what he would think of his son taking to some other profession, or going for a higher education in India or elsewhere, he reflected for a while and said "I would not mind anything he does provided it makes him happy." After a pause, he continued, "we are businessmen, and we can be happy only in carrying on the business our elders started. This will be my son's pride, too, one day, when I am gone."

The head-clerk of the merchant was a jovial old Gujarati brahmin, who gave me a delightful little sermon one morning, full of genuine, folksy, forceful logic and metaphor. He chanted some Vedic hymns in excellent Sanskrit, with an almost ideal pronunciation—a thing no Panjabi brahmin in East Africa seemed to try to do—and then gave his own commentary on some of the passages from various periods of Indian literature. "A man has a *first class* (he used the English phrase interspersed in his tête-a-tête speech which he conducted in Hindi) wife, good looking, works like a strong bull, cooks like Laxmi (the goddess of wealth and the home); but he has no son— then what's the use of her, he feels, it is all useless; then a man has a fine Peugeot[24] but in the midst of the road on safari, he runs out of petrol; then what's the use of even a Mercedes Benz? Another man has three sawmills and huge sisal estates, but he is stupid and stubborn—then what is his use to himself, his family, and the world?" He then told me he made 470 shillings per month (about 67 U.S. dollars) as head-clerk and accountant; from this he must support his son who is going to school in India. When I offered him a little sum in lieu of a *dakṣiṇā* (brahmin's ritualistic fee), he declined it politely and left the room with another pleasant Sanskrit chant on his lips.

This man was a rarity among my subjects. His boss was religious in the style of Renaissance Hinduism; he did not know the primary sources of the tradition—his and his family's incantations were partly in Sanskrit, but their understanding came from translations and from popularistic preachings. (To an educated Gujarati who has not studied Sanskrit formally, the latter language is about as comprehensible as Latin is to an educated Italian who has not studied Latin.) But the brahmin was a man who had not lost his grass roots; here was the genial, pleasantly exhibitionist, humorous, sensitive deliberation of a man who knew his primary sources, and whose mind had not been tinged by the phony and pompous English of the Hindu Renaissance. Nor was he in any sense a modernite; but he knew how to compare a Peugeot with a Mercedes, in order to illustrate a very classical, very Indian type of exhortation. He was not a puritan like his more modern master, who would never have used a simile of the kind "he who has a *first class,* good looking wife. . . ." This brahmin was atypical among East African Asians; their cultural alienation cannot simply be pegged as a blend of puritanism, technocracy, and the eclecticism of the Hindu Renaissance—there are subtler shades to all this, however strongly these particular elements may operate. The student must intuit the complex world-view of the Asian expatriate by heeding what he says, to whom, and in which situation. But the encounter of the brahmin clerk gives one pause; for in this person, there were none of the complex inhibitions and frustrations which the more typical Asians display. He did not have a problem of cultural identity. He was a simple, learned, outgoing Hindu priest without a priestly estate.

As in India, the chaste monk, the *sādhu* and the *sannyāsi* or any person who is reputed to be celibate, is a perennial cynosure of the Hindu settler. A man in his forties, who owned a medium-size *dūkā* in a settlement near Mombasa, said that his father had come under the influence of His Holiness the Śaṃkarācārya who had visited East Africa a couple of years ago. "Since then, my father had been wanting to leave and settle in Amarnāth in the Himalayas." I told the man that no one could live at Amarnāth as the place was well over 15,000 feet high, that there were no accommodations of any sort, and that the pilgrims from the plains came to worship and leave, since the place was not one where people could stay at all with the present amenities. The subject then began to ramble, and said that he had had many affairs with "low-type" women; and that he drank a lot every day—but he asked me very earnestly not to tell his father about this as "it would destroy everything." After he had lost his first wife, he went to Dar-es-Salaam to find a new bride; he found a girl who was not only fair and attractive and of wealthy parentage, but she even belonged to exactly the right caste and the right *gotra*.[25] Her parents would not allow her to marry him, they did not want her to go to a despotic father-in-law; they did not want her to live in a joint household.

All his meandering might have seemed beside the point if we viewed it from the outside. Things fall in line, however, if we look for the kind of explanation which Carstairs, and more recently Spratt have suggested.[26] We could then speculate that the man really wanted his father out of the way, that he wanted him to go to the Himalayas and freeze and die; but so long as he was with him and had to put up with him under one extended roof, his father was still the master of the fates of everyone, including the subject: the father must not know that his son had an independent sex-life, and he must not know that his son drank, or "it would destroy everything." There was also an incarnate superego watching over both father and son: the Saṃkarācārya, chief abbot and monk of the most highly respected monastic Order of Hinduism—who had or had not given the father a directive; but if he did, it was probably quite different from what the son reported, for the Saṃkaracarya knows better than anyone else that the region of Amarnath is not inhabitable, and that not even the hardiest ascetics can make their abode there. The Śamkaracarya is the epitome of celibacy, he is the charismatic teacher *par excellence,* not only must his word not be doubted and his orders obeyed implicitly, but if his orders suggest the withdrawal of one person from the family unit, so that this person may dedicate himself to spiritual things full-time, then the rest of the family, however large, has to redefine its further actions and reactions in accordance with that supreme command. The personal or the family-directed concerns of the individual lose importance, and if the father thinks that their private interests obstruct his lofty quest as enjoined by the Samkaracarya, then private concerns of the other members of the family must cease to exist. Drinking, women, and other worldly things, forbidden or reprimanded by society even under ordinary conditions, at the appearance of a direction-changing charismatic teacher become heinous vices; and if a man feels that he is victim to them, when his father is seeking the noblest achievement with which all worldly desires conflict, he feels annihilated—his words, describing the situation, turn incoherent, the mystical and the domestic become inextricably interwoven, and the person can no longer relate normally to his kin who condemn his callousness.

Reducing such events to a minimal cause, we now have an important clue to the *sādhu*-complex in the culturally endemic fear of the loss of semen, a pervasive syndrome throughout India's cultural and religious history. Several anthropologists and other authors have studied this specifically Indian complex during the past few years.[27] The student of magic and supernaturalism will know that this can be tied to the "loss of soul" theme which pervades many of the world's supernatural concepts.[28] In East Africa, this fear is directly formulated only by such religiously and ideologically vocal groups as the Ārya Samāj, and by some individuals who are practicing some form of *yoga* on their own, though usually inspired and instructed by some established specialist, or group of specialists. The orthodox, classical formulation of this complex centers on the term *brahmacaryam*, literally "walking in the Supreme Spirit [*brahma*]" originally implying a life of spiritual cultivation and contemplation without necessary reference to sexual continence. However, the one and only present connotation of *brahmcaryam* is sexual continence, and a person who lives as a celibate is a *brahmacāri*. Ideally, all "twice-born," i.e., upper caste Hindus are *brahmacāris* previous to their initiation through the investiture with the sacred thread *(upanayana)* which is performed by almost all Ārya Samājis and by some other East African Hindus for

222

their sons around the age of twelve, except that in many cases the ceremony is deferred until the day of his marriage, so that the considerable expenses through the obligatory feeding of guests are incurred on one rather than two separate occasions. But the traditional pre-initiate student of the Veda is not what attracts the Asian. It is the person who lives as a *brahmacāri* throughout his life, the man who "never drops a single drop of semen," in the words of a Nairobi leader of the local *Brhat Bhāratīya Sangh*. At a meeting of that cell, a speaker explained the cause of over-population and of the threatening explosion "when the Aryans came to India 20,000 years ago, they kept *brahmacaryam* up to forty-eight years of their lives. Thus, India was never overpopulated. But when the Muslims came in, things changed, and men no longer preserved their sperm, but let it go here and there all the time. Hence, India is now so overpopulated and everybody starves. We do not believe in the "loop" and in the other dirty things Americans are smuggling into India. There is only one contraception, the contraception of the Aryans, and that is *brahmacaryam.*" Not particularly original words; Mahatma Gandhi preached just this.

Readers should realize that this was not just a minor piece of a sporadic sermon in a religiously committed section of the Asians. All Asians—Hindu, Muslim, and others, perhaps not even excluding the Catholic Goans—identify the ideal man with the man who does not drop semen at all, or very very rarely, and then only with the express purpose of creating offspring. I mentioned the disappointed and somewhat hostile reaction which I encountered when I told Asians that Netājī Subhas Chandra Bose had a daughter. This was an instance of the seminal retention syndrome: the ideal charismatic hero has no daughter.

The extensions of this complex are extremely wide, and not apparent to the subjects. Rarely is loss or the retention of semen directly brought into the discussion. I believe that many statements of loss of personal power could be reduced to loss-of-semen language even where this is not cognitively present to the mind of the subject. An old, pious Gujarati of the *darzī* (tailor) caste said: "when I was a very young man in India, my *guru* gave me the *mantra* of Śakti[29] and told me to repeat Her secret name all the time; then for many years, even when I had moved to Tanga, I saw gods and goddesses whenever I looked into the light. I could heal sick people with the power this gave me. I have many certificates of great people whom I cured. But then things went wrong. My first wife was very good, she agreed to live with me like brother and sister after our first child. But after her death my father insisted I marry again and he got me another wife, who was very bad. She insisted on intercourse and I had to do it at least once a week. She was after my semen, she knew she was making me weak . . . then very soon, I could not cure people any longer; I saw nothing when I looked into the light and now, although I do repeat the *mantra* quite often, all this is gone. *Mantra* is useless for a man who lets his sperm drop. If one retains it all one's life, one becomes a *mahātma,* and a *mahāpurus"* (great man).

But most statements are far less direct. Many years ago, a rich Jain merchant at Jaipur had told me the secret of his wealth: "I do not go to cinema, Mahārāj; I do not listen to songs" (i.e., to performances of song and dance at houses of prostitution). "And I open my *dhotī* (loincloth) only when I must beget a son. I do not drop any semen otherwise. That is why God has blessed me with too much wealth."[30] At Tabora, Tanzania, a Hindu audience turned deadly silent one evening when I told them that I had gone to see *Saṅgam,* the latest Indian movie, famous for the first actual kissing on the Indian screen which had not been censured. Some younger men and women in the audience giggled with embarrassment. All this reaction, of course, was due to the "loss" syndrome: all Asians go to the movies, which is the evening entertainment *par excellence,* just as in India and Pakistan. But men of religious standing do not, or should not go; for the movie is full of dancing and singing women who make alluring gestures; these excite the male. A religious person must meditate at night; but when he has seen the "ladies on the picture," he cannot concentrate, and finally he loses his semen at night, and all his power with it. *Sādhus* in India do go to mythologicals (some 30 percent of Hindi and other Indian language moves were mythologicals until 1960, enacting photogenic versions of the Puranas and other mythological texts); but they should not go to a movie like *Sangam,* and *a fortiori,* they should not be seen attending an American movie where "the women kiss and dance naked."

A surgeon at Nakuru, Kenya, took his wife on a tour abroad. She was a graduate from an Indian university, spoke excellent English, and had a fair command of Sanskrit which she had studied in college. Both of them owned expensive Japanese cameras, the doctor an 8mm movie camera, his wife a Nikkon, and they had done some good amateur shooting. "I like Europe, especially Rome and London," the doctor's wife reminisced. "But I did not like Paris at all, except the Eiffel Tower. . . . we went to a horrible place at night, called the Folies Bergeres. . . . I was shocked, I don't know what these women do . . . they dance naked in front of all men, and they are not ashamed. . . ." Talking about movies, the surgeon said with a twinkle in his eye "we don't omit going to a single one" (*ham to ek bhī nahin chorte*; the Hindi phrase suggests a kind of gentle, humorous avidity which is lost in translation), "but actually it is not really good for grown-up people, except for good pictures, like *Rāmrājya*.[31] But nowadays they don't show such good spiritual pictures anymore. They only show what appeals to the sensual men." Here the good doctor was patently wrong, for up to this very day, and perhaps in an increasing rather than in a decreasing number, the Indian movie industry keeps producing "good, spiritual," i.e., mythological movies or else *sāmājik* (social message containing) movies, some of which are quite good by any standard.

We may have a parallel to this configurational paradox in the western world: in some societies, the officially "conservative," say, for instance, the Roman Catholics, take life easier and in a more hedonistic mode than Protestant groups in the same area; this is not the case in North America, where the Catholics have assumed the puritanical role of the European Protestant prototype; but *La Dolce Vita* in Latin Europe, it seems to me, is eminently compatible with a Roman Catholic background. If we regard the Ārya Samāj as a Protestant movement—and it is that on all counts—and the *sanātanis* as the traditionalists, the Hindu "Catholics," so to speak, then a similar phenomenon obtains: the traditionalist *sanātani* tends to be less antagonistic about sensuous delights than the Arya Samaji. That does not mean that the *sanātani* is not also a puritan—puritanism is the quintessence of the modern Asian value orientation; but statements of *sanātani* Asians and Arya Samaji Asians of the same social and economic niveau tend to show that the Arya Samaji reformist is more averse toward the senses than the *sanātani*; the former condemns movies and the modern ways of young people more vehemently and certainly with more conviction than his *sanātani* peer.

There is a built-in notion of ethical relativism in traditional Hindu doctrine and homiletic, chiefly on internal grounds—ethics not being the essential part of the religious life, the ancients and the scholars found it easier to tolerate a relativistic, or at least a casuistic attitude about common morals. Not so with the Ārya Samāji and for that matter, the Ramakrishna and other recent reform movements: for them, black is very black indeed, and there is no doubt as to what is black: sex, both marital and extramarital, fun, and games. When I quoted *śruti* (canonical texts) in an Ārya Samāji assembly at Dar-es Salaam, showing that certain actions which some people think evil are not always evil, but can in fact be highly meritorious, two elderly women stood up and left with the proper *namaskār*;[32] the ladies who had been sitting beside them later on told me that the two had been deeply perturbed and upset by me and said, "If Śri Krṣṇa really made love to married women, and to thousands at that, then he was not an *avatāra* of God, but of *śaitān*" (i.e., the Devil—a strangely alien notion; *śaitān* is a Semitic term cognate with "Satan" and the only source from which these ladies could have derived it was either Muslim or missionary Christian—there are unpleasant demons in Hinduism, but there is no Satan). A statement like this could hardly have been made by a *sanātani*, either in India or in Africa. When the amorous tales of Śri Kṛṣṇa came up in religious and secular discourse with the *sanātani*, there were smiles and nods, and among the less involved, shrugs, but condemnation of this most delightfully unpuritanical deity of the Hindu pantheon seems to be common to nineteenth century and later reform movements.

One of the best measuring rods of conservatism in an Indian society is the consumption of meat versus vegetarianism or rather, the attitude toward these two types of diet. Vegetarian food, in all Indian societies, either means or is intended to convey higher caste-status. The "upcasting" of low-caste groups through their joint, protracted rejection of meat has been thoroughly studied and reported in anthropological literature.[33] This process does not directly work in East Africa. Caste rank was completely defined from the time of immigration, and no group can "climb" in the manner in which obscure groups have climbed in India. But whether the individual eats meat or not has a lot to do with the respect he commands among his peers and his kin. A *sanātani* Panjabi woman of about forty-five said "the Ārya Samājis sometimes eat meat[34] but if they don't, they are proud of it and make it known. We (i.e., the *sanātani*) shouldn't eat meat, but those of us who do think it is not right. Some ladies say that those who do *bhakti* (i.e., lead an actively religious life) should not eat meat, but for those who do not, it is irrelevant whether they eat meat or not. If a modern holy man tells us 'go and eat meat' we are very glad, because then the *pāp* (sin) will attach to him, not to us who eat it on his advice."

One might expect that radical modernization and exposure to western social models would tend to soften the negative assessment of behavior which has long lost its moralistic dimension in the West. The one custom which the modern

Asian has most thoroughly assimilated from his western friends and business partners is social drinking. And yet, quite unlike the Anglo-Saxon, whose world provided the model, the Asian still praises the teetotaller as a more highly moral man than the person who drinks. A Panjabi businessman who took me to the delightful Manyara game reserve in Tanzania equipped with a plush Lodge in the midst of the area, said that his wealthiest Gujarati friend at Arusha, fifty miles away, had never been to the Game Reserve, although he had been in India and in Europe on business. "He would never come to this place," he continued, "he is not interested in nature, and he travels only when it means making money; but for the rest, he wants to stay at home comfortably and drink whiskey."

My somewhat atypical host enjoyed nature in the sense in which occidental nature lovers do; this rarely happens in India or East Africa—people just don't go out into the forest or the bush for pleasure, nor do they visit the four or five magnificent game reserves which are among the most impressive sights anywhere in the world. If they do go, it is usually to take an Indian relative or a western friend or associate and to show them around. Of a dozen interviewees of high economic status in the three large cities, only two had been to one or more of the game reserves more than once; half of them had never been to any at all. A Lohana businessman in Nairobi had never visited the game reserve which lies at the outskirts of the city; "This is for the children," he said, "we do not have time for such things."

Asians of all economic levels, including professional men, are profoundly concerned with cosmological problems. A heart specialist at Nairobi mused: "If you climb up the stairs to your bedroom, there must be a bedroom to climb up to." The question had been that of the existence of a personal God who guides man's fortunes. This speculative pseudo-ontological statement could not have been inspired by Hindu nor any other scriptures; but the desire to believe in a theistic matrix of the universe is quite as strong as among the Asian professionals as it is, say, among fundamentalists in the West.

Now this doctor, as most men in the professions, had hardly ever been exposed to theological discourse; he was not a religiously committed person; rather, like most middle-class Asians he thought that religion was a matter for the women. His strange analogy seemed out of place; its logic was bad, but there was no way to show him that there were alternatives to the theistic position in a modern man's world view. The absence of any interest in "ideas" per se is quite striking among the Asians. Attitudes have changed radically among comparable groups in India; they have not in East Africa.

One would expect political ideologies prevalent in a society to reflect reactions to immediate political problems. This, however, is not borne out in India nor among Asians in the East African area. The general, non-historical, diffuse, metaphysical attitude toward affairs seems to prevent engagement in political ideology, except on the level of naive discourse. Some of the one-time political leaders of the Asian community no doubt have well-informed political notions; some Asian trade-unionists are orthodox socialists or communists, and display a considerable degree of familiarity with the involved doctrines. But the Asian population, by and large, does not get excited about conflicting political ideologies, because the political world view held by the majority is a sort of extended reflection of the religious—views that might be classed as "political" in a wider sense. It focuses upon charismatic individuals, and there is little feeling for those impersonal processes which constitute modern political life and doctrine in which persons are, at best, variables in a functional system.

It is hard to say whether or not there is a modal difference between a quasi-political world view and private notions held by members of the different communities. I think the question of whether the Ismaili, the Patel, the Lohana, the Sikh, etc., hold political views markedly divergent from one another, can be answered in the negative. No doubt there is a lot of difference in the attitudes toward Indian and Pakistani *politics* between Hindus and Muslims among the Asians, but one often gets the feeling that these attitudes are automatically engendered rather than acquired through political ratiocination, through experience or discourse. In other words, most Ismailis, Bohras, and Ithna Asharis would think Pakistan was basically right in its political struggle with India and in the Kashmir dispute; Hindus and Jains would hold Pakistan was wrong and that India's title to Kashmir should not be challenged. But in matters of international dialog beyond Southern Asia, as in matters of political ideology in the narrower sense, there is hardly any variation of ideas between members of the different groups.

If a political world view were to be adumbrated for the Asians in general—except for those few who are politically or ideologically committed—it would run somewhat like this: good politics should enhance the wealth and the well-being of the nation whose leaders legislate and implement political ideas and policies. The leaders and their followers must be nationalists, and they must identify themselves with the culture of their ancestors. If politics and statecraft are to be beneficial, then the leaders must lead a moral life—they must be continent, simple in their habits, frugal, or, if they happen to be of actual or fictive royal descent, they should spend in lavish splendor. They must be religious: a man who does not worship God—an atheist, an agnostic—is not acceptable as a leader. Democracy is talked about, but it is not something that is really wanted—a strong leader who tells people what to do and who breaks down impious opposition, aided by a band of strong, righteous, serious ministers or vassals—this is the ideal conception of a ruler. The impersonal administrator is not understood, the advantages of a non-charismatic, memo-based administration are not perceived and their efficacy is doubted. The Asian talks about communism, capitalism, American imperialism or British colonialism, but by and large, none of these subjects are emotionally charged and they do not evoke awe, fright, or hope. Those who have been abroad, particularly in England, seem to wish for democracy in a somewhat utopian fashion; for when the chips are down, most of them still admire the hero and crave his presence, and long for a time when justice and equity will be dispensed by a ruler or a minister or a statesman like Rama the divine hero; Gandhi talked about *Rāmrājya* as the ideal state of affairs—a true benign theocracy, in memory of the *Rāmāyana* Epic of ancient India which set the perennial model for the Indian people at large. The man who leads in spirit should also rule the state: ideally, he should be either a king in golden raiments or an ascetic, a monk in sacred rags. But the bespectacled, briefcase carrying government official, the unobtrusive looking public administrator, is just not the person who would give inspiration and prompt action for the benefit of the nation. Rationally, modern Asians know that the administrator will prevail sooner or later if things go right. But the *dūkā*-owner and his kin, the *fundi* and the small-scale entrepreneur, hope for return of the hero to administer and to lead, much as American Indians are said to hope for the return of the buffalo.

The democracy suggested by Indian governmental exhortation "is not for us here"; this seems to be the common view of all but the highest-brow Indian society. Political views correspond entirely to those of the articulate, but unsophisticated urban middle class on the subcontinent. At the time of *uhuru*, the Asian political organizations, the various regional Congress groups, discarded any further political activity by their own decree. Since then, there has been no political dialog in the manner previously conducted by leaders of the former Kenya National Congress and their erstwhile followers; that dialog reflected views that were structurally identical with those of the moderate wing of the Indian National Congress. With the creation of Pakistan, the Muslim groups of East Africa were at a loss at deciding where to anchor their political notions that hitherto had been geared to an undivided India.

The only ideologically motivated and organized group which holds a definite political viewpoint is probably not conscious of its being more political than "cultural" or religious. The *Bṛhat Sevā Sangh* "Great Service Party," though officially and constitutionally nonpolitical, entertains a clear-cut, nationalistic, ethnocentric doctrine exactly in line with the radical Hindu rightists in western, and now in Northern India. The model organization in India was the R.S.S. *Rāṣṭriȳa Svayam-Sevā Sangh* "National Self-Help Party" founded by a Maharashtrian Brahmin, Guru Golvelkar, inspired by Fascist models and by a chauvinistic, hypertrophically puritanical reading and application of the concept of *Hindu Rāj,* "Hindu Rule" as read into the Hindu Epics, the *Rāmāyana* and the *Mahābhārata.* In India, the R.S.S. was proscribed for a long time, its leaders were kept confined under the Preventive Detention Act, and although the official or unofficial membership of the R.S.S. is not large and is restricted mainly to Marāthī-speaking areas, its ideological influence is considerable, it being the most outspoken Hindu political revivalist organization in India. It has considerable financial backing, as some of the wealthiest *Marwāri* industrialists have been supporting the R.S.S. by large donations. Though their views are less highly politicized than the Maharashtrian ideologies, there are quite a few Northern spokesmen, foremost among whom is Professor Balraj Madhok.[35] It is probably due to his writings, of which I saw copies in several Panjabi houses in East African cities, that some active sympathy with the East African B.S.S. has been created among Panjabis. Most of the members, however, are Gujarati, Patels, Lohanas, and some few Maharashtrians, their number being quite small in East Africa. Membership is open to anyone, even to Muslims in theory, provided they subscribe to the ideology of *Hindu Rāj,* radically rejecting Nehru's idea of a "composite culture." Even this highly articulate organization does not contemplate political action in East Africa, overtly or covertly. All those who were politically vocal in pre-*uhuru* days, working or at least speaking for some sort of political identity, now insist on retaining purely cultural interests in the Asian community; "cultural" not in the sense of creating works of Indian culture or importing them, nor in any anthropological sense, but by identification with what they know of contemporary urban Indian life styles.

The B.S.S. holds regular meetings, whose style and tone document the members' allegiance. The *Br̥hat Sevā Sangh* is perhaps the only indigenous Asian organization in East Africa which attracts people across caste—and language lines, for purposes other than business and commerce. The caste organizations discussed earlier do not attract, nor aim to attract, membership on religio-political or ideological grounds. The B.S.S. meets at private homes on a rotating basis, in the style of the Indian R.S.S., though this emulation is not dictated by any secrecy such as that which the R.S.S. had to observe when it was outlawed in India.

The B.S.S. has members of all age groups; young men and boys have their own sub-units in each chapter. Women cannot be members. When I pointed out to a large B.S.S. meeting that they were addressing only one-half of the world, their spokesman looked puzzled. I then elaborated, saying that one-half of the world were women; where were they today and at other meetings? At first, there was embarrassed silence, then sporadic giggles, but then the situation was handed to me in detail by another functionary, a man of about thirty-five: "Women have their separate meetings; we do not mix with them." Did they actually have separate meetings and if so, what was their organizational link with the *Sangh*? It then appeared that the women did not actually have an organization of their own, but they *could* have one if they wanted to. At present they did not meet, though all of them were sympathizers with their kinsmen who were members. "To meet and walk around with one another (i.e., men and women) is against Hindu culture. For the boys are pupils, students, and when women are around, then . . . (here he hesitated for a moment) the boys' minds would be distracted from their work and their *vyāyam* (P.T. and military drill) . . . and what you, sir, said about men and women being together for such functions as ours, that does not seem right to my mind, it does not add up in my mind (*hamāre man meṇ jajtā nahin*) . . . to *mix* the two together" (*donon mix karnā*—he used the English word *mix* in his Hindi response, in line with the modern urban Indian tendency to use English words to refer to undesirable behavior) "that seems to me a difficult thing to do. . . . this (i.e., "mixing" them together) had been tried here, but not in this Sangh . . . there was an organization of Ārya Samāj women, but that was stopped, and I believe it was stopped for that reason (i.e., for the distractive effects of "mixing") in India, for the meetings of the *Rāṣtriya Sevā Sāngh,* the wives and sisters of the members started their own organization. . . . what we do here is that we assemble about twenty-five families together by suggesting they live in the same area of the town. . ." The implication was that in this manner the womenfolk could also meet and be instructed in religio-political "cultural" thought and ideas, without the danger presumably inherent in getting both sexes to share the same meetings.

This situation gives rise to thought. In Hindu temples and at the Ismaili *jamātkhāna,* both in East Africa and on the subcontinent, men and women pray and worship in the same hall, though they are seated in two separate sections facing the speaker or the sanctum. This is quite universal, at weddings and other religious and secular occasions—the women sit on one side, the men sit on the other, the children commute constantly between the two groups. Now the B.S.S. aimed to be a modern, nationalistic, religious reformed politico-cultural organization, and yet women were completely excluded from the meetings. My reading is that any Indian movement, however organizationally structured, must act more puritanically than the old-established religious organizations if it is to be accepted as Indian *and* modern.

Another person then said, "They say, that Hinduism will not be the religion of the twentieth century; that it will not survive this century." Where had he heard that? Some missionary had told his father. "This we must fight with all our power. We must show the world that Hinduism will not only last, but that all people of *Āryavarta* ("the land of the

234

Aryans," i.e., India) must accept, defend, and preach it." Here again, we have an attitude which is less than a century old, for until the beginnings of the Hindu Renaissance, prose-lytization was not part of any form of Hinduism; in fact it was even theoretically impossible, since one must be born into a Hindu caste in order to be a Hindu. The Ārya Samāj does indeed convert people to be *Āryans,* but traditional Hindus tend to be more than skeptical about it.

These are the functions of the B.S.S. in East Africa, as reported by one of its senior founder-leaders, a man of about fifty, a railway employee who came from India with his father, at the age of four: "We arrange for speeches to be given by great men, famous people, by scholars, saints, and by leaders visiting from India; we arrange for and hold the "festival of Hindu rule" (*Hindu samrāj kā utsav manāte hain*)—during that festival, we show them how Maharaja Pratāp Singh and other heroes lived and taught their people to be brave and to follow the *śāstras* (Hindu scriptures in general). The more learned among us, those who read English, read the works of Dr. Radhakrishnan, and C. E. M. Joad;[36] we all read Swami Vivekānandajī's works, but of course we are all aware that none of us has the *Jñān*[37] which the Swamiji had; but we try and regard him as the *ādarś* (illustrious example) for all Hindus. Apart from the 'festival of the Hindu rule,' we also arrange and celebrate *Makar Sankrānt,* and *Vijay Daśamī'* (more commonly known Hindu festivals with nationalistic in-interpretability).

If hero worship is ubiquitous in the South Asian world, the B.S.S. like its model organization the R.S.S. in India, put worship and obeisance to the charismatic hero on its official banners. On the walls of the houses belonging to B.S.S. members, we find the same polychromes as everywhere, the various gods and goddesses, with film actresses interspersed between Indian political leaders; but the pictures of Subhas Chandra Bose, B. G. Tilak, and of Guru Golwelkar were prominently displayed in almost all the B.S.S. houses I visited. These three men were the Hindu charismatic heroes *par excellence.*

Mahatma Gandhi is accepted as a *mahātma,* but just only as that—the fact that he preached *samjhautā* (mutual understanding and acceptance) with the Muslims militates against his being accepted to the fullest charismatic status. "He was a *mahātma,* no doubt," a young B.S.S. member said, "but there were greater *mahātmas* than him, powerful, stronger.

A typical Hindu living room, in East Africa.

236

You could see it on their faces: there is a divine brightness on their faces, their bodies exude lustre, they are strong and tall. . . ." When I remarked that some *mahātmas* had no doubt had small bodies, with no particular shine on their faces, and that I had also encountered people who did have lustrous faces with bodies of knights in shining armor but who were total *budhūs* (idiots), this did not seem to register. "No," the man said "something is always visible; every great man has his *lakṣaṇa* (physical sign) by which he can be recognized." The idea that some very inconspicuous men may be *mahātmas* and that some exquisite looking people may well be imbeciles was unacceptable. This was a more radical axiom than I had encountered in India; for Mahatma Gandhi was small and ugly, and had no heroic *lakṣaṇa*-s whatever on his body. But then in India, there is always an answer to this kind of fact: his eyes, his smile, his movements, etc., bespeak his *mahātma*-status even if his body has no heroic stature. I had the feeling at this specific B.S.S. assembly, that most men were committed to a kind of *kalo k'agathia* vision, for just as the ancient Greeks believed that physical beauty (*tà kalá*) and goodness (*agathá*) must go hand in hand, the Hindu fundamentalist believes that to be truly godly or saintly also means to be physically powerful, corpulent, robust, and light-complexioned. At least at two other occasions, not B.S.S. meetings, I elicited annoyed and angry reactions when I said that some tiny dark people had been very great men indeed, and that some very handsome light-colored men had been fools and knaves. When a famous person's exact features were not remembered or when there never was a personal confrontation, physical traits were ascribed to him even where they had not been present. Netājī Subhas Bose provides the best example: he was medium-size, slightly flabby, and bald-headed, also about as dark as the average Kāyasth Bengali. But in the ascriptive memory of the Asians, he was over six feet tall and fair. Bose was the arch-hero, and it is hard to find any Indian, Pakistani, or an East African Asian, who would not exalt Bose. When talking to a schoolteacher in Jinja, Uganda, who had taken a course in Political Science at the New Delhi Campus of Panjab University, I finally succeeded in getting him to see that Bose was not a statesman, nor a political thinker of the caliber say, of Nehru or Rajagopalachari. "He may not have been the greatest political brain, but he was a hero, a spiritual genius, and an intellectual giant. . . ."

The "intellectual giant" diction is modern Indian Renaissance style, transferred *in toto* to East Africa. Usually, the term is countervailed by a negative apodosis, "he is an intellectual giant, but, . . ." the final, slightly detracting clause being that the person in question lacks certain spiritual qualities which make a hero a charismatic and a perfect man. But then, just as both the village Vaidya—the locally trained, traditional herbalist curer and the visiting Sir J. B. S. Haldane were "intellectual giants" for the chairman who introduced them on the same rural platform, it does not make too much difference in the Asian's world view whether a person qualifying for this apparently superlative epithet is some itinerant monk-preacher from India or Dr. Radhakrishnan, former President of India and foremost exponent of the Indian scriptures to the lay West. Also, to be an "intellectual giant," one must be Indian or occidental: I tried to elicit similar eulogy for some of the top African leaders as well as for some Chinese leaders who were visiting Kenya—but none of them seemed to be eligible for this status. If the "intellectual giant" is an occidental, he is equally a ". . . but . . ." case: that is to say, he lacks spiritual qualities of the sort the Hindu giants and other saints, members of the religious profession, own by ascription. The great Šamkarācārya was both an "intellectual giant" and a saint, a "realized soul," etc.—all this being Vivekanandian jargon used by one and all when talking Indian apologetic in English. None of these idioms could be said in any of the Indian languages. The Asian world view is formulated, linguistically, in the English of the Indian Renaissance, not through primary and grass root sources which remain the domain of some very few, like the *pandit* mentioned earlier in this chapter.

Interviews with the more radical elements in East Africa, such as members of the B.S.S., reinforced an old hunch of mine: that the Indian Renaissance, regardless whether its proponents are talking about religious matters or about politics and other secular themes, has created a sort of linguistic dualism: things that are communicated in English, the proper medium of the Renaissance, cannot be said in an Indian language without injecting neologistic patterns into an alienated vernacular speech. When a Gujarati or Panjabi informant of the radical type conducted his speech in Gujarati or Panjabi or Hindustani, he either inserted English terms into his Indian speech, or else, if he happened to have been engaged in vernacular reading and in the study of religious texts which use Sanskritic vocabulary, he spoke in the closed, predictable code of cultural jingoism. Madhok's writings provide the best example; the Panjabi Hindu radical right in East Africa quote him profusely: anyone born in India, or descending from those who were born there, is a Hindu if he believes that Hinduism and its values should guide all conduct, individual and societal; he has to work for *Hindu ektā* "Hindu unity," but *ektā,* though lexically unobjectionable Sanskrit, is a neologistic retranslation of the English politicized sememe "unity." He should be proud of and should preach Hindu *saṃskṛti* "culture"—but again, although *saṃskṛti* is a good Sanskrit word (in fact, it incorporates the same morpheme as "Sanskrit," which meant the codified language of scholars, courts, and of learned commentary), "samskriti" was never used in India in the sense in which modern Indians use the term, again as a neologism meant to translate the nineteenth century English evaluative term "culture."

The B.S.S. and non-aligned Hindu rightist notions about the inclusiveness of the term "Hindu" go back to Tilak and his less scholarly followers. "A true Hindu is he," said an elderly Maharashtrian B.S.S. member at Dar-es-Salaam, "who prays the God *(sic)*, leads a pure life, does not drink and womanize, worships Mother India, and reveres the saints and heroes of India from Ramcandraji[38] to Netājī (Subhas Chandra

Bose); he should not think in terms of *jāt* (caste), but only in terms of glorious Hinduism." This contrasts with the pre-Renaissance formulations of what constituted a Hindu; but when I told a large B.S.S. gathering that the only qualification for being a Hindu, apart from being born into Hindu society, was the acceptance of the Veda as canonical, there was disbelief and disappointment all over. Somehow, the feeling is that a traditional, textual claim of this sort is too narrow to inspire the young and those who would be political, or "cultural" Hindus.

A highly respected elderly Maharashtrian gentleman was aggressively outspoken about all he felt: that Hindu culture was supreme, that the Africans had missed out on a good chance to learn about or even to adopt Hindu culture, that African culture was inferior, and that all the great cultures in the world, including western culture, had their origin in India. That rather impressive gentleman said "I beseech you, sir, to do your work as a real scholar, and to contribute to the glory of Hindu culture: you must prove that the Africans received their culture from early Hindu settlers thousands of years ago. The Chaga, Masai, Watutsi, and other tall, fair tribesmen of the interior were descendants from northern African Hamitic peoples, whose first ancestors had come from India." Though these views might have been shared by quite a few concerned Hindus, this specific person was a very genuine man who courted martyrdom. After he had published some highly critical, sharply worded statements about the African rulers in an English language daily, his passport was taken from him, and further recriminations were threatened. "Many of us feel this way," a Panjabi trader commented, "but we have wives and children to think of." However, there is no doubt that this expression of extreme ethnocentrism is becoming that of a minority view. Insistence on the old-time Hindu glory, if it were to operate at all, would mean complete isolation both from the hosts and from the more liberal Asians who may well constitute the majority of the vocal Asians in a few decades. My views were echoed by one of the most knowledgeable and highly respected Asians in East Africa, a man who is given high regard by the African leaders even at this moment. He referred to the aforesaid Maharashtrian gentleman as "that R.S.S. man"—he did not even say "B.S.S.," for, as he told me, he saw no difference whatever between the Hindu fascist R.S.S. in India and the local B.S.S. cells in East Africa, except that the latter had no power and no consistent ideological backing from the rest of the minority.

There are, however, quite a few political thinkers of quite a different ilk. Comrade Makhan Singh was a trade union leader in Nairobi. He had been jailed by the British both in India and in East Africa, and he certainly was of the stuff political heroes are made of. He was a Sikh—beard, turban and all—living in a modest but pleasant urban house. In his autobiographical self-introduction,[39] he described himself as of a carpenter's family (i.e., he belonged to the Rāmgaṛhiā caste); and he was "deeply religious and poor." Makhan Singh meant it when he spoke about integration; there are no Asians in East Africa, only Africans. When I asked him if he would support intermarriage between Africans and Asians, he got quite irritated and repeated that there were only Africans here; his implication seemed to be that he would not object to miscegenation; however, no one in his family has entered into liaison with an African girl. There is no doubt in my mind that if most Asians proclaimed similar views, unilaterally for a number of years, the African leadership might well be induced to take a more lenient attitude toward the Asians. Makhan Singh gravely resented anthropological interests. His resentment was shared by quite a few scholarly Asians, and quite understandably. The study of topics which are crucial to anthropological reporting—kinship, geneaology, social structure and organization, and in the case of all Indian societies, caste, cannot but be highly disturbing to the subjects who must impress upon their non-Indian contemporaries that theirs was as egalitarian a society as they believe western societies to be. "You should not be allowed to come to this country or to India," Comrade Makhan Singh told me with

241

controlled irritation. "There are no Sikhs and Jats and Patels and Lohanas and Hindus of which you write; there are only Africans here, and Indians in India, and Pakistanis in Pakistan, just as there are only Americans in America. When you go on writing about these people they will say with useless pride, 'Look, a foreigner and a scholar writes about us Patels in an English book—we are a great community' and you will make bad things worse." When I remonstrated that the anthropologist would opt out of his profession if he ignored these basic things, Makhan Singh retorted "To hell with anthropology and all your social sciences. What would you say if an Indian or an African asked you questions about American society or religion and negro-white relations?" When I tried to hint that quite a few American and non-American social scientists were doing just that, Makhan Singh ignored it—quite probably, he just did not believe me. An Ismaili coed from Tanzania, studying at an American university, said to a friend of hers "Of course the Asians are mad at Bh., if he constantly criticizes them and writes about their ancient ways; Americans would be mad too, if anyone wrote such nasty things about Americans." Quite amazing that otherwise well-informed people like Makhan Singh or that coed should not be aware of the fact that criticizing America on every level has become one of the most popular creative and lucrative pastimes of American and non-American writers.[40] Yet this is not really the point: a deep dislike for an objective statement of Indian social structure and the caste-system is part of a syndrome which I have tried, on several occasions, to explain in terms of modern ordinary language philosophy. "Caste no longer exists," "caste has been abolished" "what should we do in order to get rid of caste," and similar statements which I have encountered, solicited and unsolicited, in India and East Africa many dozen times, belong to a pseudo-indicative order: in other words, when a modern English-speaking Indian, wherever he is, makes a statement of the form "caste has been abolished," what he really means to say is *caste ought to be abolished.* This does not mean that this corrected statement would make sense to the student of Indian society, for it cannot be made operational. "Caste is abolished" would imply "social structure has been abolished" and "caste ought to be abolished" would mean "social structure ought to be abolished." The simplest test for the non-operationality of such statements is that they can be made *only* in English; if a speaker tries to express them in any Indian language, he cannot do so or he says something quite different, as for instance "feelings of discrimination on the basis of caste *jātibhed* ought to be abolished."

It is by no means only the politically committed or the intellectually naive who oppose anthropological taxonomies. Of about half a dozen of the most highly knowledgeable persons in East Africa, only one agreed that the objective study of society was important, even if only for "the pleasure of intellectuals who have not much else to do." Field anthropologists from virtually all areas of the former colonial world have the same problems; the leaders of the newly emergent nations simply do not want themselves and their people to be used as paradigms for anthropological theories, regardless of whether the anthropologist applies the same tools of analysis to his own compatriots or not. "Indians today are Indians of progress (*unnati*) not of caste (*jāti*)," as a B.S.S. member tried to persuade me with a not-too-well rhyming pun created *ad hoc*.

Sights and Sounds

The aesthetic world view of modern Indian society anywhere is highly stereotyped, and as I have not seen any radical departure from the way Indians and Pakistanis look at things of beauty—or ugliness. Let me restate briefly what I have said in greater detail in another publication,[41] then demonstrate it by East African Asian situations, and thereby incorporate paradigms for the presentation of conservatism and modernity from yet another critical angle. With the decline of feudal and traditional sponsorship of the arts in India, the aesthetic perception of middle class Indians lost the acute discriminating taste medieval India displayed. With anti-sensuous puritanism

Gods and ads adorn the walls.

as the official culture of nineteenth and twentieth century urban India, the understanding and appreciation of the arts became fossilized. With the exception of a small though growing section of musical specialists who continued the tradition of classical music and dance, and the virtually unchanged traditional religious sculpture and architecture in certain parts of India, particularly in some one-time princely states in the South, urban Indians failed to attend to the artistic component in any artifact; the incredible polychromes and oleographs of gods, goddesses, politicians, and film actors which penetrate every nook and corner in India and Pakistan, were about the only pictorial artifacts which urban Indians bought to have in their homes and offices. This is paralleled by most of the enormous output of the Indian screen, ranking second in quantity of all movie-producing nations today; *Pāther Pañcāli* and the other works of Satyajit Ray are shown and enjoyed in the West, reintroduced into Indian cities and then enjoyed with reluctance through the "pizza-effect".[42] Some amount of classical and not-so-classical "oriental" dancing is taught to daughters of the wealthy, with decreasing resistance against it at least in metropolitan India. To make it short, let me report an episode for an ostensive definition: when you ask a modern, English-speaking resident of Delhi, a banker, or a university teacher, what sights one should see in the Capital, he will enumerate the Red Fort, The Qutb Minar, the Muslim rulers' tombs, and more likely than not the Birla Temple. The latter is a recent edifice erected by the late Seth Jugal Kishore Birla, a top industrialist—this temple has considerable negative aesthetic and artistic merit, if I may say so. The connoisseur of Oriental or any architecture has to see it in order to believe it; it is pure *kitsch,* albeit highly expensive marble *kitsch,* and reminds one of Disneyland rather than of a Hindu shrine. But it is just that, and it is well visited by Hindus and non-Hindus alike; it is clean, well looked after, and so puritanical that even the God Śiva is represented as an alabaster icon, not by the prescribed *liṅga* (phallus). Of my East African Asian informants who visited Delhi during the last decade, there was only one out of about two dozen who had anything critical to say about the Birla Temple. All others thought it was delightful, on a par with the tenth century Qutb Minar, a magnificent structure. When it was suggested that this sort of modern Hindu art, and the ubiquitous polychromes, on calendars, wall-hangings, or embellishing color-ads of various mercantile firms, were *bad* art, there was surprised silence in East Africa as in India: the best apologetic idiom I heard about these artifacts was "these are photos of God, they are beautiful and inspiring." The notion that even a "photo of God" may be bad art is simply not understood cognitively or metaphorically, because the distinction between presentation and content is atrophied in modern Indian urban culture. Some young people in East Africa did learn to appreciate classical Indian music, though I met only two men below thirty who rejected *filmī* music outright, but this did not mean that they could transfer a more general aesthetic standard to other genres; a young woman who performed *bharata nāṭyam* with fair competence and who could sing one or two classical *rāgas* quite pleasantly, resented the suggestion that the polychromes of the multiarmed Jagadambā (World Mother) of Śiva, Kṛṣṇa, and Pandit Nehru did not improve the chaste beauty of the whitewashed walls inside her father's house.

A wealthy Patel merchant in Mwanza showed his guests the large, elaborate shrine which his wife had set up in honor of the God Puruṣottama (Viṣṇu); as everywhere the place was replete with large size polychromes and other reproductions of icons of very recent origin, all of them belonging to the same genre—the Ravi Varma[43] type of painting, mythologically correct, but aesthetically quite exasperating, both by modern critical standards and by those set in the Hindu tradition of icon making. When this was pointed out to the merchant, he made a remark that seemed to me quite cryptic at first: "It is our weakness that these *mūrtis* (icons) are ugly." His daughter had been studying art in Bombay, and she had admitted reluctantly that the icons in her father's house were poor art—but "I would never tell him that; why should I hurt my father who wants the best for me?" The connecting link between these two utterances should be sought in the culturally endemic separation of art form and art content: at first, no image of God could be "bad"; but then there could be bad *art*, whatever bad art consisted of; then comes a scholar who points out that bad art can also be used to fashion good Gods: that this was not seen before, and that the artists did not see that they were not doing a good job, that was "our weakness." The daughter knew intuitively that things were bad, aesthetically speaking, about the house; but the person who had given her the opportunity to *see* that things were bad, was her father; hence she must persist in accepting what she *knew* to be bad. The modern Indian apologist has this stance: we cannot say things that would hurt our elders, even if these things are true.

In all houses, photographs of the family members, dead

Crowding each other for wall space are Saint Chella Ram, other gods, a family photo and a diploma.

and alive, filled the walls and the mantlepieces. In the plush, large living room of a Panjabi merchant in Nairobi, there were no less than two large-size, framed pictures *each* of himself and his wife, in addition to a post-wedding picture taken many years earlier. Both of them were alive, and sat in the living room alone or in company, every day. A sugar merchant at Arusha, Tanzania, who had lived abroad for several years, had the following photographs lining his large living room: himself as a boy, himself and his wife at their wedding, after the wedding; alone in Britain with his wife disembarking from a BOAC jet; with his oldest son as a little boy; with his wife and his three sons, the oldest now a boy of about eleven. Questions about the reason for this multiplication of self-portraits were absorbed with some astonishment, "When we look at these pictures, we are glad that we are here, and we can think of the important days in our life"—or statements to this effect. One woman, a Panjabi Hindu of about thirty-five, said, referring to the numerous photographs of her in-

247

laws spread evenly over the spacious living-room, "I often told them: take these things away, you are cultured people." Though this was an atypical remark which went unheeded, it does seem to imply that there is a feeling of potential rebellion at times against these rustic excesses. No doubt Spratt's theory that the basic personality type of the Indian is narcissistic[44] would find some support here. The showing of the family and marriage album with badly-posed photos to one and all who come, has remained part of the compulsory and compulsive host-guest ritual, just as in middle-class urban India and Pakistan. Ritual dictates how people pose for any amateur shot. Many men have the most expensive Japanese and German cameras (they travel to Aden, a free port where the Leica and the Canon cost one-third less than in the countries of their manufacture). Still, the suggestion that one might take pictures of people in action or any candid shot is not only unacceptable, it fills the amateur photographer with indignation. Group photos are taken on many occasions, and everyone stands and sits at his assigned place, a redundant discipline from a time when lenses were weak and long exposures necessary. In the scores of family albums one has to survey in Asian houses, there is no such thing as a candid shot, except perhaps of a baby in its carriage.

Sartorial matters have been touched on in a previous chapter, but there is place for another look at them, as reflecting Asian aesthetics. Asian women are the best dressed in Africa; grudgingly or admiringly, Africans and whites will admit this. The elegant, never gaudy *sārīs* of the Panjabi women (whose sisters in India tend to overdress), and the simple elegance of less ascetic Gujarati women—female attire is sheer delight to anthropologist and laymen alike. Ismaili women and Goan women dress in western styles. Male dress, however, presents a crass contrast. The conservative Gujarati, as well as some *"chotī jāt"* people and some *fundi* wear Indian garments—*dhotī* or *pajāmā*, and a shirt over them. Businessmen wear suits and ties. The suggestion that British tailoring, heavy suits, boots, and especially neckties are a silly remnant of bygone times and ought to be discarded both from a modern viewpoint and for comfort in a tropical land, was rejected by most men. "You have to wear coat and tie if you want to make business," said a Panjabi food-importer, "if you dress like a *fundi* (artisan) or like an American tourist or run around naked, no one will want to make business with you." "It is ugly for a man to go without coat and tie. We want to look decent, like decent people," said another. When I pointed out to a group of merchants at a sundowner that all this sartorial anachronism was a remnant of the British *Rāj*, both in South Asia and here, one of them nodded assent and said, "Yes, we are under British influence," and left it at that.

At Kampala, I left my host's hospitable house one evening to attend a Hindu ceremony in town; I had my monastic garb on. My host's daughters were sitting on the verandah and shrieked with laughter when they saw me get into the host's Mercedes 300. "Why aren't you dressed decently?" the oldest of them exclaimed; "what is the meaning of running around like this?" "Decently," of course, meant English style— suit and shoes and tie. These girls vaguely knew about the robe of the Indian monastic, but they obviously couldn't square this memory with the image of a modern man. "Photos" of Saint Chella Ram,[45] Swami Dayānanda, and others in ochre vestments were hanging all over the house; but a modern man who spoke English could not possibly wear those things—they were *not* decent. There is a big difference here between upper middle class Hindu girls in East Africa and their collaterals in India, where the Hindu Renaissance has been sufficiently pervasive to permit wider eidetic tolerance—it is no longer thinkable that Hindu city girls in India would take objection to a monk's wearing his robe, regardless of whether or not he spoke English and wore a watch. In fact, the numerous successful swamis in India bear witness to their acceptance as modern men, compatible with traditional demeanor. Some of the Asian girls were quite orthodox in their ritualistic behavior, participating in many of the domestic rituals, possibly more diffusely than among their Indian collaterals. We have here, once again, an interesting example of selective opting for some cultural traits: an identical situation—sartorial in this case—evokes mutually incompatible responses in very similar audiences on both sides of the Indian Ocean. If Indians and East African Asians were to be analyzed as one contiguous society, anthropologists might well refer to this as a case of cultural lag. At the time when the Asian's grandparents settled in East Africa, there were indeed no "holy men" who rode in cars, spoke English, and listened to the BBC. At that time, the role and the image of the ascetic was far less complex than in later years on the sub-continent. Since the information which the young Asians have in matters of religious tradition has not been modified and amended in the African domicile, they share their grandparents' image of the practitioners of traditional things.

At Tanga, a group of Asians invited me to attend a music *baithak* at the home of an Ismaili. A *baithak* is quite literally a "session," a soirée, and for about three hours, three or four persons, one woman among them, sang and played classical and semi-classical North Indian music passably well; this was preceeded by an exquisite hot chicken dinner; the Ismaili ladies in the house wore western dress, but they knew no English, and very little Urdu. The performance was satisfying, and I learnt that there were indeed some very small groups of music-lovers in various cities, though in no way organized; in each location, they clustered around a person or persons who provided the home and the atmosphere, or the participants rotated from house to house, with about a session per week. The instruments used were the one-hand harmonium (*bājā*), and a *tablā* (two-part finger drum); the *bājā* is not a classical instrument, but the *tablā* is, and the songs performed belonged to the *ghazal* and *thumṛī* genre, styled "light classical" in the programs of All-India-Radio today.

Unfortunately, these small groups are quite atypical. There are no Asians who do not like music; but "music" means Indian film music, which is a hodgepodge of some basic *rāgas* or traditional mode-types, mixed with elements of Viennese waltz, Dixieland, Indian folksong, and Prussian military march, to isolate just a few components. Once in a while, a *filmī* tune is really quite lovely, but from among roughly a hundred hit-parade tunes produced in Hindi movies every year no more than half a dozen would satisfy any sophisticated musical standard in India. Of course, *filmī* music is the joy of the masses and of the lowbrow urban dwellers as well; but again, in India today there is a fast growing number of people who have taken to active and passive participation in classical music—"classical," incidentally, in the Indian context, is not an historical term like in western music; it is a synchronic designation for music composed and performed in the perennial *rāga*-tradition of India. In East Africa, there does not seem to be any parallel development. Obviously, the Asian settlers could afford to buy indigenous Indian culture, and the best of it. But so far, music-teachers and classical performers have not been invited to stay in East Africa. There were one or two excellent religious musicians touring the region during 1964, but their genuine musical skills were incidental to the religious purpose of the invitation. In all houses, rich and poor, there lurks a phonograph, and many many H.M.V. and Columbia 78 rpm shellacs made in Dum Dum, India. I browsed through well over a hundred collections in all the three countries, and found a total of ten classical or semi-classical records at various places; the rest were *filmī,* and it is this style that is largely identified with music to listen to.

On several festive occasions, Gujarati girls and boys, pupils at the various schools and some young adults, performed delightful folk dances—especially the Gujarati *garbhā* and *rās,* for such illustrious audiences as the joint diplomatic corps and the dignitaries of the big cities; they wore gorgeous silks, and the dances, albeit easy, were beautifully performed. But only about four girls in East Africa had studied some *bharata nātyam* or any of the modern compromises with the classical dance form of India. Again, this points to the suggested transmaritime cultural lag: comparable social groups

251

in India have now begun to let their daughters learn classical dance—and what used to be looked down upon as a thing a girl of good family should not do, viz., dancing and singing, is being increasingly encouraged in urban middle class society of India—due perhaps to the salutary effect Rabindranath Tagore has had on the resuscitation of the traditional arts and

Gujarati girls dance the *garbhā* to entertain ambassadors and high commissioners in Kampala, Uganda.

the concomitant creation of respect and regard for artists. There was a South Indian dance instructor at Nairobi, and he had an excellent disciple, a Panjabi Hindu girl born in that city. But he had to look for additional income very soon, as his initial expectations of finding a wealthy, keen audience that would rally to support and engage a harbinger of India's artistic traditions and skills were shattered in less than a year.

Now a good percentage of the wealthier adolescents, boys and girls, are both admirers and performers of such alien imports as the Twist, the Frug, and Rock 'n Roll: it takes an American choreographic creation less than a year to get firmly established in East Africa. These are tolerated by the elders. Paradoxically, it appeared as though the Twist and similar dance forms, as well as jazz and Indian *filmī* music, caused less anxiety among the conservative and the parent generation in East Africa than the potential pursuit of classical Indian dance and music. In trying to elicit some response about this lack of culture import, I suggested that culture had to be bought, and could be bought, by the wealthier Asians. Though this was admitted, there were afterthoughts: "we do not want that our daughters should dance and sing like professional musicians; if we did, who would marry them? No one wants to marry an artist." Translated into culturally explanatory language, the statement means something like this: in India, the professional singers and dancers were the *bāijī* (prostitute-singers and dancers) and the *barwā* (music and dance instructors and procurers) throughout the centuries since Muslim rule. The South Indian *bhāgavatar* and the *devadāsī* had direct ritualistic significance, but the Asians of East Africa know nothing about it, there being no South Indians among them. Hence, any woman who sings might be likened to a *bāijī,* and of course, nobody marries a *bāijī.* A young Panjabi woman complained that her parents found it almost impossible to find a suitable husband for her because she was thought to be a "club-type," i.e., a girl who likes social dance and gatherings of peers of both sexes; now she was too old— twenty-one to be exact—to get married to the right man and she thought she would have to "make her own arrangements," go to India and look for a husband among the senior student or professional groups in Delhi, or embark on some journalistic or teaching career.

I pointed out that the elders do not really object to the Twist, Frug, and Rock 'n Roll, etc., and there is good reason for this: these transatlantic imports have no cultural connotation one way or the other, for the conservative Asians. They are culturally neutral, whereas classical Indian music and classical Indian dance are not. Indian *filmi* music is all right, and there is nothing wrong with a daughter singing film tunes; nor, of course, with her dancing the *garbhā* or *rās* with other Gujarati girls or boys in a group, at festive occasions under the watchful eyes of the elders. Twist, Frug etc. belong to the same gestalt; though they may be frowned upon as too fast, too joyous and immodest, they are tolerated; *Bharata nātyam* or *kathak*, i.e., the traditional Indian dance forms are not, because of their concatenation with the *bāijī* and the *barwā* as culturally known, undesirable agents.

There may be an even subtler implication in the neutrality of the elders' feelings about modern dance and *filmī* music. A Sikh farmer in Eldoret, who had bought a 3,000-acre wheat farm from a departing white South African, was doing an impressive job as a true rancher. His thirteen-year old daughter went to the Duke of Gloucester School in Nairobi, the most fashionable, elegant, and expensive of all girls' schools. She too learnt modern dance, Twist and all, as part of social dance curriculum. She did not want to learn any Indian dance, although there was an option to learn it through the school's auspices. Both her parents agreed that there was nothing wrong with modern social dance, although the mother, a simple, barely literate Sikh woman, confided that she just did not understand the meaning of modern dance. During a pleasant post-dinner talk on that lovely farm, the father suggested that it might be good to let the girl learn classical Indian dance; for this, he had heard, was now being done among good people in India. But the mother strongly ob-

254

jected to it. When I asked her why she would rather let her daughter dance modern American dances, and didn't she think they were considerably more daring than the Indian dances, she shook her head and said "with these *pardesī nāc* (foreign dance), it's just movement, and no one knows what it is all about; but Indian dances show bad things, Rādhā and Kṛṣṇa making love. . . ." This statement was highly revealing and should add grist to our theoretical mills.

When I criticized the poverty of *filmī* music at a tea-party given by some Asian school teachers at Mbeya, Tanzania, they got quite excited and said "You do not understand our Indian culture; you cannot appreciate our music." I then proceeded to illustrate *bhūpāli*, a classical North Indian pentatonic *rāga*, and one of them said "This is good music, too, but one can't go on attaching one's heart to these old-fashioned things; Indians must be modern. Film is good for them." And on went the talk about love and women and true romantic feelings; none of these men were under thirty, all were married and had numerous children, and all derived their knowledge about male-female relationships and the importance of romantic love exclusively from the Hindi movies; whether Nutan, the film actress, really wants wealth and a car and lovers, as the film magazine hinted, or whether she did not really represent her true self as in the movie *X* the other night—such speculation gave profound concern to the teachers, some of whom had taken their master's in English literature from an Indian university.

Again, the rule underlying these utterances is quite simple to state: in a literate society, where the father arranges for the marriage, no actual choice for autonomous courtship is left to the young men and the women. Hence when it comes to talking about male-female relationships, the source of reference cannot be any actual experience of the young people who never courted, but their clandestine ego-ideal internalizations from the screen; and most of the hundreds of novels that litter newsstands in India, and that are shipped to East Africa, are written versions of film plots, not the other way around.

My hosts at Nairobi took me to *Saṅgam,* a four hour long Hindi color movie, with the famous Raj Kapoor and the charming dancer-actress Vijayantimala in the main roles. This was the movie where the first perfunctory kissing occurred on the screen; in thousands of movies previous to *Saṅgam,* kissing was out, as the Board of Censors in India would not stand for it.[46] American and other foreign movies are hardly ever censored, and one has the feeling that the Board does not object to foreigners doing wicked things, if only to show their audiences how much purer the Indian movies are in spite of an equal amount of feminine loveliness spread before them. *Saṅgam* was the talk of the towns, in India and East Africa, for over a year; its numerous songs, some of them quite delightful though none too highbrow, were being sold on the inevitable 78 rpm shellac labels, sung and whistled not only by Asians but also by African men who like Indian movies. Part of the movie was shot in Europe, with schmaltzy love and despair scenes, mixed with an unusual degree of patriotism, the Sino-Indian conflict providing the thematic jumping board for the plot and the hero, Raj Kapur, wouldn't you know it, acting as an ace-pilot in the Indian Air Force. In addition to the unequivocal display of patriotic feelings and songs, there was quite a bit of Hindu mythology and even some Hindu metaphysics, with hints at metempsychosis, diffusely present in the unending movie.

As my hosts and I arrived at the theater, there was a long queue around the building. There are first and second-class seats in Indian and East African movie theaters. My host got in line and waited for about forty-five minutes to get to the box office; then he came over to us and announced with disappointment, that all first-class seats had been sold out. Why hadn't he bought second-class tickets, then, I demanded? My host was aghast: How could I or he and his wife sit downstairs with those rotten people? "They are procurers and pimps (*sic*—I didn't have the heart to ask the difference) they would insult you by soliciting for their horrible women." I saw the movie alone, second class, the same evening—unfortunately, nobody insulted me, nor do I think there were many procurers and pimps at that particular performance. Most of the people around me were students, bank clerks, etc., though there were no women. The notion that the front rows in a "cinema" are populated by the denizens of a meretricious inferno is an unchecked take-over from India where, in the purely non-western theaters at least, there is indeed a constant percentage of members of the second-oldest profession in the audience, in the first ten rows from the screen. But not in East Africa; here, an Indian situation has been diffused to Africa as a myth of form, with no content.

Let me align some aspects of Asian conservatism with the aesthetical perception of the people as outlined in this chapter. So long as the conservative elements in the household, joint or nuclear, control the purse strings, the "moderner" inside the fold cannot cathect any but the most superficial, marginal elements of modern life as it surrounds him. This is most evident in the men's judgments about beauty, both in the arts, and with reference to physical attractiveness. As in India, the ultimate criterion for beauty in the human face is the lack of pigment—less pigment, more beauty, more pigment, less beauty, and the "black" is the radically ugly. But again, in a society where the father decides the son's marriage and where there is no scope for individual courtship, just occasional fornication with prostitutes or with women well beneath the man's social status where no courtship and little aesthetic judgment are required, and where the contact is made on the sneak, there can hardly be any graded appreciation of the female physiognomy. The simplistic standards which do not extend beyond the "fair = attractive, dark = ugly" identification cannot be broken so long as the choice of the mate is not consequent upon individual assessment in which the aesthetic must play a part.

Mr. V. a banker in Arusha, had been living in his large, depressing, shabby ancestral house and could not be persuaded to move to something more pleasant—which he could very well have afforded—for fear of "leaving his luck behind."

257

"He has become rich in that house," a friend of his confided, "and he believes that if he ever leaves the house and builds himself a new mansion like his younger, more modern brothers, luck will leave him." There is a barely visible chain between these two themes: in his ego-image, the conservative Asian refuses to undertake any move away from the conservative pattern if that means risking the one thing that counts: wealth acquired, augmented, and held over two or three generations. In his alter-image, and particularly in the transference of a traditional conceptual nexus, we find thriftiness, rejection of aesthetic improvement and fear of annoying the powers that gave wealth at a particular location. The power-devolving actor is the eldest brother, head of a one-time joint household. We witness that the conservative scheme of things still regulates Asian life in East Africa.

The Asians' view of their cultural homeland is complex. The image of India and Pakistan, as political and cultural bodies, as well as prospective havens of refuge in case of dire emergency, has undergone drastic changes within the past few decades. Apart from the Ismailis there is hardly an Asian who does not regard the subcontinent as his spiritual point of reference, regardless of whether he has been born there or whether he is a member of the third Asian generation in East Africa. This, of course, is quite radically different from, say, Irish settlers in the United States, or even from Indian settlers in Guiana or Trinidad.[47] More than in any other region of the world where Indians have permanently settled, the East African Asians have preserved their native languages, Gujarati or Panjabi, with a considerable knowledge of Urdu among Panjabi speakers. Books and magazines in these Indian vernaculars are read at least as much as English-language publications; and dozens of periodicals as well as some books and a considerable number of monographs relating to the Asian settlers themselves, are being published in Gujarati in East Africa. Before embarking on my field trip, I had assumed that the ritualistic link provided by Sanskrit for the Hindu life cycle and other ritual and, for the Ismailis, the use of

258

Gujarati for their common prayers, would account for a cultural orientation toward the subcontinent, at least among the more traditionally oriented people. This, however, proved to be dubious: there is no real interest in Sanskrit, and its use in Hindu ritual is tolerated with the same sort of impatience with which lay Hindus in India, even the pious among them, view the *pandits'* long incantations at home. However, the intensive use of the modern vernacular was a point to be reckoned with. Now, as Gujarati will no longer be taught in the public schools, this may change; but then it may not, as witness the fact that Panjabi was spoken in East Africa in spite of there having been no official instruction in that language or even in Hindi-Urdu, in Asian schools previous to *uhuru*. Panjabis all over the world, of course, have a specifically strong attraction to their speech-form, in spite of the fact that they do not hesitate to call it rustic, literarily poorer than Urdu which has always been the language of sophistication among them; but all Panjabis will tell the professional linguist that Panjabi cannot be learned the way the Panjabis speak it, unless you happen to be born there. This claim is not proferred for Urdu or Gujarati.

Of all the Asians who claim that they consider themselves African, the Ismailis' claim is to be taken literally. Short of intermarriage with Africans, there is no area of potential cultural and social interchange which they would not in principle adopt toward the African hosts. There are two opinions about the modal reaction of the Africans toward the Ismailis: some observers hold that the Africans accept the Ismailis because they feel their African identification is sincere; others feel that African leaders tend to be particularly suspicious about the Ismailis precisely because they regard East Africa as their inalienable home which they will not leave, by their own religious decree. Whatever the case, we can maintain safely that this community does not regard India or Pakistan with any kind of overt or covert nostalgia, nor with the sort of novel love-hate emotion other sections of the Asian population now display.

The politicians of both India and Pakistan have made it abundantly clear that they will not carry any brief on behalf of the Asian settlers. During the independence celebrations of various countries around Africa, top-level Indian and Pakistani statesmen passed through the East African capitals addressing, somewhat reluctantly, large crowds of Asian settlers. In each case, they left no doubt in the minds of their audiences that their governments considered the settlers as East Africans; they advised them to take out East African citizenship, and to "integrate" completely. These pious admonitions have been gravely resented by the Asians, and there were many harsh words directed toward the dais when an Indian minister suggested intermarriage with Africans. "You are dark and ugly yourself, madam," an Asian heckler called out from the audience; "why don't you go and marry an African?" When I discussed the settlers' feelings about such and similar unsolicited nonchalant exhortations on the part of Indian and Pakistani leaders with a high-ranking Indian administrator serving in Africa, he frowned and said "so the Asians here are angry with her, because she said the truth?" The truth, however, is that the Asian settlers, at least the more vocal among them, know pretty well what integration may mean, and what it ought to mean for themselves, and for the Africans; they are not ready to take counsel from outsiders. "Panditji is a great man," an Asian woman mused a few months before Mr. Nehru's death, "He has done too much ("too much" is Indian English for "very much, a good deal") for India and the Indians; but for us he has done nothing. For us here, he is useless. The Indian politicians who come here are hopeless, too."

There is quite a simple test to prove the fundamentally negative feelings of the Asians toward the governments of India and Pakistan. The two High Commissioners and their staff attend all the major functions of the Asian community; Asian businessmen like to invite them to their sons' and daughters' weddings, schools like to have the High Commissioner put in an appearance at such events as folk dances and convocations, where they are invariably required and requested to distribute prizes to the pupils. But the High Commissioner's personnel are never regarded as belonging to the community in any cultural operative sense. True, people are cognitively aware that the Indian and Pakistani politicians and public administrators are part of their own culture; and they also feel that these people ought to share with the settlers more than just formal events. The situation is particularly delicate if personnel at the High Commission happen to be Gujarati or Panjabi rather than native speakers of Hindi or other Indian languages. Settlers belonging to any of the small linguistic groups—Maharashtrians, Sindhis, etc.—find it hard enough to be accepted as local Asians; but Indian and Pakistani persons temporarily residing in East Africa reported that their relations to individuals and families from among the settlers were more difficult if they happened to speak Gujarati or Panjabi as their mother-tongue. But, then, the governments of India and Pakistan cannot really encourage any greater intimacy between their personnel and the Asian citizens or residents of East Africa, than, say, with Africans or Europeans, the Asian settlement being incidental in the diplomatic sense. Since High Commission personnel must identify with the statements and the policies of their governments, and since the official policies of these two governments vis-a-vis the Asian settlers is not to the latters' liking, High Commission personnel are viewed with misgivings and kept at bay, except for formal occasions.

Obviously, attitudes toward the cultural homeland are emotionally loaded. From the economic angle the two countries are pitied and feared: they are poor, the living standard is incomparably lower than that in East Africa; not only do the Asians, whose standards are estimated to be about three times higher than those of comparable communities in India and Pakistan, know that their kin across the Indian Ocean cannot even dream to afford the relative luxury they themselves enjoy; even the indigenous African poor are better off than the poor in India—a fact that is known to Asians and Africans alike.

Thus, in economic and technological matters, the land

of the forbears is poor and pitiable—feared if there is the prospect that one might have to relocate oneself there in case things do not work out in Africa. Many have moved to the two countries, and their reports are not happy ones.

Contrary to the facts, all but the best informed Asians entertain the notion that primary and secondary education in India and Pakistan lag behind that in East Africa. They are aware that there are universities in the old countries, and that there is increasing college education. But modally speaking, this does not really concern most of the Asians, as the college-oriented among them are a small fragment. The not-too-wealthy middle class, and quite a number of the more affluent, have begun to send their sons and daughters—the latter much less frequently—to India for college education; the affluent prefer to send them "abroad" which means to Europe or America—the term "abroad" is not usually used for India and Pakistan.

A school teacher was hired from India for a period of three years to teach at a high school at Jinja, Uganda. "When I first came," he said, "everybody thought I was coming from a land of *budhus* (rustic yokels), that there was no good schooling in India. Now I have convinced them that this is not so, and that people at home are far more educated and cultured than people here." If this is really what the Jinja Asians had said to the young teacher, it must have been the expression of an ambivalent feeling—for school teachers like this one are regularly hired from India, on a temporary basis, as are the Brahmin priests and assistants to the local Brahmin specialists.

In matters of traditional and moral culture, of course, the Hindus look to India for their inspiration. The religiously *engagé* try to perform a pilgrimage to India to see the great shrines of the North at least once in a lifetime. Hīrjī Bābā, (see the chapter on Religion) collected over a hundred Gujarati pilgrims to charter space on a boat to conduct an extensive pilgrimage to some shrines in India. The young, however, do not seem to share the desire for pilgrimages. I have not met a single man or woman under twenty-five who wanted to go on a pilgrimage to India. Modern people, i.e., those who do not profess any traditional or religious interest or commitment, would like to go to India—not to travel through the country, but to visit relatives and to see the big cities—Delhi, Bombay, perhaps Amritsar. There is no desire at all to see regions where there is no kin. The large tracts of India from which there have been no emigration or indenture to East Africa—Uttar Pradesh, Bihar, Bengal, and particularly the South, might as well not exist except for the more adventurous who might like to see Calcutta because it is said to be a big, swinging city. My suggestion that those who could afford to travel to India would do well to see the marvellous religious and secular edifices of the land was rejected with some disgust: "We want to see Bombay, Delhi, yes, and Calcutta, and the Taj Mahal in Agra. But the old cities are dirty. We do not like Banaras and those 'holy cities'—they are dirty and unhealthy. They are full of frauds. We want to see new things." This attitude, of course, is well known to perceptive tourists, Peace Corps volunteers, and other serious travellers to India. City people, even university teachers, dissuade the keen traveller from seeing Banaras, Hardvar, Rameshvaram, and the other places of historical and aesthetic importance. "You must see the Bhakra Nangal Dam," Panjabis will tell you; "The Damodar Valley Project is worthwhile," some will suggest.[48] India wants to be known as a modern country by its not-too-sophisticated urbanites; this attitude is shared by those in East Africa who have traveled to India, except for those who had some religious interest.

This does not mean that Indian contemporary culture does not diffuse to East Africa. The very opposite is true—in fact, there is nothing in the private and public doings of the settlers, that could not also occur in India or Pakistan today, without the slightest modification, except in the sense that many activities would not be accompanied by the same display of technological advancement and automation: fewer men and scarcely any women in Indian and Pakistani cities drive cars, and Asians in East Africa use a multitude of electric gadgets about the house which are simply unknown to their kindred on the subcontinent. But this is a trivial difference, so long as the contents of cultural behavior and activity are identical. To this author, this is one of the most fascinating aspects of East African Asian society—for the entire cultural interaction, the total complex of cognitive, conative, volitional, and affective behavior, has been transplanted from South Asia to the Asians in East Africa. Or to put it more bluntly, the Asians have brought all these things along with them and have not altered them in any significant manner. Whatever is appreciated in India and Pakistan, relating to the human frame, literature, movies, the ego-image and the alter-image, all the cultural things which are being discussed in this study are seen and reacted to just exactly as they are in the old country. More poignantly, things that are disliked and rejected in the old country, are disliked and rejected in East Africa: the Satyajit Ray trilogy (*Pāther Pāñcali, Aparājita,* and *The World of Apu*), which was ignored and scorned in India previous to its phenomenal success in Europe and America, was ignored by the Asians when it was presented in East Africa for a brief period. When these movies became famous abroad, a section of Indian movie-goers began, reluctantly as it were, to see and declare some merit in these movies; then quite recently, when they were rerun in Nairobi and Kampala, a small section of Asians lauded them with the same reserve as did the more numerous converts in India. Dark complexion in India and Pakistan means ugliness and implies low-caste origin; dark complexion elicits precisely the same response from the Asians in East Africa, and *a fortiori,* this institutionalized aesthetical sentiment pattern extends to cover the Africans.

I would estimate that the next five decades will bring about a radical change toward an overall situation in which the conservative elements will no longer set the rules which the young must circumvent with reluctance and embarrassment. At this moment, the conservative element still dominates in all fields, social, religious, and economic, and most importantly, in the sphere of ideology.

CHAPTER SEVEN

Religion and
the Supernatural

One of the most delicate problems in the study of Indian society relates to the fact that many of my prospective readers are Indian and are gravely concerned about their image abroad. Modern sophisticates from the Indo-Pakistani sub-continent do not readily appreciate the anthropological table of contents. They might object to the emphasis placed on the study of religion in modern Asian society. The oft-quoted "Great Tradition-Little Tradition" dichotomy is obviously an outsider's crutch. Few people would appreciate a large section of their countrymen's activities being referred to as "Little Tradition" activities, where "Little Tradition" might seem to imply relative inferiority. The terminology goes back to Robert Redfield,[1] the renowned British scholar and preceptor of some of the most famous anthropologists of today, including some Indian writers. I have made an exhaustive statement about "Great Tradition-Little Tradition" usage elsewhere,[2] but since the terms have been used throughout this book, I think it is appropriate at this point to state the idea in out-line. The conceptual basis for this somewhat jargonistic dichotomy is really quite simple: in literate societies, particu-larly where there is an old ecclesiastic tradition, there are two concurrent types of religious behaviour, partly overlapping, and partly contradicting each other. The "Great Tradition" is based in the cities, the shrines, the temples, and in the canonical and exegetical literature. Its spokesmen are priests, doctors, monks, learned and not so learned. Their religion is normative—they tell the people how they should behave and believe, ideally. In the villages, however, we find a very different picture. Though the villagers, or other people inhabiting areas remote from the "Great Tradition" centers, are vaguely familiar with the official doctrines, they have their own religious, parochial cults and ideas; village curers, shamans, and other part-time religious or magical practitioners are the agents of these "Little Traditions." The Latin countries provide excellent examples: neighboring villages, in Southern Italy have their "separate" madonnas, with their separate, parochial types of worship and propitiation. The priests, agents of the "Great Tradition," may or may not remind the villagers that there is only one madonna—to the villagers, the local saints, madonnas, holy spots, etc. are in a way more important, since they are closer at hand than the Vatican. In the case of India and Asian East Africa, the analogy should be quite clear at this point—we have "Great Tradition" Hinduism and Islam—the Veda, the high-ritual of marriage, the worship in the temples, the Quran, the Mosque, the *Jamātkhāna*—these are "Great Tradition" institutions; but we also have sorcery, localized methods of diagnosis and therapy, possession, divination—these are things of the "Little Traditions." It is almost impossible to convince the modern Asian that the anthropologists' use of such terms is *not* derogatory in any sense; the contrary assertion that "primitive," "Little Tradition," etc., are, if anything, commendatory terms to many anthropologists, will hardly improve the situation. Nobody wants to be "primitive," nobody wants to belong to a "Little Tradition," when there is a "Great Tradition" in one's society. The fact that a proliferating polytheism, polydemonism, and an intensively particularized ritual have great aesthetic charm, and that they reinforce powerful grass roots, thus serving as an antidote against alienation, means absolutely nothing to the modern Indian who wants to be a chemical engineer or a politician, and wants his society to be viewed as one of potential engineers and statesmen. That such things as sorcery, divination, witchcraft, etc., should be mentioned at all in a book about an Indian community, is highly offensive to a modern Indian audience. However, there is hardly any remedy for this. The anthropologist's job is to report on human cultures, not to disguise those elements in it which happen to displease its subjects. Super-chauvinistic new-nation governments may stop issuing visas to social scientists who want to study subjects which are no longer "modern," but that does not diminish the importance of those topics. Indians feel the subtle distinction between doctrinaire religion and the marginal elements of supernaturalism. The Asian tailor or cobbler in Dar-es-Salaam knows quite well that the spells and the pills which some local expert in supernatural matters hands to a member of the community with the hope of remedying some physical, mental, or economic ailment have nothing to do with the Hinduism of the *Bhagavadgītā* or with the sermons of itinerant *sādhus* who come from India from time to time. But he is also aware of the fact that these things are not necessarily incompatible with the behests of the nobler doctrines which he imbibes from a very early age. In the case of Hinduism, there is a built-in propulsion toward compatibility: what anthropologists would class as "Little Tradition" elements, are seen by the Hindu as a lower manifestation of the central doctrines. Magic, healing, sorcery, etc., cut across denominational and secular lines, in East Africa just as on the sub-continent. We shall here analyze East African-Asian religion by matching it against its predominant "Great Tradition" suppositions.

Hinduism

The great majority of the East African Asians are Hindus. The distinctions between Hinduism, Jainism, and Sikhism, which have been blurred or stressed, as the case may be, in different social and political settings on the subcontinent, are brought out more clearly in the East African milieu. Facing the outsider, the East African Hindu would refer to himself and his kin as "Hindus," regardless of whether he belongs to a Panjabi or any other Indian language-speaking group in East Africa. He might also include Jains as "Hindus" when talking to a non-Asian. But within the Asian community, Hindus hardly refer to themselves as just that; they would qualify the term either by using a caste-group name which automatically classifies them as Hindus for any Asian audience, or they would specify their particular type of Hinduism by a linguistic, regional, or sectarian reference. The difference between Gujarati and Panjabi Hinduism is quite radical from any analytic viewpoint. Gujarati Hinduism and Jainism are much closer to each other in style than Gujarati and Panjabi Hinduism. In India, this never became quite so apparent, because large Gujarati and Panjabi Hindu communities hardly ever live together in a single region—except perhaps in metropolitan areas like Delhi or Bombay, where they do not interact as exclusive co-respondents in social and economic contexts. In East Africa, they all face each other in a constant and exclusive symbiosis. There is very little actual religious participation between the Gujarati and Panjabi Hindus in East Africa, and the sectarian identification of the Hindus in all the three countries is quite delicate and different from that in India. The most obvious fact is that Gujarati Hindus do not take Panjabi Hinduism seriously. When the expatriate Gujarati Hindu speaks about "Hindus" to another Gujarati speaker, Hindu *or* other, he means Gujarati Hindus *only,* and does not include Panjabi or other Hindus, unless he is prompted to include them in guided discourse. Checking this experimentally, we found that all Gujarati respondents corrected themselves so as to include Panjabi and other Hindus when told that they also shared the Hindu ritual and the Hindu traditions. But the fact remains that the unconscious identification of most Hindus in East Africa is that of Gujarati Hindus exclusively.

One could of course adduce all sorts of reasons why this

intra-religious exclusiveness is prevalent in East Africa. Gujaratis take Hindu ritual far more seriously and practice it far more intensively on all levels than the Panjabi Hindus in East Africa. Even in India itself, Gujarati worship is intensive, occupying much of the spare time, whereas Panjabi Hinduism is a happy-go-lucky affair, unless there are specially vested interests in religious activities as in the case of the Ārya Samāj, to be discussed in greater detail further down.

On the other hand, the worldlier Panjabis—and they are the unquestionable majority in that group of settlers—tend to be somewhat contemptuous about the ritualization of Gujarati Hinduism, and those Panjabis who are aware of the tremendous involvement of the many Gujarati Hindus in religious cult and its domestic ramifications, will regard these rituals as outmoded and out of step with the needs of the time, incongruous with the daily life of the same Gujarati businessman, who to the Panjabi is a money-grabbing, egotistical merchant. If the critical Panjabi happens to belong to the Ārya Samāj, he will tend to regard Gujarati religious practice as basically irreligious or "superstitious," much in the manner in which the fundamentalist Protestant in the western world tends to regard the Catholic as basically irreligious *because* of his ritualistic involvement. The analogy could be pressed even further—just as the fundamentalist, unsophisticated Protestant tends to identify Catholicism with blind sacerdotalism, the Ārya Samāji, as well as the noncommitted Panjabi Hindu in East Africa, tend to regard much of Gujarati Hinduism as superstitious traditionalism. The hired religious specialist, the Brahmin *purohit* who consecrates marriages and performs other official rites is not necessarily the key figure in the alleged sacerdotalism. There are the *sādhus* and other visiting "holy men" and there is the charisma attaching to a person who is reported to have had some special vision or some specific contact with the deity.[3] Not that Panjabis would normally refuse to listen to a "holy man"—but if they do listen, the men would say they were listening reluctantly, and to please their conservative, pious elders and their womenfolk.

The Gujarati merchant is thought to act woman-like in these matters: he goes all out to serve and to humiliate himself before the alleged "holy man" and before religious charismatic leaders within his society and from India. As we shall see, there is some justification for the religious alter-image the Panjabi Hindus entertain about their Gujarati fellows. Most Muslims and Goans reject Hinduism per se, and more than their more universalistic and more tolerant urban kindred in India, they regard it as unholy, as undignified, and as barely disguised idolatry and polytheism. None of them would know, or care to know, the fundamental differences between Panjabi and Gujarati Hindu practice. I tried to test if there was any knowledge about these differences; but each time the reaction among non-Hindus was one of withdrawal and of embarrassed non-interest. The most that western-oriented non-Hindu Asians would say by way of a positive appraisal of Hinduism, was that "all religions are the same" and "they also worship God in their own way," generalities hailing from the cultural noncommitment so well entrenched in India by the teachings of the Hindu Renaissance.[4]

Let us then turn to the all-over doctrines of East African Hinduism. The notions that are shared by all Hindus—which would include Sikhs, but not Jains—are "Great Tradition" notions. One aspect of "Great Tradition" modern Hinduism is its vagueness and de-emphasis on theological particular.

There is a fine distinction, however, between modern Judaeo-Christians in the western world and their Protestant-inspired aversion to theology, and the East African Indians' dislike for systematic Hindu theology. While the occidental Protestant has learned the axiom that words and rituals are vain and that active piety or faith are the things that count in the face of God, the East African Hindus' dislike for theology is a direct heritage of the Hindu Renaissance, which rejects theology and ritual which were inextricably merged in classical Hinduism. They were the domain of specialists; such specialists are either not present in East Africa, or their number is negligible. To put it more drastically—whereas the mod-

ern Protestant rejects the theologian as a man of words rather
than of faith or action, the East African Hindu rejects the
sādhu and the priest (*purohit*) because they are either thought
to be fraudulent or to utilize their special sacerdotal skill for
self-aggrandizement. Switching eras for a comparison, I would
think that the average East African Hindu's feelings about
the sacerdotal specialists is comparable to the early reforma-
tion's feelings about the lower levels of the Catholic ecclesiastic
hierarchy.

The articles of faith, if we may borrow this not too felicitous term from Christian homiletic, are rather simple for the
non-specialist East African Hindu: there is one God (*Īsvar,
Bhagavān*), who is the origin of the universe, and who mani-
fests himself in all living beings. Although Isvar is neither
male nor female, because he is essentially impersonal, he appears in many divine forms, some of which are male, others
female—i.e., the gods and goddesses of the Hindu pantheon.
With the exception of the Ārya Samājists and the Sikhs, to
whom we shall turn later, this is the basic theology, and it
does not differ in any substantial way from the average contemporary urban notions of popular theology on the subcontinent. It does, of course, differ enormously from the
Judaeo-Christian and Islamic concept: Īsvar is not a creator
god, as the concept of a historical creation is quite alien to
all schools of Hinduism, classical and modern. The responses
of the modern Hindu, when questioned by a non-Indian, must
not confuse us: the East African Hindu when speaking English
uses the terms he or his immediate forebears have heard from
Christian missionaries or from teachers who had been taught
by Christian missionaries in India. Thus, in any putative
Hindu-non-Hindu dialog about religious matters, the Hindu
will not reject the term "creator," unless the inapplicability
of the term for the Hindu concept of the deity is pointed out
to him. It may of course also be that he simply uses the term
loosely, to include notions of manifestation or emanation
which are an intrinsic part of Hindu theology.

The East African Hindu takes rebirth for granted, and

possibly more literally than his theologically more sophisticated kindred in India. His notions about the workings of rebirth as linked with the laws of karma or automatic retribution are quite vague, and from the "Great Tradition" viewpoint not quite correct. In the first place, East African Hindus assume that a human being could conceivably be reborn as an animal—whereas more sophisticated Hindu teaching denies this, the conventional doctrine being that an individual who has acquired merit sufficient to be born in human form would find it virtually impossible to fall back into the lower kingdoms of life.

The linking of moral and religious themes is as naive and natural to the East African Hindu as it is to his relatives in India. Whenever I asked middle class Hindus in the East African cities what they thought was the *purpose* of the Hindu religion, all but some people with committed interest in religious matters said that Hinduism teaches one to be good, and a good Hindu is he who leads a decent life in society, does not commit theft and adultery, does not take advantage of others in his business, worships God, and is not interested in cinema, drinking, gambling and women; or, to quote a recurrent phrase, Hinduism, when properly followed, makes a man desist from "bad habits"; in line with the Hindu Renaissance in India, "bad habits" include about all the things psychologists recommend. They are the simple deviations from the official moral norm, which is radically puritanical.

That classical Hinduism as theology is not primarily concerned with the good life, that it is a redemptive religion geared to asceticism and asocial behavior aimed at the cessation of rebirth, is known to specialists only, though it is vaguely apprehended by most Hindus, more so by the women who are exposed to the specialists.

The only statement that does indeed differ from any contemporary Judaeo-Christian view elicited by the casual-sounding interviewer who wants to get at radically divergent views, is that the Hindu declares a good, i.e., a religious man to be one who has *samādrsti*, i.e., who views all living beings alike, not because they are creatures of God, but because the same divine spirit is manifested through them. This must not be pressed too hard, and the interviewer must avoid mixing levels of elicitation: the notion of *samādṛṣṭi,* as a traditional Hindu theme, includes all living beings by definition. Just as with "all men are equal, though some are more equal," to quote occidental facetiousness, *samādṛṣṭi* does not in practice extend to all beings; for if the East African Hindu says that *samādṛṣṭi* should extend to non-Indians and Africans, this is a theological statement with very little pragmatic relevance. However, one stance is shared by all people with a South Asian cultural background, not only Hindu: this sort of ideological contradiction, which puzzles the outsider, does not bother the Asian speaker in the actual social context. He may believe in the merits of poverty and the sharing of all goods as he walks through lanes filled with massive poverty, and he may believe that he views all beings alike, and yet distance himself totally from the African or the American or the European. It would be wrong to label this as a double standard or ascribe it to poor memory. The reasons for this dichotomy are complex; succinctly—the logical and the social contexts are particularly unrelated in Indian culture. Insistence on their compatibility, or the extension of logical structuring to social themes, is a peculiarly Judaeo-Christian, or Greek-occidental, humanistic obsession; its universality is not apparent to the cultural anthropologist.

The East African Hindu's attitude toward other religions is that of his modern, English-speaking kindred in India: all religions lead to the same goal, all teach man to be moral, to be non-violent, to be kind to fellow-beings. He avers that differences in theology are unimportant. This goes so far as to cause embarrassment to most of those I interviewed: when they were told that Jainism, the religion of many of their business associates, denied the existence of God, they were puzzled. And Jain persons I spoke to were equally puzzled about the fact that their own teaching was atheistic—it did not seem to have occurred to them, somehow, that there was

273

a very crucial doctrinary distinction between Jainism and Hinduism, whose followers were culturally indistinguishable from each other. The more learned among my Jain informants would use a stratagem well established among modern educated Jains in India: they would say that although there was no notion of an Isvar or personal deity in the Hindu sense, the function of divinity was occupied by the Jain "pathmakers," the *tīrthaṅkaras*, i.e., the saints who found emancipation by their ascetic life throughout the long history of Jainism—and in fact they have been given the same epithets as Hindu divinity, viz. *Īsvar, Bhagavān,* etc. One of the reasons why this kind of information causes uneasiness among East African Jains and Hindus alike is that there is free and possibly even preferential intermarriage between Hindu and Jain *mārwārīs* and Gujarati speaking *banyās* in India. The two Jain communities in East Africa, as was shown in an earlier chapter, are somewhat atypical of the Jain groupings in the original setting; in India, people of *mārwārī* or *banyā* caste status intermarry, regardless of whether they are Hindus or Jains; in such inter-denominational alliances, married women carry on the ritual of their natal home—so that a Jain girl would continue to worship the Jain *tīrthaṅkaras* (founders) in her Hindu husband's house, giving additional ritualistic attention to the Hindu deities worshipped by her affines.

Though the more subtle elements of the doctrine of *karma* and rebirth are not present to individuals' minds, many events and situations in society are explained by quoting the doctrine perfunctorily. The question of whether *karma* is a genuinely impersonal force of reward and retribution, or whether it is an instrument of the divine, is as unsolved here as it is in India. But the average idea seems to be that God is somehow the regulator of *karma*; this is in tune with the more personalistic sects in India; the East African Hindus are ideologically much closer to these than to the more speculative, abstract schools of Hindu thought.

Views about the place of formal worship are disparate and ambiguous, but this sort of ambiguity is pretty well predictable: the influence of the Hindu Renaissance movements makes itself felt with the men more than with the women—the former tend to look down, or pretend to look down on ritualistic worship when done by men—however, they not only consent to their women's regular performance of *pūjā* (formal worship), but they seem to prompt them to perform some sort of ritual in their homes. The statement made to me by an artisan (*fundi*), a Gujarati low-caste man in Kampala, "It is good for our women to do the worship of the gods in our house, so that they do not become too modern and spoilt," represents a pervasive feeling about the prophylactic propriety of ritual for women.

Only a fraction of the male Gujarati Hindu population follows intense ritual, and this, as we shall presently see, occurs when people have come under the influence of some teacher or of some proselytizing sect. Once a man turns to "religion," he is well respected for it by his more mundane compeers—I have not noticed any sort of ridicule toward such persons even from those who flaunt their worldliness. No matter what form of religious innovation a member of the Gujarati Hindu groups may espouse, there is a preference for ritualized cults among the less modern, though by no means less affluent. The modern, westernized men who turn to religious interests, tend to seek out the more recent, anti-ritualistic cults—such as the Aurobindo movement, the Shivananda "Divine Life" Society, and other groups whose medium of propaganda is English rather than an Indian vernacular.

Once a person—or more usually, members of a nuclear family following their senior male—have turned their interest to one of the available forms of religious specialization, their theological world view becomes more elaborate, much less vague, and begins to fall in line with the preachings and writings of the founding institutions on the subcontinent. It is perhaps only in such situations that some interest in greater India emerges: for otherwise "India," to traveling Asians, is coextensive with those Gujarati and Panjabi sub-areas where kinsmen and business associates reside.

This has led to resumption of pilgrimage, even among some of the most modern and the most affluent, countering the more pervasive trend against ceremonial visits to India. Parents or grandparents who lacked "English"—sophistication, might have sailed to one of the shrines frequented by their elders once or at the most twice in their lifetime. The neo-religious sophisticates, both men and women, have begun to visit the *āśrams* of their chosen preceptors—Hrishikesh, Pondicherry, Bangalore; and at least half a dozen influential Hindus have moved permanently to such centers of the Hindu Renaissance.

Let me add that reaffirmation of religion and the reinterpretation of traditional values follow the model set by the middle-class Renaissance movements in India itself. The peculiar grass root nostalgia pointed out by E. Shils[5] is responsible for much of this behavior.

On the level of religious discourse, I found that questions and arguments are as frequent as in India.

"If man is a part of *Īsvar* (the Lord), then what is the need of working for the attainment of *Īsvar?*" asked a young Patel merchant. The monistic-absolutistic style of Hindu parlance is evident even where there is no specific alignment with the non-dualistic schools of Indian thought. This particular informant was a Vaiṣṇava, and the worshippers of Viṣṇu belong to a speculative tradition which strongly rejects the monistic notion of essential, numerical oneness of the individual and divinity as taught by Advaita Vedānta. But as this latter school has had the highest prestige in India over many centuries (it was formulated and systematized by Śamkarācārya in the eighth century A.D.), its diction seems to have suffused religious speech throughout India. The same person then asked "If a man has attained Īsvar, will he be reborn, too?" Now the official "Great Tradition" version is that the "realized" soul, the person who has found God, is thereby exempt from rebirth, which is axiomatically painful. In the various popular *bhakti* (devotional) movements of the past few centuries, this classical stand has been somewhat modified, and Śrī Ramakrishna, the Bengali saint of the late nineteenth century, declared that a liberated soul, one that has found God, to use the Christian idiom shared by English-speaking Hindus, may choose to merge with the divine and hence not return in a human form; or else, he may choose to come back with the sole intent of teaching humanity to find the goal of liberation and divine vision. Something of this modernized, eclectic teaching must have seeped through to this informant and, presumably, to some East African Hindus—his question makes sense in this light, though it might evoke a frown from the orthodox *pandit* in India, for whom the vision of the Divine is virtually synonymous with cessation of rebirth.

The age-old problem of theodicy is by no means a purely Christian concern, and though we do not find much mention of it in traditional Indian parlance, contact with missionary schools and other diffusive mechanisms might conceivably have impinged on the modern East African Hindus' religious notions. Various subjects in different locations, asked questions like the following: "Atom for atom, this universe is totally of divine essence (*sṛṣti sab aṇu aṇu īśvarsvarūp hai, sakal svarūp hai*), then why can there be evil in it?" (or, "Why should one see evil in it?" which gives the question a slightly different twist). The classical view is that evil, like good, is basically illusory, superposed on the supreme substance in a dreamlike fashion.

The fusion of meat-eating with killing and of a vegetarian diet with a higher form of morality is, of course, something ubiquitously Indian, shared even by Muslims *against* orthodox Islamic tradition. Indian Muslims eat meat, but they tend to admire people who do not, and some Hinduized Muslims have taken to vegetarianism in emulation of high-caste Hindu friends. There is an intra-Hindu critique of the vegetarian philosophy; *jīvo jīvasya jīvanam* "life is life's life," viz., life feeds on life, is an old Sanskrit dictum, used by meat eaters as an apologetic adage which states that as the life-force is present in vegetables as well as in animals, one might just as well eat meat. To this, an East African Gujarati informant replied "the life force which is in flesh (i.e., in the animals before they are killed), the self, intelligence and cognition, these are not present in cereals. . . . in plants, there are fewer of the sense organs than in animals and men. . . . plants cannot move hither and thither of their own; animals have no intellect (*buddhi*), men have; yet animals have one sense organ (*indrīya*) more than plants"—the implication being that one does not have the same moral right to destroy and eat animals as one has to eat cereals. This statement presupposes a good amount of familiarity with classical doctrine. I would think that many Hindu males in East Africa share this degree of theological knowledge, or they evince comparable theological interest.

On the other hand, there is little or no acquaintance—even among the professional ritualists—the *pandits* in East Africa—with the types of canonical legitimizing well known to their peers in India. The tradition distinguishes between the canonical texts (*śrutī*) and the non-canonical scriptures (*smrti*); most of the religious literature known to the Hindus in East Africa is *smrti,* including the well-known *Bhagavadgītā,* so often translated into English and other western languages;[6] but one of the most powerful sects, the *Ārya Samāj* denies the importance of any *smrti* text, and asserts that only the Veda is binding on the Hindu. However, the *Ārya Samāj* has a special slant, in that it denies the canonical status of the *Upaniṣads,* which are regarded as part of the Veda by all other Hindus, hence binding in doctrinary matters, in whatever manner one may wish to interpret them. It is the *Upaniṣads* that contain the speculative interpretation of the Vedic hymns, but hardly any East African lay Hindu knows the importance of the *Upaniṣads.* He assumes that the *Bhagavadgītā* is all that there is to them; though this text is really a day-to-day moralistic *vademecum,* whereas the *Upaniṣads* provided India with whatever sophistication its saints and scholars have had. The East African Hindus are deprived of their benefit. The *Ārya Samāj,* perhaps unconsciously, plays upon this ignorance. To its own followers, comprising a highly vocal percentage of the minority, it preaches the Veda as a corpus of simple prayer and social rule, with a tinge of reformed asceticism and a strongly anti-hedonistic world view, and belittles the *Bhagavadgītā* and the other Hindu scriptures which constitute conservative lore.

Generally speaking, the Hindu population in East Africa can be divided into two sectors, the admittedly conservative *sanātani,* the "eternal"—religion followers, and the *Ārya Samāji,* the followers of the "Society of the Aryans." The *sanātani* constitute the large majority of the total Hindu population, since most Gujarati and over half of the Panjabi Hindus are *sanātani.* They accept all scriptures and all forms of Hindu worship in an eclectic fashion; this means that they accept the *Upaniṣads* as canonical—the only trouble being that they do not know them, nor do local preachers speak about them. They worship the *avatāras* (incarnations) of the God Visnu (especially those of Rama and Kṛṣṇa), the Goddess (Devī, Ambā, Jagadambā, etc.), and whatever other deity had been their *kuladevatā* (clan or tutelary deity of their ancestors in India); they also accept, in theory at least, the possibility of worshipping divinity through "philosophy," as the modern thinkers among them would say, i.e., in the abstract, impersonal mode propounded by the various modern versions of Vedanta, emphasized by the Sivānanda "Divine Life Society," the Aurobindo movement, and some smaller movements that have gained audiences in East Africa.

Whilst the technical distinction between the *sanātani* and *Ārya Samāj* views—i.e., the inclusion of the *Upaniṣads* as Vedic, or as part of the canonical literature by the *sanātani,* and its exclusion from canonical status by the *Ārya Samāj*— is important in India, it does not affect the East African denominational situation at all. But there is a fascinating paradox which causes considerable irritation to *Ārya Samāji* respondents: the *Ārya Samāj* is supposed to be "modernized," anti-ritualistic, anti-traditional, whereas the *sanātani,* is thought to represent reactionary ritualism. The *Ārya Samāji,*

279

in East Africa as in India, censure the *sanātanis* for being gullible and superstitious, and for their idolatrous worship of non-divine objects. However, the fact of the matter is that in practice, the *sanātanis* are *less* traditional, less "ritualistic," and certainly far more tolerant and open to new views than the rigid, self-conscious, iconoclastic *Ārya Samāj*. Much depends on the internal definition of "ritual"—the *Ārya Samājis* use what they think is "pure" Vedic ritual, a twice-a-day fire ceremony with Vedic incantations picked rather randomly, and with little poetic discrimination, by Swami Dayananda, the founder of the *Ārya Samāj*, who lived in northern India in the mid-nineteenth century. The *sanātanis* tend to have more elaborate rituals—during my field trip, the *Sanātan Dharm Sabhā* at Nairobi conducted a seven-day, highly impressive observance, based entirely on Vedic usage and Vedic texts with quite a few delightful improvisations. The *Ārya Samāj* fire-ritual, though performed daily in the more highly motivated homes, is somewhat drab and rustic in comparison to the occasional *sanātani* performance.

The distinction between *sanātani* and *Ārya Samāj* has proper meaning only where there is a large group of Panjabi Hindus. In the Panjab, the people who did convert to Islam or embrace Sikhism during the past four centuries, were the *sanātanis*; then in the last century the *Ārya Samāj* engendered a fundamentalist Hindu revival in that area—accompanied by overt denigration of the *sanātanis* as those who had been lax and had not opposed conversion from the indigenous religion to Islam. In East Africa a few influential Gujaratis have joined the *Ārya Samāj*; thus, the distinction is no longer one that applies to an approximately even bifurcation between *sanātanis* and *Āryas* among Panjabis only; in a very true sense, this local, parochial Indian distinction has been de-ethnicized in East Africa. Here one might say that every Hindu who is not an *Ārya Samāji* is *ipso facto* a *sanātani*, regardless of which particular sect or form of worship he favors.

Whereas *Ārya Samāj* religious parlance is amenable to Indian vernacular discourse, the *sanātani* adherents seem to

280

feel much more comfortable when they discuss religious matters in English. Again, we have an apparent paradox: the *sanātani* are "conservative" by etymological definition, but their eclectic attitude has caused them to read *all* that the teachers of the Hindu Renaissance have been putting out over the past fifty years—and all of it is in English, only quite recently retranslated from English into the Indian vernaculars. Let me present a few typical instances of religious talk among East African *sanātanis*:

"*ādmī* (man) *minus* mind is desire, mind *minus* desire is God"—a neat statement of modern Hinduism inspired by Swami Vivekananda, the doyen of English-thinking Hinduism. The classical ascetic emphasis has been taken over into modern discussion, and modernizing trends come to a halt before the ascetic claim. Gadgets and cars, democracy and what-not are all right, but basically, they are not "spiritual"—they are "materialistic"—the truly great man gives up all desires, including presumably the desire for gadgets and other modern things.

This kind of discourse is stereotyped and predictable as in the equivalent milieux in India. A narrow set of questions is asked, and an equally narrow set of replies is expected; unexpected replies cause consternation.

At religious meetings of various kinds, the discussion invariably touches these points: is *bhakti* (devotion) or *jñan* (intuitive knowledge, "philosophy") preferable for the search of God? *Jñan,* all ask and agree, is respected, difficult, but not really feasible in this day and age when people live in a state of constant pollution ("because they eat all sorts of things and have many bad habits"), and only *sannyāsis* (monks) can really achieve God through *jñan*. For all of us here, *bhakti* is the right thing—you can live in the family, fulfill your duties to your kin and to society, and perform *bhajan* and *kīrtan* (religious congregation and litany, and listening to religious talk or conversation) at the same time, thus developing a great love for the Lord Who will then grant his *darśan*[7] in good time. The *Bhagavadgītā* teaches *bhakti,* and its main message, at least as the Hindu laity sees it, is "how to live in the world and yet be a devotee of the Lord." The book has all-Indian appeal, and verses from it are quoted by some well-informed non-Hindus as well. At the Dar-es-Salaam headquarters of the Ismailis there is a large photograph of the present young Aga Khan in tails, surrounded by aphorisms from scriptures of the world—the *Bhagavadgītā* among them. The sympathetic non-Hindu Indian identifies Hinduism, more or less, with the *Bhagavadgītā* or its popular, lay interpretation. Every Saturday morning at 7 A.M., the Kenya Broadcasting Corporation has a ten-minute program on the *Bhagavadgītā* (the present writer was a speaker on this program on several consecutive Sundays during 1964), and the estimated radio-audience is 6,000 including quite a few non-Hindus in the Nairobi area.

There is a remarkable deviation, however, from the more general religious tone among the East African Hindus' kindred in metropolitan India. Most Gujaratis in East Africa worship the *Devī* in one form or the other, the mother-goddess, also called *Ambā* or *Ambikā* ("mother"). Although many groups in the Gujarat also regard the Goddess as tutelary, there is more direct emphasis on mother-goddess worship in East Africa. I would assume that this is due to the great interest in magic and healing, which again may be partly due to the presence of African servants. The mother-goddess is magically potent, and worshipping her is thought to promote diagnostic, divinatory, and therapeutic powers. In India, worship of the mother-goddess on the village level often has strongly shamanistic overtones, and though the official Hindu culture identifies the village goddesses, say, of the Dravidian South (such as Mariyamman and the "seven sisters") with the goddesses of the "Great Tradition" pantheon, we find that shamanistic practitioners have a goddess as their tutelary spirit more often than not. In East Africa, possession is fairly frequent among certain Hindu groups, and four fascinating and highly relevant series of events occurred during my field trip in 1964, which I observed in person.

The Hindi and Gujarati term for possession by a deity is *lagnā,* the root *"lag"* both in Gujarati and Hindi meaning literally "to stick" "to be affixed"—the phrase for those possessed is "this or that deity has affixed itself . . . on the person," the most frequent expression being *mātā lag gayī* (Gujarati *"ambā* or *mātā lageche"*), literally "the mother has affixed herself." Although some persons were possessed by other deities like *Kṛṣṇa, Rām, Hanumān,* the names of these deities do not seem to be readily incorporated in the token phrase; one does not hear *"Rām lag gayā"* or *"Kṛṣṇa lag gayā"* though I did hear *"Hanumān lag gayā."* The more general phrase is *Devatā lag gayī,* i.e., "a divinity has affixed itself," i.e., any deity to be specified. I heard the phrase about a man who was possessed by Śiva—the man who reported it said about the possessed person *"Usko māta lag gayī"* and then went on to relate that the person saw and communicated with Śiva on certain days, not mentioning the "mother" at all. This may have been a slip of the tongue, but there is a possibility that the "mother" is the stereotype subject of possession and that the term thus covers all types of *lagnā.*

The first case was that of a Lohana petty merchant in Mombasa, Kenya. Since World War II, "God has visited his house," *Īśvar ghar mān aveche,* as the Gujarati Hindus around the place kept saying. Years ago, the man told me, he noticed that incense was repeatedly missing from his 'supply,' and then he saw that many incense sticks were burning spontaneously in front of the "foto" of Kṛṣṇa, an oleograph depicting that god in the little house-shrine. When he started speaking to the god, after several repetitions of "O Lord, why do you take my merchandise away from me?," the deity stepped down from its picture and entered the devotee's body through his mouth. "From that day on," he reported, "I have been seeing Kṛṣṇa regularly, and whenever I see him, I forget everything else." The people around the house, mostly Lohanas, some Patels, and other Gujaratis, accepted the phenomenon as a regular occurrence. They reported that the man lost consciousness, that he sometimes fell on the floor and lay motionless for an hour, or alternatively he sat erect in front of the Krsna image, and "his body turns cold as ice," in the words of my informants. The day of Krsna's birth (*janmāstami*) was said to be a day of particularly powerful possession, and I went to Mombasa to observe the spectacle on that day. There were well over three dozen people in the tiny room in front of the shrine—the man's house was a sort of simplified duplex where he lived with his wife and three children, aged 7 to 11 and his unmarried younger brother. He waved incense in front of the Krsna painting, and chanted a single-line prayer in Gujarati, meaning "O Lord, have pity on me" (*Dayā*—the word means pity, compassion, mercy, not in the sense of a Christian *miserere,* but in the same sense of *bestow Darśan,* or Your vision, upon me); he stood with folded hands, after having thrown the burning incense on the altar; then he leaned over very slowly, and came to lie flat on his face, in the *dandavat* "sticklike" posture common to many modes of worship. He remained in this position for over twenty minutes, during which time he seemed neither particularly rigid nor particularly excited—there was no tremor of any sort, nor any irregular breathing which accompanies other cases of possession. He then stood up and distributed *prasad* (food offered to the deity and redistributed among the devotees) which was accepted in a devout mood. And then a rather strange thing happened—he came up to me and said in a matter-of-fact tone: "Today I had a specially good vision of the Lord" (*Āj prabhu kā bahut acchā darśan huā*). I then asked some men in the audience if this was the manner in which he usually had his *darśan*; they all said yes, that was about it.

This man did not do any divination, nor did he claim to heal any disease; but people said that he had become a wealthy man ever since the Lord entered his house the first time, and that people who worshipped regularly at his shrine became affluent, too. Let us mark the fact that the attending informants did not insist on having witnessed any more dramatic syndromes than the ones I observed. It is therefore not unthinkable that it was a type of performance which might well have been planned and practiced without any clinical or traumatic cause, by way of conscious or planned religious attention-drawing.

The next case I observed was in the township of Tabora, in Tanganyika; this case attracted considerable attention in East Africa; in fact I first read about it in the newspaper. A school teacher, aged about fifty, had had constant visions of Krsna. He was reported to feed milk to the painting of *Gopāla,* i.e., Baby Krsna, one of the most frequent mythological foci in popular Hinduism. I got to the place at 7 A.M., when the ceremony took place, every day, ever since about two years before when Krsna appeared to the man in a dream asking him to feed him milk whenever he, Lord Krsna, would "enter the house." After some initial prayers, at least two of which were standard Sanskrit invocations including the hymn *Sāntākāram bhujaga śayanam* known to millions of Visnu worshippers all over India, the man's hands began to tremble, though there was no perceptible change, nor any rigor, in his body. He then took up a *lothā* (brass vessel) of milk and held it to the mouth of the painting of Baby Krsna— as he held it thus, the man whispered in a coaxing voice, prompting the god to drink as a mother would coax her little child; at one point, the teacher attempted a falsetto, so as to imitate Mother Yaśodā's voice, so people told me—Yaśodā being Lord Krsna's foster mother. The milk poured down the front side of the picture, but when this was pointed out by me to the audience afterwards, all but one denied it and rejected my observation as false; the one person who sided with me was a follower of the *Ārya Samāj.* After the feeding was over, the man sat erect for about half an hour without uttering a word. "He is in *samādhi,*" i.e., in a deep state of consummate meditation, I was told. His wife and the (antagonistic) Ārya Samājist told me separately that the man now entered *samādhi* without any warning, and that each time he did so he looked about the same as he did when I was present. When I asked some of the devotees whether contact with this man had any special effect on the followers who came in great numbers, they said that bad people who had been fond of women, whiskey and gambling, had turned away from these bad habits and had acquired *bhakti,* i.e., devotion to religious pursuits, and to the Lord Kṛṣṇa. No divinatory or healing powers were reported about this person.

The most bizarre case was that of a Lohana woman in Mwanza, Tanganyika. She had several write-ups in the East African press. A Patel lady doctor, an MBBS from Bombay, aged about forty, visited me and requested me to attend the "prayers" of the said woman, who was her protegée; a day earlier, in a talk to the Hindu community at Mwanza, I had criticized the gullibility of many Hindus, directly referring to the Lohana woman whose fame had spread so far. I found that I would receive lively and highly informative responses to such mildly antagonistic sermons. The Ārya Samājis in the audience were highly pleased with my criticism; the more conservative were silent, but the said lady doctor was decidedly disturbed. With a complete medical training and the usual degree, and after a decade of medical practice, she seemed to believe in the Lohana woman's "power", which was proven to her by the feats which she had been witnessing for many months. Since "the mother had affixed herself" about two years earlier, strange things had been happening in the woman's house: the children—she was a mother of eight—heard the sound of music one night on the upper floor, and when they went up the next morning, *kuṅkum* (red cinnabar powder, sacred to the Goddess) was all over the place, on the walls and on the floor. Later, there were several *kuṅkum* footprints of a woman's foot, and the polychrome painting of the tiger-mounted Goddess had a triangular blotch of *kuṅkum* emerging from the feet of the Goddess. When the woman prayed, people reported, she became motionless like the statues of the Goddess in the temple; and, so they maintained, *kuṅkum* came forth from the woman's hands after she had folded them in prayer; and sometimes, regular heaps of *kuṅkum* would fill the prayer room after the woman had completed her observance. The *kuṅkum* effusion seemed to be the most amazing thing to the audience, and though similar feats are said to occur in India, few were reported in East Africa. I then requested the lady doctor to bring the Lohana woman to me for an interview, which she did. To me, the woman appeared to look disturbed, though she spoke in a pleasant, eager tone of voice. The lady doctor got quite annoyed at my suggestion that the woman might be a psychopath: "She has many children and a husband and she looks well after them—could a madwoman do these things?" Of course she could, I said, but that did not impress the doctor. In matters relating to the situation the doctor's parlance was fully that of the Hindu Renaissance, which I define as the English-using Hinduism since 1900. I pretended to show reluctance, but both the woman and the doctor insisted I attend the former's prayer in the morning. She told me that whenever she prayed to the Goddess, she saw a great light, but no (anthropomorphic) shape, and that great peace descended on her. The woman spoke in a soft, pleading voice, but her utterances were in stereotyped Hindu parlance, so that nothing about her personal feelings concerning these experiences could be ascertained. Unless we posit that the whole pattern was pathological—which some of us might be inclined to do—there was nothing abnormal in the manner in which she spoke or acted. She did talk nervously, but that might have been due to the fact that she had heard from someone that I had criticized the whole procedure in front of a Hindu audience a day earlier. Anyway, I think I assuaged her fears, for now she was quite eager to have me at her home the next morning, though, she added "I am not sure whether the Goddess will put *kuṅkum* into my hands—She does not always do it."

I arrived at the woman's place about one hour before her daily *pūjā* was due. About twenty people had assembled, which I was told had been the average crowd for the past few months. The woman came out, told me she would have to take her bath and put on fresh clothes—very much a "Great Tradition" feature—and when she came back I observed the palms of her hands; there was no *kuṅkum* nor any unnatural coloration on them. She then proceeded into her little cubicle, where the painting of the Goddess, an oleograph torn from a calendar, not even framed, was placed in the center of the inverted box which served as her altar. A triangular blotch of *kuṅkum* emerged from the toes of the Goddess. There was a *kuṅkum* footprint on the floor, and a crude *trisul* as well as an inverted *swastika* by its side, all made of *kuṅkum,* all allegedly left behind by the Goddess on her last nocturnal visit—the woman had placed small glass panes over this footprint in order to preserve it. When I asked why the *swastika* was inverted, she said the Goddess made it this way—(the Hindu *swastika* points, against the annoyingly wrong notion of some Indophiles, in the same directions as the Nazi *swastika* though with shorter hooks), this *swastika* was inverted, i.e., it ran counterclockwise. The *trisūl*, i.e. Śiva's and the Goddess's trident emblem, was about five inches long, quite irregular, and looked as though it had been drawn by a child.

The woman then stood in front of the little altar lighted by a bare 150-watt bulb, and began her incantation. It was a short Gujarati prayer meaning simply "O Mother, be gracious, give me *darśan,* be benign to all in this house"—she clapped her hands several times during the first four or five repetitions of her chant—then her voice became louder and shriller, she opened her hands which began to tremble visibly, then her body shook quite strongly, her eyes were closed.[8] After these incantations, which lasted exactly five minutes and twenty seconds, she stood perfectly still, looking quite beautiful and very calm, her hands still outstretched. Finally, she prostrated herself before the shrine, touched the altar with her hands, rubbed her palms together for a few seconds, stood up, and left the room. "It is over," she said to me. Without my asking her, she showed me her palms which were full of *kuṅkum!* The lady doctor then asked me with a smile if I was convinced.

The woman did give general advice to people who solicited it; there was no actual prediction or divination, but guidelines for specific, individual behavior. The counsel she gave was of the form "If you offer this and that to the Goddess on this and that date, and if you fast on that day, your baby will get well; or your husband will stop playing around with other women, or drinking too much with other men."

Unless the Goddess did actually dispense it, the *kuṅkum* phenomenon may have been caused by the woman's touching the altar and the floor both of which were full of *kuṅkum,* some of which might have spread from the protuberances of her palms, *kuṅkum* having the body of very finely ground flour. I do not think that the woman lied when she told people about the Goddess's coming to her house, leaving footprints, *swastikas* and *triśūls* of *kuṅkum.* Whether schizophrenic or not, behavior like this woman's is fairly frequent in Indian possession contexts. The possessed subject forgets her actual part in preparing the artefacts at some earlier time and introjects only those segments of her ritualistic activities which create a complete gestalt in her mind and in that of her audience. The fact that she obviously functions in society— as a mother of eight children and wife of a lower middle class husband with earnings just barely sufficient to keep the house and the children going—does not necessarily conflict with a possibly pathological matrix. Her conduct is "normal" in the Hindu scene: it is not uncommon, and it has an audience and self-perpetuating prestige.

The fourth case I observed was that of a Gujarati Brahmin, all of whose clientele were Lohana and Patel. When the "mother had affixed herself" to him several years earlier, he put a red flagpole on top of the house, thus formally converting it into a temple of the Goddess. Regularly every Sunday at 9 P.M., he worships the Goddess in a "Great Tradition" formalistic way, with incense and chants—including portions of the *Candī,* a Sanskrit hymn to the Goddess much in vogue among Brahmin worshippers of Durga all over India. The ceremony itself lasted about half an hour, never much longer or shorter. Then the man sat down and "let the Mother descend on me" (*Ambā ko praveś hone detā hūṇ*), as he put it. He did not go into any visible trance that evening, but informants told me that he frequently danced and sang, though most of the time he kept as quiet as he did on that particular Sunday. He then got up, and without any further ceremonial ado he informed the audience that the Goddess now spoke in him and that they should address their questions to Her. From that moment on, the assembly resembled the astrological buzz sessions frequent in certain *jyotiṣī* (astrologer) circles in India. The audience put quite specific queries, though some one or two asked standard Hindu Renaissance questions, such as how to find peace (*śāntī*) in the midst of a householder's life of worldliness and turmoil. But most of the questions were mundane and specific, and the answers were sufficiently vague so as to cover possible vagaries in the predicted outcome. A few examples: "My son wants to go to school in Britain, but I want him to get married here—shall I send him or insist he should marry first?" Answer: "My child, let your son go but make him promise to get married when he comes back." Question: "I am suffering from arthritis and doctors tell me there is no cure. Will the Mother heal me?" Answer: "The Mother will certainly relieve your pain if you pray with a devout heart." A sophisticated Lohana girl who had just returned from "schooling" in Britain was very much in love with a boy, but his parents thought she was a "club-type," and they were trying to wean the lad from her. She had asked the Brahmin what she should do about it. He had told her that she should make a gift of money to the shrine of the Goddess, and that she should observe the *Sūryānarāiṇ* vow, i.e., not to take any food or a bath before the sun was clearly visible in the sky for half a year—quite a tough proposition during the rainy period. The six months passed and the boy got engaged to another girl. She then went to reproach this diviner, but he said "My child, whatever the Mother dispenses is the best for you." That clinched the matter. The fee for these services was a minimum of 20 E.A. shilling (slightly over two dollars), but

290

affluent people frequently paid him up to two hundred shillings.

A final assessment of these occurrences might show that there has been no ritualistic change, nor any assimilation to non-Indian models. My expectation that possession and divination might have incorporated certain African elements had to be written off. The only possible approximation or assimilation of certain African forms seems to occur in the use of spells and in child-curing, where I observed successive Indian and African treatments of Indian children, always inspired by African domestic servants. All the cases of possession and divination I have observed or reported could happen in India without any modification, even after two or three generations of East African residence.

Such phenomena get a lot of publicity in Africa, as they do in India. Actually, I was steered to Mwanza by a report in an English language daily in Dar-es-Salaam. That paper brought a report about another case, which I quote verbatim:

> Hindus in Tabora have been visiting the house there of Mr. Manishankar Joshi where a miracle is said to have occurred, and to worship at an altar (i.e., set up in the house, Bh.) in the present month of Purushottam of the Hindu calendar. Children playing in the courtyard of the house heard dancing and singing coming from the room where Mr. Joshi had erected the family altar to God Purushottam (a name of Viṣṇu, Bh.) and they told Mr. and Mrs. Joshi, who later also heard the sound of dancing and music which stopped as soon as they opened the door. They then knelt at the altar together in prayer. On opening her eyes, Mrs. Joshi's attention was drawn to four unusual prints—those of a small hand distinguished by the absence of a thumb, which had been formed into the form of red powder directly in front of the altar. Two mornings later Mr. Joshi turned away from the radio after listening to the morning news and saw two palm prints in oil similar to the footprints near to the radio. On further investigation, they discovered two further sole prints in red powder on the floor beside the nearby bed.
>
> A similar "miracle" occurred elsewhere in East Africa on the occasion of the previous Purushottam festival. Mr. Joshi had come

from India in the early thirties and lives as a trader and police canteen contractor in the town. When he first arrived, he was a teacher at the H. R. Primary school, which was then known as the Indian Primary School.

"Miracle in a Tabora House," *The Sunday News, Dar-es-Salaam*
April 12, 1964.

That the reporter must have been Indian is evident from the style. Yet, in order not to be taken as one who identifies and sympathizes, he uses such misleading phrases as "they knelt . . ."—nobody kneels in a devotional setting in Hinduism—one either stands, prostrates himself completely, or sits crosslegged; he also put "miracle" in quotes. This is a camouflaging device—in order to be taken seriously as a modern journalist by Indian, African, and white readers, the Indian author attempts to write "outsider style."

My host at Mombasa on the day when I read this report was a Lohana petty merchant; he showed the article to me. My host's hearsay description was more colorful and succinct than the paper report; he said "the daughter of the house

An African servant and a Hindu shrine share this kitchen.

was exuding (*sic*) *kuṅkum* (red cinnabar powder) from her palms and this happens to her every day."

The attitude of younger, more modern Hindus toward these phenomena and the persons who display them vacillates between ambivalence and antagonism. "We don't believe in any of that stuff," most would say; but that does not mean that some would not seek advice from their performers if secular efforts failed. When I showed the pictures I had taken of the woman in Mwanza during her trance, a young Hindu woman said, "I am afraid to look at this picture. It is horrible." She then continued saying that she did not believe in religion. But on another occasion, the same young lady said "I have done a lot for God." She then elaborated: in order to get her wish she had observed many vows which some older people had mentioned to her casually. She also chanted the *mantra* (mystic syllable, spell) *hrīṃ hrīṃ cāmuṇḍāyai namaḥ,* which is a *mantra* of the *tantric* lore, supposed to be highly potent and occasionally dangerous among practitioners in India—a fact not known to her. When I asked who had taught her this formula, she said that nobody had, that she had read it "written on a temple." This was an incorrect statement, since no temple in East Africa can bear this inscription, and she had never been to India. Also, the elaborate detail of the involved observances required some sort of personal instruction. An astrologer, she said, had told her that the *mantra* would bear fruit only after a certain date, and that if it didn't, she would have to switch to another *mantra* and to a different type of observance.

Such highly eclectic, elaborate statements from within an orthodox Hindu framework, coupled with a denial of any interest and concern with religion, must seem incongruous idiosyncrasy. Yet this type of vacillation between assertions and denials in the religious realm is quite typical and the subjects do not seem to feel any constraint or uneasiness about what would appear to be inconsistent notions to the non-Hindu.

Young people speak against religious traditions. This is

the complaint of those older Hindus who are religiously committed in one way or another. An Ārya Samāji leader in
Kampala said "we cannot really blame our children if they
like rock 'n roll and other dirty things; we parents do not
teach them the right things." By "right things" he meant
direct religious instruction. An affluent Lohana merchant in
Tanga was known and censured for his stinginess in business
transactions, and for his excessive thrift at home. "But," so
a critic said, "he is a good man, a pious man—he makes his
family pray." But when I asked one of his sons if he thought
religion was important in modern life, he said, "I dislike religion—it is hypocrisy; I want to be modern and travel and
study. The old people do not let us do these things."

A young woman of the *sutāria* (carpenter) caste was
hanging her wash on the clothesline in the small courtyard of
her husband's shop in Bukoba—a poor dwelling, slightly better
than a hovel, and much less comfortable than the dwellings
of some African traders two blocks away; she chanted, to my
amazement, a Sanskrit hymn. When I asked her what language
she thought the song was, she said, "Why, Gujarati of course—
the only language we know!" But when I told her the song
was really in Sanskrit, she said, "Yes, it may be Hindi, like
in the films." Did she know that this specific hymn had reportedly been composed by Śamkarācārya, a famous ascetic
many hundred years ago? "My *guru* taught me this prayer,"
she said with a shrug. "My *guru* taught me all the good
things," she continued: "how to heal the baby by waving
hot peppers over his head, how to ward off the evil eye . . ."

When this Hindu woman included Sanskrit hymns in her
daily worship, this was a "Great Tradition" procedure regardless of whether or not she knew the linguistic and literary
provenance of the formula. But when she used that same
hymn to break down the opposition of her mother-in-law and
her other affines banding against her, then this was an instance of "Little Tradition" Hinduism, because she would
choose some African or some non-Sanskritic Indian magical
device for the same purpose, were such a device available to her.

The temple plays a role which is totally different from the church or the mosque. The man who does not go there but "worships in his heart" or "meditates on God" ranks higher in the Hindu vision than the person who has to go to the temple to have *darśan* or "sight" of the deity. Of a dozen young, English-educated people interviewed in three East African cities, nine said that young people do not go, or are not supposed to go to temples. Elaborating on this, one of them—a twenty-two-year old male—said "If young people go to *mandir* (Hindu temple), then the elders will ask 'what's wrong with him anyway? Why should he go to the temple? That is for old people, women, and widows.'" Two young women, after their return from secondary school in Britain, made a habit of going to the local temple once a week, but they were obviously following the pattern set by compulsory chapel attendance during their British education. One of the informants, a man of twenty-five, who ran a *dūkā* in Tabora, Tanzania, said "old people disapprove of us going to temples, because they think we want something special from God." By "something special" he meant some favor which could not be had, or some object that could not be achieved through natural efforts—and "the old" are suspicious of such behavior, particularly when they think it must have something to do with "romance" and with the seeking of a marriage partner not selected by them.

However, the roughly 120 temples in East Africa are visited by people of all age groups and of all economic levels; over a period of ten days, the Hindu temple at Moshi was visited by an average of 110 people every evening during the *āratī*, the weaving of lights and incense to the beating of drums and the chanting of religious songs in honor of the temple deity. The song used for this occasion was the modern hymn *Om Jaya Jagadīśa Hare,* sung all over northern and western India at daily ritualistic functions. It was originally a hymn to Visnu, but the text was modified by substituting terms referring to other deities, or the deity of the specific shrine. In East Africa, all non-specialized chanting is in Hindi, because the Hindi *bhajans* (litanies) are most easily available from India, and many of them have quite recently been set to the highly popular tunes of Hindi movies (a process vaguely reminiscent of rock 'n roll tunes sung in the more avant-garde churches here and there in the United States). For more specialized types of ritual, Gujarati and Sanskrit hymns or chants were used, but very few of the participants were fully aware of this—they seemed to think that they were singing a sort of hieratic or archaic Gujarati.

Both Gujarati and Panjabi Hindus have their own professional ritualists who serve only their linguistic group. Gujarati Hindus—Patels, Lohanas, and "small castes"—have their brahmins, usually of the Audic caste. This replicates sacerdotal hiring by kindred groups in India, where the Audic brahmins enjoy the highest prestige in ritualistic specialization. There are other brahmin groups in East Africa; the *Brahma Samāj* (unrelated to the famous Bengali organization of similar name) is the fraternal or parochial organization of the Gujarati brahmins in East Africa, but not too many of them are Audic brahmins. Some are Nagar brahmins, who do not perform any professional ritual. Panjabis are less fastidious, partly due to the fact that there are not so many brahmin castes in the Panjab, partly because the *Ārya Samāj* has succeeded in blurring the distinction between actual brahmin castes and ascriptive "brahmins" as part of the pan-brahmanizing ideology which is nuclear to the *Ārya Samāji* doctrine.

Let me report on two highly typical East African brahmin ritualists, an Audic and a Panjabi *purohit* (priest). Both of them were well known in their respective communities—with all their virtues actual and alleged, and all their shortcomings, actual and alleged. The Gujarati Audic conducted almost all the weddings of the Gujarati Hindus in Nairobi and he traveled to cities and "bush" locations within a radius of at least 150 miles to marry and bury people, and to conduct the occasional *upanayana*—the investiture with the sacred thread, the initiation of high-caste boys. He wore an ochre-colored turban, wound in such a fashion that all Gujaratis recognized him as a priest. He was well versed in Sanskrit, not only the ritualistic scriptures, but also the *vedāṅgas,* the "limbs of the Veda" i.e., the extra-canonical genre which deals with a variety of topics such as *ayurveda* or the traditional Indian *materia medica* which is diagnostic and symptomatic with a mild infusion of magical notions. It is chiefly based on the concept of the three humors—wind, bile, and phlegm; more importantly this *purohit* was a master of *jyotiṣ* (astrology) in which he claimed to be the foremost expert in East Africa. "Other *pandits,*" he said, "charge and get only 25 shillings for setting up the astrological chart of a boy, and 30 shillings for matching the horoscopes for prospective brides and grooms. But I get 100 shillings each, and more, if I ask for it." (As a true brahmin, he is not supposed to take any salary, and whatever he receives is *dakṣiṇā* or a ritualistic fee, or else

A one-year-old boy's head is shaved in a Hindu ceremony.

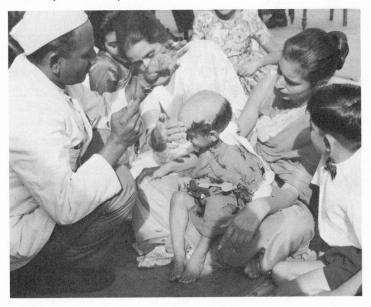

tokens of esteem, alms-like donations from the Hindu public.) I asked him why he did not try to teach some Sanskrit and other cultural things to young wealthy Gujaratis. "I tried several times," he said, "but the interest subsided after a few weeks every time I began, so I gave up in the end." He complained that interest in religion was quite passive and much more lax than in his days. His father had been born in India, and' was hired for five years by the Patels in Nairobi; but they so liked his work that they made him stay on. He brought his wife from India, and the son was born in Nairobi. He went on pilgrimages to India on two occasions, once with his father in order to have his thread-ceremony conducted at Baroda, his family's ancestral home; and once again as an adult in order to fetch a wife, after having looked into her horoscope from a distance.

This priest was learned even by Indian standards; his training was orthodox and did not exceed the average requirements for ritualistic specialists, but the mass of material he knew by rote was impressive by any standard. This was all the more amazing as he had never obtained any formal instruction in India; his father and the holy books, shipped from India, were his only guides. His visits to India had been short. He did not have any fellow-specialists to talk to. Infrequent visits by "saints" and other religious experts from India hardly sufficed to keep him abreast of things cultural and religious.

Pandit D., the priest of the Panjabi Hindus in a large city, was a very different sort of man. He was knowledgeable in the ritualistic texts, and had an average command of the literature of popular Hinduism, especially the ubiquitous *Bhagavadgītā,* on which he based the aforementioned weekly radio broadcast over the Nairobi station, since discontinued along with other Asian programs. His command of Sanskrit was good, but like that of most Panjabi *pandits,* his pronunciation and his chanting were atrocious. Unlike his Gujarati colleague, he was neither a teetotaller nor a vegetarian, and his flock criticized him for these lapses. He was reputed to have

298

considerable knowledge of magic, and several women confided that they consulted him regularly in order to obtain potent means to control hostile affines.

This brahmin was an enterprising person. He conducted a large-scale *yajña* (sacrificial rite) sponsored by wealthy merchants in the Hindu community. This was very much a "Great Tradition" event undertaken for the general welfare and improvement of the affairs of the *yajamāna,* the sponsors of the rite; it lasted a whole week, with printed programs, hundreds of invitations, lots of food and fanfare, oratory contests, masquerade competitions for the children, etc. The *yajña,* ("sacrifice") consisted of a daily *havan,* the focal ceremony in which large quantities of melted butter (*ghī*) were poured into the sacrificial fire as Vedic hymns were chanted. At this particular *yajña,* the daily hymn selected by the *pandit* was the *puruṣasūkta* from the Black *Yajurveda.* This was broadcast inside and outside the temple, via a fairly good and certainly very loud amplifier and loud speaker system. The incantation, joined occasionally by a few knowledgeable men in the audience, was interspersed by Panjabi exclamations as the brahmin instructed his assistant, a young brahmin ritualist hired from India for a period of five years; *hon caṛh jā* "now pour it on" (i.e., the *ghī*) *jaldi karo tūū* "hurry up, man," *ag jalā,* "light the fire now," *nāl phūnko* "blow vigorously," etc. Although this *pandit* was the head-priest of the Panjabi *sanātani* in the whole region, his style of worship, the highly Panjabicized pronunciation, and the choice of the texts, was close to *Ārya Samāji* ritual. The reason is not far to seek: apart from Sikhs and Muslims, the *Ārya Samāj* represented Hinduism during the past eighty years almost single-handedly in that region of India; the revival of *sanātani,* i.e., conservative Hinduism, leaned heavily on the *Ārya Samāj* model in spite of its ideological opposition. There was no other model. The pattern was transferred without any modification to the East African Panjabi *sanātani* Hindus.

Toward the end of the *yajña,* the sponsors and their wives threw the remaining *ghī* into the fire, repeating with the *pandit* the Vedic sacrificial call *svāhā,* a dissemantic *mantra.*[9]

This particular ceremony took place in the large Hindu temple run by the Panjabi *sanātani* people in the city. An elementary and a high school were attached to the temple. Each *sanātani* community has its own temple establishment in the larger cities of East Africa; there is no operative centralization, the temples are managed autonomously by the individual parochial communities in the cities. A board of trustees, consisting of wealthy members of the community, the priest, and usually one or two teachers employed by the school attached to the temple, function as the executive body. At the *Sanātan Dharm* Temple in Nairobi, an almost completely Panjabi organization, suggested innovations were looked at askance. Some of the younger men in the community proposed that there should be a "ping-pong hall" and a playground for the children and students attached to the temple "like the *Ārya Samāj* and the H.H. The Aga Khan's people do." But the most powerful member of the board rejected it, and mused "If I know that there will be some *bhajan* (litany) or *pūjā* (formal worship) in the temple, I will come. But what has it to do with football?" Yet, such antiquated attitudes are no longer shared by many of those who belong to an avowedly conservative group like the *sanātani.* There is a feeling, prompted and reinforced by reports from religious institutions in India at this time, that "something modern" has to be done to keep the young attracted to traditional things.

Few of the many temples in East Africa are works of aesthetic merit; however, the Jainas in Mombasa went to enormous expenses to have an exact replica of the famous Dilwara Temple of the Gujarat erected in that city, and it tops all other buildings in the area. According to one report, the marble was imported from Carrara, Italy—the most expensive marble in the world; the artists were traditional Jain architects and sculptors hired from India. Some of them stayed on to become part of the community; some young men of the "small castes" were actually trained by those exquisite craftsmen, which should enable them to build temples of more refined style, and to sculpt icons, whose direct import from India has become very expensive.

All shrines are kept very clean—a comment that cannot be made about Indian shrines in general. A Panjabi doctor from Nakuru, Kenya, and his wife had just returned from a visit to India. She complained bitterly about the filth in the temple of Lord Viśvanāth, the main shrine in Banaras, and probably the most important Śivite sanctuary in India.[10] The "cleanliness-godliness" adage which she quoted is of western

African women pass the Swāmīnārāyana Temple in Kampala, Uganda.

provenance, for ritualistic purity refers to the ritualistically relevant sections of the precincts only, not to the area surrounding the shrine. The complaint about "dirt and filth" in India—secular and sacred—is ubiquitous among Asians returned from trips to the old country.

The icons installed in the various Hindu and Jaina temples in East Africa were all made in India by professional icon-makers; in most cases, these men belong to castes whose exclusive craft has been the fashioning of icons. Although the Jaina temple in Mombasa now reportedly employs a sculptor born in Mombasa and trained by craftsmen who were hired from India, no locally made image has been installed in any of the public Hindu temples in East Africa. The architecture of the Hindu temples is modern and eclectic; some of them are more or less exact replicas of a specific temple in India, one favored by the India-born elders of the present-day Hindu settlers. Some temples—especially the highly modernistic, yet definitely attractive temple of the Swāmīnārāyan sect in Kampala, are innovations upon Indian styles. The notion of a temple being built in some modern style, not copied from traditional patterns, may have been inspired by close symbiosis with the Ismailis, whose *jamātkhānas* were built quite recently on non-Indian models; also, some Christian denominations built churches in highly modernistic styles in some East African cities, and these have provided additional models.

The Śaṅkar (Śiva) temple in Dar-es-Salaam, has the *liṅga* (the obligatory phallic representation of Śiva) in its *garbhagṛha* (*sanctum sanctorum*) in the center of the temple; this is flanked on its left by a full image of Rāmacandra, the seventh incarnation of Viṣṇu and the hero of the epic *Rāmāyaṇa,* with Sītā, his spouse, and Laksman, his brother, to his right and left. This accords with the North Indian tradition of ritualistic diffusion: the main deity of a shrine is accompanied by deities belonging to a different mythological set. And, just like in Northern and western India, where the temples of Viṣṇu usually do not have Śiva installed as a co-deity, the large temple of Lakṣmīnārāyana (i.e., Viṣṇu) at Dar-es-Salaam has only Hanumān, the simian warlord and companion of Rama-candra, the epitome of devotion, as his accompanying deity.

The critical, intellectualizing elements which challenge puritanism in India today are absent in East Africa. The God Siva, according to the ritualistic scriptures and the in-structions used for his formal propitiation must not be wor-shipped except in the form of the *liṅga,* his phallic representa-tion. At the Birla Temple in New Delhi, India, however, this rule has been broken and Śiva is worshipped as an anthropo-morphic icon at that new temple, built by one of the wealthiest Hindu merchants. When I asked him in 1954 whether he was aware of the fact that this iconization was in conflict with ritualistic injunctions, he shrugged his shoulders and ad-mitted it; "but," he said, "we can no longer go on with these dirty things which no one understands." "Dirty things" of course is a blasphemy, of which Mr. Birla did not seem to be aware; it reminded me of the Czech nursemaid taking the holy communion; when the baby—who happened to be this author—whom she carried with her tried to snatch the host, she brushed his hand aside and said "No, Poldi, this is *kaka*" (i.e., excrement). Indian puritanism was transmitted and has remained unchecked among East African Hindus. There are *liṅgas* in some of the Gujarati Siva temples, but not in the Panjabi-run *sanātani* shrines. Panjabi men, however, "mod-ern"—or perhaps just because of their modernity—were elo-quently embarrassed when the topic of the *liṅga* was brought up. A Sikh lawyer, just back from India, related with glee and a smirk that he saw "thousands of these things" (sic—he spoke English) in Banaras. The wife of the Panjabi Brahmin doctor in Nakuru, Kenya, who had just come back from an extended trip to India, complained about the dirt in the temple of Viśvanāth in Banaras. She kept comparing the dirt of that famous temple with the spotless cleanliness of the *Barā Darbār Sāheb,* the "Golden Temple," the main shrine of the Sikhs at Amritsar. "There ought to be a cleaning com-mittee in those dirty temples," she said. She also complained that the *pāndās* (the officiating priests and priestly guides of the Viśvanāth temple in Banaras) began to fleece her of money the moment they found out she was a "foreigner." This woman happened to be quite knowledgeable about religious matters and Hindu doctrine; but even she did not like the idea that Siva should be worshipped in the form of the *linga,* however correct the injunction may be from a ritualistic viewpoint. Somehow the feeling is that there should be nothing in "modern" Hinduism that reminds people of "superstition" and "bad things"; all the erotocentric ritual of the tradition is "superstition" and "bad" in modern Hindu English.[11]

"I was fed up with Banaras," the woman then concluded, "I did not even take the boat trip." It has to be understood that Banaras is the Hindu Rome or Mecca; also, that it has become one of the main tourist attractions on an international scale. Literally thousands of genuinely foreign tourists take "the boat trip" and visit the Viśvanāth temple. They have to view it from outside, as no non-Hindus are permitted to enter; an aperture in the wall permits Hindus of the former untouchable castes and foreign tourists to look at the *linga* from the outside.

When an American Peace Corps volunteer told a Hindu bank clerk at Kisumu that he would return to the States via India at the end of his contract, and that he would like to see Banaras, Hardvar, and other cities of sacred fame, the clerk got quite upset and exclaimed: "Why do you people always want to see the filthy things in India? Indians never visit the slums in England. Why don't you go to see the Bhakra Nangal or the Damodar Dam or Tatanagar?".[12] The clerk had neither been to India, nor to England or the States; but his reaction was quite typical, and is shared by much more sophisticated people in India itself. The argument that there are more river dams and other installations in the western world than in India, and that what the West is lacking is places like Banaras, etc., is not understood, or not appreciated. This discrepancy between pietism and technocentric modernism accounts for some fairly traumatic discourse between modern Hindus and informed western observers.

We have mentioned the *Ārya Samāj* quite frequently. Let me repeat that it is a reform movement which had gained momentum in the Panjab, and that a fairly high percentage of the Panjabi population adheres to this form of renascent, aggressive, fundamentalistic Hinduism; it was founded by Swami Dayananda who was born a Gujarati brahmin. However, less than a hundred Gujarati families in East Africa belong to the *Ārya Samāj.*

The *Ārya Samāj* is highly activistic. Its leaders insist on physical exercise with a certain militant overtone, though less so than the *Brhat Seva Sangh,* which is overtly militant and fascist. In the minds of East African Hindus, the *Ārya Samāj* is modern and progressive. Objectively, this is quite true if simple social reform is the issue. However, in matters of aesthetical and refined religious experience, the *Ārya Samāj,* with its profound iconoclasm, its routinized and standardized minimal Vedic ritual, falls way behind the traditionalist groups. When the male-oriented power structure in modern Hinduism came up during a conversation, an *Ārya Samāji* woman exclaimed with visible annoyance: "the *Ārya Samāj* is modern. They do not regard men as better than women. They let their daughters free!" (*sic*). She had been born in an *Ārya Samāj* household, but was married to a *sanātani.* Her *sanātani* husband, a sophisticated, quite worldly man, nodded assent. The feeling seems to prevail that simplicity in ritual and the forensic of male-female equality correspond to an actually different treatment of women in the Asian patrifocal households. Nothing could be farther from the truth: perhaps more than in India, the treatment of women in East Africa does not depend on sectarian provenance within the Hindu fold, but on their linguistic-and-caste background, apart of course from idiosyncratic differences which are accidental. Gujarati Hindus and Jains tend to perpetuate the patrifocal situation which assigns women a secondary place in ritual, interpersonal relations and societal interaction.

The East African *sanātani* Hindus, unlike the *sanātani*

of the equivalent social groupings in India today, accept the *Ārya Samāji* censure of religious reactionism. In India, things have changed considerably: literate *sanātani* have recently become aware of the multiplicity and aesthetic richness of traditional Hinduism; this awareness was reinforced by the agents of the Hindu Renaissance, particularly by the Ramakrishna-Vivekananda movement, and most recently, by the fame of Dr. S. Radhakrishnan, writer, philosopher, orthodox Hindu scholar, and second president of India. The East African Hindus know nothing about this reinstatement of a *sanātani*-type Hinduism. Perhaps more importantly, the specialists invited from India belong to the old order: they usually lecture in Gujarati or Hindi, and they do not participate in the modern, overtly anti-ritualistic current of modern Hinduism. Since the East African *sanātani* Hindus do not have any dialectic repertory to counter *Ārya Samāji* criticism, which is refuted as stale and naive in India today, they demurely accept this criticism. To illustrate this situation by an analogy: in some rural areas of North America, there may be Catholic and Protestant Christians. If the latter keep criticizing the former in the manner in which fundamentalist Protestantism has been criticizing naive Catholicism, the Catholics cannot really answer in full force. But if there were Catholics in the area who kept abreast of modern Catholic writing and the modernizing efforts of the Catholic Church, there would be a very different discourse between the two. Similarly, *sanātani* Hindus—comparable to Catholics—have been getting involved in the homiletic of modern Hinduism in India, and they have come to rebut and refute *Ārya Samāji* critics, who would be comparable to the Protestant group. In East Africa, however, the *sanātani* have no answer, simply because they do not know that *sanātani* thought and ideology have undergone a tremendous resurgence in India during the past few decades, with more fuel added by western admiration and emulation.

About four years ago, the *sanātani* and the Gujarati Hindus invited a Śamkarācārya, one of the supreme abbots of the monastic, scholarly *sannyāsi* tradition in India. He came to

East Africa and stayed for over two months, preaching orthodox Hinduism with all its demands for austerity and sense-
control, and with no compromise with modern ways. It is
the custom in India to touch the feet of a senior or highly
respected person in token of profound respect. When women
touched the Samkaracarya's feet—they had been instructed not
to do so—he would not drink water, nor eat any food, for
twenty-four hours. He said his mind and his body were pol-
luted through such contact. In orthodox India, stories like
this tend to enhance the status of those concerned; but *Ārya
Samāji* and other "modern" critics in East Africa used this
and similar incidents to rebuke the "superstition" and backwardness of the *sanātani* world view.

There was a fascinating and rather amiable "saint" in
Nakuru, Kenya. Hīrjī Bābā, a Lohana petty merchant, was
a pious old man, wearing quaint garments of his own design.
He had established numerous temples and other places for
worship and *bhajan* (religious litany) in all parts of East
Africa. Most interestingly, he has also made a small number
of converts among indigenous Africans. A group of Kikuyu
and Luau men and women took Hindu names, dressed Indian
style, and learned enough Gujarati to participate in the
bhajan and other devotional observances. Some of them even
renounced the consumption of meat and began to live as strict
vegetarians like conservative Gujarati men and Hindu women.
This is quite unusual and extraordinary in the African milieu;
from the point of view held by the African leadership, it
would hardly be regarded as desirable. Africans convert to
Islam and Christianity—there is as yet no alternative to be
converted to. Islam and Christianity are not unilaterally
linked with India: Hinduism is. I often tried to draw educated Africans' attention to the fact that much in the *sana-
tana* kind of Hindu religious practice is closer in style and
content to indigenous African religions. There was no "modern" African who seemed convinced except a few African
graduate students in anthropology: for "indigenous" can only
mean tribal, and tribal means old-fashioned, reactionary,

something to forget and to remove; the Swahili word was *chenzi*—"wild"—a term formerly used by the Christian missionaries to deride tribal lore. It seems that the politicized African would rather accept Christianity or Islam—both imported from outside Africa—than conform to or refine autochthonous, tribal modes of viewing the world and the supernatural. Hence, I had no audience among either Hindus or Africans: *sanātani* "Little Tradition" ritual has much in common with certain tribal African ceremony—but this is knowledge for the anthropologist only; it cannot be used "practically," to get Africans and Asians together on a more intimate, personal level. However, the dozen or so African converts to Hīrjī's intensely devotional Hinduism were total converts; their enculturation into the typically Gujarati-Cutchi style of fervent personalistic religion (*bhakti*) occurred rapidly; they shared the typical Hindu style of approaching the charismatic for *darśan*—power-giving, blessed "vision."

Among Hindus, Hīrjī was accepted as a saint by those who identified with Hindu grass roots. At their *bhajan* (litany) party, some participants came very close to trance; Hīrjī himself fell down at the feet of a visiting *sādhu,* and kept lying prostrate *dandavat* "like a stick"; and the audience—at least three of them millionaires—washed the itinerant *sādhu's* feet with water, milk, sugar, jaggery, and other ingredients, which they then drank as *prasād*—as a "gift" accepted by the god or the deity in human form, the *sādhu,* and then redistributed among the audience.

Active involvement in supererogatory religious practice of this kind is quite common among Gujaratis over thirty in East Africa. There is a sharp decline of such involvement among younger people. Panjabis had no such involvement in the first place—Sikhs visit the *gurdvāra* (the Sikh "gate of the preceptor," i.e., their temple) on Sundays and for the more regular festivals. Except for some religious specialists among them, the religious involvement of the Gujarati community is viewed by them with a mixture of disparagement and mistrust; quite a few Sikhs and non-Gujarati Hindus regard the total, time-consuming religious engagement of Hirji and his followers, as well as of other Gujarati religious activist groups, as anachronistic and vaguely pathological.

Yet the most religious among the East African Hindus do not go to the extremes some of the South Indian settlers in the Union of South Africa do; there are no piercings of the cheeks in fulfillment of certain vows,[13] and there are probably no extreme ascetic practices which entail the infliction of physical pain on the individual who undertakes a vow.

Most Hindu women, however, do vow occasional observances during periods of their lives, not necessarily in states of mental or other duress, but in line with the many traditions of austerity which have remained more or less incumbent on Hindu women. A middle-aged Lohana woman who did not have any English education, said "Some women do not make any vows because their men no longer believe in these things. But most women who do not take any vows do so because their health does not permit it." But then, a younger, extremely sophisticated, English-speaking woman of the same community told me that she had given up a fourteen days' fast—which was part of a particular vow in honor of the God Nārāyaṇa (a name of Viṣṇu)—because her peers began to tease her about it; then she corrected herself and added: "The reason why I started eating again, was that I lost health." Overt omissions of traditional observances or claims of non-observance are part of the modern Hindu's defense against his peers' suspicion of "being old-fashioned." Yet, the pattern changes as young modernites grow older. A large number of those who "did not care for religion," either in the sense of not doing anything at all that could be construed as "religious" by their peers, or by performing vows clandestinely, tend to take to religious reading and conversation as they turn forty, or when they get established in their occupations.

Mr. P. of Tanga, a wealthy Lohana merchant of about fifty, put his initials in red *kuṅkum* (cinnabar powder or paste) on every drinking glass in the house. Although he claimed that this was done to indicate the ownership of the glasses—he did not state who might possibly dispute it—these were actually ritualistic markings, as his name was that of the *kuladevatā* (tutelary deity) of his agnatic family; such markings are *kuśala* (auspicious) and some such markings, though less prominently displayed, can be found in most Gujarati Hindu households, modern or "old-fashioned."

Anthropologists have described Hindu ritualistic hierarchies in terms of purity and defilement. In India, any physical contact with organic matter pollutes, and some sort of purification has to be undergone to reinstate the person into "normal ritualistic status." Thus, there is a feeling of extreme discomfort attached to leather. It is almost impossible to enter a temple in India with anything made of leather—the temple authorities' opposition to cameras is not so much due to their fear of desecration through pictorial profanization, as to the fact that camera cases are made of leather or look as though they were made of it. This sort of apprehension is hardly existent in East Africa. On several occasions, my hosts removed my briefcase from me as I entered a temple—not to hide it, but to relieve me of the burden; they carried it upstairs and right into the shrine, depositing it in the hall without any qualms. This behavior would be unthinkable in India, even in such modern shrines as the Birla Temple in New Delhi, where leather items have to be checked—much like coats in occidental restaurants.

Leaders in the various Hindu communities have a fairly extensive knowledge of theological detail pertaining to their specific group. The president of the Lohana Society told me that he worshipped the God Viṣṇu personally, but that the Goddess in her various forms as Jvālā ("flame"), Ambājī ("venerable mother"), etc., was the *kuladevī* (family deity) not only of his own agnatic group, but of other Gujarati groups with whom Lohanas do not intermarry, and he specified those groups.

If we return to our "Great Tradition"-"Little Tradition" polarization, we can assign the various ritualistic groupings in East Africa pretty well to the one or the other pole. One of the most interesting "Little Tradition" examples is provided by the followers of Sāī Bābā, who was a low-caste, Gujarati-speaking mystic, probably a Muslim. It is virtually impossible to find out exactly when he died, from his East African Indian followers; for as in India, anything that is holy and revered is preferably ageless. And just as almost all Hindus think that the Veda is uncreated; or if a historical response is urged, say it is "many thousand years old," followers of Sāī Bābā told me "he lives eternally" or "he died many hundred years ago." Sāī Bābā lived in the late eighteenth century. He must have been a man of considerable mesmeric powers, and many miracles are attributed to him. In the religious tradition, the line of teachers must never be interrupted. The present Satya Sāī Bābā is a man in his late forties, of humble social background. He lives in Puttupati, Podanur District, South India, and rides in a gold-sprayed Rolls Royce given to him by his devotees. He wears long hair but no beard, and a golden robe. He was to visit East Africa a few years ago and his followers prepared for the welcome of a charismatic hero. "He is Kṛṣṇa, Rāma, Mohammed, Allah (*sic*), Christ, and much more," a devottee, a bank clerk, told me. A surgeon trained in England asserted that "He can heal everything when you just beseech him even from a great distance. There was a case of terminal cancer here, all doctors had given up; I had operated twice. Then the patient invoked Satya Sāī Bābā, worshipping his photo. He recovered within three days and runs his petrol pump again." The present Sāī Bābī is said to be an incarnation of the original saint. He has the power of *parakāyapraveś* (entering and taking possession and use of another person's body). He is omniscient and knows what every human being thinks at any time, anywhere, when he concentrates on it. When his devotees from Kampala visited him in India, they saw that he took *bhasma* (wood ashes, used for ritualistic purposes) from a pot, which has never become empty of *bhasma* ever since, although the devotees use this *bhasma* for their devotions all the time.

I had met this present Satya Sāī Bābā in Bangalore a

few years before my field work in East Africa. I thought that his golden robe meant to imply that he was the personification of *hiranyagarbha* "the golden foetus," an aspect of the universal deity in the Vedic tradition. But His Holiness had never heard about *hiranyagarbha*; in fact he was theologically illiterate. The next day a Brahmin devotee of his came to me and told me that His Holiness had given some thought to my suggestion and that he wanted me to know that I was right: he was indeed the manifestation of *hiranyagarbha*.

We find a totally different constellation in the *Swāmīnārāyana* cult, which is popular among Patels, Lohanas, and other dominant castes in East Africa. The founder was 'a Gujarati brahmin turned *sannyāsi*, by the name of Sahaja nanda; he lived in the early eighteenth century. This is very much a "Great Tradition" cult: thoroughly ascetic, it demands a high degree of ritualized observance from its followers. When the present leader, supposed to be the incarnation of the founder, visited East Africa, he had his dais screened in one direction, so that the women who sat separately from the men, as in all religious meetings, could not get into his field of vision. Neither did he set his eyes on any woman during his sojourn, nor presumably in India. The reaction to this rigorous saintly behavior was mixed: the Swāmīnārāyana followers praised him for his purity, and even four years after his visit, this particular feature was pointed out every time the topic came up. On the other hand, the reformed sects, especially the *Ārya Samāj* and its members, censured and ridiculed the Swami for this show of austerity. "What is the use of his penance and saintliness, and where is his control of mind," an *Ārya Samāji* lady said to me, "if he feels that the sight of a woman will disturb his meditation! Our men who are no saints, but live in the world and do worldly business are not particularly disturbed by our sight, they do not commit impure acts, and they do not need a screen to keep their eyes from women!" "If a man can get all excited and perturbed by the mere sight of a female being," another woman suggested, "then what is the use of *yoga*? That Swami is worse than us ordinary people, for we do not get excited and perturbed by looking at people of the other sex."

A very small but highly influential segment of the Gujaratis, particularly Patels, are devotees of the late Bengali mystic-poet-writer Sri Aurobindo. He was a political terrorist during the independent movement; previous to that, he had studied in England. He took refuge at Pondicherry, which was then a French possession, gave up politics and became a philosopher-saint. He wrote and published voluminous tracts, some amount of poetry, and an epic, all in English. He was subsequently joined by a French woman who established mystical contact with him. Within two decades, his *āśram* ("refuge," monastery-like institution) became world-famous and under the able administrative leadership of "The Mother," the place has become one of about half a dozen of genuinely important *āśram* centers of Hindu Renaissance religiosity. The teachings of Aurobindo[14] are eclectic to a high degree, as are those of all other modern Hindu movements; but they are intellectually more sophisticated than the Ramakrishna Mission, the Śivānanda and Yogānanda movements, all of which have national and international following. Aurobindo taught a blend of Vedānta with mildly esoteric overtones; his teaching is not so radically puritanical as those of the *Ārya Samāj* or the older Swāmīnārayaṇa sect. Aurobindo died in the early fifties, and "The Mother" now reigns supreme at Pondicherry. Quite a few East African Gujaratis have visited the place more than once, and at least one wealthy, well-known Patel leader moved permanently to Pondicherry after retiring from active life in East Africa. There are only about 300 active followers of the Aurobindo movement in the three East African countries, all of whom belong to the top echelon of the minority—professionals, lawyers, former politicians, and wealthy businessmen. A photograph of Sri Aurobindo and "The Mother" was kept on the mantlepiece, or, in some cases, in lieu of the regular altar in some niche of the house, and *pūjā* or some surrogate formal worship was conducted by the occupants, both husband and wife. Wealthy nuclear households often seem attracted to Aurobindo: people who served in the upper civil agencies, or professionals with occidental training who have gained a fair degree of affluence, tend to live in nuclear family settings which they created by moving out from the previous joint or extended household of their parents. I did not see any large joint household where the Aurobindo cult was focal. Somehow, the cosmopolitan sophistication of the movement appeals to people who have already moved away from the original social setting. The more traditional cults, especially Swāmīnārāyan among the Gujaratis, have some extremely wealthy followers, most of whom live in the traditional joint family setting.

The conservative cults tend to be ritualistically and homiletically exclusive; the Swāmīnārāyanis do not usually invite outside speakers, although the well-designed, expensive-looking Swaminarayana temples are open to all. At Kampala, I saw and photographed an African man who was moving along the tiled floor of the Swāmīnārāyan temple on his hands

An African man seeks a cure at a Hindu shrine.

and knees; "he wants to be cured from some disease and has come to know about the power of Swāmi Sahajānanda," one of the attendants informed me.

The Ramakrishna-Vivekananda movement, which has a large number of followers in other countries where there are Hindu settlers, has no organized votaries in Africa; the reason is simple, and unknown to the Asians. In order for a Ramakrishna-Vivekananda chapter to be created, there have to be Bengalis or South Indians, monastic or lay, in the area. In all centers in the USA and Europe, the monks are exclusively Bengali or Dravidian by birth, many of them American citizens. There are no South Indians or Bengalis in numbers among the Asian settlers in East Africa, and the dozen or so individual Bengalis and South Indians thinly spread through the large cities are not regarded as part of the Asian settling community, which identifies only Gujarati, Panjabi, Konkani, and Cutchi speakers as proper settlers. But in spite of the fact that the otherwise international Ramakrishna-Vivekananda movement has no institutionalized following in East Africa, the "modern" Hindus, particularly the followers of Aurobindo, Swami Sivananda and other Hindu Renaissance cults, know Vivekananda's writings. They also believe that the teachings of Vivekānanda, Sivānanda, and the other modern swamis are known to the people of India at large. This is an error: no movement that did its core-preaching and writing in English has come to be absorbed in the Hindu grass roots; neither the Ramakrishna-Vivekananda movement, Sivānanda, nor Aurobindo have touched the Indian masses.

A Gujarati Hindu woman suggested that outcaste people should be allowed to enter the *sanātani* temple in Nairobi. There were not more than about three hundred people in East Africa who belonged to what are now called the "scheduled" castes in India, the former "untouchables". They used to do the lowest menial jobs, but many of them have gone to India as the first victims of Africanization—their jobs are now done entirely by Africans. But when there was a suggestion about permitting temple entry to those *Vālmīks*—a Panjabi

315

euphemism for the "untouchables" (Valmiki was the mythical author of the *Rāmāyana,* and a low-caste man by tradition) one of the trustees of the *Sanātani* temple in Nairobi got quite upset and said he would withdraw his sponsorship from the institution if that were done. "Let them have their own temple," he said. This has been the view of the orthodox in India at all times. Somehow, the feeling is that a temple is by definition a high-caste, private institution, and that one cannot force entry into it by decree, because, as that same man put it, "when you want to join a club for red-haired people, only red-haired people can join, and no offense could be taken by others."

Across sectarian lines in Hindu East Africa, we find quite a few instances which cannot be ascribed to the influence of any particular sectarian doctrine. A Gujarati merchant once mused "When the *guru* passes away, his soul lives on the astral plane. There he retains responsibility for his disciple." This sort of statement is a curious melange of heterogeneous teachings, hardly found anywhere in India except perhaps among the few theosophists who follow the mixed code of Mme. Blavatsky and Col. Olcott. But the notion of an "astral plane," thus expressed, is definitely not of Indian origin— it must have come to this man through some European esoteric reading. Moral responsibility beyond death does belong to the Indian eschatological complex—the fact that these two ideas present themselves as a single conceptual unit indicates the high degree of eclecticism to which Hindus have been exposed through the Hindu Renaissance in India. But where-as there are growing checks against eclectic hypertrophy in India, no such checks are forthcoming in East Africa, because "modernization" does not touch the traditional core among the settlers. Their Hinduism has become culturally isolated and the "modern" are not exposed to the intra-religious critique generated in India today.

Islam

Although Muslims of several sects make up slightly over one-fourth of the Asian minority in the three countries of

East Africa, we can give them much shorter shrift than the Hindus. In the first place, a good study of them has recently been published, and a detailed account at this place would mean duplication;[15] but more importantly, Islamic religion and the social implications of the Islamic law (*šari'a*) and of the teachings of the Prophet on the later bodies politic are much simpler and much more homogeneous than those of the Hindu complex. The theology of Islam stems from the same root as Judaism and Christianity; the Muslim tends to consider the Hindu, a *kāfir,* sotto voce perhaps, because he has no "book"—at least not the Book the Muslim is thinking of; also because he is thought of to be an idolator who "sets up partners for Allah"—which is the greatest sin in Islam.

However, Indian Islam has moved away in many respects from the original Arab model—and this has been a matter of grave concern to the Arab and Near Eastern scholars of Islam for many centuries. I shall concentrate on the one school that is ritualistically and ideologically most removed from orthodox Islam—the Shi'a Khoja Ismailis, or just Ismailis, as they are referred to in East Africa. In previous sections of this study, we have already become acquainted with this amazing community. Through a chain of historical accidents, the Ismailis in East Africa have become modern and prominent, and the transition within three generations from the state of the community in the Cutchi-speaking areas of Western India to their present situation verges on the miraculous. Contrary to the view that factors other than the rise of a single, charismatic, influential individual are instrumental to thorough-going social change, it can be shown that the Ismailis in East Africa today are what they are largely through the efforts of the late Aga Khan. We cannot here go into the personal history of that amazing man,[16] but shall take our departure from a single functional aspect: he issued a series of *firmān*s, i.e., canonical injunctions to the community, and since the *firmān* of the leader of the Ismailis, who is the "living Imam" (*hāzir imām*) has binding effect very much like the Pope's *ex cathedra* decrees, it was the contents of the *firmān*s that changed the life of the community

over a period of a few decades. The Aga Khan, according to
the faith of his followers, is born in the direct line of descent
from Ali, kinsman and close associate of the Prophet Muhammad. But more than that, they hold—and this is radically
contrary to orthodox teachings—that revelation did not come‹
to an end with the death of the Prophet or the codification
of the Qur'an, but that it is an ongoing process. The Aga
Khan's *firmān* is as binding on Ismaili as any injunction
of the Qur'an. Had the Qur'an given "modern" orders to
the faithful, the Muslims would have been modern. The
firmāns given by the late leader ("the late His Highness" as
his English-speaking followers put it) were not only modern
but quite revolutionary. Overnight, he ordered that women
of all ages should wear western dress on almost all occasions,
but particularly for their domestic chores. This was hard
going for the traditionalists—and almost everyone at that
time was just that. Elderly women who were young wives at
the time the *firmān* was issued felt most uncomfortable. Three
women of over fifty to whom I talked separately at different
places, said "we felt naked" when they had to put aside their
traditional long wear covering all their bodies and much of
their faces. Such radical sartorial modification also brought
about a rapid change in the self- and alter-image of the Ismaili
women. The present Aga Khan, a Harvard graduate and
"His Late Highness's" grandson, increased the amount his
grandfather had permitted for Ismaili brides' wedding gowns
through a recent *firmān* to match the rising cost of clothing.
The original *firmān* had been revolutionary, as much more
than pomp and show were symbolically connected with the
inordinately expensive gowns of the daughters of the rich
contrasting with the outfits of the poor. "His Late Highness
passed many democratic orders like this," as an Ismaili teacher
at Dar-es-Salaam put it.

The more conservative Muslim sections in East Africa—
the Khoja Shi'a Ithna-As'ari, the Ahmaddīyas, and the *sunni*
groups, regard Ismaili religious practice and belief with considerable misgivings, mixed no doubt with some envy. All

Muslims share a basic, simple theology—God is one, no partners may be set up for Him, and His greatest Prophet is
Muhammad. But the differences lie in the assessment of the
Prophet's uniqueness. While all Muslims recognize Prophets
before Muhammad, Ibrahim (Abraham), Noah, Moses, and
Jesus, Son of Mary (but NOT of God—this is the heresy
Muslims never forgave the Christians), there is a radical
schism on the point of succession to Muhammad. The *sunnis,*
who form the great majority of Muslim's in the world, believe
that the revelation came to a close with Muhammad, when
the Qur'an laid down the ultimate canon of guidance. Not
so the Shi'a sects. The Khoja Shi'a Ithna-Asaris, of whom
there are roughly 30,000 in East Africa, all of Lohana Hindu
descent, believe that the Imam, the successor of the Prophet, has
been living in hiding since the assassination of Hassan and
Hussein in the twelfth century; the Bohras, Gujaratis of
Brahmin or Lohana descent who number about 20,000 in East
Africa, hold a similar view—they respect a living leader, the
Da'i-ul-mutlaq, who lived in Bombay in undeniable splendor, and who may or may not have been the Imam himself—
his official function is that of a caretaker of the Faith. But
the Khoja Shi'a Ismaili *have* their living Īmam—H.H. The
Aga Khan. "When we know that the Imam lives among us,
that we can write to him, hear him, and even see him when
he blesses us with his *darsan* (sight, charismatic vision, personal appearance—a Hindu term), then our hearts are filled
with such sweet love and trust that all our problems are
solved," a senior Ismaili leader confided to me. In Indian
society charisma is something different from the Weberian
concept. A holy man is a holy man by his own declaration,
not by any special deed or set of deeds; charisma is ascriptive
in India. Thus, the fact that the late Aga Khan was a great,
although a highly conservative man, who did many things for
his community, has little to do with his charismatic status
which, in a very definite way, is a *character indelebilis* once
it is established through such due process as inheritance,
ritualistic installation, etc. The present Aga Khan is not a

genius, but a very modern, well-educated person, hardly distinguishable by achievements and by qualification from other
rich, well-educated, but non-scholarly men of this generation.
Yet his status with the Ismailis is quite identical with that of
his illustrious grandfather. It is not diminished by the fact
of his marriage to an English divorcee. It seems to me that
the physical presence of the leader of the faith lends tremendous support to the community as it enhances its self-
image, and the identification of its members in a manner in
which other Muslim, or for that matter non-Muslim groups,
cannot share. They have the book or books, they have occasional visiting saints, they have "faith," and they have as many
sermons as they want. But the Lord, so to speak, is not cor-
poreally amongst them.

The wisdom of the Aga Khan, when viewed in present-day
perspective, might seem to bound on the miraculous to his
followers. As we already stated, one of the most important
firmāns issued by him was that all Ismailis must regard themselves as citizens of the land where they live and work. When
the British Government passed unexpected and, so it seemed,
highly discriminatory legislation in March 1968, which virtually stopped the immigration of Kenyan Asians into Britain,
those who held British passports rushed to the airports to
beat the deadline. Most of them did not make it. But among
those who fled, there was not a single Ismaili: for all Ismailis
are Kenyan, Tanzanian, and Ugandan citizens, following their
late leader's behest. This does not guarantee, of course, that
the African governments will not recriminate against Asians
holding African citizenship some day; but that is another
matter. At this time, the Ismailis are safe as East African
citizens. The majority of the more affluent among the other
communities opted for British citizenship, when the British
Government permitted this option immediately before *uhuru*;
that proved to have been a wrong move.

Attendance at the *jamātkhāna* on Fridays is 100 percent;
all Ismailis go—those who pray several times a day (as the
oldest among them do) as well as those who do the Twist and

the Frug on weekends, and who "enjoy," as modern Indian English parlance refers to dating and romantic behavior. This by itself makes the Ismailis different from Hindus and non-Ismaili Muslims. Modern Hindus, particularly the "England-returned," tend to feel embarrassed when they have to participate in domestic or temple ritual; I met over a dozen young non-Ismaili Muslims in several East African cities who did the *namāz* (the Muslim formal prayer), but they did so on the sneak, lest their peers should think them "old-fashioned." The Ismaili does not have any such problem: quite openly, and proudly, and with much verve, does he or she attend the weekly meetings at the *jamātkhāna* where, along with prayer and sermon, there are food, auctioned and eaten, fun and games, even social dance resembling the new American church pattern, but without any conscious or unconscious emulation of it. For a while, Ismaili prayers were conducted in Gujarati, but the community has now reverted to a variety of Arabic which none but some of their preachers understand. The prayer manuals are now bilingual, in Arabic and in Gujarati translation. The service at the *jamātkhāna* is simple, the style is eclectic, including quite a few assimilated Hindu elements.

Summary

In their religious style, the Sikhs are close to the Panjabi Hindus, and previous to the rise of separatistic political movements in India, hardly any Sikh rejected the commonly held notion that Sikhism was part of Hinduism. Theologically, however, it has strong Islamic overtones.[17] The founder of Sikhism, Guru Nānak, deliberately wore garments of both Hindu and Muslim saintdom with a view to obliterating doctrinal distinctions between the two religions. The fact that Sikhism was set up to stem the tide of Muslim conversion in Northern India, and that the tradition of mutual warfare really never subsided until it blew up to hideous dimensions during partition in 1947, does not contradict the extreme theological similarity of Sikh and Muslim teachings. There is a wide area of overlap—a strongly monotheistic tendency, a highly verbal iconoclasm, and a stress on faith and on the community of the faithful, the *khālsa,* (an Arabic word) are things Islam and Sikhism share; yet the doctrine of rebirth, a simplified reading of the law of *karma,* and the tacit acceptance of Hindu mythology, are indigenous elements. At all times, Sikhs have regarded themselves as Hindus rather than as Muslims, when the decision was forced upon them. Sikhs and Hindus intermarry, provided they belong to the same caste; Sikhs and Muslims do not intermarry even in regions where the Muslim's ancestors shared the same caste as those of the Sikh.

To the other Asians, the East African Sikhs appear as a single group; but the two castes represented in East Africa do not intermarry; nor do they worship at the same place. The Rāmgarhiā *gurdvarās* (temples) are usually smaller but fuller than the *Singh Sabhā gurdvārās* of the *Jaṭs.* Their ritual is identical; reading of the *Guru Granth Saheb,* the one and only canonical book of the Sikhs,[18] the chanting of *kīrtan* (litanies based on texts from the *Guru Granth*), and the distribution of ritualistic food (*prasad*) which is again a

Sikhs carry the *Granth Sahib,* their holy book, in a procession.

feature common with all Hindu ritual. There is a very close religious and cultural symbiosis between the *Ārya Samājis* and the Sikhs, both in the Panjab and in East Africa. Both feel closer to each other than to the *sanātani* Hindus, because the *Ārya Samāj* and the Sikhs do not worship idols. The Book is set out on an altar and worshipped very much like a Hindu idol, but this is not felt to be a felicitous comparison by the Sikhs. The theology of the *Ārya Samāj* and the Sikhs is simple, and indisputably monotheistic; the ritualistic and theological sophistication of *sanātani* or any other orthodox Hindu doctrine with its resilience in face of other doctrines and its multiple interpretability on almost all issues of religious concern, is repugnant to the theologically naive Sikhs and *Ārya Samājis*.

The Goans are fundamentalist Roman Catholics. East African Goans are conservative; their priests wield undisputed judgment in the field of morals. There is no religious interaction between the Goans and any other Asian group. In tune with the conservative missionary style no longer encountered in India, Hinduism is still regarded as evil superstition and devilry by East African Goans. The Goan Catholics' attitude to Islam is indifferent, and though no Goan is interested in theological distinctions of any sort, he somehow knows that Islam is closer to Christianity in many ways than Hinduism. Some additional lenience toward Islam may stem from sartorial perception: Ismaili women, like Goan women, wear western dress. Of over twenty Goans I interviewed independently, only one knew that there was a considerable difference between Ismailis and other Muslims; another male adult did not know that the Ismailis were Muslims at all. This is interesting on several counts; one often gets the feeling that the East African Ismailis stress their distinctness from other Muslims rather than their basic religious oneness. This is parallel to the Sikhs, many of whom now tend to emphasize their difference rather than their basic cultural identity with the Hindus as a religious body. When Goans meet non-Goan Asians, religious discussion is painstakingly avoided, even after occasional proddings by Hindus who are eager to conduct theological dispute. When I observed Catholic and secular festivals among the Goans, I did not at first notice anything different from a Latin European or Latin American function—boys and girls are given their first communion, the bishop confers confirmation at about the same age as with non-Asian Catholics, and people dress up for mass on Sunday. But the Goan priest has more charismatic status than the Catholic Father in other communities, African or white. This is a carry-over from the Hindu forbears of the Goans; quite unconsciously the *sādhu's* ascriptive charisma works on in the figure of the Catholic priest, himself a Goan and a celibate.

To summarize and conclude this final crucial chapter: there has been little if any change in religious actions and attitudes among the Asian minority, and there is no doubt some cultural lag in matters of religious ideology, if we juxtapose the contemporary Asians with their collaterals in India and Pakistan, and if we regard all of these as one large cultural body. Whether Hindu, Muslim, Sikh, or Roman Catholic, the people in East Africa have not been exposed to the intensive religious and secular dialog in which comparable groups in India and Pakistan now engage. This accounts for the religious naiveté of the Asian groups as contrasted with their South Asian kin. Ritual has been both fossilized and weakened among the less highly specific Hindu groups—the *sanātani,* the non-sectarian Gujarati forms of ritualistic and other religious observance, the weekly worship of the Sikhs in their Rāmgarhia and Singh Sabhā *gurdvarās.* However, there has been no decrease of intensity in religious attention among such Gujarati groups as the *Swāmīnārāyanis,* the followers of *bhakti*-cults (as that of the Sindhi saint-merchant Chella Ram,[19] whose picture is seen in almost all Lohana and many Patel houses throughout East Africa) of Sri Aurobindo, and Satya Sāī Bābā or of that led by the contemporary Lohana saint Hīrjī Bābā. The main problem that seems to mar objective reporting lies in the disaffection of the younger and the more cosmopolitan sectors of the minority. Although they share the modernistic, anti-traditionalist and overtly nonchalant parlance of similar groups in South Asia, they have no means of backstopping religious information which makes it possible, and even attractive, to modern South Asians to display a new degree of religious concern. With the exception of the Ismailis and the Goan Catholics, both of whom follow their respective religious observances without any embarrassment, regardless of their age or economic status, most modern Asians are quite alienated from the attitudes and acts of their elders; thus, they will reluctantly participate in religious functions, they will pretend or even believe that they are not interested in religion, and they will take pains, if confronted with questions and with pertinent discussion, to show that their values are secular and modern, and that they regard the religious involvement of their elders and their not-so-sophisticated peers as irritating, superstitious, and a waste of time. This holds good for the male population; very few women within any of the constituent religions make bold statements of any secularity—in fact if they did, it would be held against them by the men who claim secularity for themselves; for whereas religious involvement is thought to be somewhat sissy for a modern male, detachment from religious values on the part of women is interpreted as potentially mischievous, and as an attempt to loosen kin and marriage ties.

All this overt antagonism, however, dissimulates a persistent, culturally transmitted anxiety in religious matters. Indian society has not yet made the transition to a genuinely secular world view, and this is largely due to the historical accident that South Asia never created an autochthonous secular tradition. Modernisms which pervade Asian parlance, the values of democracy, nationalism, the concept of an Indian or Pakistani nation, the various forms of socialism and communism, all these were recent imports into South Asia, and even more recent arrivals in East Africa, where they came via India. Hence, when we analyze the dominant cultural themes in this expatriate community, it becomes futile and impossible to extricate the religious from the non-religious. The Asian's insistence that he is not concerned with religion and the occidental's statement of non-concern may sound alike, but they have entirely different implications. At this time, the western intellectual, if he makes such a statement at all, feels rather sad about it, being aware of his alienation from whatever grass roots he might think desirable; but the Asian's statement emerges from an opposite pole: he genuinely wants to be emancipated from religion, as the prototype of a retarding past, but he cannot, chiefly because no negotiable alternative presents itself to him. There is no Sartre, no Kafka, no Tillich to set a standard, and his means of choice range between embracing his ancestral religion as modified, however slightly, in East Africa, or trying to jettison it, but without any other value option to fill the vacuum. What he sees and knows of the West are the lowbrow European expatriates and their modest ideological equipment, the gadgets supplied by the West, the "sundowners," and other shattered remnants of the erstwhile *Pax Britannica,* whose agents were no more acquainted with the secular alternatives of western thought than the Asian settlers are.

NOTES

Chapter One

1. Hollingsworth, L. W. *The Asians of East Africa*. London: Macmillan Co., 1960; Delf, G. *Asians in East Africa*. London: Institute of Race Relations, Oxford University Press, 1963; J. Mangat. *A History of the Asians in East Africa*. Oxford: Clarendon Press, 1969; Gregory, R. G. *India and East Africa*. Oxford: Clarendon Press, 1971.

2. Morris, H. S., "Indians in East Africa," in *British Journal of Sociology*, V. 7, 1956, pp. 194-211; Pocock, David F., "Differences in East Africa: a study of caste and religion in modern Indian society," in *Southwestern Journal of Anthropology*, V. 13, 1957, pp. 289-300.

3. R. R. Kuczynski, *Demographic Survey of the British Colonial Empire*, London, Oxford University Press, 1949.

4. H. Kuper, *Indian People in Natal*, Durban: Natal University Press, 1959. p. 3.

5. See also A. Bharati, "Ideology and Content of Caste among the Indians of East Africa." in *Caste in Overseas Indian Communities*, ed. B. Schwartz, San Francisco: Chandler Publishers, 1967. pp. 267-320.

6. This is the Sanskrit spelling; without exception, the East African Jainas refer to themselves as *Jain*, in the Hindi and Gujarati version of the term. Depending on the context, i.e., scriptural or oral reference, I have used both "Jaina" and "Jain," respectively.

Chapter Two

1. A. K. Ingutia, "Caste: in India and Africa."

2. "Ideology and Context of Caste: the Indians in East Africa".

3. "India's Political Idiom" in *Politics and Society in India,* ed. C. H. Philips, New York: Praeger, 1962, pp. 134-148.

4. At the time of publication of this study, the best account is Prof. L Dumont's *Homo Hierarchicus,* and A. Beteille, *Castes: Old and New.*

5. The Arabic word *qaum* means "tribe" rather than caste, in Arabic; yet this term had been adapted to Muslim usage in certain areas to sup-plant the Indian word *jāti*: in large portions of Pakistan and India, however, Muslims still use *"jāti"* for their own endogamous groups.

6. All caste studies listed in the bibliography attach great importance to the defining role of pollution in accounting for caste hierarchies; but see especially H. Orenstein, *Gaon: Cohesion and Conflict.*

7. McKim Marriott, "Caste Ranking and Community Structure."

8. D. Pocock, "Differences in East Africa."

9. "Harijan" means "people of God," a term created by Gandhi and con-summately applied ever since, to all former untouchables as well as to some tribal groups.

10. See Kannan, C. T., *Intercaste and Intercommunity Marriages in India,* Bombay: Allied Publishers, 1963; also his "Intercaste Marriage in Bombay," *Sociological Bulletin* (Bombay), Vol. X, Sept. 1961, pp. 53-68.

11. A *gotra* is a patrisib with a mythical agnatic, apical ancestor. Re-gardless of religion and caste, the *gotra* system cuts across all Hindu or one-time Hindu sections of Indian society; the apical ancestor is usually one of the many Vedic seers (*ṛṣi*). Gotras are exogamous units. As is shown in this study, very few people are quite clear about the meaning and the extension of their *gotra*; the officiating brahmins and the matri-monial go-betweens usually know just about as much as is needed to ensure exogamy.

12. The 'second birth' is the young high-caste Hindu man's investiture with the holy thread, Sanskrit *(yajñopavīta),* which follows a course of sacred instruction and which introduces the person into adult member-ship of a "twice-born" caste.

13. The complex process of "Sanskritization" has been explored by many authors, including Milton Singer, McKim Marriott, Harold Gould, and others; it has been ingeniously criticized by J. F. Staal.

14. See note 11.

15. See note 9.

16. There are few concentrations of *digambara* Jains in the Gujarat, but more in the distant South, around Sravana Belgola in the State of Mysore.

No *digambara* monks or laymen, however, had actually been living in the nude for at least five centuries. Their founders are represented as nude, in sculpture and painting, as well as in literary reference, since nudeness stands for complete detachment in the religious universe of discourse. The only monks who actually walk around in the nude belong to the Naga group of Śaivite ascetics in the North of India.

17. The actual etymology of *visa ośvāl* is analogous to all caste nomenclature which refers to numerical units: *visa* is Middle Indic for 'twenty,' and *visa osval* simply means 'belonging to the twenty *Ośvāl* villages.' There is another Jain group, not represented in East Africa, called the '*dasa ośvāl*' or the people belonging to the 'cluster of ten (villages).' Professor David E. Sopher of Syracuse University suggested yet another etymology: the numbers '10,' '20,' etc. may refer to the actual or alleged percentage of 'pure' *ośvāl* origin, i.e., 10 or 20 percent, in relation to a stipulated total 'purity' of the caste. This could relate to a previous process of hypergamy, in which case the *higher* number would indicate a *lower* or less frequent occurrence of matrimonial alliances contracted with women of relatively lower caste status over a long period of time. *Oshwal,* or *Ośvāl,* or *Osavāl* (all the three spellings occur) is an area located in western Rajasthan bordering Gujarat. *ujjvala* 'bright' is therefore not really the derivand of *Oshval,* but is simply a loconymic, like hundreds of caste names in India. At one time, both the Visa Oshval and the Navanīt Vanik might have had genuine *banyā* or *marvārī*-like caste status. It is unlikely that the Jaina core-teaching, that of non-violence to all living beings including insects and the microbes of the soil, would have been disregarded in earlier days. I would suggest that these two groups might have been alienated at one time from their mercantile pursuits, which are standard for the Jainas; these two then turned to agriculture, both as landholders along with the non-Jaina *Patidārs* (Patels), or as laborer-tenants working on the land, but not owning it. In due course, this would have accounted for their being classed as agriculturists. Frequently, when the previous status of an agricultural caste whose members own land is not known, or doubtful, its leaders succeed in creating a quasi-martial ranking for it; but in the case of Jainas this was impossible, for although the ancient founders of Jainism were *kṣattrīyas,* the Indian image of the Jains has been that of merchants for at least one thousand years, probably much longer. In modern western India, therefore, the Navnit Vanik and the Visa Oshval could not have regained their *banyā* ranking. In East Africa, of course, their final return to the pursuit of trade and commerce came too late to have any effect on their caste ranking. The few *banyā* Jains in East Africa do not regard the Visa Oshval or the Navanīt Vanik as on a par with themselves, nor do they usually exchange brides with them in India. Exceptions have occurred

in East Africa, but those liaisons were between the extremely rich, where questions are hardly asked. This is a fairly pervasive syndrome in India: a group becomes 'down-casted,' as it were, when it has modally deviated from the traditional occupations of the neighboring groups with whom there had been matrimonial exchange, until the new occupation has become well-established—unless, of course, this occupation happens to be 'lower' or more polluting than the previous one. If the group then reverts to its previous occupation, it takes a long time for it to be readmitted to its previous status—and at times, castes once downgraded never regain their original status even after reverting to their erstwhile occupation.

18. See chapter "On Mantra" in my *Tantric Tradition*.

19. *prasād* is food offered to the deity in the ritualistic setting, then redistributed to the congregation. See my "Pilgrimage Sites and Indian Civilization," pp. 88-94.

20. As Khushwant Singh, *The Sikhs*, bibliography. More recently by the same author, *A History of the Sikhs*, 2 vols., Princeton: University Press, 1966.

21. Richard G. Fox, "Resiliency and Change in the Indian Caste System: the Umar of U.P." in *Journal of Asian Studies*, XXVI/4, 1967, pp. 575-587.

22. In fact, the first printed or published edition of the Rgveda was due to Max Müller at Oxford, and the *Sacred Books of the East* Series. No complete text ever appeared in India before the late 19th century.

23. This highly Christianized movement, which had its origin and its continuity entirely in the urban middle and upper classes of Calcutta, was created by Raja Rammohun Roy in the early 19th century. Until recently, Brahmos referred to themselves as such, *not* as Hindus; and although they would hardly call themselves a caste or a *jāti*, being too 'western' or 'modern' for that, they tended to become endogamous until the early decades of the present century; and village Bengalis certainly do refer to them as a *jāt*.

24. See Morris, H. S. "The Divine Kingship of the Aga Khan."

25. The Muslim call to prayer, done by the *mu'ezzin* who climbs on to the minaret for that purpose. I have witnessed two mosques in the city area, where the *azzān* has indeed been prerecorded, and is relayed from the minaret by a loudspeaker-cum-amplifier system. The believers who heard about it admitted it was true, but they frowned upon the situation.

26. Literally, the title means "he to whom the authority of the mission has been delegated." The sect publishes an organ in Gujarati and Urdu, *Gulšān-e-Da'udī* "Rose Garden of the Daudis" which is printed and distributed from Bombay. Whereas the Ithna Ašari, as their name implies, stress the 12th Imām; the Bohras historical leader was the 21st Imām Tayyid. Similar to the Ithna Ašari, the Bohras also believe that the actual

Imām is alive, but that he must live in hiding. Some followers think that the late Dr. Syedna *might* have been the actual Imām, not just his caretaker; but most Bohras deny this.

27. The best introductory study of the system still is Th. Beidelman, *A Comparative Analysis of the Jajmani System,* New York: J. J. Austin, 1959. Also published as Monograph No. VIII of the Association for Asian Studies.

Chapter Three

1. Fred Riggs, *Administration in Developing Countries.* Boston: Houghton Mifflin, 1965.

2. N. Spulber, *Development, Entrepreneurship and Discrimination: Antisemitic and Anti-sinitic Aspects.* Bloomington, Ind.: Indiana University, IDRC, Mimeo., 1965.

3. Willem F. Wertheim, "The Trading Minorities in Southeast Asia" in his East-West Parallels: *Sociological Approaches to Modern Asia* (Quadrangle Books, Chicago, 1965), pp. 39-85; for a critical summary of the work, see my review in the *Journal of the American Oriental Society,* Vol. 86/2, pp. 222-3.

4. Ambu H. Patel, *Struggle for "Release Jomo and His Colleagues."* New Kenya Publishers, Nairobi, 1963.

5. The manner in which the rising indigenous intelligentsia replaces the alien, and a scheme of possible universal applications, in which the indigene himself becomes the new entrepreneur, is well outlined in N. Spulber's paper.

6. Lord Hailey, *An African Survey,* Oxford University Press, London 1957, contains an excellent statement for the time it was written; two small books, G. Delf, *Asians in East Africa* (London 1963) and L. W. Hollingsworth *The Asians of East Africa* (London 1960) have some rudimentary material; most revealing is perhaps a study "Indian Immigrants in Kenya" by Raghava Rao, and the rejoinder plus surrejoinder of Chanan Singh (now a judge in the Kenya Supreme Court), both trained economists; in *The Indian Economic Journal,* 1957-1958, Bombay; and H. S. Morris, "Indians in East Africa," in *British Journal of Sociology,* Vol. 7, 1956; also Ann Evans-Kolars, *The Alien Town,* Geographical Dissertations Series, University of Chicago, 1959.

7. M. F. Hill, *The Permanent Way.* East African Railways and Harbors, Nairobi, 1949.

8. R. C. Thurnwald, *Black and White in East Africa,* Routledge, London 1935.

9. G. Delf, *Asians in East Africa,* London 1963, p. 45.

10. Ibid., p. 52ff.

11. Guy Hunter, *The New Societies of Tropical Africa: A Selective Study*. London: Oxford University Press, 1962, p. 147.

12. *Op. cit.*, p. 143 and p. 1.

Chapter Four

1. David Pocock "Differences in East Africa," and H. S. Morris, "The Indian Family in Uganda."

2. The custom of calling or referring to a spouse or any other related person by the name of his or her children rather than by direct naming.

3. *The Twice-Born*, especially p. 39-77.

4. Literally "assembly of the virtuous;" the most general Indian term for a religious congregation of any kind.

5. *Op. cit.*, pp. 282 sqq.

6. See my essay "Culture, Persons, and Non-Persons: the Anthropology of Hindi Movies."

7. For an exhaustive treatment, see chapter on "Mantra" in my *Tantric Tradition*.

8. For a good general survey, see E. Norbeck, *Religion in Primitive Society*.

9. This is the famous anthology of poems written by Ghalib, no doubt the most popular, if not necessarily the most outstanding, and certainly not the most prolific, among the Urdu poets of the classical period.

10. Anthropological literature on drinking behavior is on the increase. The most important periodical in this field is the *Quarterly Journal of Alcohol*, Yale University Press; it is a cross-disciplinary publication and presents the most objective reporting on the topic. For an excellent study, see also MacAndrew, *Drunken Comportment*.

11. "He who has never been drunk is not a good man." It loses in translation although it is not any more profound in the original.

12. Personal communication from Prof. Hellmut Wilhelm, Far Eastern Institute, University of Washington, 1961.

13. See McKim Marriott (ed.), *Village India*, passim.

14. Personal communication, January, 1962.

15. Personal communication from the late M. N. Roy, Dehra Doon, India, March, 1953.

Chapter Five

1. This was the presupposition of both Hollingsworth and Delf.

2. David G. Pocock, "Factions in Indian Society."

3. Ambu Patel 'compiled' and published a pathetic little book which

contains well over a hundred statements of varying length, by such very different people as Ashok Mehta, Odinga Oginga, Indira Gandhi, and a motley symposium of East African Indian leaders, businessmen of stature, etc. Patel published the volume at his own expense, in a press which he himself had set up; he also acted as his own printer, sales manager, and producer. See *Struggle for "Release Jomo & His Colleagues"* (correct: the imperative clause is hyphenated in the title of the book), Nairobi: New Kenya Publishers, 1963 (12th December, i.e., Kenya's Independence Day). The publishing firm, Ambu Patel's own, is now defunct.

4. The 160 or so definitions of 'Culture' were collected and edited with thorough annotations, See A. L. Kroeber & Clyde Kluckhohn, *Culture: A Crtical Review of Concepts and Definitions,* New York: Random House paperback V-226, 1963.

5. See Morris, H. S. "The Indian Family in Uganda," in *American Anthropologist* V. 61, 1959, pp. 779-789.

6. Lord Hailey, *An African Survey: Revised 1956,* London: Oxford University Press, 1957, pp. 404 sqq.

7. See note 1 above.

8. W. K. Hancock, *Survey of British Commonwealth Affairs,* Vol I., London 1937, p. 193. Like many of his contemporaries, Hancock echoed the objectively unfounded notion that Indians were somehow unclean and unhealthy. Previous to that, an official report was published, one that several Asian leaders remembered well, and quoted against the former government; it is likely that Hancock had seen this report and, lacking any anthropological knowledge or interest, he saw nothing wrong in perpetuating a stereotype once set by official records. Thus, the *Economic Commission Report* of 1919 (H. M. Stationery Office, London), read "physically the Indian is not a wholesome influence because of his incurable repugnance to sanitation and hygiene . . . the moral depravity of the Indian is equally damaging to the Africans. . . ," quoted in W. K. Hancock, *Survey,* p. 215.

9. *Post Office Directory,* East African High Commission, The Postmaster General of East African Posts and Telecommunications Administration, Kenya 1959-60. These figures show a steady increase until the 1965 edition, and a slight decline in 1966-67, probably but not necessarily due to Asians leaving the territories in numbers.

10. *Op. cit.,* p. 409 sqq.

Chapter Six

1. Louis Dumont, *Contributions to Indian Sociology,* Vol. I., The Hague: Mouton & Co., 1957, introduction.

2. The most eminent—and prolific—scholars in that School are Profs.

Milton Singer, McKim Marriott, and Barnhard S. Cohn.

3. G. Morris Carstairs, *The Twice Born,* Bloomington: Indiana University Press, 1958. This book was devastatingly criticized by Prof. Morris Opler (*American Anthropologist,* Vol. 61/6, 1959). Most of Opler's criticisms are well taken; still, the book has its value due to its author's felicitous selection of autobiographical statements which represent an important cross-section of the population in the area studied by him.

4. Bharati, "Patterns of Identification among the East African Asians," in *Sociologus* (Berlin), Vol. 15/2, Fall 1965, pp. 128-142.

5. Sanskrit "sacrifice"—a highly elaborate set of rituals with a defined purpose.

6. For an excellent restatement of 'Sanskritization,' see J. F. Staal, "Sanskrit and Sanskritization," in *Journal of Asian Studies,* Vol. XXII/3, 1963, pp. 261-275. Staal's article, however, should be read in conjunction with M. N. Srinivas, who first suggested these terms in *Religion and Society among the Coorgs of South India,* London: Oxford University Press, 1952.

7. Personal communication, taped in Nakuru, Kenya, May 12, 1964.

8. Literally "a coil, circle"; it is the horoscopic diagram drawn by astrologers for each client—on order, that is. It is from this chart that astrological calculations for the person are made.

9. See the author's monograph *Aesthetical Norm and Value-Modification in Modern India.* Calcutta: Indian Renaissance Institute Monograph N.I., 1962.

10. Edward Shils, *The Intellectual between Tradition and Modernity: The Indian Situation.* The Hague: Mouton & Co., 1960. This is an important, though very brief study.

11. See the author's autobiography *The Ochre Robe,* Doubleday-Anchor, New York, 1970, chapter "The Indian Legion." Also, "Hindu Scholars, Germany, and the Third Reich:" in *Quest,* Bombay: January-March 1965, pp. 74 sqq.

12. Personal communication by the late M. N. Roy, at Dehra Doon, India, March 1951.

13. This author knows Anita Bose quite well. She is now Mrs. Pfaff, wife of an economics professor at Michigan State University, East Lansing, Michigan.

14. See "Hindu Scholars, Germany, and the Third Reich."

15. *satsang,* literally "assembly of the virtuous" is the common name for religious meetings of any kind, both at a shrine or at a devotee's home.

16. Food offered to the deity as part of the ritual, and then distributed among the congregation. For an analysis of the function of *prasād,* see A.

Bharati "Pilgrimage Sites and Indian Civilization" in *Chapters in Indian Civilization*, Madison, Wisc.: Indian Studies Syllabus, 1967.

17. I have coined the term *pizza-effect* and used it with some heuristic success over the past few years. Pizza in the American diet is not quite what is used to be in Calabria, Southern Italy, where the majority of Italo-Americans came from. There, it had been a simple bread-dish. In the U.S.A., it was highly modified and embellished. Since World War II, the American *pizza* has become a popular dish all over Italy, not only in Calabria. Similarly, many things began to be appreciated in India only after they had been accepted in the West; this covers such diverse fields as Sanskrit scholarship, Indian music, and the film trilogy by Satyajit Ray, which was a complete flop in India before it received numerous occidental awards.

18. *Ardhamāgadhi* is technically a Prakrit, one of the ancient and Middle Indian languages of Northeastern India, quite as complex as Sanskrit and less well-studied than Pali, the Buddhist canonical language.

19. These priests have brahmin status, and they are accepted as such by Hindu brahmins as well. I could not, however, establish conclusively whether or not the ritualistic functionaries in Mombasa were actual Jaina brahmins, or Jainas of the dominant non-brahmin castes deployed for ritualistic office. Most of my Jaina informants insisted that any Jaina person who is pious and devout and well versed in the texts can perform the ritual. This, of course, would be in radical contrast to what Hindus and Jainas in India maintain.

20. The term is a Gujarati garbled form of the Arabic-Persian-Urdu word *mulāqāt* "a meeting, an encounter;" though this girl handled Hindi fairly well, and though she knew and used the word *mulāqāt* correctly in other contexts, she would not believe that *murakat* was borrowed, with its meaning changed, from *mulāqāt*.

21. A very austere vow observed by women who feel that they are in crucially critical situations. The person undertaking this vow must not eat, drink, or bathe before she sees the disc of the sun in the sky in the morning—which means considerable delay during the monsoons; and she must not eat cereals of any sort, thus virtually living on milk, fruit, and vegetables.

22. *bhajan* or *kīrtan* are synonymous; 'litany' is a somewhat narrow translation; a *bhajan* or *kīrtan* can include the recitation of some hagiographic account, a religious discourse, and a performance of religious music and dance. For a fine statement about *kīrtan*, see Milton Singer's *Krishna* book.

23. see note 16 above.

24. The French Peugeot sedan and station wagon are the most popular

cars in East Africa; small British cars and the Volkswagen, in this order, are the runners-up. Rich and sophisticated Asians frequently own Mercedes Benz models, which have the highest prestige of all cars in the area.

25. The exogamous unit in the kinship system; for an explanation of *gotra,* see Chapter II.

26. Philip Spratt, *Hindu Culture and Personality.* Also, my review of this book in *Journal of Asian Studies,* Vol. XXVI/3, May 1967, p. 519 sq.

27. By far the best account is that of P. Singer, *Sadhus and Charisma.* (Unpublished dissertation: Syracuse University, New York.)

28. See E. Norbeck, *Religion in Primitive Society,* p. 138 *et passim.*

29. A *mantra* is a mystic syllable, or chain of syllables, with or without lexical meaning; it is the instrumental base of meditation. For a thorough analysis, see this author's *Tantric Tradition,* chapter on Mantra. *Śakti* 'power' is the female aspect of the Supreme Deity.

30. The Indianist might have caught the theoretical incongruence of this statement. There is no 'God' in Jainism. But in this type of parlance, the Jain speaker uses the linguistic code of the majority, i.e., the Hindus; if he were challenged on the point, he would probably elaborate and state something to the effect that the *tīrthaṅkaras* 'ford-makers,' the founders of Jainism are referred to as *Bhagavān* 'Lord, God,' hence a statement like the above does not conflict with Jaina doctrine.

31. *Rāmrājya* was a mythological movie classic, produced well over three decades ago; it was a filmed version of the Epic *Rāmāyaṇa,* the account of the life and the deeds of Rāmacandra, the seventh incarnation of Viṣṇu. This movie was the only one Mahatma Gandhi ever saw; he commended it, and is reported to have seen it several times. In style and conceptual sophistication, it ranked, say, with *Ben Hur.* However, one of the most highly revered spokesmen of the Hindu Renaissance, the late Swami Śivānanda, would not even concede mythologicals: "One should not even attend the so-called religious movies. They are not really religious films. . . . What is the spiritual calibre of the actors there?" and a bit earlier "Cinemas produce an evil tendency in man. He cannot remain even for a day without attending a show. His eyes want to see some half-nude pictures and some kinds of colours. . . . Young girls and boys become passionate when they see the actors on the films kissing and hugging." *Sure Ways for Success in Life and God-Realization.*

32. The Hindu greeting of entrance and departure; it means "I honor thee" and it is accompanied by folding one's hands in front of one's chest.

33. See McKim Marriott, *Village India*; almost all the sections of this important anthology deal with this particular theme.

34. She was referring to two things: there are two groups in the Samāj,

the "*mās* (i.e., meat) party" and the "*ghās* (i.e., grass) party," each of them deriving their different inspiration from different leaders in the movement; the first reference was to members of the *mās* party; the second, implicit reference was to those members of the *ghās-party* whose members ate meat although they know they shouldn't.

35. Madhok's booklet *Hindu Rashtra* "Hindu Empire" is more of a credo than a study in political theory. It outlines the modal views of all radical Hindu rightists, and is significantly more sophisticated and better informed than most of the pamphleteering literature the Hindu right puts out in an unorganized, haphazard fashion.

36. Indian and Pakistani intellectuals prefer popular, eclectic, survey-like writings to primary texts. Joad's popularity in India, hence among East African Asians, is comparable perhaps to Will Durant's popularity in non-scholarly Britain and America. East African Asians read books that are read in India; they do not venture out on their own, though the purchase of books directly from Britain is financially much easier than in India due to increasing restrictions on imports in that country. At the time when C.E.M. Joad and a host of other British philosophical popularizers were in vogue in Britain, books could still be bought in India from British book agents; this came to a halt—both in India and Pakistan—around 1960; hence even if Indian students and college teachers were to direct their attention to more recent and superior works published in English, they could not buy them. No such restriction obtained in East Africa in 1964, when this research was conducted; books and other cultural goods could have been bought directly from Europe; but somehow, this was not done, as the intellectual model is set in India, even where western products of thought are concerned.

37. *jñān*, the modern North Indian pronunciation of Sanskrit *jñāna* means intuitive perception or knowledge of the supreme religious truth; the word is cognate with the Greek and Latin roots—*gno* (as in 'cognosco', 'cognition' etc.) but it refers to a religious universe of discourse, and never applies to mundane knowledge. Technical or semi-technical terms of Hindu theological provenance are always adduced in the Indian original, partly because they have no real English equivalent, partly because a basic theological vocabulary was constantly used by Swami Vivekananda and the other founders of the Hindu Renaissance, when they spoke English or their vernacular; English discourse among Indians is shot through with these Indian theological terms, some of which are now being picked up by the hippy-counterculture in the West.

38. Rāmacandra, the seventh incarnation of Viṣṇu, is the quintessence of the human that is divine; the hero of the *Rāmāyaṇa*. His image has been reinforced through the nationalist movement; Gandhi's last words were *he Rām* "o Rāma", subsequently laid out in Devanagari script

mosaic on his *samādhi* or burial place in New Delhi.

39. In *Struggle for "Free Jomo Kenyatta,"* pp. 138-150.

40. See preface to M. McGiffert, *The Character of Americans,* Homewood, Ill., Dorsey Press, 1964. Also, Kouwenhoven's article "The Disparaging of America" in the same book.

41. *Esthetical Norms and Value Modification.*

42. See note 17 above.

43. Ravi Varma was a 19th century painter of royal blood; he belonged to the family of the Nayer princes of Kerala. He was inspired by some embarrassingly mediocre Victorian painters who marketed their wares in India; the style has come to stay—and Ravi Varma was no doubt the most powerful single inspiration for South Asian contemporary polychrome art.

44. In *Hindu Culture and Personality.*

45. Chella Ram (also spelled Jhella Ram and Jhela Ram) was a Sindhi saint; a petty merchant like many other saints of the post-medieval and more recent rural, as well as the incipiently urban areas of India, he never embraced monasticism formally. Though originally known regionally only to Sindhis and Lohanas, his fame has spread, and his sainthood is accepted all over western India. He died around 1946. His life story is quite reminiscent of that of Guru Nānak, the founder of Sikhism, who lived four centuries earlier in a different part of India.

46. Strangely enough, kissing was not forbidden in the oldest Indian movies, produced between 1930 and 1940. There was mild osculation in such classics as *Sakuntalā* and *Candīdās*; see my article "Culture, Persons, and Non-Persons."

47. See the works of M. Klass, A. Niehoff, C. Jayawerdene.

48. Located in the Panjab, and Bihar respectively, these are indeed models of modern technological cooperation between countries supporting underdeveloped regions.

Chapter Seven

1. R. Redfield & M. Singer, "The Cultural Role of Cities," and R. Redfield, *Peasant Society and Culture,* Chapter 3.

2. Bharati, "Great Tradition and Little Traditions: an Anthropological View of Eastern Societies".

3. '*darśan*' is the focal term in the patron-client relationship between divinity and holy men, or between the latter and ordinary people. Though it means 'vision' quite literally, the *darśan*—theme is complex, and crucial to the Indian religious setting. See my elaborate statement on *darśan* in "Pilgrimage Sites and Indian Civilization."

4. I use the phrase 'Hindu Renaissance' in a sense radically different from

the way in which modern Indian apologists have been using it. For peda-
gogical reasons, I do not use it as a laudatory term; *see* my *Ochre Robe,*
and *Aesthetical Norms and Value Modifications in Modern India,* and
"The Hindu Renaissance and its Apologetic Patterns." This is an extremely complex topic, but quite briefly, the Hindu Renaissance covers
all the religious views and the concomitant religious practices of English-
speaking, urban Hindus since the middle of the 19th century; it is this
Hinduism which is most evident in East Africa.

5. Edward N. Shils, *The Intellectual between Tradition and Modernity:
the Indian Situation.*

6. The most reliable, scholarly, and ideologically unslanted modern
translation is that by the late Franklin Edgerton, *The Bhagavadgītā,*
New York: Harper Torchbook TB 115, paperback, 1964.

7. See note 3 above.

8. Just for the record: against the assumption of several psychiatrist
friends to whom I related this episode subsequently, I do not think this
woman was a pathological case, unless one calls all the millions of cases
of "possession" pathological by a decree of lexical synonymity. This,
however, does not seem to be at all justifiable, for it would blur the
distinction between genuinely pathological cases which do occur in the
world of possession, and the more frequent situations where the person
functions quite normally within his or her society at all other times.

9. See my *Tantric Tradition,* Chapter "On Mantra."

10. See my "Pilgrimage Sites and Indian Civilization."

11. See my "The Use of 'Superstition' as an Anti-Traditional Device."

12. The Railway Directory lists Tatanagar, but the more frequent name
of the place is Jamshedpur; both names, of course, commemorate the
founder of the Tata industrial empire, Sir Jamshedji Tata. Now nationalized, with a Tata scion as the Government-appointed director, the Tata
steel plant is one of the most up-to-date in the world, and certainly
among the most highly advanced in Asia.

13. *vrata* in Sanskrit, *vrat* or *brat* in the modern North Indian vernaculars means a 'vow'. Some *vrat* have strongly psychosomatic components,
as for instance the vows for Subbramania, the tutelary God of the
Tamilians, where men and women pierce their cheeks and tongues with
iron skewers (see H. Kuper, *Indians in Natal,* pp. 221 sqq.); but by and
large, the term *vrat* does not have the sinister overtones of certain Roman
Catholic patterns; perhaps 'observance' might be a more felicitous translation. Most Hindu women perform *vrats* of many kinds on certain days
in the month, especially on *ekadaśī,* the eleventh day of each lunation.
Many people, both men and women, perform *vrat* for special reasons,
seeking divine favor for many things—recovery from sickness, wealth,
love, etc.

14. Sri Aurobindo's *magnum opus* is *The Life Divine,* which has had over a dozen editions, and which has been translated into many western, and into all Indian languages.

15. See Morton Klass, *Indians in Trinidad,* and Arthur Niehoff, *East Indians in the West Indies.*

16. The late Aga Khan produced a somewhat stylized autobiography of the 'as told to' type—and Somerset Maugham's co-authorship helps. Apart from the Aga Khan's amusingly [or embarrassingly] open and somewhat naive admiration for royalty and for an international aristocracy already on the wane in his days—an aristocracy of which he was very much part— the book is valuable and highly informative. See *Memoirs of the Aga Khan.*

17. Gopal Singh, *Guru Granth Sahib*; complete translation in four volumes.

18. See above; also, Khushmant Singh's excellent material.

19. Dada Chellaram, the latter-day Hindu saint (1904-1946), should be of great interest to any student of contemporary religious movements in India. A Sindhi merchant, follower of Guru Nanāk, the founder of Sikhism (1469-1539 AD), he was brought up in the *'sahajdhāri'* "light-wear," i.e., the non-turban tradition of Sikhism prevalent in non-Muslim Sindhi society. His teachings, including his intentionally archaic wording, was that of the simplistic, pious, anti-intellectual, anti-ritualistic, puritanical Sikh gurus. His letters to a Panjabi Sikh friend have been published in English (*Niraguna Patra*), along with his other tracts, sermons, and aphorismic writings. Chellaram spoke the theologically naive medium of much of the Hindu Renaissance and there is not a single line in his writings which could and would not also have been written by most of the other leaders of the Hindu Renaissance. Here are a few samples: "Man is prone to fall. He is weak at resisting desires." (*Niraguna Patra,* p. 43); "avoid discussions on religious matters. They lead nowhere." (ibid., p. 123). Such, and only such stereotype exhortations in a low key fill Chellaram's writings. He has become the modern patron-saint not only of Sindhi Hindus, but of a majority of Lohanas and of many Patels, within less than three decades after his death. His oleograph photographs invariably adorn a wall in thousands of East African and Indian Hindu households, together with pictures of other saints, ancient and modern, gods, Indian national leaders, and film actresses. Theologically simple, anti-Sanskritic, puritanical modes of homiletic are avidly interiorized by modern Hindus, unless they choose a more complex and sophisticated Renaissance doctrine (Aurobindo, Ramakrishna-Vivekananda). There does not seem to be any intermediary choice. Chellaram appeals to all Gujarati and Sindhi Hindus who would be modern without being deprived of some sort of ideological grass roots identity.

BIBLIOGRAPHY

H. H. The Aga Khan, Sultan Muhammad Shah. *The Memoirs of Aga Khan: World Enough and Time.* Told by Somerset Maugham. New York: Simon & Schuster, 1954.

———. *Glimpses of Islam.* 2nd enlarged ed. Lahore: Sh. Muhammad Ashraf, 1961.

Agnihotri, V. "Workers of Indian Origin Abroad." *Indian Labour Journal* (Delhi), Sept. 1962, pp. 737-48.

Agrawal, K. G. "Marital Choices in India." *Indian Journal of Psychology,* Vol. 39, Sept. 1964, pp. 107-11.

Ahsan, Syed R. "East Indian Agricultural Settlements in Trinidad: A Study in Cultural Geography." Thesis, University of Florida, 1963.

Alsdorf, Ludwig. *Beitraege zur Geschichte des Vegetarismus und der Rinderverehrung in Indien.* Wiesbaden: F. Steiner Verlag, 1962.

Amin, R. K. Mogri. *Socio-Economic Study of a Charotar Village.* Anand Bombay: Charotar Book Stall, 1965.

Ansari, Ghaus. *Muslim Caste in Uttar Pradesh.* Lucknow: The Ethnographic & Folk Culture Society, 1960.

Archer, John C. *The Sikhs in Relation to Hindus, Moslems, Christians, and Ahmeddiyas.* Princeton: Princeton University Press, 1946.

Aurobindo, Sri. *The Life Divine.* Calcutta: Arya Publishing House, 1947.

Aurora, G. S. "Process of social adjustment of Indian immigrants in Britain." *Sociological Bulletin* (Bombay), Vol. 4, Sept. 1965, pp. 39 sqq.

Bailey, F. G. *Caste and the Economic Frontier*. Manchester: Manchester University Press, 1957.

———. "Closed social stratification in India." *Archives of European Sociology*, Vol. 4, 1963, pp. 107-24.

Barber, B. "Social Mobility in Hindu India." Mimeographed. New York: Barnard College, 1961.

Benedict, Burton. "Factionalism in Mauritian Villages." *British Journal*, Vol. 8, 1957, pp. 328-42.

———. *Indians in Plural Society* (Indians in Mauritius). London: H. M. Stationery Office, 1961.

Berghe, Pierre van den. "Indians in Natal and Fiji: A 'Controlled Experiment' in Culture Contact." *Civilizations* (Brussels), Vol. 12, 1962, pp. 75-87.

Bernatizik, Ingrid. "Was machen die Inder in Afrika?" *Westermanns Monatshefte* (Germany), No. 103, Nov. 1962, pp. 67-73.

Berreman, G. D. "Caste, Racism, and Stratification." *Contributions to Indian Sociology*, ed. L. Dumont, 1963, pp. 122-25.

———. "The Study of Caste-ranking in India." *Southwestern Journal of Anthropology*, Vol. 21, 1965, pp. 115-29.

———. "Stratification, Pluralism and Interaction: A comparative analysis of Caste." In *Ciba Foundation Symposium on Caste and Race*, edited by A. V. S. deReuck and J. Knight, pp. 45-73. London: J. & A. Churchill, 1967. Available separately, Center for South Asia Studies, Univ. of California reprint No. 259.

Beteille, A. *Castes: Old and New*. New York: Asia Publishing House, 1969.

Bharati, A. *The Ochre Robe*. New York: Doubleday, Anchor Books, 1970.

———. *Esthetical Norm and Value Modification in Modern India*. Indian Renaissance Institute Monograph, No. L. Calcutta: 1962.

———. "Cultural Criticism as a Tool for Social Studies." *Quest* (Bombay), No. 33, 1962, pp. 15-22.

———. "The Indians in East Africa: A Survey of Problems

of Transition and Adaptation," *Sociologus* (Berlin), Vol. 14, 1964, pp. 170-77.

———. "Problems of the Asian Minorities in East Africa," *Pakistan Horizon* (Karachi), 1964, pp. 342-49.

———. "Political Pressures and Reactions in the Asian Minority in East Africa." Maxwell Overseas Center Occasional Papers, 1964.

———. "Patterns of Identification among the East African Asians." *Sociologus* (Berlin), Vol. 15/2, 1965, pp. 128-42.

———. "A Social Survey." *In Portrait of a Minority: The Asians in Africa,* edited by D. P. Ghai, pp. 13-65. London: Oxford University Press, 1965.

———. "Possession and Divination Among Lohana Hindus in East Africa." *Abstracts of the 63rd Annual Meeting of the American Anthropological Association,* Vol. 64, 1965, p. 8.

———. "The Unwanted Elite: The Asians of East Africa." *Transaction,* July-August 1966, pp. 17-24, (illustrated).

———. "Ideology and Content of Caste among Indians in East Africa." In *Caste in Overseas Indian Communities,* edited by Barton M. Schwartz, pp. 283-321. Chicago: Science Research Associates, 1967.

———. *The Tantric Tradition.* New York: Doubleday, Anchor Books, 1970, particularly the chapter "On Mantra."

———. "The Use of 'Superstition' as an Anti-Traditional Device in Modern India." *Contributions to Indian Sociology* (New Series), Dec. 1970.

———. "The Hindu Renaissance and its Apologetic Patterns." *Journal of Asian Studies,* Vol. 29/2, Feb. 1970, pp. 267-87.

———. "Pilgrimage Sites and Indian Civilization." In *Chapters in Indian Civilization,* Vol. I., edited by J. W. Elder, pp. 83-126. Dubuque (Iowa): Kendall-Hunt Publishing Co., 1970.

———. "Modes of Cultural Identification in Modern India." In *Great Tradition and Little Traditions: Indological Investigations in Cultural Anthropology.* Banaras: Chowkhamba Sanskrit Series Publications, 1972.

———. "Culture, Persons, and Non-Persons: The Anthropology of Hindi Movies." In *The Movie in Asian Folk Cul-*

ture, edited by C. Leslie. To be published, 1973.

Brelvi, Mahmud. *Islam in Africa.* Lahore: Institute of Islamic Culture, 1964.

Carstairs, G. Morris. *The Twice Born.* Bloomington: Indiana University Press, 1966.

Chanan Singh. Review of *Indian Immigrants in Kenya* by G. Raghava Rao. *Indian Economic Journal* (Bombay), Vol. 4, No. 3, Jan. 1957, pp. 295-98.

———. "Asians in East Africa: The Historical Background." In *Portrait of a Minority,* edited by D. P. Ghai, pp. 1-13. London: Oxford University Press, 1965.

Chandrashekharayah, K., "Mobility within the Caste." *Sociological Bulletin,* Vol. IX/1-2, 1962, pp. 62-67.

Chellaram, Dada. *Niraguna Patra.* Saproon (Himalayas): Niraguna Balik Satsang Mandal, 1964.

Chettiar, T. S. Avinashalingam. *Vivekananda and Gandhi.* Coimbatore: Sri Ramakrishna Mission Vidyalaya, 1962.

Cohn, Bernard S. "Changing Tradition of a Low Caste." *Traditional India* edited by M. Singer, pp. 207-16. Philadelphia: American Folklore Society, No. 9, 1959.

Coopan, S. "Indian population: a Small but Significant Minority." *Economic Opinion* (Johannesburg), No. 9, Feb. 1962, pp. 37-42.

———. "The Indian Outlook." In *Africa in Transition* edited by P. Smith. London: 1968.

Dadoo, Y. M. "India's Role in the Struggle Against Apartheid." *Afro-Asian and World Affairs,* Vol. 1, Summer 1964, pp. 272-75.

Datta, Kalikinkar. *Renaissance, Nationalism and Social Changes in Modern India.* Calcutta: Bookland, 1965.

Davids, Leo. "The East Indian Family Overseas." *Social and Economic Studies,* Vol. 13, Sept. 1964, pp. 383-94.

Delf, G. *Asians in East Africa.* London: Institute of Race Relations, Oxford University Press, 1963.

Derrett, J. Duncan. "East Africa: Recent Legislation for Hindus." *American Journal of Comparative Law,* Vol. 11/3, 1962.

Desai, I. P., and Damle, Y. B. "A Note on the Change in Caste." In *Ghurya Felicitation Volume* edited by K. M.

Kapadia. Bombay: Popular Book Depot, 1964.

Desai, R. H. *Indian Immigrants in Britain.* London: Institute of Race Relations, Oxford University Press, 1963.

Dodge, Peter. "Comparative Racial Systems in the Greater Caribbean." *Social and Economic Studies* (Jamaica), Institute of Social and Economic Research, Vol. 16/3, September 1967, pp. 249-62.

Dotson, Floyd & Dotson, Lilian. "Indians and Coloureds in Rhodesia and Nyasaland." In *Race* (London), Vol. 5/1, 1963, pp. 61-75.

————. *The Indian Minority of Zambia, Rhodesia, and Malawi.* New Haven: Yale University Press, 1968.

Drieberg, Jack H. *The East Africa Problem.* London: Williams & Norgate Co., 1930.

Driver, Edwin D. "Caste and Occupational Structure in Central India." *Social Forces,* Vol. 41, Oct. 1962, pp. 26-31.

————. "Family-structure and Socio-economic Status in Central India." *Sociological Bulletin* (Bombay), Vol. 11, 1962, pp. 112-20.

D'Souza, Victor S. "Caste and Endogamy: A Reappraisal of the Concept of Caste." *Journal of the Anthropological Society of Bombay,* Vol. 11/1, 1959, pp. 11-42.

Dumont, L. and Pocock, D. F. "Pure and Impure." *Contributions to Indian Sociology,* Vol. III, 1959, pp. 9-39.

————. *Homo, Hierarchicus: essai sur le systeme des castes.* Paris: Gallimard, 1966.

————. "A note on locality in relation to descent." *Contributions to Indian Sociology,* No. 7, March 1964, pp. 71-6.

Edgerton, Franklin, The *Bhagavadgita.* New York: Harper & Row, Torchbooks, 1964.

Enthoven, R. E. *The Tribes and Castes of Bombay.* Bombay: Government Central Press, 1920-2, 3 vols.

Federation of Indian Chambers of Commerce and Industry. East Africa. 1st. ed. New Delhi, 1964.

Firth, Raymond et al. "Factions in Indian and Overseas Indian Societies." *British Journal of Sociology,* Vol. 8, 1957.

Ghai, D. P. and Ghai, Y. P. "Asians in East Africa: Problems and Prospects." *Journal of Modern African Studies* (Cambridge, England), Vol. 3, May, 1965, pp. 35-51.

————. eds. *Portrait of a Minority: The Asians in East Africa.*

London: Oxford University Press, 1970.

———. "An Economic Survey." *In Portrait of a Minority: The Asians in East Africa* edited by D. P. Ghai and Y. P. Ghai, pp. 91-113. London: Oxford University Press, 1970.

Ghai, Yash P. "The Future Prospects." In *Portrait of a Minority: The Asians in East Africa* edited by D. P. Ghai and Y. P. Ghai, pp. 129-54. London: Oxford University Press, 1970.

Ghurye, G. S. *Caste and Race in India.* Bombay: Popular Book Depot, 1950.

———. "Bombay Suburbanites: Some Aspects of Their Working Life." *Sociological Bulletin* (Bombay), Vol. 13, Sept. 1964, pp. 73-83.

Gillion K. L. *Fiji's Indian Migrants: a History to the End of Indenture in 1920.* Melbourne: Oxford University Press & Australian National University, 1962.

Goldthorpe, J. E. "Asians." In *Outlines of East African Society,* Chapter 55. Kampala: Makerere College Publications, 1958.

Gould, Harold A. "Sanskritization and Westernization: Further Comments." *Economic Weekly* (Bombay), Vol. 14, Jan. 13, 1962, pp. 48-51.

Green, Helen Bagenstose. "Socialization Values in the Negro and East Indian Subcultures of Trinidad." *Journal of Social Psychology,* Vol. 64, Oct. 1964, pp. 1-20.

Gregory, Robert G. "Churchill's Administration of East Africa: A Period of Indian Disillusionment." *Journal of Indian History,* Vol. 44/2, 1966, pp. 397-416.

———. *India and East Africa: A History of Race Relations Within the British Empire, 1890-1939.* Oxford: Clarendon Press, 1971.

Hailey, Lord. *An African Survey.* Rev. ed. London: Oxford University Press, 1957.

Hallen, G. A. and Theodorson, G. A. "Change and Traditionalism in the Indian Family." *Indian Journal of Social Research,* Vol. 6/2, 1965, pp. 122-31; and Vol. 6/3, 1965, pp. 208-11.

———. "Change and Traditionalism in the Indian Family" (Part 3). *Indian Journal of Social Research,* Vol 4/2, 1963, pp. 105-10.

Harder, Kelsie B. Descriptions of Marriages in the Panjab. Chillicothe: Ohio Valley Research Project, Ross County Historical Society, 1963.

Harper, Edward B. "Ritual Pollution as an Integrator of Caste and Religion." *Journal of Asian Studies,* Vol. 23, June 1964, pp. 151-97.

Hazareesingh, K. "The Religion and Culture of Indian Immigrants in Mauritius, and the Effect of Social Change." *Comparative Studies in Society and History,* Vol. 8, 1966, pp. 241-57.

Hazlehurst, Leighton W. *Entrepreneurship and the Merchant Caste in a Panjabi City.* Durham: Duke University Press, 1966.

Hey, Peter. *The Rise of the Natal Indian Elite.* Pietermaritzenburg: University of Natal Press, 1962.

Hill, M. F. *The Permanent Way.* Nairobi: East African Railways and Harbours, 1949.

Hollingsworth, L. W. *The Asians of East Africa.* London: MacMillan Co., 1960.

Hsu, Francis. L. K. *Clan, Caste, and Club.* New York: Van Nostrand, 1963.

Huttenback, Robert A. "Indians in South Africa 1860-1914." *English Historical Review,* Vol. 81, 1966, pp. 273-91.

Hutton, John H. *Caste in India.* 3rd ed. Bombay: Oxford University Press, 1961.

———. *Caste in India, Its Nature, Function, and Origin.* Cambridge: Cambridge University Press, 1946.

Ibbetson, D. Ch. J. *Panjab Castes.* Lahore: Government Printing Press, 1916.

Inayat, Ullah. "Caste, *Paṭṭi* and Faction in the Life of a Panjab Village." *Sociologus* (Berlin), Vol. 8/2, 1953, pp. 170-86.

Ingutia, A. K. "Caste in India and Africa." *Transition* (Kampala Uganda), Vol. 5, 1965, pp. 15-19.

Ishwaran, K. and Mogey, J., eds. *Family and Marriage.* Leiden: E. J. Brill, 1963.

Jaina Deravasi Organization. *Śrī Pārśvanātha Pratiṣṭhā Mahotsav Khaṇḍ.* (In Gujarati.) Commemoration Volume of the Inauguration Festival of the Jain Pārśvanāth Shrine. Mombasa: Jaina Śvetāmbara Derāvasī Sangh, 1963.

Jayawardena, Ch. "Religious Belief and Social Change: Aspects of the Development of Hinduism in British Guyana." *Comparative Studies in Society and History,* Vol. 8, 1966, pp. 211-40.

Joshi, P. S. *The Tyranny of Colour: a Study of the Indian Problem in South Africa.* Durham: E. P. & Commercial Printing Co., 1942.

Joshi, V. H. *Economic Development and Social Change in a South Gujarat Village.* Baroda: University of Baroda, 1966.

Kannan, C. T. *Intercaste and Inter-community Marriages in India.* Bombay: Allied Publishers, 1963.

———. "Intercaste Marriage in Bombay." *Sociological Bulletin* (Bombay), Vol. 10, Sept. 1961, pp. 53-68.

Kapadia, K. M. *Marriage and Family in India.* 3rd ed. London: Oxford University Press, 1966.

———. ed. *Ghuyre Felicitation Volume.* Bombay: Popular Book Depot, 1964.

———. *Hindu Kinship: An Important Chapter in Hindu Social History.* Bombay: Popular Book Depot, 1947.

———. *Marriage and Family in India.* London: Oxford University Press, 1955.

———. "The Growth of Townships in South Gujarat: Maroli Bazar." *Sociological Bulletin* (Bombay), Vol. 10, 1961, pp. 69-87.

———. "Caste in Transition." *Sociological Bulletin* (Bombay), Vol. 9, 1-2, 1962, pp. 73-90.

Karve, Irawati. *Hindu Society: an Interpretation.* Poona: Deccan College, 1961.

———. *Kinship Organization in India.* Bombay & New York: Asia Publishing House, 1965.

Khan, Nasir A. "Emerging New Pattern of Marriage in Indian Society." *Indian Journal of Social Research,* Vol. 4/2, 1963, pp. 89-96.

Klass, Morton. *East Indians in Trinidad: A Study of Cultural Persistence.* New York: Columbia University Press, 1961.

Kolars, Ann Evans. *The Alien Town: Patterns of Settlement in Busoga, Uganda.* Chicago: Department of Geography Research Publication, No. 55, 1958.

Kolenda, Pauline. "A Multiple Scaling Technique for Caste Ranking." *Man in India,* Vol. 39, No. 2, 1959, pp. 127-47.

————. "Religious Anxiety and Hindu Fate." *Journal of Asian Studies,* Vol. 23, June 1964, pp. 71-81.

Kondapi, C. *Indians Overseas.* Bombay: Oxford University Press, 1951.

Kuczynski, R. R. *Demographic Survey of the British Colonial Empire.* London: Oxford University Press, 1949.

Kudryavtsev, M. K. "On the Role of the Jats in India's Ethnic History." *Journal of Social Research* (Ranchi, Bihar), Vol. 7, Sept. 1964, pp. 126-35.

Khushwant Singh. *The Sikhs.* London: Allen & Unwin, 1953.

Kunhi, Muhammad M. "Indian Minorities in Ceylon, Burma, and Malaysia." *Indian Yearbook of International Affairs* (Delhi), 1964, Vol. 1, pp. 405-72.

Kuper, Hilda. *Indian People in Natal.* Natal (South Africa): University Press, 1960.

Lakshmanna, Ch. "Caste, Democracy, and the Social Order." *Indian Journal of Social Research,* April 1964, pp. 41-7.

Lakshmipathy, S. "Future of Indians in Malaysia." *Indian Review* (Madras), Vol. 64, Oct. 1965, pp. 517-18.

Leach, E. R. "What Should we Mean by 'Caste'." In *Aspects of Caste in South India, Ceylon, and Northwest Pakistan* (Cambridge Papers in Social Anthropology, No. 2.) London & New York: Cambridge University Press, 1971.

Leys, Norman M. *The Colour Bar in East Africa.* London: Hogarth Press, 1941.

MacAndrew, C. and Edgerton, R. B. *Drunken Comportment.* Chicago: Aldine Publishing Co., 1970.

Madan, T. N. "Is the Brahmanic *Gotra* a Grouping of Kin?" *Southwestern Journal of Anthropology,* Vol. 18, 1962, pp. 59-77.

Madhok, Balraj. *Hindu Rashtra: A Study in Indian Nationalism.* Calcutta: Swastik Prakashan, 1955.

Mahajani, Usha. *The Role of Indian Minorities in Burma and Malaya.* Bombay: Vora, 1960.

Majumdar, B. B. *Militant Nationalism in India and its Socio-Religious Background.* Calcutta: General Printers & Publishers, 1966.

Majumdar, D. N. *Caste and Communication in an Indian Village.* Delhi: Asia Publishing House, 1959.

Mamoria, C. B. "Marriage and Family in India." *Indian*

Journal of Social Work, Vol. 23, July 1962, pp. 199-208.

Mangat, J. S. *History of the Asians in East Africa, 1896-1965.* Oxford: Clarenden Press.

Marquet, J. *The Premise of Inequality in Ruanda.* London: Oxford University Press, 1961.

Marenco, E. E. "Caste and Class among the Sikhs of Northwest India." Thesis, Columbia University, 1963.

Marriott, McKim. *Caste Ranking and Community Structure in Five Regions of India and Pakistan,* Monograph Series No. 23. Poona: Deccan College, 1958.

———. "Interactional and Attributional Theories of Caste-ranking." *Man in India,* Vol. 39, 1959, pp. 92-107.

———. *Village India—Studies in the Little Community.* Chicago: University of Chicago Press, 1966.

Mason, Ph. *An Essay in Racial Tension.* London: Royal Institute of International Affairs, 1954.

Mathur, K. S. *Caste and Ritual in a Malwa Village.* New York & London: Asia Publishing House, 1964.

Mayer, Adrian C. "Association in Fiji Indian Rural Society." *American Anthropologist,* Vol. 14, 1958, pp. 97-108.

———. "The Dominant Caste in a Region of Central India." *Southwestern Journal of Anthropology,* Vol. 14, 1958, pp. 407-27.

———. *Caste and Kinship in Central India: A Village and its Region.* London: Routledge, 1960.

———. *Peasants in the Pacific: A Study in Fiji Indian Rural Society.* Berkeley: University of California Press, 1964.

———. *Indians in Fiji.* London: Institute of Race Relations, Oxford University Press, 1963.

Mehta, Subhas Chandra. "Persistence of the Caste System: Vested Interest in Backwardness." *Quest* (Bombay), No. 36, January 1963, pp. 20-27.

Mishra, K. C. "*Gotra* and Exogamy." *Prajna* (Banaras Hindu University), *Vol.* 9/1, 1965, pp. 155-62.

Misra, B. *The Indian Middle Classes: Their Growth in Modern Times.* London & New York: Oxford University Press, 1961.

Misra, Satish Chandra. *Muslim Communities in Gujarat: Preliminary Studies in their History and Social Organization.* New York: Asia Publishing House, 1964.

Mookherji, S. B. "Indian Minority in Southeast Asia." *Mod-*

ern Review (Calcutta), No. 111, Jan. 1962, pp. 22-30; Feb. 1962., pp. 127-35.

———. "The Exodus of the Overseas Indians." *Eastern World* (London), Vol. 18, Nov. 1964, pp. 13-15.

Morris, H. Stephen. "Indians in East Africa." *British Journal of Sociology,* Vol. 7, 1956, pp. 194-211.

———. "The Plural Society." *Man* (London), Vol. 57, 1957.

———. "The Divine Kingship of the Aga Khan."·*Southwestern Journal of Anthropology,* Vol. 14/4, 1958.

———. "The Indian Family in Uganda." *American Anthropologist,* Vol. 61, 1959, pp. 779-89.

———. "Communal Rivalry among Indians in Uganda." *British Journal of Sociology,* Vol. 8, 1967, pp. 306-17.

Mukherjee, Ramakrishna. "Indian Tradition and Social Change." *Patna University Journal,* Vol. 20/1, 1965, pp. 56-80.

Mutatkar, R. K. "Caste, Leadership, and Group Dynamics." *Bulletin of the Deccan College Research Institute* (Poona), Vol. 23, 1962/3, pp. 83-93.

Mwulia, N. D. E. *"Indians' Role in Uganda Economy and Politics: 1900-1962."* Thesis, Howard University, 1966.

Nanavati, M. B. "A Village in Gujarat: A Study." *Indian Journal of Agriculture and Economics* (Bombay), Vol. 16, 1961, pp. 1-11.

Napal, D. *Manilall Maganlall Doctor: Pioneer of Indo-Mauritian Emancipation.* Fort Lewis (Mauritius): Neo Press Service, 1963.

Narain, Iqbal. *The Politics of Racialism: A Study of the Indian Minority in South Africa.* Agra: Shiva Lal Agarvala, 1962.

Niehoff, Arthur and Niehoff, Juanita. *East Indians in the West Indies.* Milwaukee: The Public Museum, 1960.

Norbeck, E. *Religion in Primitive Society.* New York: Harper & Row, 1961.

Opler, Morris E. "The Problem of Selective Culture Change." In *The Progress of Underdeveloped Areas,* edited by Hoselitz, pp. 126-34. Chicago: University of Chicago Press, 1952.

———. Review of *The Twice Born,* by G. M. C. Carstairs. *American Anthropologist,* Vol. 61/6, 1959.

Orenstein, Henry. *Gaon: Conflict and Cohesion in an Indian*

Village. Princeton: Princeton University Press, 1965.

Pachai, P. L. "South African Indians and Citizenship: A Historical Survey." *Africa Quarterly* (New Delhi), Vol. 4, Oct. 1964, pp. 167-78.

Patel, Ambu H. and Thakur, N. S., eds. *Struggle for 'Release Jomo Kenyatta.'* Nairobi: New Kenya Publishers, 1963.

Patel, Tara. "Caste as a Factor in Social Tensions." *Seminar on Social Integration in India,* Agra 1961, pp. 73-80.

Pather, S. R. ed. *Centenary of Indians.* Durban: Cavalier Publishers, 1961.

Pocock, David F. "Differences in East Africa: A Study of Caste and Religion in Modern Indian Society." *Southwestern Journal of Anthropology,* Vol. 13, 1957, pp. 289-300.

———. "Factions in Indian Society." *British Journal of Sociology,* Vol. 8, 1957, pp. 315 sqq.

———. "Indians in East Africa." *Economic Weekly* (Bombay), Vol. 10, 1958, pp. 863-4.

———. "Race and Racism in East Africa." *Economic Weekly* (Bombay), Vol. 10, 1958, pp. 999-1004.

———. "Generations in East Africa." *Economic Weekly* (Bombay), Vol. 12, 1960, pp. 153-62.

———. "The Hypergamy of the Patidars." In *Ghurya Felicitation Volume,* edited by K. M. Kapadia, pp. 195-204. Bombay: Popular Book Depot, 1964.

Prabhu, P. N. *Hindu Social Organization.* Bombay: Popular Book Depot, 1954.

Prasad, Amba. "People of Indian Origin in Uganda." *Africa Quarterly* (New Delhi), Vol. 2, 1963, pp. 240-50.

Rai, K. B. "India's Stake in Africa." *Africa Quarterly* (New Delhi), Vol. 4, Oct. 1964, pp. 152-56.

Rajkumar, N. V. *Indians Outside India.* New Delhi: All India Congress Committee Publications, 1951.

Rao, G. Raghava. "Indian Immigrants in Kenya: A Survey." *Indian Economic Journal* (Bombay), Vol. 3, July 1956. (See Also Chanan Singh's review of this article.)

Rastogi, P. N. "Functional Analysis of Sanskritization." *Eastern Anthropologist* (Lucknow), Vol. 16, Jan. 1963, pp. 10-19.

Rattansi, P. M. "The Asians in East Africa: An Educational Survey." In *Portrait of a Minority,* edited by D. P. Ghai and Y. P. Ghai. London: Oxford University Press, 1970.

Rivers, W. H. R. "The Origin of Hypergamy." *Journal of the Bihar and Orissa Research Society* (Patna), Vol. 8, 1921, pp. 9-24.

Rogers, C. A. Frantz, Ch. *Racial Themes in Southern Rhodesia.* New Haven: Yale University Press, 1962.

Ross, Allen D. *The Hindu Family in Its Urban Setting.* Toronto: Toronto University Press, 1961.

Rothermund, Indira. *Die Politische und Wirtschaftliche Rolle der Asiatischen Minderheit in Ostafrika,* Afrika-Studien No. 6. Berlin & New York: Springer Verlag, 1965.

Sabikhi, Vanita. "Indian Minorities in South Africa." *Afro-Asian and World Affairs* (New Delhi), Vol. 2, Spring 1965, pp. 57-60.

Sangave, V. A. *Jaina Community: a Social Survey.* Bombay: Popular Book Depot, 1959.

Saraswati, B. N. "Caste, Craft, and Change." *Man in India* (Ranchi, Bihar, India), Vol. 43, July 1963, pp. 218-24.

Sauldie, Madan M. "Indian Settlers in East Africa." *All India Congress Committee Economic Review* (New Delhi), Vol. 17/13, 1966, pp. 29-30, 37.

Schneider, David M. and Gough, Kathleen. *Matrilineal Kinship.* Berkeley and Los Angeles: University of California Press, 1961.

Schwartz, Barton M. "Differential Social and Religious Adaptation." *Social and Economic Studies* (Jamaica), Institute of Social and Economic Research, University of the West Indies, Vol. 16/3, Sept. 1967, pp. 237-49.

———, ed. *Caste in Overseas Indian Communities,* Chicago: Science Research Associates, 1967.

———. "The "Failure of Caste in Trinidad." In *Caste in Overseas Indian Communities,* pp. 117-45.

Shah, A. B. and Rao, C. R. M., eds. *Tradition and Modernity in India.* Edinburgh: W. & R. Chambers, 1965.

Shah, A. M. "Caste, Economy, and Territory in the Central Panchmahals." *Journal of the M. S. University of Baroda.* Vol. 4/1, 1955, pp. 65-95.

Shah, B. V. "Gujarati College Students and Caste." *Sociological Bulletin* (Bombay), Vol. 10, March 1961, pp. 41-60.

———. "Gujarati College Students and Selection of the Bride." *Sociological Bulletin* (Bombay), Vol. 11, 1962, pp. 121-40.

———. "The College Student and Adult Boy-Girl Relationship." *Journal of the Gujarat Research Society* (Bombay), Vol. 24, April 1962, pp. 134-44.

———. *Social Change and College Students of Gujarat.* Baroda: M. S. University, 1964.

Shanti, Pandit. *Asians in East and Central Africa.* Nairobi: Panco Publications, 1963.

Shils, Edward N. *The Intellectual Between Tradition and Modernity: The Indian Situation.* The Hague: Mouton & Co., 1960.

Singer, Milton, ed. *Traditional India: Structure and Change:* Philadelphia: American Folklore Society No. 9, 1959.

———. ed. *Krishna: Myths, Rites, and Attitudes.* Honolulu: East West Center Press, 1966.

———. and Barnhard S. Cohn, eds. *Structure and Change in Indian Society.* Chicago: Aldine Publishing Co., 1968.

Singer, Philip. "Hinduization and Creolization in Guyana." *Social and Economic Studies* (Jamaica), Institute of Social and Economic Research, University of the West Indies, Vol. 16/3, Sept. 1967, pp. 221-37.

———. *Sadhus and Charisma.* Unpublished dissertation. Syracuse University, 1961.

Singh, A. K. *Indian Students In Britain: A Survey of their Adjustment and Attitudes.* New York: Asia Publishing House, 1963.

Singh, Gopal, ed. and trans. *Guru Granth Sahib: Complete Translation in Four Volumes.* New York: Asia Publishing House, 1965.

Singh, Narain, et al, eds. *Souvenir of the Opening Ceremony of the Sikh Temple in Nairobi.* Nairobi: Shri Guru Singh Sabha, 1963.

Singh, T. R. "Some Aspects of Ritual Purity and Pollution." *Eastern Anthropologist* (Lucknow, India), Vol. 19/2, 1966, pp. 131-42.

Sivānanda, Swami. *Sure Ways for Success in Life and God-Realization.* Hrishikesh, India: Divine Life Society, 1966.

Smith, M. G. *The Plural Society in the British West Indies.* Berkeley: University of California Press, 1965.

Smith, Roger J. "Muslim East Indians in Trinidad: Retention of Ethnic Identity Under Acculturative Conditions." Thesis, University of Pennsylvania, 1963.

Spratt, Philip. *Hindu Culture and Personality*. Bombay: Manaktalas, 1966. See also this author's review of the book, in *Journal of Asian Studies*, Vol. 26/3, 1967, pp. 516-7.

Srinivas, M. N. "Varna and Caste." *In Caste in Modern India*, pp. 63-9. Bombay: Asia Publishing House, 1962.

Srinivas, M. N. "Sanskritization and Westernization." In *Far Eastern Quarterly* (now *Journal of Asian Studies*), Vol. 14/4, 1956, pp. 481-96.

Srivastava, S. K. "The Process of De-Sanskritization in Village India." In *Anthropology on the March*, edited by Bala Ratnam, pp. 263-67. Madras: Social Science Association, 1963.

Staal, J. F. "Sanskrit and Sanskritization." *Journal of Asian Studies*, Vol. 22/3, 1963, pp. 261-75.

Tandon, Yash. "The Asians in East Africa: a Political Survey." In *Portrait of a Minority*, edited by D. P. Ghai and Y. P. Ghai. London: Oxford University Press, 1970.

Tangri, Roger K. "Asians in Kenya: a Political History." *Africa Quarterly* (New Delhi), Vol. VI/2, 1966, pp. 107-27.

Theroux, Paul. "Hating the Asians." *Transition* (Kampala), No. 33, Vol. 7, Nov. 1967, pp. 46-51.

Van de Berghe, P. L. *Caneville: the Social Structure of a South African Town*. Middletown, Conn.: Wesleyan University Press, 1964.

Waiz, S. A. *Indians Abroad*, 2nd ed. Bombay: Imperial Indian Citizenship Association, n.d.

Wolf, Elinor. "Indian Students in the United States: an American's View." *Indian Management* (New Delhi), Vol. 3, Jan. 1963, pp. 22-5, 40.

Wood, Evelyn, "Caste's Latest Image." *Economic Weekly*, Vol. 16, June 1964, pp. 951-2.

Yalman, Nur. "The Flexibility of Caste Principles in a Kandyan Community." In *Aspects of Caste in South India, Ceylon, and Northwest Pakistan*, edited by E. R. Leach, pp. 78-112. Cambridge: Cambridge University Press, 1971.

Zinkin, Taya, *Caste Today*. London: Oxford University Press, 1962.

Index

Aesthetics, 243–258
Africanization, 109–110,
Aga Khan, H.H., 80, 150, 282, 317–20, 340
Aggarwāl (merchant subcaste), 42
Ahmedabad, 44
Ahmedīyas, 18–19, 87–88, 157
Amin, 40. *See* Patel(s)
Amin, S. G., 43
Arab traders, 10, 105, 168
Ardhamāgadhī (Jaina canonical language), 335
Ārya Samāj, 46, 58, 67, 77, 132, 199–201, 269, 278–81, 313
astrology, 185–186, 290, 297
atomic bomb: an Indian invention, 187–188
Aurobindo, Sri, 275, 313–314, 324
Austin, J.L., 4

Banaras, 303–304
Bandung Conference, 178
banks, 106
banyā (merchant castes), 42–43, 45, 53, 59, 75, 169
Baroda (Varodra), 44

Bhagavadgītā, 58, 182, 207, 218, 267, 281–282
bhajan (litany), 216, 296, 335
bhakti (religious devotionalism), 276–277, 281–282
Bhatia (name of a caste), 53, 59, 91, 160
Bhrgu-samhitā, 184–185. *See also* astrology
Birla Temple, 245, 303
Bohras (Shi'a Muslim caste), 26, 85–87, 143, 319
Bombay, 22, 86, 127–128, 246
Bose, Anita, 192–193
Bose, Subhas Chandra "Netāji," 191–193, 237
Brahmo Samāj, 330
brahmacāri, a celibate, 194, 223
brahmins, 27, 77–80, 86, 213, 269, 296, 335; Desāstha 22, 55–56
Brhat Sevā Sangh (BSS), 194, 232–237, 239–241, 243

Candī, a hymn to the goddess, 289
Carani (name of a caste), 93
Caribbean, 9, 16. *See also* Guiana

356

357